CAMBRIDGE STUDIES IN
ANGLO-SAXON ENGLAND

31

TEXT AND PICTURE IN ANGLO-SAXON ENGLAND

CAMBRIDGE STUDIES IN ANGLO-SAXON ENGLAND

FOUNDING GENERAL EDITORS
MICHAEL LAPIDGE AND SIMON KEYNES
CURRENT GENERAL EDITORS
SIMON KEYNES AND ANDY ORCHARD

Volumes published

1 *Anglo-Saxon Crucifixion Iconography and the Art of the Monastic Revival* by BARBARA C. RAW
2 *The Cult of the Virgin Mary in Anglo-Saxon England* by MARY CLAYTON
3 *Religion and Literature in Western England, 600–800* by PATRICK SIMS-WILLIAMS
4 *Visible Song: Transitional Literacy in Old English Verse* by KATHERINE O'BRIEN O'KEEFFE
5 *The Metrical Grammar of* Beowulf by CALVIN B. KENDALL
6 *The Irish Tradition in Old English Literature* by CHARLES D. WRIGHT
7 *Anglo-Saxon Medicine* by M. L. CAMERON
8 *The Poetic Art of Aldhelm* by ANDY ORCHARD
9 *The Old English Lives of St Margaret* by MARY CLAYTON and HUGH MAGENNIS
10 *Biblical Commentaries from the Canterbury School of Theodore and Hadrian* by BERNHARD BISCHOFF and MICHAEL LAPIDGE
11 *Archbishop Theodore: Commemorative Studies on his Life and Influence* edited by MICHAEL LAPIDGE
12 *Interactions of Thought and Language in Old English Poetry* by PETER CLEMOES
13 *The Textuality of Old English Poetry* by CAROL BRAUN PASTERNACK
14 *The 'Laterculus Malalianus' and the School of Archbishop Theodore* by JANE STEVENSON
15 *The Text of the Old Testament in Anglo-Saxon England* by RICHARD MARSDEN
16 *Old English Biblical Verse* by PAUL G. REMLEY
17 *The Hymns of the Anglo-Saxon Church* by INGE B. MILFULL
18 *Scenes of Community in Old English Poetry* by HUGH MAGENNIS
19 *The Old English Apocrypha and their Manuscript Source: 'The Gospel of Nichodemus' and 'The Avenging of the Saviour'* edited by J. E. CROSS
20 *The Composition of Old English Poetry* by H. MOMMA
21 *Trinity and Incarnation in Anglo-Saxon Art and Thought* by BARBARA C. RAW
22 *Heathen Gods in Old English Literature* by RICHARD NORTH
23 Beowulf *and the Old Germanic Metre* by GEOFFREY RUSSOM
24 *Ælfric's Letter to the Monks of Eynsham* by CHRISTOPHER A. JONES
25 *The Intellectual Foundations of English Benedectine Reform* by MECHTHILD GRETSCH
26 *Apocryphal Gospels of Mary in Anglo-Saxon England* by MARY CLAYTON
27 *Representations of the Natural World in Old English Poetry* by JENNIFER NEVILLE
28 *Anglo-Saxon Gestures and the Roman Stage* by C. R. DODWELL
29 *Literary Appropriations of the Anglo-Saxons from the Thirteenth to the Twentieth Century* by DONALD SCRAGG and CAROLE WEINBERG
30 *Rewriting Old English in the Twelfth Century* edited by MARY SWAN and ELAINE M. TREHARNE

TEXT AND PICTURE IN ANGLO-SAXON ENGLAND

NARRATIVE STRATEGIES IN THE JUNIUS 11 MANUSCRIPT

CATHERINE E. KARKOV

Miami University

CAMBRIDGE
UNIVERSITY PRESS

PUBLISHED BY THE PRESS SYNDICATE OF THE UNIVERSITY OF CAMBRIDGE
The Pitt Building, Trumpington Street, Cambridge CB2 1RP, United Kingdom

CAMBRIDGE UNIVERSITY PRESS
The Edinburgh Building, Cambridge CB2 2RU, UK
40 West 20th Street, New York, NY 10011–4211, USA
10 Stamford Road, Oakleigh, Melbourne 3166, Australia
Ruiz de Alarcón 13, 28014 Madrid, Spain
Dock House, The Waterfront, Cape Town 8001, South Africa

http://www.cambridge.org

First published 2001

Printed in the United Kingdom at the University Press, Cambridge

Typeset in Garamond 11/13pt [CE]

A catalogue record for this book is available from the British Library

Library of Congress Cataloguing in Publication data

Karkov, Catherine.
Text and picture in Anglo-Saxon England: narrative strategies in the
Junius 11 manuscript / Catherine Karkov.
p. cm. – (Cambridge studies in Anglo-Saxon England ; 31)
Includes bibliographical references (p.) and index.
ISBN 0 521 80069 2
1. Caedmon manuscript. 2. English poetry – Old English, ca. 450–1100 – Criticism,
Textual. 3. English poetry – Old English, ca. 450–1100 – Illustrations.
4. Christian poetry, English (Old) – Criticism, Textual. 5. Illumination of books and
manuscripts, Anglo-Saxon. 6. Christian poetry, English (Old) – Illustrations.
7. Bible. O.T. – History of Biblical events. 8. Manuscripts, English (Old).
9. Caedmon – Illustrations. 10. Bible – In literature.
11. Narration (Rhetoric) I. Title II. Series.
PR1625.K37 2001
829′.109–dc21 20011025201

ISBN 0 521 80069 2 hardback

Contents

Plates

Plate section between pp. 116 and 117.

Acknowledgements

I am grateful to Michelle Brown (British Library), Gill Cannell (Parker Library) and especially Martin Kauffmann (Bodleian Library) for their assistance with photographs, and to Pamela Fox and the Miami University School of Fine Arts for a generous grant towards their reproduction. I would also like to thank Rolf Bremmer, George H. Brown, Patrick W. Conner, Helen Damico, Carol Farr, Antonette di Paolo Healey, John Higgitt, Hilda, Nick Howe, Karen Jolly, Sarah Larrett Keefer, Alison Kettler, Éamonn Ó Carragáin, Katherine O'Brien O'Keeffe, Fred Orton, Bill Schipper, Paul Szarmach and Kelley Wickham-Crowley for help and advice of various kinds; and Tom Seiler and the Medieval Institute Press (Western Michigan University) for permission to reproduce sections of chapter 5. I am especially grateful to Andy Orchard for his keen editorial eye, and to Simon Keynes for his practical assistance. Any errors that remain are, of course, my own.

Plates I–XLIIIb are reproduced by permission of the Bodleian Library, University of Oxford; plates XLIVa–XLVa, and XLVIa–XLVIIIa by permission of the British Library; plate XLVb by permission of the Bibliothèque Municipale de Boulogne-sur-Mer; plate XLVIIIb by permission of the Master and Fellows of Corpus Christi College, Cambridge.

Abbreviations

ASE	*Anglo-Saxon England*
ASPR	Anglo-Saxon Poetic Records, ed. G. P. Krapp and E. V. K. Dobbie (New York, 1931–42)
ASNSL	*Archiv für das Studium der neueren Sprachen und Literaturen*
ASSAH	*Anglo-Saxon Studies in Archaeology and History*
BL	London, British Library
Bull.	Bulletin
CCCC	Cambridge, Corpus Christi College
CCSL	Corpus Christianorum Series Latina (Turnhout)
CH	Ælfric, *Catholic Homilies*
CSASE	Cambridge Studies in Anglo-Saxon England
CSEL	Corpus Scriptorum Ecclesiasticorum Latinorum (Vienna)
Dan.	*Daniel*, Junius 11
EEMF	Early English Manuscripts in Facsimile
EETS	Early English Text Series
ELN	*English Language Notes*
Ex.	*Exodus*, Junius 11
Gen.	*Genesis*, Junius 11
HBS	Henry Bradshaw Society
HE	*Bede's Ecclesiastical History of the English People*, ed. B. Colgrave and R. A. B. Mynors (Oxford, 1969)
JEGP	*Journal of English and Germanic Philology*
Jnl	Journal
JWCI	*Journal of the Warburg and Courtauld Institutes*
MÆ	*Medium Ævum*
MLN	*Modern Language Notes*
NM	*Neuphilologische Mitteilungen*

N&Q	*Notes & Queries*
NS	New Series
OS	Old Series
PG	Patriologia Graeca, ed. J. P. Migne, 1–16, (Paris, 1857–86)
PL	Patriologia Latina, ed. J. P. Migne, 1–221 (Paris, 1844–64)
PMLA	*Publications of the Modern Language Association*
SS	Supplementary Series

1

Introduction: problems and solutions

In libris mortuos quasi vivos invenio; in libris futura praevideo . . .[1]

Richard de Bury, *Philobiblon*

Oxford, Bodleian Library, Junius 11 is the only one of the four major Anglo-Saxon poetic manuscripts to be illustrated. It has been studied for its literary content and for the style and iconography of its drawings, but it must also be understood as an historical text. The four poems which make up the text, as has been noted many times, contain passages from older works that have been combined, rearranged and reworded to create a new poetic narrative in which the voices of the dead speak again, as if they were alive. Figures from biblical history appear in the drawings accompanied by attributes of Anglo-Saxon life, ensuring that they too become as if alive, and reminding us that the same figures we see here were very much a part of Anglo-Saxon 'historical' texts such as genealogies and chronicles. Their actions and histories also provided moral and spiritual exempla for their Anglo-Saxon readers – with whom they stood united in expectation of the Last Judgement. These people, the characters within the poems, the poets, artists, scribes and compilers of the manuscript, and the book's original intended audience have fascinated scholars since the rediscovery of the manuscript in the seventeenth century. Scholarship on the book has helped to keep its varied dead alive, but has provided relatively little concrete information on when, where, why and for whom Junius 11 was produced. Questions and problems remain concerning all

[1] 'In books I find the dead as if they were alive; in books I foresee things to come . . .' R. de Bury, *Philobiblon*, trans. E. C. Thomas (Oxford and New York, 1970), pp. 16–17.

aspects of this manuscript. This book will leave many questions unanswered, but will, it is hoped, provide some solutions as well.

Junius 11, written and illuminated *c.* 950–1000, possibly at Christ Church Canterbury, is one of the most studied and most controversial of Anglo-Saxon manuscripts.[2] The majority of scholars today would agree that the manuscript was deliberately compiled according to a predetermined plan in order to create a narrative centred on the theme of Fall and Redemption. Yet questions still remain about the date and sources of the individual poems, the sources of the drawings that accompany them, and the relationship of the drawings to the text. Of central concern to this analysis of the Junius 11 manuscript is the relationship of the images to the text. Although only forty-eight drawings, covering the Creation to Abraham and Sarah's approach into Egypt on page 88 of *Genesis*, were completed, blank spaces left for pictures throughout *Exodus* and *Daniel* indicate that at least the Old Testament poems were originally to have been richly illustrated, and that these three poems, with their drawings, were envisaged as a unified book. The final poem, *Christ and Satan*, the

[2] Because of the unity of design and regularity of the punctuation in Junius 11, all passages cited are taken directly from the manuscript, and manuscript punctuation has been retained. Translations are my own. Any emendations to either text or translation are noted, and the reader is directed to the editions of the separate poems noted below for information on variant readings. For a discussion of the poems and their relationships to one another see: A. N. Doane, *Genesis A: A New Edition* (Madison, WI, 1978); A. N. Doane, *The Saxon Genesis: An Edition of the West Saxon Genesis B and the Old Saxon 'Vatican Genesis'* (Madison, WI, 1991); R. T. Farrell, ed., *Daniel and Azarias* (London, 1974); E. B. Irving, Jr., ed., *The Old English Exodus* (New Haven, CT, 1953; reprinted and revised New York, 1970); P. J. Lucas, ed., *Exodus* (London, 1977); M. D. Clubb, ed., *Christ and Satan: An Old English Poem* (New Haven, CT, 1925); R. E. Finnegan, *Christ and Satan: A Critical Edition* (Waterloo, 1977); I. Gollancz, ed., *The Cædmon Manuscript of Anglo-Saxon Biblical Poetry: Junius XI in the Bodleian Library* (London, 1927); C. W. Kennedy, *The Cædmon Poems Translated into English Prose* (Gloucester, MA, 1965); J. R. Hall, 'The Old English Book of Salvation History: Three Studies on the Unity of MS. Junius 11' (unpubl. PhD dissertation, University of Notre Dame, 1974); J. R. Hall, 'The Old English Epic of Redemption: The Theological Unity of MS. Junius 11', *Traditio* 32 (1976), 185–208; P. G. Remley, *Old English Biblical Verse*, CSASE 16 (Cambridge, 1996); B. J. Timmer, *The Later 'Saxon Genesis' Edited from Manuscript Junius 11*, 2nd edn (Oxford, 1954); F. Junius, *Cædmonis monachi paraphrasis poetica Genesios ac præcipuarum sacrae paginae historiarum, abhinc annos M.LXX. Anglo-Saxonice conscripta & nunc primum edita ...* (Amsterdam, 1655); B. Thorpe, *Cædmon's Metrical Paraphrase of Parts of the Holy Scriptures in Anglo-Saxon* (London, 1832).

product of three scribes working within a generation of the scribe of the Old Testament poems, ends with the rubric 'Finit Liber II. Amen', and has no spaces left for pictures within its text; nevertheless, illustrations may have been intended for it too. Israel Gollancz in the facsimile of the manuscript,[3] Merrel Clubb in his edition of the poem,[4] J. R. Hall in his study of the overall unity of the manuscript,[5] and Barbara Raw in her analysis of the construction of the manuscript,[6] have all suggested that *Christ and Satan* may have been illustrated with a series of three to five full-page drawings designed to accompany the major divisions of the poem.[7] It is impossible to determine now whether such illustrations existed, or were ever intended; however, as the iconography of many of the surviving drawings is typologically related to the themes of the final poem, it is clear that the artists, like the compiler and/or scribes, understood that *Christ and Satan* was an integral part of the manuscript's narrative. Moreover, with its apocalyptic subject matter and descriptions of the Last Judgement it provides a New Testament counterpart to the Old Testament *Daniel*. It should also be noted that the number and distribution of the planned illustrations in *Christ and Satan* would have worked as a visual indication that this final poem, with its New Testament content, was a continuation of, yet also separate from, the preceding poems in which the drawings were integrated throughout the text.

How closely the illustrations relate to the text, however, has also been a matter of some debate. Junius did not include them in his 1655 edition of the manuscript, and indeed they were not reproduced in their entirety until Sir Henry Ellis's 1832 study of the poems.[8] Gollancz's treatment of the illustrations was largely descriptive, cataloguing the ways in which individual drawings and details accorded with the textual account of the events they were meant to 'illustrate', but failing to see the drawings as

3 Gollancz, ed., *Cædmon Manuscript*, p. cv.

4 Clubb, ed., *Christ and Satan*, pp. ix–x.

5 Hall, 'The Old English Book of Salvation History', pp. 25–43.

6 'The Construction of Oxford, Bodleian Library, Junius 11', *ASE* 13 (1984), 187–207, at pp. 191 and 203; reprinted in *Anglo-Saxon Manuscripts Basic Readings*, ed. M. Richards (New York and London, 1994), pp. 251–75.

7 See below, p. 206.

8 H. Ellis, *Account of Cædmon's Metrical Paraphrase of Scripture History*, *Archaeologia* 24 (1832). See ch. 5 for a more extensive treatment of these editions. For information on Junius, see ch. 6.

creating a narrative in their own right. Barbara Raw was primarily interested in the sources of the drawings, and the possible reasons for their occasional 'dislocation' from the text.[9] She suggested that the majority of the illustrations were derived from an Old Saxon exemplar which the Anglo-Saxon artists had, in places, misunderstood or had difficulty relating to the reworked text. In her analysis, for example, the illustrations and the texts of '*Genesis A*' and '*Genesis B*' (two parts of *Genesis* which some see as separate poems) form three awkwardly integrated narratives:

> A comparison of the Junius drawings of the rebellion and fall of the angels and of the descendants of Adam with the text of *Genesis A*, *Genesis B* and the Old Saxon *Genesis* confirms this view. The drawings of the rebellion and fall of the angels correspond in detail to *Genesis B*, and hence to its Old Saxon original, even when they ostensibly illustrate *Genesis A*. The drawing on p. 2 shows God enthroned between two seraphs. To his right are two angels of whom one is haloed. The halo is appropriate to Satan of *Genesis B*, who is described as next in rank to God himself; the *A* text says nothing of Satan's special position.[10]

Why should we expect the artist to provide line-by-line, literal illustrations of the text? The details of the halo and crown worn by Lucifer may be intended simply to help us identify him in the visual narrative of his fall (pls. IIa, IIb).[11] Similarly, Raw believed that details that were not in accord with any of the texts were derived from separate visual or textual sources – the ladder in the drawing of the creation of Eve (pl. IV) from an illustration of Jacob's ladder, or the scene of ploughing in the drawing of Noah and his family on page 77 (pl. XXXIX) from a separate literary source – but she offered no explanation as to why such details may have been incorporated into the manuscript.[12]

George Henderson contributed the first in-depth analysis of the 'programme' of illustrations intended for the manuscript as a whole, not just the *Genesis* poem, though he saw that programme as 'very irregular,

[9] 'The Probable Derivation of Most of the Illustrations in Junius 11 from an Illustrated Old Saxon *Genesis*', *ASE* 5 (1976), 133–48.

[10] *Ibid.*, pp. 146–7.

[11] The turning position of God and the downward gesture of his right hand also provide a visual transition from the frontal, iconic image of God enthroned on page 1 to the vertical narrative of the fall of the rebel angels.

[12] Raw, 'Probable Derivation', pp. 140 and 136.

with marked dense patches of illustrations and one surprisingly bare patch'.[13] Like Raw, Henderson attributed what he interpreted as problems with the programme to the artists' copying of a model that provided 'an elaborate but only partial programme of scenes'.[14]

Thomas Ohlgren and Herbert Broderick were the first to consider the illustrations as forming a significant narrative cycle in their own right, though Broderick remained more interested in source study than visual narrative.[15] While attributing a high degree of originality to the artists, Broderick identified three principal sources for the Junius drawings: a lost Early Christian Genesis manuscript with illustrations in the Cotton Genesis tradition,[16] the Utrecht Psalter (Utrecht, Biblioteek der Rijksuniversiteit, MS 32, produced at Reims *c.* 830 and brought to England sometime before the year 1000), and contemporary Anglo-Saxon illuminations.[17] Following Raw and Henderson, however, he concluded that the manuscript contained an 'odd and often unsuitable apportionment of picture-spaces', and that the synchronization of text and picture was

[13] G. Henderson, 'The Programme of Illustrations in Bodleian MS Junius XI', in *Studies in Memory of David Talbot Rice*, ed. G. Robertson and G. Henderson (Edinburgh, 1975), pp. 113–45; reprinted in G. Henderson, *Studies in English Bible Illustration*, 2 vols., vol. I, (London, 1985), pp. 138–83, at p. 146. All references are to the 1985 reprint.

[14] *Ibid.*, p. 160.

[15] T. H. Ohlgren, 'The Illustrations of the Cædmonian Genesis as a Guide to the Interpretation of the Text' (unpubl. PhD dissertation, University of Michigan, 1969); H. R. Broderick III, 'The Iconographic and Compositional Sources of the Drawings in Oxford Bodleian Library, MS Junius 11' (unpubl. PhD dissertation, Columbia University, 1978); H. R. Broderick, 'Observations on the Method of Illustration in MS Junius 11 and the Relationship of the Drawings to the Text', *Scriptorium* 37 (1983), 161–77.

[16] On the 'Cotton Genesis tradition' see K. Weitzmann and H. L. Kessler, *The Cotton Genesis: British Library Cotton Otho B.VI* (Princeton, NJ, 1986). According to Weitzmann and Kessler the drawings in Junius 11, along with the images in several other medieval Genesis cycles, were ultimately derived either directly or indirectly from the illustrations in the late-fifth-century Cotton Genesis.

[17] 'Iconographic and Compositional Sources', pp. 365–6; 'Observations on the Method of Illustration', pp. 162–3: 'Careful study of the distribution of picture-spaces in the text as well as the methods of illustration employed by the two artists has enabled us to conclude that it is more than likely that these artists were not working from an illustrated exemplar with text and illustration combined, but were probably supplying this collection of biblical poems in the vernacular with a set of pictures for the first time' (p. 162).

further marred by the artists' reliance on independent pictorial models.[18] In 1969, Ohlgren interpreted the illustrations as more complex visual glosses that in some cases added additional layers of meaning to the text, an argument that he has expanded in subsequent articles.[19] Yet Ohlgren too has tended to understand the drawings as ultimately remaining within the Cotton Genesis tradition, and has continued to explore the sources and meaning of individual details and scenes rather than reading the pictorial narrative as one level within the manuscript's larger narrative structure. Source study, in other words, continues to fragment this manuscript by failing to consider the poems and drawings as part of a coherent whole.[20]

As vital as the search for sources and exemplars may be to many contemporary scholars, such issues, if they concerned the manuscript's Anglo-Saxon audience, would have concerned them differently. As with Anglo-Saxon homiletic writing,[21] references to the writings of earlier authors, as well as traces of the oral in the written text created a complex and highly learned intertextuality while at the same time giving the text the weight of authority; nevertheless, the function and overall content of the manuscript would have been primary.[22] The preoccupation of art historians with the apparent lack of coherence between the manuscript's visual and verbal narratives has led us to assume disorder, and perhaps to ask the wrong questions as a result. In asking why episodes that we feel should be illustrated are not and episodes that strike us as unimportant are copiously illustrated,[23] we are assuming that the 'authors' and readers

18 Broderick, 'Observations on the Method of Illustration', pp. 162–3.

19 T. H. Ohlgren, 'The Illustrations of the Cædmonian Genesis: Literary Criticism through Art', *Medievalia et Huministica* 3 (1972), 199–212; 'Some New Light on the Old English *Cædmonian Genesis*', *Studies in Iconography* 1 (1975), 38–73.

20 See most recently Remley, *Biblical Verse*. Remley's detailed study of the Old Testament poems in Junius 11 fails to consider the role of the illustrations, the inclusion of *Christ and Satan* in the manuscript, and the way in which sources might have been used by the poets as tools in the construction of a new and larger narrative rather than as simple exemplars.

21 See C. Lees, *Tradition and Belief: Religious Writing in Anglo-Saxon England* (Minneapolis, MN, 1999), p. 103.

22 For an excellent consideration of this issue see W. Noel, *The Harley Psalter* (Cambridge, 1995), pp. 1–27.

23 Henderson, 'Programme of Illustrations'; Broderick, 'Observations on the Method of Illustration'.

of the manuscript shared our tastes. It would be more productive to ask why the illustrations are distributed in the way that they are, and whether there might not be reasons why certain episodes may have been more appealing to an eleventh-century audience than they are to us today. That is not to say that we should ignore modern readings and interests, but simply that we must be open to alternative ways of considering such things as composition, structure and textual unity. Similarly, rather than looking for reasons to explain the apparent disunity between text and illustration, it might be more rewarding to ask if there is a unity of design, function or content that our assumptions about what constitutes an illustration have prevented us from seeing. If there are logical reasons for the copying of charters, letters, and other types of additional material into the pages of gospel books,[24] there are likely to be similarly logical reasons for poems clearly related by biblical themes to be bound together and illustrated with drawings that pick up on those related themes.[25]

EXEMPLAR VS INTERPRETATION

Crucial to an understanding of the role of the drawings within the manuscript is a consideration of the ways in which picture and text relate to each other in Anglo-Saxon art. 'Illustration' is the conventional term used to describe the images in a book or manuscript, and is retained here for the sake of convenience; however, in the Anglo-Saxon world an image was rarely intended as nothing more than a literal illustration of an accompanying text, and an illustration or illustrated cycle was rarely nothing more than a copy of its model.[26] Recent analysis of manuscripts as diverse in time and function as the Book of Cerne (Cambridge,

[24] See S. Keynes's comments on the Old English additions to the York Gospels in *The York Gospels*, ed. N. Barker (London, 1986), p. 81.

[25] The repetition of motifs, words and phrases in *Genesis* and *Exodus* has led some scholars to see the two poems as written to accompany each other, with *Exodus* most likely written or emended to accord with a preexisting *Genesis*. See especially C. Stévanovitch, 'Envelope Patterns in *Genesis A* and *B*', *Neophilologus* 80.3 (1996), 465–78, esp. 474–5.

[26] Even the Harley Psalter (London, British Library, Harley 603), generally described as a copy of the Utrecht Psalter (Utrecht, University Library, MS 32), differs dramatically from its exemplar. See Noel, *Harley Psalter*.

University Library, Ll.1.10),[27] the Benedictional of St Æthelwold (London, British Library, Add. 49598)[28] and the Tiberius Psalter (London, British Library, Cotton Tiberius C. vi),[29] has revealed that in each case the miniatures function as a visual gloss or exegesis of the text, and are one of the primary tools used by scribes and artists to relate different texts or portions of texts to each other. Kathleen Openshaw and Robert Deshman have shown how Anglo-Saxon psalter illustration is often symbolic, with individual miniatures used to establish a typological programme that relates Old and New Testament events.[30] The psalter was an extremely popular form of book in Anglo-Saxon England, as it was throughout early medieval Europe, and the text of the psalter was one of the most important sources for the Junius 11 poems.[31] The influence of illustrated psalters on other types of manuscript is undoubted, and many of the details in the Junius 11 illustrations, along with those of other eleventh-century Anglo-Saxon manuscripts, have been traced back to the Carolingian Utrecht Psalter,[32] but there was also an Insular tradition of symbolic psalter illustration that seems to have been equally influential.[33] A significant number of the Junius 11 drawings have a typological function, yet they work in a slightly different way from the psalter illustrations, combining symbolic and literal content to create a visual narrative that both illustrates the poetic text and translates it into a new pictorial language. Like the poems they accompany, the drawings require

[27] M. P. Brown, *The Book of Cerne: Prayer, Patronage and Power in Ninth-Century England* (London and Toronto, 1996). See particularly ch. 4, 'Decoration as Elucidation'.

[28] R. Deshman, *The Benedictional of Æthelwold* (Princeton, NJ, 1995). Deshman identifies a series of interrelated programmes related to the liturgy, monastic life and the court, that run throughout the manuscript. He also notes that 'the miniatures are iconographically interrelated on various levels', and that repetition of motifs and themes is used to create what he terms a 'cyclic symbolism' (p. 7).

[29] K. M. Openshaw, 'The Battle between Christ and Satan in the Tiberius Psalter', *JWCI* 52 (1989), 14–33.

[30] K. M. Openshaw, 'The Symbolic Illustration of the Psalter: An Insular Tradition', *Arte medievale* 2nd series 6 (1992), 41–60; R. Deshman, 'The Galba Psalter: Pictures, Text and Context in an Early Medieval Prayerbook', *ASE* 26 (1997), 109–38.

[31] Remley, *Biblical Verse*, pp. 69, 175–8 and 257–8.

[32] See especially Raw, 'Probable Derivation', and Broderick, 'Iconographic and Compositional Sources'.

[33] Openshaw, 'Symbolic Illustration'. See also Deshman, 'Galba Psalter'; J. O'Reilly, 'Early Medieval Text and Image: the Wounded and Exalted Christ', *Peritia* 6–7 (1987–8), 72–118, esp. pp. 86–93.

an audience capable of reading and interpreting correctly;[34] indeed the need to read and interpret properly is one of the central themes of the manuscript. At every level the manuscript itself demands the active participation of each reader/viewer at each new reading.

The poetic and pictorial narratives are not the same, but there are stylistic similarities between them which help us to create a unified reading that bridges the gulf between the verbal and the visual. Like the text, which includes different types of voice (description, dialogue, gnomic sayings, authorial interventions), the illustrations address both text and audience in different ways. Raw, for example, questioned why Enoch should be depicted on page 60 (pl. XXIX) haloed, holding an open book and standing on a dragon, when none of these details is mentioned in the poem.[35] All three details, however, help to identify Enoch as a type of Christ, and to establish the relationship of this episode to the Harrowing of Hell and the Last Judgement, New Testament events that are both foreshadowed in verbal and visual motifs throughout the Old Testament poems and recounted at length in *Christ and Satan*. Enoch stands over the dragon as does the Christ prefigured in Psalm XC who tramples on the beasts, an episode repeatedly linked to the Harrowing of Hell and the Last Judgement in Anglo-Saxon art and literature.[36] Moreover, as a symbol of the devil and Antichrist, the dragon is a reminder that Enoch returns to earth to do battle with the Antichrist, at which time he will be slain and ascend to heaven for a second and final time. In his treatise 'On the Old and New Testaments', a text roughly contemporary with the Junius 11 manuscript, Ælfric explains:

Enoh wæs geciged se seofoða man fram Adame; he worhte Godes willan and God hine ða genam mid andsundum lichaman of þisum life upp, and he ys cucu git, swa swa Helias, se æðela witega, þe wæs eal swa genumen to þam oðrum life, and

34 For an analysis of the relationship of audience to narrative in Anglo-Saxon poetry, see C. B. Pasternack, *The Textuality of Old English Poetry*, CSASE 13 (Cambridge, 1995); P. Head, *Representation and Design: Tracing a Hermeneutics of Old English Poetry* (Albany, NY, 1997); R. Frank, 'Some Uses of Paronomasia in Old English Scriptural Verse', *Speculum* 47.2 (1972), 207–26; S. Lerer, *Literacy and Power in Anglo-Saxon Literature* (Lincoln, NE and London, 1991).

35 Raw, 'Probable Derivation', p. 136.

36 See below, p. 61. See also K. M. Openshaw, 'Weapons in the Daily Battle: Images of the Conquest of Evil in the Early Medieval Psalter', *Art Bull.* 75 (1993), 17–38; and Openshaw, 'Battle between Christ and Satan'.

hi cumað begen togeanes Antecriste, þæt hig his leasunga alecgon þurh God, and beoð þonne ofslegen þurh ðone sylfan feond, and hi eft arisað, swa swa ealle men doð.[37]

The open book not only connects Enoch with the image of God and Christ as Creator and Judge, and particularly with the image of Christ in majesty holding the book of judgement, but also mirrors the open manuscript we read. It has been suggested that the open book and text displayed by Enoch may refer to the tradition that Enoch invented writing,[38] certainly a possible interpretation as this is the only drawing in the manuscript in which the artist has indicated writing on the open pages of a book. But beyond this, the image is also an example of the motif of reading and writing that runs throughout the manuscript, creating a self-referentiality that unites the writing of the first story with the writing of this manuscript and its continual reading and interpretation (each a form of rewriting) by its audience. The open book might also be understood as reflecting Enoch's loyalty to God ('him wæs þeoden hold, rodera waldend', *Gen.* 1202b–1203), which leads to his salvation. The image refers us back to the opening words of the manuscript which instruct the reader to love and to praise God as a means to salvation. The drawing thus serves to unite the beginning and end, Creation and the Last Judgement, *Genesis* and *Christ and Satan*, and helps to locate narrative and reader within the continuum of Christian history. Katherine O'Brien O'Keeffe, Martin Irvine and Carol Pasternack have emphasized the fact

[37] 'The seventh man from Adam was called Enoch, he did God's will, and God took him up with his whole body, up from this life, and he is living yet, just as is the noble prophet Elias, who was also taken to the other life, and both shall come against Antichrist, to conquer his lies through the power of God. They will then be slain by that same fiend, and they will rise again just as all men will do.' *The Old English Version of the Heptateuch, Ælfric's Treatise on the Old and New Testament and his Preface to Genesis*, ed. S. J. Crawford, EETS OS 160 (Oxford, 1922; repr. 1969 with additional texts transcribed by N. R. Ker), p. 23. All translations from Old English are my own. See also Augustine, *De civitate dei* xv. 19 (CCSL 48), pp. 481–2; Bede, *In Genesim* (CCSL 118A), p. 96; and P. Clemoes, 'Cynewulf's Image of the Ascension', in *England Before the Conquest: Studies in Primary Sources Presented to Dorothy Whitelock*, ed. P. Clemoes and K. Hughes (Cambridge, 1971), pp. 293–304 (repr. in *Cynewulf: Basic Readings*, ed. R. E. Bjork (New York, 1996), pp. 109–32).

[38] Gollancz, ed., *Cædmon Manuscript*, p. xliv; T. H. Ohlgren, *Anglo-Saxon Textual Illustration: Photographs of Sixteen Manuscripts with Descriptions and Index* (Kalamazoo, MI, 1992), p. 95.

that compiling, writing, reading and hearing texts in Anglo-Saxon England were interactive, creative processes that were both intellectually and theologically demanding.[39] Each reading or retelling of a text created a new narrative that echoed earlier tradition, or, in Irvine's words, presented 'a special rearrangement of the larger library'.[40] For the compilers and readers of Junius 11, the illustrations were an integral part of this process.

PICTORIAL DISLOCATION

It has also been argued, even by those who understand the importance of the illustrations to a reading of the manuscript as a whole, that in at least two places (pages 20–4 and 76–8) the illustrations are out of step with the text,[41] yet careful analysis of the drawings indicates that this is not the case. The first problem arises with the illustrations on pages 20 and 24, both frequently interpreted as misplaced depictions of the Temptation of Eve. The full-page drawing on page 20 (pl. Xa) serves as a visual preface to the events recounted in the following pages. Far from being out of place in the narrative, it provides an eloquent summary of the actions leading up to the central drama of the Temptation. The artist has arranged the figures to lead our eyes in a circular motion from the figure of Satan bound in hell, to his servant passing through the gates of hell, to the serpent and Eve in the upper left part of the drawing and on to the figures of Adam and Eve in the upper right. Together Adam and Eve point towards the large decorated initial on the facing page (pl. Xb) that begins the phrase 'Ac ðoliaþ we nu þrea on helle' ('but now we suffer pain in hell', *Gen.* 389), part of Satan's lament. Adam and Eve will also suffer pain in hell, and the drawing serves to unite Satan's desire for their fall with

39 K. O'Brien O'Keeffe, *Visible Song: Transitional Literacy in Old English Verse* , CSASE 14 (Cambridge, 1990); M. Irvine, *The Making of a Textual Culture: 'Grammatica' and Literary Theory, 350–1100* (Cambridge, 1994), esp. pp. 428–9; Pasternack, *Textuality of Old English Poetry.*

40 *Making of a Textual Culture*, p. 429.

41 Raw, 'Probable Derivation'; Henderson, 'Programme of Illustrations', esp. pp. 147–51 and 153–6; R. Gameson, *The Role of Art in the Late Anglo-Saxon Church* (Oxford, 1995), pp. 37–8, 43–5, 112 and 151; Broderick, 'Observations on the Method of Illustration'. Henderson (p. 156) feels that the pictures are so at odds with the text that at least the second artist may have been illiterate, while Gameson (p. 38) describes his work as representing the 'nadir of the physical relationship between text and image'.

the means by which it will be achieved and the suggestion of its fulfilment. Colette Stévanovitch has drawn attention to the way in which the poet has used envelope patterns to give a circular structure, symbolic of its circular logic, to Satan's lament. The pronounced circular motion of the drawing may well be intended to reflect the verbal patterns of the accompanying text. It may also serve to document the passing of circular logic, or flawed reasoning, from Satan to the Tempter, and then to Eve and Adam.[42] In a more general context, the circular motion of the drawing produces a diagram of the cyclical pattern of Fall and Redemption that the text of the manuscript records, and that will end with Christ's smashing of the gates of hell, an event to which the bound Satan already makes visual reference.[43] Furthermore, it is not necessary to interpret the combination of serpent and Eve as a representation of the Temptation. Rather, it suggests the entry of evil into the world that begins with Satan's words and continues with the entry of his messenger into paradise and his adoption of the form of the serpent, until this moment a perfectly innocent animal.[44] The serpent is presumably one of those animals over which Adam and Eve were given dominion; it operates according to their will, as they operate according to God's. The serpent's transformation into, or acceptance of the words of, Satan's messenger thus parallels the Fall of Adam and Eve.[45] The detail introduces a motif echoed twice more in the next five pages of the manuscript: on page 23 the description of the messenger's journey into paradise is introduced by a biting beast-head initial (pl. XIa), while on page 25 its end is marked by the poet's words:

> Wearp hine þa on wyrmes lic.   and wand him þa ymbutan.
> þone deaðes beam.   þurh deofles cræft.[46]

[42] Stévanovitch, 'Envelope Patterns in *Genesis*'.

[43] The drawing may also have an interesting connection with the images of *Mors* in the Tiberius Psalter (BL, Cotton Tiberius C. vi, 6v) and Leofric Missal (Oxford, Bodleian Library, Bodley 579, 50r) in which dragons or serpents are depicted emerging from the body of Death. Here the devil's messenger merges into the body of the serpent in order to bring death to mankind.

[44] But see below, p. 43.

[45] A. LaCocque and P. Ricoeur, *Thinking Biblically*, trans. D. Pellauer (Chicago, IL, 1998), p. 12.

[46] 'Then he turned into the body of the serpent and wound himself about the tree of death with devil's cunning' *Gen*. 491–2.

In the next line the Temptation of Adam begins. The repetition of the image of the serpent helps to keep the true source of evil, Satan and his words, and the process by which evil and death are brought into the world, firmly in the reader's mind. Compositionally, it is but a visual extension of the way in which Anglo-Saxon poets used anaphora and other rhetorical devices to unite and add emphasis to individual parts of their texts.

The illustration on page 24 (pl. XIb), as I have argued elsewhere, is most likely to be understood as a representation of the Temptation of Adam, rather than the Temptation of Eve.[47] While the human figure in the drawing does appear to be female, the androgyny of the first couple prior to the Fall is one of the characteristic features of this Genesis cycle.[48] Both Adam and Eve are shown with long hair, prominent breasts and no genitalia. Eve's nipples are usually more pronounced than Adam's, but the artist is by no means consistent in his use of this detail. Moreover, the text on this page describes the tree of death, its dark and bitter fruit, and the punishment that awaits those who eat the fruit:

sceolde on wite a.
mid swate and mid sorgum. siððan libban.
swa hwa swa gebyrgde. þæs on þam beame geweox.[49]

This is to be Adam's punishment, and the text on the facing page goes on to recount the Temptation of Adam. While it is true that illustrations such as that of the messenger's journey on page 20 can be used to foreshadow events described later in the text, the artist has included several details in this drawing to indicate that here text and illustration belong together, that this is indeed Adam rather than Eve, and further to suggest Adam's successful resistance to this first Temptation. Adam

47 C. E. Karkov, 'The Anglo-Saxon Genesis: Text, Illustration and Audience', in *The Old English Hexateuch: Aspects and Approaches*, ed. B. Withers and R. Barnhouse (Kalamazoo, MI, 2000), pp. 187–223; C. E. Karkov, 'Margins and Marginalization: Representations of Eve in Oxford, Bodl. Lib. MS Junius 11', in *Texts in Margins*, ed. S. L. Keefer and W. Schipper (forthcoming).

48 Compare the depictions of Adam and Eve in BL Claudius B. iv, where Adam is distinguished by his beard and Eve by her breasts and long flowing hair. But see also M. Dockray-Miller, 'Mixed Pairs: Gender Construction in Anglo-Saxon Art and Poetry' (unpubl. PhD dissertation, Loyola University, 1996).

49 'He should ever after live in punishment, with sweat and with sorrow, whoever tasted that which grew on that tree' *Gen.* 481b–483.

stands on higher ground looking down on the messenger who hands him the fruit, a traditional way of indicating a superior position in medieval art. The messenger is shown with dark hair and a prominent hooked nose, his thin cloak revealing his legs in a somewhat less than angelic way. A bit of drapery flies out behind him suggesting the demonic tail that will reappear after the Fall. Adam quite rightly remarks that he is *unlike* any angel he has ever seen ('þu gelic ne bist ænigum his engla þe ic ær geseah', *Gen.* 538b–539).

In marked contrast to his appearance on page 24, the messenger in the scene of Eve's Temptation on page 28 (pl. XII) has the appearance of a traditional beautiful angel. He is tall and slender with fair hair and a finely drawn face. The tail-like bit of flying drapery has disappeared and his cloak flutters elegantly about him. Rather than being unlike an angel he is here, as he emphasizes to Eve, *not* like a devil ('ne eom ic deofle gelic', *Gen.* 587b).

The second instance of pictorial displacement is more problematic. The illustrations of Noah's covenant with God on page 76 (pl. XXXVIII), Noah ploughing on page 77 (pl. XXXIX) and the drunkenness of Noah on page 78 (pl. XL) do seem to be out of step with the text, as the drunkenness of Noah appears in the poem on page 76 but is not depicted until page 78. However, the poetic account of Noah's drunkenness extends over several pages, and the illustration does coincide with the end of the story. Such an arrangement is not unprecedented; Michelle Brown notes, for example, that the evangelist portraits in the ninth-century Book of Cerne preface extracts from the conclusions of the four gospels rather than the more usual opening texts.[50] It is, then, more than likely that these three drawings provide an interactive visual gloss, rather than a literal and passive illustration of the text. In a similar vein, the illustration of the sacrifice of Isaac in the Old English Hexateuch (London, British Library, Claudius B. iv, 38r) is placed at the end rather than the beginning of the episode. The three-line capital that begins the sentence 'Ða Noe ongan niwan stefne' ('Then Noah began once again', *Gen.* 1555) at the bottom of page 75 marks a new beginning for both Noah and biblical history. For Noah it is the beginning of his agricultural life and a new fertility of the earth worked by human labour; historically it is the

[50] Brown, *Book of Cerne*, p. 73.

beginning of the second age of the world.[51] Both poem and illustrations repeatedly place emphasis on moments or cycles of Creation and Fall, and within this larger programme it is possible to interpret the illustration of God's covenant with Noah, along with the drawing of Noah offering sacrifice to God, as both framing and illustrating the moment of rebirth and thanksgiving, and the next two illustrations as documenting both the fertility of the land and man's next fall from grace.

Richard Gameson has commented on the fact that the illustration of Noah working the land is clearly the work of a sloppy artist who has placed his drawing randomly over the words of the text, completely disregarding the discrete spaces left for illustrations at the top and bottom of the page, but this need not necessarily be the case. Even the most incompetent of artists could hardly have been unaware of the words written on the page and the fact that he was drawing over them,[52] and perhaps we should turn to the unusual nature of the picture for help in explaining its unusual placement on the page. Traditionally, illustrations of Noah at labour showed him working in the vineyard rather than ploughing, and did not usually include the detail of his family looking on from their house. The text on this page is devoted to Sem and Japheth's obedience to and consideration of their father, and ends with the words 'gode wæren begen sem and iafeð' ('both were good, Sem and Japheth', *Gen.* 1587b–1588a). As Doane notes in his edition of the poem, the emphasis of the text is on the contrast of the two good sons and the harmony of their actions with Cham, the inconsiderate third son, and the disharmony created by his actions.[53] Cham's grandson Nimrod, his seed, will further the wrongdoing through his pride and the construction of the tower of Babel, bringing linguistic disharmony, the loss of a common language, to his people. The illustration sets up just such a contrast. On the left, two sons stand together beneath a single arch watching their father at work. The third son walks ahead of his father and turns back to look at him, disrupting the flow of both the pictorial and the textual narrative. Cham's servile position in the picture looks forward to Noah's

[51] Bede, *In Genesim*, ed. C. W. Jones, CCSL 118A (Turnhout, 1967), pp. 127; Ælfric, 'On the Old and New Testament', in *Heptateuch*, ed. Crawford, p. 24.

[52] The same artist had no trouble ordering his illustrations to correspond with the text in the Anglo-Latin *Psychomachia* manuscript (Cambridge, Corpus Christi College 23) produced around the same time.

[53] Doane, ed., *Genesis A*, p. 278.

curse upon him, that he should be a servant to his higher kinsmen (*hleomaga þeow*, *Gen.* 1595b). A similar reference to Cham at labour occurs in the prose *Solomon and Saturn* in the question and answer: 'Saga me, hwylc man aþohte ærest mid sul to erianne? Ic ðe secge, ðæt wæs Cham, Noes sunu.'[54]

The clear correspondence between text and image is restored with the illustration of the drunkenness of Noah on page 78. Coming at the end of the episode of Noah's drunkenness and Cham's disrespect for his father, the picture recapitulates the story we have just read in the poem, while the luxuriant vegetation and uncovered genitals of Noah prefigure the fertile land and future generations to come.

STRUCTURE AND COHERENCE

One of the characteristics of the text of the Junius 11 manuscript is its complete and carefully structured organization, from the intra- and intertextuality of its poems[55] to its 'unusual systematic and metrical pointing'.[56] With questions of incompetent artists, servile copyists and misplaced drawings out of the way, the chapters that follow will demonstrate that the manuscript was not only carefully compiled to create a series of interrelated narratives, but that the illustrations were meant to be an integral part of that narrative and an aid in establishing the overall unity of the manuscript. As paraphrases of the biblical books of Genesis, Exodus and Daniel, the Old Testament poems imply and incorporate their sources. They are also translations into the vernacular of (for the Anglo-Saxons) an originally Latin text.[57] *Christ and Satan*, the manuscript's only New Testament poem, can also be understood as a paraphrase of selected passages from the gospels. The Junius 11 drawings

[54] 'Tell me, which man first ploughed the land. I tell you that was Cham, Noah's son.' See Raw, 'Probable Derivation', p. 136; J. M. Kemble, *The Dialogues of Solomon and Saturn* (London, 1848), p. 186. See also J. E. Cross and T. D. Hill, *The Prose Solomon and Saturn and Adrian and Ritheus* (Toronto, 1982).

[55] See Hall, 'Old English Epic of Redemption'; Remley, *Biblical Verse*, p. 23; and Pasternack, *Textuality of Old English Poetry*, pp. 179–93.

[56] O'Keeffe, *Visible Song*, pp. 151–2.

[57] On the theory and practice of paraphrase and translation, see R. Copeland, *Rhetoric, Hermeneutics, and Translation in the Middle Ages: Academic Traditions and Vernacular Texts* (Cambridge, 1991), esp. ch. 4.

constitute yet another level of paraphrase and translation, referring not only to the poems they accompany and their textual sources, but to a range of other texts and pictorial traditions as well. This function of illustration as translation is inherent in the very terms 'image' and '*re*presentation'.[58] Together, poems and drawings create a new and unique version of biblical history and suggest ways in which biblical history relates to Anglo-Saxon history, as well as to the manuscript's Anglo-Saxon audience – a process which theoretically extends to include contemporary history and the contemporary reader. We can thus identify a metonymic compilation of text and illustrations which creates a dialogue that echoes back and forth throughout the manuscript, while also making reference to a series of other related texts and images that would have been familiar to an Anglo-Saxon reader. Metonymic composition (or compilation) is characteristic of Anglo-Saxon art and literature and can be traced in works as diverse in date and content as *Beowulf*[59] and the Ruthwell 'cross'.[60] The resulting narratives are never completely open-ended and, in the case of Junius 11, they are carefully structured by aspects of pictorial design, as well as narrative technique. With this in mind, the chapters that follow will first examine the design of the illustrated portion of the manuscript before going on to consider the manuscript as a whole, the relationship between the pictorial and poetic narratives and the intertextuality and intervisuality of each. The term 'intervisuality' was introduced into medieval studies by Michael Camille as a visual parallel to the intertextuality of literary texts.[61] It is used here to refer to images that call to mind 'other images that are formally similar, but which have different

[58] See R. Barthes, 'Rhetoric of the Image', in *The Responsibility of Forms* (New York, 1985), pp. 21–40.

[59] G. Overing, *Language, Sign and Gender in Beowulf* (Carbondale, IL and Edwardsville, 1990). See also C. Pasternack, 'Stylistic Disjunctions in *The Dream of the Rood*', *ASE* 13 (1985), 167–86; Pasternack, *Textuality of Old English Poetry.*

[60] C. E. Karkov, 'Naming and Renaming: The Inscription of Gender in Anglo-Saxon England', in *Theorizing Anglo-Saxon Stone Sculpture*, ed. C. E. Karkov and F. Orton (Morgantown, WV, forthcoming).

[61] M. Camille, 'Gothic Signs and the Surplus: The Kiss on the Cathedral', *Yale French Studies*, special issue: *Contexts: Style and Values in Medieval Art and Literature* (1991), pp. 151–70. Camille defines intervisuality as 'a process in which images are not the stable referents in some ideal iconographic dictionary, but are perceived by their audiences to work across and within different, even competing, value systems' (p. 151).

contexts and thus different connotations',[62] as well as to images that may have different meanings or connotations in different contexts. The final chapter will turn to the issue of the history and historiography of the manuscript, taking up two of the main subtexts that run throughout this manuscript: reading and writing as forms of creation, and the continuum of history constructed in and around this set of texts and images. As the drawings form an original translation of the text, so modern scholars have created, and continue to create, their own translations of the manuscript and narratives of its role in Anglo-Saxon culture according to their own interests and desires, keeping the dead before us as if they were alive.

[62] J. J. G. Alexander, 'Dancing in the Streets', *Jnl of the Walters Art Gallery* 54 (1996), 147–62, at p. 156.

2

Structure, style and design

Before turning to the function and meaning of the pictorial narrative it is necessary to consider briefly the structure and design of the manuscript as a whole. In the study of Junius 11, as in the study of all manuscripts, codicology is crucial to an understanding of how books work as books and not simply as sets of assembled texts. Moreover, there are places in which elements of structure, style and design will have profound ramifications for our interpretation of the poetic and pictorial narratives.

STRUCTURE

The Junius 11 manuscript is divided into two books with the Old Testament poems *Genesis*, *Exodus* and *Daniel* comprising Liber I, and the New Testament poem *Christ and Satan* Liber II. While the end of *Daniel* may be missing, the fact that the manuscript was intended to comprise two books is indicated by the words '*Finit Liber II. Amen*' at the end of *Christ and Satan*, as well as by the thematic difference of this final poem.

Gatherings

The manuscript consists of seventeen gatherings. *Genesis* occupies the first eleven; *Exodus* the twelfth, thirteenth, and the first three pages of the fourteenth; *Daniel* the end of the fourteenth and the fifteenth and sixteenth, ending on the first page of the seventeenth gathering; and *Christ and Satan* the remainder of the seventeenth gathering. The 'normal' gathering seems to have been of eight leaves, though only four gatherings now conform to this structure. The composition of the gatherings is as follows:

I	(pp. 1–8), a bifolium followed by three singletons[1]
II	(pp. 9–12), two singletons
III	(pp. 13–24), two bifolia and two singletons, 6 and 7 wanting[2]
IV–VI	(pp. 25–40, 41–56, 57–72), complete
VII	(pp. 73–90), an extra leaf after 7[3]
VIII	(pp. 91–104), 3 wanting[4]
IX	(pp. 105–16), 3 and 5 wanting[5]
X	(pp. 117–28), 1 and 5 wanting[6]

[1] A. N. Doane, ed. (*Genesis A: A New Edition* (Madison, WI, 1978), p. 5) suggests that an entire gathering has been lost or removed between the first and second gatherings, on the basis that there is 'a gap and general weakening of the binding' at this point. The two leaves of what is now the second gathering (pages 9–12) are all that remains of the missing gathering. They were joined together by a parchment slip prior to rebinding and loosely sewn to the third gathering at the time of rebinding in the fifteenth century. The lost material might have included an account of the third to sixth days of Creation, and would certainly have included the description and (presumably) depiction of the creation of Adam and, possibly, his naming of the animals. Page 9 contains the creation of Eve.

[2] A. N. Doane, ed., *The Saxon Genesis: An Edition of the West Saxon Genesis B and the Old Saxon 'Vatican Genesis'* (Madison, WI, 1991), pp. 30–1; B. C. Raw, 'The Construction of Oxford, Bodleian Library, Junius 11', *ASE* 13 (1984), 187–207, at p. 193. Stitching patterns suggest two leaves cut out at this point after the thirteenth-century resewing. The stubs of the cut-out leaves can still be seen before page 19. It is impossible to say what, if anything, is actually missing in terms of the content of the poem. There is no break in the sense of the narrative between pages 22 and 23 (lines 441–2). Doane's belief that the text jumps awkwardly from 'Satan's speech inveigling his retainers to seduce Adam and Eve to a scene in which one of the minor devils is already preparing to make the journey' (p. 31), is indicative only of a change in action, and not necessarily of a gap in the narrative.

[3] The added leaf (pages 87 and 88) contains two full-page illustrations of Abraham building an altar and Abraham and his people approaching Egypt. These drawings, the work of the second artist, are the last of the completed illustrations.

[4] Doane, ed., *Genesis A*, p. 10. A leaf has been cut out after page 94. There is no break in the sense of the text and the missing page may have been left blank for illustrations.

[5] Doane, ed., *Genesis A*, p. 10. Knife-marks indicate that leaves have been cut out after pages 108 and 110. Again, there is no break in the narrative sense of the poem, though significant episodes are missing from the biblical story. The page missing after 108 is likely to have contained an account of the visit of the three angels to Abraham and the annunciation of the birth of Isaac, and that after 110 the dialogue between Abraham and God over the destruction of Sodom.

[6] Doane, ed., *Genesis A*, pp. 10–11. Knife marks and projecting tags provide evidence for the two missing leaves (the first after page 116 and the second after page 122). Both

XI (pp. 129–42), 4 wanting[7]
XII (pp. 143–54), 4 and 5 wanting[8]
XIII (pp. 155–68), 6 wanting[9]
XIV (pp. 169–80), 8 wanting, and one leaf inserted at centre (pp. 175/6)[10]
XV (pp. 181–94), gathering of six, one leaf inserted after 5[11]
XVI (pp. 195–210), complete
XVII (pp. 211–29), gathering of ten, two singletons at 4 and 7 (pp. 217/18)[12]

The apparent lack of uniformity created by the various missing and inserted pages led Farrell to argue that Junius 11 was 'an excellent example of non-conformity to quires of eight'.[13] Lucas, Doane and Raw have, however, presented cogent arguments for the validity of most of the

leaves may have been left blank for illustrations as there is no sign of a break in the sense of the narrative nor a significant gap in the Genesis material recounted.

7 Doane, ed., *Genesis A*, p. 10. A leaf has been cut out after page 134. Again, this is likely to have been a blank leaf intended for illustration, and presumably removed by someone in need of blank parchment. There is no break in the sense of the poem.

8 P. J. Lucas, ed., *Exodus* (London, 1977), p. 7. The central bifolio of the gathering is lost, and there is clearly material missing after line 141, which breaks off in mid-sentence. I. Gollancz suggests that the missing material may have covered the story of Joseph in Egypt, though this is far from certain. Gollancz, ed., *The Cædmon Manuscript of Anglo-Saxon Biblical Poetry: Junius XI in the Bodleian Library* (London, 1927), p. cxii.

9 Lucas, ed., *Exodus*, pp. 7–8. A leaf has been cut out after page 164, and its stub is still visible. There is a clear change of subject between lines 446 and 447, and it is likely that the missing material covered the final stages of the crossing of the Red Sea and the Egyptians' pursuit of the Israelites (Lucas, p. 131).

10 R. T. Farrell, ed., *Daniel and Azarius* (London, 1974), p. 3; Gollancz, ed., *Cædmon Manuscript*, p. cxiii. A fragment of parchment at this point appears to be the remains of a leaf cut from the manuscript. There is also a break in the sense of the poem. The missing material is likely to have contained Daniel III.2–6, and possibly an illustration. Page 175/6 is a singleton inserted at the centre of the gathering.

11 Farrell, ed., *Daniel*, pp. 4–5; Gollancz, ed., *Cædmon Manuscript*, p. cxiii. There is no break in the sense of the poem, and no evidence of illustrations missing from this gathering. There is no evidence that the inserted leaf was a later addition.

12 R. E. Finnegan, ed., *Christ and Satan: A Critical Edition* (Waterloo, 1977), p. 4. The composition of this gathering continues to be a problem. The single leaves between pages 216 and 219, and 222 and 225, may be insertions, or may indicate that material has been cut from the manuscript. There is no indication that any text is missing, but it is possible that illustrations were intended. See below, page 205.

13 Farrell, ed., *Daniel*, p. 4.

losses and insertions, and hence the overall uniformity of the gatherings in their original format.[14] Though crucial to a reading of the poems, the uniformity of the gatherings has little bearing on the relationship of the illustrations to the text, with the exception of the section containing *Christ and Satan*. Therefore, only those instances in which missing or inserted leaves impact on the narrative structure of the manuscript will be considered in the chapters that follow. Detailed analysis of the structure of the individual gatherings is readily available in the facsimile edition of the manuscript and the editions of the individual poems.

Sections

The unity of the poems comprising Liber I is indicated by page layout and scribal practice, as well as by the lack of individual titles for the separate poems, and the section-numbers (i–lv) that run continuously through them.[15] *Christ and Satan* (Liber II) is divided into twelve sections. There are problems with the section numbering in Liber I which have led to the suggestion that they were imperfectly copied from a lost exemplar or exemplars.[16] Some section numbers are clearly errors: for example, the 'viiii' between sections xviii and xx is obviously a mistake for 'xviiii'. Other numbers have been lost due to damage to the manuscript, and still others have not been marked at all, but are indicated by spacing and capitalization. Despite the problems, the important thing – as Remley notes – is that 'the system of numeration never breaks down completely'.[17]

The manner in which the sectional divisions relate to the narrative flow of the poem is another matter. There are places in which they appear to break up the sense of the verse, and this has led to the hypothesis of at least four stages in the transmission from exemplars to final poetic text.[18]

[14] Lucas, ed., *Exodus*, pp. 7–8 and 13–15; Doane, ed., *Genesis A*, pp. 4–11; Raw, 'Construction'.

[15] On the unity of Liber II see C. Stévanovitch, 'Envelope Patterns and the Unity of the Old English *Christ and Satan*', *ASNSL* 233 (1996), 260–7.

[16] P. G. Remley, *Old English Biblical Verse* (Cambridge, 1996), pp. 24–9; Doane, ed., *Genesis A*, p. 12; Doane, ed., *Saxon Genesis*, p. 29.

[17] Remley, *Biblical Verse*, p. 25.

[18] *Ibid.*, p. 28. Remley envisages: 'First, a compositional stage, in the course of which some or all of the poems, arising under separate circumstances, may have been divided

However, some of these awkward breaks, for example section vii[i] (page 21), where the first sentence begins with the conjunction *Ac* ('but'), are clearly deliberate. The initial 'A' of *Ac* is a major decorated initial (pl. Xb) and is preceded by a full-page illustration (pl. Xa). This is no haphazard break in the text. The division here, as well as what might be seen as the awkward grammar of the sentence, can be understood as reflecting the narrative content of the surrounding verse, which moves from Satan lamenting his bonds, 'an index of words for fetters and fettering',[19] in the first person singular on page 19, to an acknowledgement of a shared fate and the beginning of his plan for revenge, all in the first person plural, on page 21. The importance of the change in voice to a reading of the poem is clear, and both scribe and artist have done everything possible to flag this to the reader. Note the change in both pronouns and metre initiated by the first line of section vii[i] on the eighteenth line of the passage:

ic eom rices leas.
habbað me swa hearde helleclommas.
fæste befangen. her is fyr micel.
ufan and neoðone. ic a ne geseah.
laðran landscipe. lig ne aswamað.
hat ofer helle. me habbað hringa gespong.
sliðhearda sal. siðes amyrred.
afyrred me min feðe. fet synt gebundene.
handa gehæfte. synt þissa heldora.
wegas forworhte. swa ic mid wihte ne mæg.
of þissum lioðobendum. licgað me ymbe.[20]
heardes irenes. hate geslægene.
grindlas greate. mid þy me god hafað.

into sections. Then followed a stage of transmission involving the circulation of the poems as separate items. This stage possibly involved the introduction of new sectional divisions or the alteration of existing ones. Next came the stage (possibly a two-part process) at which the texts now witnessed by *Genesis*, *Exodus*, and *Daniel* were brought together in a single exemplar and supplied with a comprehensive series of section numbers, possibly also involving the introduction or alteration of sectional divisions. The final stage is represented by the sole surviving witness to the whole transmissional sequence – the received text preserved in Junius 11.'

19 Doane, ed., *Saxon Genesis*, p. 132.

20 In the manuscript the final e of *ymbe* and the following point have been erased, and *utan* added above the line by the corrector.

gehæfted be þam healse. swa ic wat he minne hige cuðe.
and þæt wiste eac. weroda drihten.
þæt sceolde unc adam. yfele gewurðan.
ymb þæt heofonrice. þær ic ahte minra handa geweald. vii[i].
AC ÐOLIAÞ we nu þrea on helle. þæt syndon þystro and hæto.
grimme, grundlease. hafaþ us god sylfa.
forswapen on þas sweartan mistas. swa he us ne mæg ænige synne gestælan.
þæt we him on þam lande lað gefremedon. he hæfð us þeah þæs leohtes.
[bescyrede.
beworpen on ealra wita mæste. ne magon we þæs wrace gefremman.
geleanian him mid laðes wihte. þæt he us hafað þæs leohtes bescyrede.
he hæfð nu gemearcod. anne middangeard. þær he hæfð mon geworhtne.
æfter his onlicnesse. mid þam he wile eft gesettan.
heofona rice. mid hluttrum saulum. we þæs sculon hycgan georne.
þæt we on adame. gif we æfre mægen.
and on his eafrum swa some. andan gebetan.
onwendan him þær willan sines. gif we hit mægen wihte aþencan.[21]

In this passage, the awkward section break and sentence structure help draw attention to both the spread of evil and Satan's own flawed language and reasoning. He is not, as he claims, without sin, and his words and plans are therefore based on a false premise.[22] The hypermetric lines also

21 'I am powerless, hell chains have clasped me so tightly. Here is great fire, above and below. I have never seen a more hateful landscape. Fire, hot over hell does not move away. Chains of rings, a tormenting cord, have prevented me from moving. My power of moving has been taken from me; my feet are bound, hands fettered. The ways through these hell-doors are barred, so I cannot escape from these bonds. Hard iron forged in heat, great bars, lie about me. With them God has fettered me by the neck, so that I know he knew my mind; and that he also knows, the Lord of hosts, that there would be evil between me and Adam over that heavenly kingdom, if I had the use of my hands. vii[i].

'But now we suffer pain in hell (darkness and heat), grim and fathomless. God himself has swept us away in these dark mists. Though he cannot attribute any sin to us, any hateful thing that we did to him in that land. He has yet cut us off from that light, cast us down in the greatest of punishments. We cannot carry out any vengeance for this, repay him with something hateful because he has cut us off from that light. He has now marked out a middle earth where he has created man in his own likeness. With him he will again settle the kingdom of heaven with pure souls. We must earnestly consider this, that if ever we are able, on Adam and his descendants too we will satisfy our anger, deprive him of his will, if we can at all contrive it.' *Gen.* 372b–401.

22 And see below, p. 106.

alert the reader to the difference of his language.[23] Of equal importance to an understanding of this break is the iconography of the picture on page 20 (pl. Xa), which visually marks the shift in voice by depicting Satan's messenger (the embodiment of his false voice) moving from hell into paradise. With this drawing the Fall begins. Satan's 'us' here becomes applicable not only to his present kingdom, but stands as a warning to Adam, Eve and the readers of the text, that they too might some day be included in it.

A similar rupture in the fortunes of man is indicated by the combination of section break and initial conjunction at the beginning of section xx. Again, a major decorated capital begins the first sentence of a new fitt:

> OÐÞÆT bearn godes. bryda ongunnon.
> on caines cynne secan.[24]

This is the decisive moment that introduces the flood narrative, a second fall from grace, and the break in linguistic flow combined with the graphic break in the text helps drive this point home. Nevertheless, we cannot label such breaks unusual because they 'begin with clauses uncharacteristically introduced by conjunctions',[25] since a large initial *Oðþæt* also begins fitt xxv and line 2039 in *Beowulf*.[26]

The awkward section break and capital letter at line 107 of *Exodus* (page 148) also occurs at a dramatic juncture, the point at which the Israelites become sailors, their journey a sea voyage, and their voices raised in joy ('hlud heriges cyrm'). The space left for an illustration at the bottom of page 147 indicates that once again the break in the textual narrative was to have been signalled by an illustration. While we cannot be certain of the exact subject intended for the illustration, it is true that any illustration introduces a pause in the reading process and indicates that we must stop to study the image and its meaning before proceeding with the textual narrative.[27]

[23] As does the use of envelope patterns. See Stévanovitch, 'Envelope Patterns and Unity'; C. Stévanovitch, 'The Translator and the Text of the Old English *Genesis B*', *The Medieval Translator* 5 (1996), 130–45.

[24] 'Until the children of God began to seek wives amongst the race of Cain.' *Gen.* 1248–9.

[25] Remley, *Biblical Verse*, p. 28.

[26] I would like to thank Patrick W. Conner for drawing this to my attention.

[27] The classic study of this phenomenon is K. Weitzmann, *Illustrations in Roll and Codex: A Study of the Origins and Method of Text Illustration*, 2nd edn (Princeton, NJ, 1970).

The section numbering of *Daniel* is relatively regular. Four of the original six section numbers are recorded and each is followed by an initial capital of at least three lines. The numbers for sections lii and liv (pages 184, 199) are missing, but in both cases the section division is marked by the enlarged capital. Spaces for illustrations have been left before four of the six sections.[28] The final section (lv) is extremely short, consisting of only 89 lines. As the other sections range in length from 103 (l) to 179 (liv) lines, the noticeably shorter length of this final section supports the argument, rejected by the poem's editor,[29] that *Daniel* ends incomplete. On the other hand, there are, as we shall see, contextual and narrative reasons for accepting the poem's present ending as its intended one.[30]

In *Christ and Satan* only sections ii, iii, v, and vi are introduced by small Roman numerals. Ten of the twelve sections into which the poem is divided are marked by two-line initial capitals. Spaces for similar capitals never completed were left at the beginnings of sections vii (page 220) and xi (page 226). Section xi begins at the top of page 226. The lower half of page 225 is filled with an incomplete repeating pattern of diamonds and quatrefoils filled with foliate rosettes, a design that has been interpreted as that of a manuscript binding, possibly one intended for this manuscript.[31] The cramped letters of the last two lines of the poem above the drawing indicate that these lines have been squeezed into a confined space, and make it clear that the drawing preceded the text and in this case has no significance to the structure or meaning of the poem.

PALAEOGRAPHY AND PUNCTUATION

Junius 11 is written throughout in Anglo-Saxon minuscule. *Genesis*, *Exodus* and *Daniel* are the work of one scribe writing in a square minuscule characteristic of the late tenth century, a somewhat old-fashioned hand if the manuscript is indeed of eleventh-century date. Doane describes the handwriting as 'distinctive, clear and regular, but not particularly elegant',[32] a description that might equally well apply to the style of the

28 The exceptions are sections liii and lv.

29 Farrell, ed., *Daniel*, pp. 32–3.

30 See below, p. 139.

31 Gollancz, ed., *Cædmon Manuscript*, p. xxxvi.

32 Doane, ed., *Genesis A*, p. 13.

illustrations. The punctuation of the poems is also clear and regular. The scribe (with some help from a later corrector) has indicated the end of almost every half-line with a metrical point, and emphasized the ends of larger sections within the poem with a more emphatic triangle of three points, a *punctus versus*, or a *punctus elevatus*. In other words, the reader confronts a carefully structured text in which both sense and metre are clearly signposted.[33]

Christ and Satan is the work of three different scribes whose hands may be dated to the early eleventh century. The first scribe, responsible for pages 213–15, writes with a rounded, irregular hand, often described as 'incompetent'.[34] The second hand begins on page 216 and continues to page 228. In general the work of this scribe is clearer and more regular than that of the first, but, beginning near the middle of page 227, the text becomes cramped and more difficult to read, most likely indicating a lack of time and/or space. Abbreviations are also more frequent in the final two pages of the poem. The third hand, responsible for page 229 only, is very close to the second. The punctuation of *Christ and Satan* is similar to, but less consistent than, that of the Old Testament poems. Metrical pointing is used to indicate half-lines, with larger poetic sections marked by a *punctus elevatus* or *punctus versus*. Some of this punctuation has, however, been attributed to a later corrector's attempts to regularize orthography and punctuation with those of the scribe of the first three poems. Thus, while the three scribes of Liber II produced a text that was visually less ordered than that produced by the scribe of Liber I, an attempt was made to suggest a unified structure to the reader.

Accents have been inserted sporadically by a later corrector, and if there is a general pattern to their distribution and function it has yet to be discerned. Despite their seeming irregularity they were clearly rhetorical rather than grammatical, and they were equally clearly designed to assist in the reading aloud of the text.[35] Thornley's suggestion that the accents

33 See K. O'Brien O'Keeffe, *Visible Song: Transitional Literacy in Old English Verse*, CSASE 14 (Cambridge, 1990), particularly pp. 179–87.

34 Gollancz, ed., *Cædmon Manuscript*, p. xcviii; M. D. Clubb, ed., *Christ and Satan: An Old English Poem* (New Haven, CT, 1925), p. xii; N. R. Ker, *Catalogue of Manuscripts Containing Anglo-Saxon* (Oxford, 1957), p. 408.

35 Gollancz, ed., *Cædmon Manuscript*, p. xxiv; G. C. Thornley, 'The Accents and Points of MS. Junius 11', *Trans. of the Philological Soc.* (1954), 178–205; Lucas, ed., *Exodus*, pp. 34–5; Doane, ed., *Genesis A*, p. 16.

are derived from liturgical chant is interesting and, if true, underscores the dramatic and performative nature of the poems.

A variety of *litterae notabiliores* ('more notable letters') are used as visual cues to reading throughout the manuscript. Small capitals appear frequently as a means of indicating the beginning of *sententiae*, semantic or rhetorical units, often, but not always, grammatical sentences.[36] The situation is complicated, however, by the fact that in some instances it is difficult to determine whether or not an enlarged letter is meant to be read as a small capital. Be that as it may, Gollancz points out that nineteen of the twenty small capitals in *Exodus* mark the beginning of verse lines, with all but one being preceded by a blank space.[37] Lucas notes further that nine of the small capitals in *Exodus* mark 'positions of substantial pause'.[38] In *Daniel* small capitals are used more regularly to begin new episodes, speeches, the resumption of the narrative after a speech, etc. There are also sections of the poems, mostly in *Genesis*, in which clusters of small capitals may be designed to draw our attention to a certain passage, or a series of events or statements. For example, in the passage in which the Lord gives Adam and Eve dominion over paradise, the word *Inc* is capitalized three times in the space of seven lines: 'Inc sceal sealt water' (*Gen.* 198b), 'Inc is halig feoh' (*Gen.* 201b), 'Inc hyrað eall' (*Gen.* 205b). Similarly, in Satan's speech before the second Fall of the angels *Ic* is capitalized four times in nine lines:

Ic mæg mid handum swa fela.
wundra gewyrcean. Ic hæbbe geweald micel.
to gyrwanne. godlecran stol.
hearran on heofne. hwy sceal ic æfter his hyldo ðeowian.
bugan him swilces geongordomes. Ic mæg wesan god swa he.
bigstandað me. strange geneatas. þa ne willað me æt þam striðe. geswican.
hæleþas heardmode. hie habbað me to hearran gecorene.
rofe rincas. mid swilcum mæg man ræd geþencean.
fon mid swilcum folcgesteallan. frynd synd hie mine georne.
holde on hyra hygesceaftum. Ic mæg hyra hearra wesan.
rædan on þis rice.[39]

[36] For *litterae notabiliores* and *sententiae* in general see M. B. Parkes, *Pause and Effect: Punctuation in the West* (Aldershot, 1982), pp. 1–6 and 20–9.

[37] Gollancz, ed., *Cædmon Manuscript*, pp. xix–xx.

[38] Lucas, ed., *Exodus*, p. 19.

[39] 'I can work as many wonders with my hands. I have great power to prepare a godlier

In both cases, the series of small capitals seems intended to alert the eye to the metrical repetition of the lines and the pattern of related statements. In *Christ and Satan* a small capital is not just used as a cue for the beginning of speeches or episodes, but also serves to highlight the use of anaphora.[40] The first *Eala* of Satan's lament on page 216 begins with a small capital, and the word is repeated nine times in the space of five lines:

> Eala drihtenes þrym.   eala duguða helm.
> eala meotodes miht.   eala middaneard.
> eala dæg leohta.   eala dream godes.
> eala engla þreat.   eala upheofen.
> eala þæt ic eam ealles leas.   ecan dreames.[41]

The same pattern is used to add rhetorical emphasis to the final description of Satan's plight in hell on page 229:

> hwilum mid folmum mæt.
> wean and witu.   Hwilum se wonna leg.[42]
> læhte wið þes laþen.   hwilum he licgan geseah.
> hæftas in hylle.   hwilum hream astag.[43]
> Đonne he on þone atolan.   eagum gesawun.[44]

In his edition of the Junius manuscript, Krapp expressed his belief that the small capitals must have had rhetorical value; however, if there is a

throne, higher in heaven. Why must I serve after his favour, submit to him in such service? I can be a god as well as he. Strong companions stand beside me, heroes hard of spirit who will not withdraw from me at the battle. They, strong warriors, have chosen me as lord; with such comrades in arms one can begin to work out a plan. They are my eager friends, loyal in their hearts. I can be their lord, and govern in this kingdom.' *Gen.* 279b–288. Gollancz (*Cædmon Manuscript*, p. xx) notes the unusual number of small capitals occurring in the middle of verse lines in *Genesis*, but offers no explanation for the phenomenon.

40 On the use of anaphora and other classical rhetorical figures in *Christ and Satan* see Finnegan, *Christ and Satan*, pp. 151–61. See also Stévanovitch, 'Envelope Patterns and the Unity'.

41 'Alas the glory of the Lord. Alas the helmet of men. Alas the power of God. Alas earth. Alas the light of day. Alas the joy of God. Alas the troop of angels. Alas the heavens above. Alas that I am completely without eternal joy.' *Christ and Satan* 163–7.

42 In the manuscript æ has been erased and changed to an e.

43 The h of *hream* was added above the line by the corrector.

44 'At times with his hands he measured woes and tortures. At times the dark flame flared up against the evil one. At times he saw captives lying in hell. At times clamour arose when he looked on that horror with his eyes.' *Christ and Satan* 713b–716b.

general pattern to the use of small capitals in the poems, it is difficult to discern. Their distribution throughout the manuscript and within the individual poems is extremely uneven, and there are long sections, particularly in *Exodus*, where there is no capitalization whatsoever. Doane's suspicion that the irregular use of small capitals may be a remnant of 'a much more systematic use of small capitals in an ancestor' may indeed be accurate.[45]

In the passages cited above, however, the patterns of repetition and alliteration not only call attention to these sections of the text, but are mnemonics, ensuring that the rhythmical words remain in our memory. Ong and Pasternack have explored the ways in which such mnemonic devices are used to shape our reading and understanding of texts.[46] Pasternack describes passages like those cited above as 'incantational', noting that 'The highly rhythmic and repetitive language prevents analytical engagement with the assertions, while the chanting facilitates memory and incites belief in the truthfulness of the words.'[47] They also serve to connect the written text to the oral-formulaic tradition, lending the words the weight of time and authority.[48] In other words, as Bäuml has suggested, the oral tradition becomes a character within the written text,[49] and one whose appearance demands that the reader/listener pay particularly close attention.

Satan's two speeches are also significant in their difference from each other. In the passage from *Genesis*, the capitalization and repetition of *Ic mæg/Ic hæbbe* adds to the false confidence reflected in his words. Despite his boasts, he cannot be God and he neither does nor will have great power in heaven. The error of his language is indicated by the hypermetric nature of the entire speech in which this passage is contained, and the envelope patterns that structure it.[50] The difference between it and the

45 Doane, ed., *Genesis A*, p. 13.

46 C. B. Pasternack, *The Textuality of Old English Poetry*, CSASE 13 (Cambridge, 1995), pp. 60–9; W. J. Ong, *Orality and Literacy: The Technologizing of the Word* (London, 1982), p. 34.

47 Pasternack, *Textuality*, p. 60.

48 *Ibid.*, p. 62.

49 F. Bäuml, 'Medieval Texts and the Two Theories of Oral-Formulaic Composition: A Proposal for a Third Theory', *New Literary History* 16 (1984), 31–49, at 43; see also O'Keeffe, *Visible Song*, and Pasternack, *Textuality*, p. 62.

50 Stévanovitch, 'Envelope Patterns and Unity'.

lament from *Christ and Satan* could not be more profound. In the latter, confined to hell and fully aware of all that has been lost, Satan's true despair and the gravity of his fate are reflected in the ordered rhythm of both words and metre. Anaphora also turns the speech into a type of chant, a traditional form for lamentation.[51]

While there may be no *consistent* pattern to the distribution of small capitals within the manuscript, the major decorated initials are clearly used for rhetorical emphasis, in addition to their practical role of marking sectional divisions within the poems. In the case of the Old Testament verses, the continuity of the initials is used to emphasize the unity of the poems, visually connecting each to, as well as distinguishing each from, the others. Capitals decorated with beast and bird heads are used to introduce sections up to page 73 and, with only two exceptions, plain enlarged initials are used thereafter. There are also a number of places in which space has been left for initials never completed (thirty-three in all).

The manuscript contains twenty-one zoomorphic initials and one foliate initial.[52] All but the initial on page 226 are the work of one hand,[53] and are executed in Wormald's Type 1 (letters formed from whole creatures).[54] In four instances, all in sections dealing with the Fall of the

[51] Although anaphora is a classical form of rhetorical embellishment within a written text, its incantational effects on the ear of the listener should not be overlooked – particularly as this manuscript was clearly intended to be read aloud at some stage in its development. In his *De schematibus et tropis*, written 700–1, Bede carefully established scripture as a source of and exemplar for such rhetorical figures. See *De schematibus et tropis*, ed. C. Kendall CCSL 123A (Turnhout, 1975), pp. 142–71; trans. G. H. Tannenhaus, 'Concerning Figures and Tropes', in *Readings in Medieval Rhetoric*, ed. J. M. Miller, M. H. Prosser and T. W. Benson (Bloomington, IN and London, 1973), pp. 96–122.

[52] The zoomorphic initials occur on pages 1, 5, 8, 14, 18, 21, 23, 26, 32, 38, 42, 48, 52, 58, 63, 67, 71, 73, 79, 143, 226. The foliate initial is on page 43.

[53] Gollancz identified the first artist as the author of the zoomorphic initials (*Cædmon Manuscript*, p. xiii), but Henderson has shown that this is not necessarily the case, and that the scribe could equally well have been responsible for the initials ('The Programme of Illustrations in Bodleian MS Junius XI', in *Studies in Memory of David Talbot Rice*, ed. G. Robertson and G. Henderson (Edinburgh, 1975), pp. 113–45, at p. 140). Lucas too sees various hands as responsible for the initials ('MS Junius 11 and Malmesbury', *Scriptorium* 34 (1980), 197–220, at p. 206; and 35 (1981), 3–22).

[54] F. Wormald, 'Decorated Initials in English MSS, from A.D. 900 to 1100', *Archaeologia* 91 (1945), 107–35, at pp. 119–21.

rebel angels and the Fall of man, the decorated initials may also be thematically linked to the content of the poem. The beasts of the eight-line initial 'H' on page 14 (pl. VIIb), the nine-line initial 'A' at the top of page 21 (pl. Xb), the six-line capital 'A' at the top of page 23 (pl. XIa), and the seven-line initial 'H' on page 42 are all much fiercer looking than those contained in the other seventeen decorated initials. They have open mouths and prominent teeth with which they snap at words within the text. In the initial 'H' of the following passage on page 14, the lower of the two beast heads curls round to bite at the *lig* of *halig*, perhaps an indication of the deceit that betrays the Lord's trust and brings about the fall of the angels:

HÆFDE se alwalda. engelcynna.
þurh handmægen. halig drihten.
tene getrimede. þæm he getruwode wel.[55]

As already noted, the initial 'A' on page 21 begins the phrase 'Ac ðoliaþ we nu þrea on helle' ('but now we suffer pain in hell', *Gen.* 389). The decorated letter marks a shift in voice and somewhat unusually breaks up the sentence into an awkward grammatical unit, suggestive of Lucifer/Satan's faulty reasoning and language. Visually the snapping beast-heads become graphic signs of the pains of hell, as well as the danger that threatens Adam and Eve, both of whom gesture towards the initial from the full-page picture on page 20. The initial on page 23 occurs in the description of the messenger's departure from hell. One of its beast-heads bites at the word *hearde* of the line 'hæleð helm on heafod asette and þone full hearde geband' ('he set a helmet of invisibility on his head and then fastened it very securely', *Gen.* 444). The initial on page 42 begins the series of dialogues between Adam, God and Eve that prefaces the expulsion from paradise. Again, one of the beast-heads bites at the text, this time at the phrase 'and wrihst sceome' ('and hide in shame', *Gen.* 876b). Together, these three initials mark the conception of Satan's plot against Adam and Eve, its enactment and its result. This is, of course, one of the most dramatic sections of *Genesis*, and certainly the one that has the most dire consequences for mankind, and the text and illustrations of Junius 11 here work together to drive home that point.

[55] 'Through the strength of his hand the ruler of the race of angels, the holy Lord, had created ten in whom he trusted well.' *Gen.* 246–8.

THE STYLE OF THE ILLUSTRATIONS

Both of the Junius 11 artists[56] worked in a style of outline drawing that combined the native interest in dynamic surface patterns and flickering lines with the expressionism of the Carolingian Reims style. Their figures are energetic, portrayed in active poses and with expressive gestures, all of which help to convey a sense of narrative within and between pictures.

The first artist, who completed the drawings as far as page 68, used a firm line and worked predominantly in brown and red ink with occasional washes of brown, red, olive, blue and ochre. The lush acanthus foliage, colour washes, and frequent overlapping of figures, frames and foliage suggest the influence of the 'Winchester Style', associated with the art of the monastic reform. His figures appear somewhat short and heavy in comparison with those of the second artist, an effect enhanced by his heavier lines and more limited colour range. Iconographically, however, his drawings are far more complex than those completed by his successor. He also shows a marked preference for exaggerated gestures, twisting poses, and architectural frames and settings. In terms of conveying narrative progression he may be the more capable of the two artists. However, as the second artist completed only ten of the forty-eight drawings, such generalizations are risky.

The second artist works in a more sketchy, illusionistic style characterized by short pen strokes that give a flickering quality to his lines and a liveliness to his figures (pls. XXXVI–XLIIIb). The prominent dot he uses to portray eyes, along with the open mouths of many of his figures, draws our attention to their faces. In general, his figures are more elongated and graceful than those of the first artist, and his lighter palette of red, blue and green ink adds a sense of buoyancy to the poses. But there is also a less naturalistic relationship between his figures and their architectural settings. On page 88 (pl. XLIIIb), for example, there is a pronounced difference in scale between Abraham and his people outside the city, and the people of Egypt within it. It may be argued that in this case the artist was trying to suggest distance, or perhaps even the superiority of Abraham and his followers to the Egyptians; however, an equally

[56] The drawing of a lion on page 31, and two figures on page 96, were added by a third, much later artist and will not be dealt with here as they have no relevance to the original pictorial programme.

awkward relationship between figures and architecture is evident in the drawings of Noah and his family leaving the ark on page 73 (pl. XXXVI) and Nimrod and his men on page 81 (pl. XLI), where no such argument can be made. Only in the scene of Noah's ploughing on page 77 (pl. XXXIX) can his figures be described as properly inhabiting the architecture in which they are set.

There does not seem to be any consistent use of colour symbolism in the drawings; however, there is an exception in the scene of the Fall of the rebel angels on page 3 (pl. IIb) in which the first artist appears to have used colour to create a visual parallel to the Fall from light into darkness described in the poem.[57] The upper register of the drawing, with the crowned Lucifer, his adoring followers and desired throne, is predominantly in red ink. In the middle two registers only God, who casts spears down towards hell, and the angel standing beside him are drawn in a combination of red and brown ink, the rest of the figures are entirely in brown. In the lowest register, hell and the falling angels are all in brown, except for a few lines of red ink around the mouth of hell and among the flames surrounding the chained Satan. Similarly, the artist has used the contrast between the tempter's dark hair on page 24 (pl. XIb) and his fair hair on page 28 (pl. XII) to help suggest the change in his appearance between the Temptation of Adam and the Temptation of Eve. In general, however, there is no obvious significance to the first artist's use of red or brown ink.

There is also no clear pattern to the first artist's use of colour wash. On page 9 (pl. IV), for example, God's halo is shaded red on the right side of the page and slightly yellow on the left, while on page 10 it is a brownish-yellow with a red, rather than black, cross at the centre. On page 11 he appears with a diadem but no halo, but here his robes and book have been painted in shades of reddish-brown and green (pl. VI). It is unclear why the artist chose to use full colour for the Lord's figure here but nowhere else in the manuscript. Perhaps he simply intended to draw our attention to this final appearance of the Lord in paradise before the second Fall of the angels and the Fall of man. This may also explain why it is only here and in the poem's frontispiece (pl. I) that God is depicted

[57] T. H. Ohlgren, 'The Illustrations of the Cædmonian Genesis as a Guide to the Interpretation of the Text' (unpubl. PhD dissertation, University of Michigan, 1969), p. 206.

frontally, looking directly out at the reader rather than responding to the figures and action within the image.

The style of the drawings is unfortunately no help in establishing the origins of the manuscript. Junius 11 has traditionally been attributed to Christ Church, Canterbury,[58] although attributions to Winchester,[59] Glastonbury, and Malmesbury[60] have also been posited. The hand of the second artist has been identified in several of the drawings in the *Psychomachia* (Cambridge, Corpus Christi College 23), also traditionally attributed to Canterbury, though again the attribution has been questioned.[61] Neither the Winchester style whose influence is evident in the work of the first artist, nor the more strongly Reims-influenced work of the second artist can be linked to a specific location, as both were popular across the south of England during the second half of the tenth century.[62] Moreover, artists could also travel from monastery to monastery, making the association of individual hands with particular locales all but impossible to establish.[63]

A distinction has sometimes been made in the quality of the work produced by the two artists,[64] but such distinctions rest on modern

58 M. R. James, *The Ancient Libraries of Canterbury and Dover. The Catalogues of the Libraries of Christ Church Priory and St Augustine's Abbey at Canterbury and of St Martin's Priory at Dover* (Cambridge, 1903), pp. xxv–xxvi and 509. See summaries in Lucas, 'Malmesbury I'; Temple, *Anglo-Saxon Manuscripts*, no. 58; and Gameson, *Role of Art*, pp. 37–8.

59 Gollancz, ed., *Cædmon Manuscript*, p. xxxv. Gollancz's attribution is based largely on his desire to see the Ælfwine of the portrait on page 2 as Abbot Ælfwine of Winchester.

60 Lucas, 'Malmesbury I'; 'Malmesbury II'.

61 Lucas, 'Malmesbury I', p. 215; M. Budny, *Insular, Anglo-Saxon and Early Anglo-Norman Manuscript Art at Corpus Christi College, Cambridge* (Kalamazoo, MI, 1998), no. 24.

62 The rise in popularity of the outline drawing style has been connected with the arrival at Canterbury by the early eleventh century of the Utrecht Psalter (Biblioteek der Rijksuniversiteit, MS 32), illustrated *c.* 916–40. The Harley Psalter (London, British Library, Harley 603), the earliest surviving copy of Utrecht, was begun at Christ Church *c.* 1000. However, both Deshman and Higgitt have documented the popularity of the style in southern England by the second half of the tenth century. See R. Deshman, 'The Leofric Missal and Tenth-Century English Art', *ASE* 6 (1977), 145–73; J. Higgitt, 'Glastonbury, Dunstan, Monasticism and Manuscripts', *Art History* 2 (1979), 275–90.

63 R. Gameson, 'English Manuscript Art in the Mid-Eleventh Century: The Decorative Tradition', *Antiquaries Jnl* 71 (1991), 64–122, at p. 67.

64 See, for example, Gameson, 'English Manuscript Art', p. 69.

concerns with aesthetics and notions of what constitutes a good drawing. In terms of conveying a visual narrative and relating the illustrations to the text, both artists are successful, and this may have been of more concern to the patron (and audience) of Junius 11 than the niceties of figure style. While there are very few descriptions of what exactly the Anglo-Saxons valued in a manuscript's illustrations, a useful hint is provided by the Benedictional of Bishop Æthelwold, produced in Winchester *c.* 970. Æethelwold, it seems, was far more interested in the lavishness of the borders, the variety of colours and the number of figures that would appear in his manuscript than in the way the figures were represented. The dedication poem of the manuscript states that Æthelwold 'commanded also to be made in his book many arches well-adorned and filled with various figures decorated with numerous beautiful colours and with gold'.[65]

THE NARRATIVE STRUCTURE OF THE ILLUSTRATIONS

Neither of the Junius 11 artists conceived or executed his drawings as images that simply accompanied the text, rather they are active translations of it and can be understood as forming a narrative distinct from that of the text. As Michael Camille, amongst others, has stressed, even images within manuscripts have an existence apart from the texts they accompany, and cannot be understood *only* in conjunction with them.[66] While the pictorial and textual narratives recount the same basic story, there are visual devices and formulae used by the artists to convey ideas that cannot be expressed verbally. This is why the drawings must be understood as a form of translation rather than as mere illustration. Formal elements such as composition, pose and particularly gesture are all used to create a visual narrative (as opposed to a series of static images), and to direct the flow of that narrative. The frontal images of the Lord, and the basically symmetrical compositions of the drawings on pages ii and 11, for example, keep the reader's eye focused on the prominent central figure of God (pls. I and VI). He meets our gaze, allowing us to

65 Deshman, *Benedictional*, p. 148.

66 M. Camille, 'Seeing and Reading: Some Visual Implications of Medieval Literacy and Illiteracy', *Art History* 8 (1985), 26–49; M. Camille, 'Mouths and Meanings: Towards an Anti-Iconography of Medieval Art', in *Iconography at the Crossroads*, ed. B. Cassidy (Princeton, NJ, 1993), pp. 43–57.

read his gesture of blessing as directed towards us at least as much as towards anyone, or anything, within the drawings. Viewers tend to interpret figures facing them as looking at or communicating with them, particularly when the figure is at the centre of the composition.[67] On page 11 the full colour of the Lord's robes in addition to his positioning above Adam and Eve and directly above the central tree create a second, symbolic axis.[68] The various formal elements work together in these two pictures to suggest the transcendent figure and eternal nature of God. Both pictures also mark points in the linear narrative that represent moments of pause, the pause before we begin reading and that which accompanies the moment of rest after God's injunction to Adam and Eve. In fact, the drawing on page 11 serves almost literally as an icon of the poet's words:

neorxnawang stod.
god and gastlic. gifena gefylled.[69]

– words that capture the sense of rest at the end of God's labour.

The semi-circles containing the scenes of Creation on pages 6 and 7, on the other hand, are diagrammatic, and serve to define each moment in the process of Creation as separate, yet indivisibly linked to the moments that precede and follow (pls. IIIa, IIIb). Viewed together the two pages visually convey the idea of a series of closely related events. The effect is enhanced by the repetition of the downward-looking and gesturing Creator three times, and the downward-flying angel spilling light from a bowl twice. In terms of both form and content the pages are related to the three uniquely Anglo-Saxon representations of the Creation in the Tiberius Psalter (BL, Cotton Tiberius C. vi, 7v), the Bury Psalter (Vatican, Biblioteca Apostolica MS Reg. Lat. 12, 68v), and London, British Library, Royal I. E. VII, 1v (pl. XLIVa). In all three, as in Junius 11, it is the act of creation, rather than the things created, that is emphasized. The circles may also have been thought to convey something of the process of shaping, or becoming, as they are in marked contrast to the strongly

67 M. Schapiro, 'Frontal and Profile as Symbolic Forms', in his *Words, Scripts, and Pictures: Semiotics of Visual Language* (New York, 1996), pp. 69–114, at p. 74.

68 On the use and meaning of horizontal and vertical axes in medieval art see Schapiro, 'Frontal and Profile', p. 77; S. Nichols, *Romanesque Signs: Early Medieval Narrative and Iconography* (New Haven, CT, 1996).

69 'Paradise stood, good and holy, and filled with grace.' *Gen.* 207b–8.

rectilinear or architectural frames that characterize the rest of the first artist's illustrations. Both in terms of content and in the use of three circles the Junius 11 drawings are related to the diagrams and commentaries of Byrhtferth of Ramsey's *Enchiridion* (completed 1011).[70] On the Trinity and the Creation, Byrhtferth writes:

Primus numerus, secundus et tertius sacratus esse dinoscitur in nomine patris et filii et spiritus sancti. Prima persona a nullo est facta, secunda a patre genita, tertia a patre et filio processit, sicut diuinus promulgat apex. Ista trinitas et indiuidua unitas sua maiestate deitatis omnia penetrat, et penetrando circumdat et circumdando adimplet et adimplendo gubernat et gubernando cuncta creata regit.[71]

The circular shape does appear again, with a very different meaning, on page 36, where hell is depicted as a dark oval filled with black flames (pl. XV). In contrast to the neatly drawn circles of Creation, however, hell is a somewhat amorphous shape that literally violates the neat rectangle of the frame. The shape, along with the darkness of the ink, conveys the difference in the kingdoms traversed by Satan's messenger as he dives back from paradise into hell, as well as the confusion of good and evil that accompanies the Fall. Such juxtaposition of different shapes or borders is a common way of indicating different levels of reality in medieval art. Another example is the Annunciation on fol. 5v of the Benedictional of St Æthelwold (BL, Add. 49598) where the nebulous shape of the cloudbank surrounding the angel Gabriel contrasts with the solid architectural setting in which Mary sits.

In the majority of the Junius 11 illustrations the direction of the visual narrative is clear and mirrors the content of the poem. In the images depicting the two Falls of the rebel angels (pls. IIb, VIII) we read

70 H. R. Broderick also notes their resemblance to the six circles of the Anglo-Saxon *horologium* (a device for calculating the time of day), as exemplified by the diagram on fol. 7r of the Tiberius Psalter (BL, Cotton Tiberius C. vi). Broderick, 'Iconographic and Compositional Sources', pp. 133–4.

71 'The first number, the second and the third, are known to be sanctified in the name of the Father, Son and Holy Ghost. The first person was created from nothing, the second was born of the Father, and the third proceeded from the Father and Son, just as holy scripture declares. This Trinity and undivided unity permeates all things in the majesty of divinity, and by permeating, surrounds them, and by surrounding, fills them, and by filling, governs them, and by governing, rules all created things.' *Byrhtferth's Enchiridion*, ed. P. S. Baker and M. Lapidge, EETS SS 15 (Oxford, 1995), pp. 196–7 (text and translation).

primarily from top to bottom, our eyes repeating the motion of the falling angels. Less important poetic details, such as God or Lucifer conversing with their followers, are confined to a secondary narrative that moves horizontally within the separate spaces depicted. The ascension of Enoch (pl. XXX), on the other hand, is meant to be read from bottom to top, the repetition of the figure of Enoch on the central vertical axis portraying the idea of ascent. On other pages, however, the connection between the narrative of the poem and the direction of action within the illustrations is more subtle, often reflecting the coming together or separation of the figures depicted – that is, the drawings capture the emotional content rather than the linear progression of the story. In the illustration accompanying God's blessing on Adam and Eve, for example, God, Adam and Eve are placed so that their gazes and gestures meet at the centre of the drawing, reflecting the communication between them (pl. V). Yet, in the lower margins, a lion and a basilisk (or dragon) move out towards the edges of the page, violating the lines of the frame and possibly reflecting the coming division of the three at the moment of the Fall. Similarly, in the scenes depicting Adam and Eve immediately after the Fall (pls. XIV, XVI), the couple are shown together in one register, and separated by thick trees in the next, expressing pictorially the idea that they are united in sin, but permanently divided from each other. The gesture that the two make with their hands to their faces in the three illustrations directly following the Fall (pls. XIV, XV, XVI) is also a sign of their sorrow.[72] Adam and Eve are shown dramatically separated from each other by a standing figure four times: at the moment of Eve's creation (pl. IV), at her Fall (pl. XII), and in the two illustrations of God's judgement on Adam, Eve and the serpent after the Fall (pls. XVII, XVIII). The contextual reasons for the use of this particular composition are clear in each case, but the similarity between the images helps to underscore visually the thematic connection between the episodes depicted. The way in which these visual figures function within the pictorial narrative is akin to the way in which rhetorical figures are used to relate passages and episodes to each other in the text.

[72] C. R. Dodwell, *Anglo-Saxon Gestures and the Roman Stage*, CSASE 28 (Cambridge, 2000), p. 117. Dodwell connects this and other common gestures in Anglo-Saxon art with those found in illustrated manuscripts of the plays of Terence, and beyond that with the conventions of the Roman stage.

In a number of instances, both artists use a continuous narrative that zigzags down and across the page to suggest a more linear progression of events. The story of Cain and Abel on pages 49 and 51 (pls. XXII, XXIII) is just that, a story, a narrative in which each episode flows smoothly into the next. The second artist uses a similar type of composition for his illustration of the drunkenness of Noah (pl. XL) and the story of the tower of Babel (pl. XLIIa). In both these latter drawings we read a continuous narrative that moves in three registers down the space of the page.

Both artists also use pose to help the reader differentiate events and figures from, or relate them to, each other. Most obvious is the contrast between vertical and horizontal figures. In the first Fall of the rebel angels (pl. IIb), the change in the depiction of Lucifer from an upright angel in the upper register, to an inverted figure as he falls, and finally to the bound and horizontal Satan at the bottom, conveys the notion of a fall from grace as effectively as does the overall composition of the page. In the illustrations of the second Fall on pages 16 and 17 (pls. VIII, IX) the horizontal Satan contrasts with the upright figure of the Lord, while the shapelessness of hell contrasts with the neat curve of the heavenly kingdom. The serpent, too, changes from an upright to a horizontal creature, in accordance with God's judgement on him after the Fall (pl. XVII) and, of course, Adam and Eve's prostrate forms in the lower half of the drawing on page 31 (pl. XIII) are a literal sign of their Fall. More subtle is the use of pose in the illustration of Eve's Temptation of Adam in the upper register of the same drawing. Here, her body hunches over as she hands Adam the apple, and the artist calls our attention to the pose by locating her between the upright figures of the tempter and Adam. The contrast between her posture and theirs is not a usual feature of early medieval illustrations of the Temptation and Fall and is thus clearly meant here to convey her already fallen state.

With pose, as with composition, repetition can be used as a type of rhetorical device to establish relationships between particular scenes or figures. The figure of Eve, spindle in hand, following Adam out of paradise on page 45 (pl. XIX) is echoed by the figure of Sarah, also carrying a spindle, following Abraham into Egypt on page 88 (pl. XLIIIb). In this case the repetition establishes both a similarity and a contrast. The women are related in that both are theologically linked to Mary, yet they are also contrasted as representatives of the disobedient and obedient wife. Similarly, the poses of Eve on page 10 and Adam on page 11 (pls. V, VI) are virtually identical, down to the detail of the right foot treading on a beast. Here the repetition could be intended primarily to establish a connection between the two illustrations, which may originally have been separated by a folio or folios now lost,[73] as well as a connection between two moments in the story of God giving Adam and Eve dominion over the newly created paradise. But again, there is also a contrast, established this time by the lion that skulks out of the frame beneath Eve's foot and the ram placed beneath Adam's foot. Read together, the two perhaps suggest the lion who guards hell, or the lion that steals sheep from the fold, looking forward to the messenger's temptation of Eve, and her subsequent temptation of Adam. A ram is also a traditional part of the iconography of the sacrifice of Isaac, and the blank space that accompanies the poet's recounting of this episode indicates that the scene was to have been part of the Junius 11 pictorial programme – perhaps even the final illustration to *Genesis*. The ram beneath Adam's foot may then have helped to establish the typological relationship between him and Abraham, just as the spindle helped to establish the relationship between Eve and Sarah.

The repetition of a series of related poses is used to help portray the direct relationship between generations among the descendants of Adam down to Noah (pls. XXI–XXXII). Within this pictorial genealogy wives are shown holding their children, either enthroned or in childbed (pls. XXI, XXIVa, XXIVb, XXV, XXVI, XXXI, XXXII), while their husbands appear either standing or enthroned beside them. In this case the repetition also helps to reinforce established gender roles: men are the leaders of their families and peoples, while women are the bearers of children. The only exceptions to the pattern of paired husbands and wives are Lamech and his two wives (pl. XXIVa); Malaleel, who appears alone on page 58 and accompanied by his sons and daughters on page 59 (pls. XXVII, XXVIII); and Enoch, who appears alone on page 60 and surrounded by his kinsmen on page 61 (pls. XXIX, XXX). The difference of these depictions may be designed to reflect the difference of these men – negatively in the case of Lamech, slayer of Cain, and positively for Malaleel and Enoch, both associated with piety.[74]

[73] See below, p. 63 for discussion of this issue.

[74] See below, p. 84.

An index is literally a pointer, a sign directly and causally related to a specific subject or vehicle.[75] Gestures are thus among the most potent indices of communication in the visual arts, with the pointing finger foremost amongst them. In their discussion of the relevance of semiotics to the field of art history, Mieke Bal and Norman Bryson have noted: 'The most obvious use of the concept of the index is the pointer. Pointing elements in an image are the most convincing case against the notion that the image is still and can be "read" in a momentary punctual act. Pointers make us aware of the way our eyes move about the surface in different directions, some of which are suggested by indexical signs. When a figure points a finger in a certain direction, our look will follow the figure's direction.'[76] More than anything else, the pointing finger and gesturing hand are used to provide the figures in Junius 11 with a sense of action and interaction, and the drawings with a sense of both life and the progress of the narrative. The extended right hand of God serves as a form of punctuation from the beginning to the end of the completed drawings. It is used to suggest the enactment of the divine Word in Creation (pls. IIIa, IIIb, IV), blessing (e.g., pls. VI, XXXV), damnation (pls. IIb, VIII, IX), judgement (pl. XVII), and simply communication (e.g., pls. V, XXXIII). Many of the figures are, like God, drawn with extended fingers, particularly in scenes depicting conversation between characters. For example, in the scene of the drunkenness of Noah (pl. XL) the extended left hand and right index finger of Cham are used to depict his revelation to his brothers of Noah's nakedness, while the extended right hand and left index finger of the bearded brother in the foreground indicate their response.

Elsewhere, the motif is used more subtly and with more powerful results. A particularly dramatic instance occurs in the drawings of the Temptation of Adam and Eve on pages 24 and 31. On page 24 (pl. XIb), the tempter points with two long, thin fingers at Adam, who holds the fruit in his hand. At the top of page 31 (pl. XIII), his open hand and pointing finger direct our attention to Eve's temptation of Adam, and echo the position of Eve's hand as she gives Adam the apple. At the bottom of the same page the tempter points triumphantly at the fallen

[75] U. Eco, *A Theory of Semiotics* (Bloomington, IN and London, 1976), pp. 115–21.

[76] M. Bal and N. Bryson, 'Semiotics and Art History', *Art Bull.* 73.2 (1991), 174–208, at 190.

figures of Adam and Eve. The detail of Eve touching Adam's hand with her index finger at the same moment that she hands him the apple effectively conveys the lengthy pleading and emotional words that she directs at him in the poem. Her poignant touch, along with her hunched posture, also help to portray the fact that she has already sinned. In addition, Eve and the apple are caught between the pointing fingers of Adam and the tempter, focusing our attention on her body and her actions, and indicating her traditionally greater guilt. But there are also significant differences in the 'dynamic stress' of these gestures.[77] The gentle touch of Eve's finger on Adam's palm is a sign of the intimate and closed dialogue taking place between the two, while the open-palmed gesture of the tempter is directed at us, and serves primarily to direct our eyes towards the central pair. In contrast, the doubled gesture of the tempter on page 24 is both more dynamic and has the effect of reversing the generally left to right progression of the visual narrative. It is a powerful index of the emotional force and dramatic import of the words the tempter directs at Adam: 'nim þe þis offæt on hand, bit his and byrge' ('take this fruit in your hand, bite and taste it', *Gen.* 518b–19).

Perhaps the most complex of all the uses of the pointing finger occurs on the page depicting the tempter's journey from hell to paradise (pl. Xa), where Adam and Eve both point to the text at the top of the facing page, physically uniting image and word, and instructing the reader to relate the events depicted in the drawing directly to the words of the poem. But the two are not identical, and the emphatic pose of the couple (again the doubled gesture) underscores the fact that the illustrations and poem are different but interrelated translations of the same biblical story that the reader must combine and recreate, actively and continuously as he or she reads. This drawing can, moreover, be understood as a metaphor for the acts of reading and interpretation themselves. No matter how innocent a creature at this point in the story, to the viewer the serpent is a potent sign of the coming Fall and of the introduction of danger, evil and deceit into the world. Its duplicitous nature is reinforced by the motion of the demonic messenger shown winding his way towards it. It is Eve who will fail to see through the messenger's disguise and will misinterpret the sign (*tacen* – here quite literally a vision) that he offers her. And it is Eve who moves our eyes from the danger foreshadowed in the drawing

[77] Eco, *Theory of Semiotics*, p. 119.

towards the dangerous words of Satan related in the text. The Anglo-Saxon reader is here being cautioned against false vision and understanding, and against the model of the reader offered by Eve.[78] By combining and properly understanding word and image, what is seen and what is heard, the reader/viewer, unlike Eve, will discern that a beautiful angel can be a serpent in disguise, and that a vision that remains unrepresented is truly a false vision.

[78] See Stévanovitch, 'Envelope Patterns and Unity', for a textual parallel to this pictorial message.

3

The pictorial narrative of *Genesis*

The story of Creation, Fall and Redemption forms the primary narrative in the Junius 11 manuscript. Interwoven with this biblical story, however, are a series of secondary narratives centred on themes of production and reproduction, reading and writing, order vs disorder, and the relationship of the biblical past to the contemporary Anglo-Saxon world. These themes are treated by text and drawings in different but complementary ways. The purpose of this chapter is primarily to analyze the techniques and functions of the pictorial narrative. This analysis will then form the basis for exploring the narrative techniques of the manuscript as a whole: the way in which image acts as a translation of word and the way in which the drawings may have helped to unite the poems by picking up on the common themes that run through them. One obvious problem is that so many of the drawings were never completed; and because of the demonstrable complexity of those that were, the original programme envisaged by the scribes, artists or compilers of the manuscript is impossible to reconstruct with anything approaching certainty. Comparison with other early medieval pictorial cycles is of limited value, as the completed Junius 11 drawings are as dissimilar as they are similar to the comparative material. It is therefore necessary to attempt to get a sense of what was originally planned by clarifying the way in which the existing pictorial and textual narratives operate in conjunction with each other.

CREATION

The manuscript opens with a full-page illustration of God enthroned between seraphim (pl. I). The picture is clearly designed to accompany the poet's opening injunction to his readers to praise God, who is here pictured in majesty before them:

US IS RIHT MICEL ÐÆT we rodera weard.
wereda wuldorcining. wordum herigen.
modum lufien. he is mægna sped.
heafod ealra heahgesceafta.
frea ælmihtig. næs him fruma æfre.
or geworden. ne nu ende cymþ.
ecean drihtnes. ac he bið a rice.
ofer heofenstolas. heagum þrymmum.[1]

Both word and image help to set the poem within a universal Christian time-frame in which past, present and future merge. Moreover here, at the very beginning of the manuscript, we find a reference to both its unity and its end, as well as to the beginning and end of time. According to Ælfric, 'Ða twa seraphin soðlice getacnodon þa ealdan gekyðnysse and eac þa niwan, þe heriað mid wordum and mid weorcum æfre þone ælmihtigan God, se þe ana rixað on anre godcundnysse butan anginne and ende.'[2] The whole composition of the picture refers directly to the descriptions of the Lord in Isaiah VI.1–2[3] and Rev. IV.9–11,[4] references that unite Old and New Testaments just as the manuscript as a whole unites poems based on

1 'It is very right that we praise with words and love in our hearts the guardian of heaven, the glorious king of hosts. He is a wealth of power, the head of all high creations, the Lord almighty. There was not for him ever a beginning, or source brought about, nor never an end will come to the everlasting Lord, but he will ever rule over the thrones of heaven with high powers.' *Gen*. 1–8.

2 'The two Seraphim truly betokened the Old and New Testaments: which praise with words and deeds the almighty God, who alone reigns in one Godhead without beginning and end.' *Heptateuch*, ed. Crawford, p. 69.

3 'In the year that king Ozias died, I saw the Lord sitting upon a throne high and elevated: and his train filled the temple. 2. Upon it stood the seraphims: the one had six wings, and the other had six wings.' Translations from the Vulgate are from the Rheims-Douai Bible. See also, B. C. Raw, *Trinity and Incarnation in Anglo-Saxon Art and Thought*, CSASE 21 (Cambridge, 1997), p. 133.

4 '9. And when those living creatures gave glory and honour and benediction to him that sitteth on the throne, who liveth forever and ever; 10. The four and twenty ancients fell down before him that sitteth on the throne, who liveth forever and ever, and cast their crowns before the throne saying: 11. Thou art worthy, O Lord our God, to receive glory, and honour, and power: because thou hast created all things; and for thy will they were, and have been created.'

the Old and New Testaments in a narrative present. The reading of the book thus becomes a metaphor for the progress of time from Genesis to Last Judgement. The architectural frame of the picture adds to its visionary quality, recalling the door opened in heaven through which John saw his vision. The cloudbank evokes the sea of glass lying before the throne, and the two seraphim and two winds the four living creatures, the four symbols of the evangelists, that surround the throne in Rev. IV.6–8. In the latter passages the twenty-four elders offer praise to God just as the Anglo-Saxon readers are instructed to do by the opening words of the poem. To an eleventh-century audience these words would automatically have called to mind the preface to the eucharistic mass, itself associated with praise of God and Creation.[5] By echoing the words of the mass, words that the Anglo-Saxons would have heard regularly, the poet universalized his text, making it a part of his audience's everyday experience. The incarnation and sacrifice of Christ, reenacted in the mass, itself symbolized the hope of mankind's eventual salvation and return to the light of the kingdom of heaven, creating a cyclical linking of past, present, and hoped-for future – a link that seems to have been particularly popular in tenth- and eleventh-century England.[6] A similar combination of visual and textual references begins the preface to the mass in the Red Book of Darley (Cambridge, Corpus Christi College 422 (pp. 27–586), p. 52), a missal produced at Winchester *c.* 1061. The preface in this manuscript is introduced by the image of Christ enthroned in a mandorla, one hand raised in blessing, the other holding a book. Two angels carrying rods or sceptres support the mandorla, their wings crossing just above Christ's head (pl. XLVIIIb). The opening words of the text of the preface are written in red and green capitals around the figure of Christ indicating the manifestation of the Word in the flesh and simultaneously surrounding Christ with words of praise,[7] a composition clearly related to the image and words with which the Junius 11 manuscript opens.

5 Doane, ed., *Genesis A*, p. 225; Remley, *Old English Biblical Verse*, p. 126; L. Michel, '*Genesis A* and the *praefatio*', *MLN* 62 (1947), 545–50.

6 The cruciforous nimbus also helps to signify the preexistence of Christ *logos* with the Father. See Weitzmann and Kessler, *Cotton Genesis*, p. 37, and below p. 138.

7 'Vere dignum et justum est equum et salutare nos tibi semper et ubique gratios agere Domine Sancte Pater omnipotens.' E. Temple, *Anglo-Saxon Manuscripts 900–1066*, Survey of Manuscripts Illuminated in the British Isles 2 (London, 1976), no. 104, ill. 301; Budny, *Catalogue*, no. 44, pl. 12.

As a frontispiece to the *Genesis* poem, the Junius 11 image is an illustration of God before Creation, the God who, according to Isaiah, 'hath measured the waters in the hollow of his hand and weighed the heavens with his palm' (XL.12), the God who proclaims, 'I am first, I am also last. My hand laid the foundations of the earth and my right hand spread out the heavens' (XLVIII.12–13). In his commentary on Isaiah, Jerome argued, following Origen, that such a being cannot be contained within Creation, but had to precede it, as this image precedes the text and its Creation narrative.[8] Ælfric took up the same theme in his treatise 'On the Old and New Testament':

Næs þeos woruld æt fruman, ac hi geworhte God silf, se þe æfre þurhwunode buton ælcum anginne on his miclan wuldre and on his mægenþrimnisse eall swa mihtig swa he nu ys and eall swa micel on his leohte, for ðan ðe he ys soð leoht and lif and soðfæstnisse, and se ræd wæs æfre on his rædfæstum geþance, þæt he wircan wolde þa wundorlican gesceafta, be þan ðe he wolde þurh his micclan wisdom þa gesceafta gescippan and þurh his soðan lufe hig liffæstan on þam life, þe hig habbað.[9]

The God of the Junius 11 *Genesis* literally brings Creation to light with both his word and his hand. As was the case with Anglo-Saxon authors, scribes and artists, the act of creation is a combination of hand and word that becomes text and image.[10] As a complement to the verbal creation

8 Raw, *Trinity and Incarnation*, p. 138. Jerome, *In Esaiam* XVIII.lxvi.1 (CCSL 73–73A) (Turnhout, 1963), 769–70. See also Origen, *De principiis* I: 2, 131B and IV: 28 (PG 11).

9 'This world did not exist in the beginning, but God himself made it, he who always existed without any beginning in his great glory and in his power, altogether as mighty as he now is and just as mighty in his light, for he is true light and life and truth, and that plan always existed in his resolved thought, that he would create those wonderful beings, shaping them by his great wisdom and through his true love establishing them in the life which they possess.' *Heptateuch*, ed. Crawford, p. 17. See also S. J. Crawford, ed., *Exameron Anglice or The Old English Hexameron* (Darmstadt, 1968), lines 382–6, p. 62: 'Ælc ðing hæfð anginn and ordfruman ðurh God, buton se ana Scyppend ðe ealle ðing gesceop; se næfð nan anginn ne nænne ordfruman, ac he sylf is angin and soðlice ordfruma ealra ðinga and æfre ungeendod.' ('Every thing has a beginning and a source through God, except only the Creator who created all things; he has no beginning and no source, but he himself is the beginning and source of all things and ever without end.')

10 The combination of verbal and manual creation in the canon table sequence of the Eadui Codex (Hannover, Kestner Museum, WM XXI[a], 36) begins with the hand of God holding scales (fol. 9v) facing Christ, the Word (fol. 10r). The evangelist portraits

recorded and enacted in the text, the illustrations of the Creation of the world emphasize the role of the hand of God by the prominence they give to his right hand (pls. IIIa, IIIb). To be sure, whenever the Lord is depicted in Junius 11 his right hand is used to indicate blessing or communication, but nowhere else does he appear with the sweeping gesture seen in the drawings depicting the Creation of the physical world. This is indeed the God of Isaiah XL.12–13 whose right hand spread out the heavens. The texts of the Junius 11 poems also place a great deal of emphasis on hands and the ability or inability of the protagonists to use them effectively, making the image of the hand one of the most important of the recurring motifs in the manuscript.

Another frequent motif is the contrast between light and darkness. The picture of the enthroned Creator surrounded by seraphim and angels is followed immediately by the rebellion of Lucifer and his angels, and their descent from the light of heaven to the darkness of hell (pls. IIa, IIb).[11] Lucifer through his pride, or presumptuous pride, literally 'overthinking' (*oferhygde*, *Gen.* 22b),[12] desires to establish a throne for himself in the northern part of the kingdom of heaven:

him þær sar gelamp.
æfst and oferhygd. and þæs engles mod.
þe þone unræd. ongan ærest fremman.
wefan and weccean. þa he worde cwæð.
niþes ofþyrsted. þæt he on norðdæle.
ham and heahsetl. heofena rices.
agan wolde.[13]

in the same manuscript show the four evangelists preparing to write (fols. 17v, 65v), writing (fol. 96v), and triumphing through the written word (fol. 147v).

11 The fall of the rebel angels also serves as a visual preface to Creation in Claudius B. iv, though it is not mentioned in the text; see below, nn. 18, 22. Augustine wrote that the creation of the angels occurred simultaneously with the creation of light and that the separation of the faithful and rebel angels was simultaneous with the separation of light from darkness. See Augustine, *De genesi ad litteram* (CSEL 28), iv.21; *De civitate Dei* (CCSL 47–48), xi.9, 14–20.

12 On the meaning of this and similar terms see H. Schabram, *Superbia: Studien zum altenglischen Wortschatz. Teil I: Die dialektale und zeitliche Verbreitung des Wortguts* (Munich, 1965); H. Schabram, 'Das altenglische *superbia* – Wortgut. Eine Nachlese', *Festschrift Prof. Dr. Herbert Koziol zum siebzigsten Geburtstag*, ed. G. Bauer *et al.* (Vienna, 1973), pp. 272–9.

13 'Pain befell them there, envy and pride, and the pride of that angel, who first began to

He and his ill-counselled followers are deprived forever of the bright light of heaven and cast into hell, where they are enveloped in endless night (*synnihte beseald*, *Gen.* 42a) and covered with darkness (*þystrum beþeahte*, *Gen.* 76a). In the illustration that accompanies this episode (pl. IIb) the artist, as we have seen, has used the change from red to brown ink to indicate the descent from light into darkness.[14] The spindly sceptre held by Lucifer in the upper register of the drawing also contrasts with the rich, feathery leaves of the palms held by the angels and the massive sceptre (or scroll) held by God, and provides a visual sign of Lucifer's difference prior to his fall. The energetic gesture with which God aims his spears at the falling angels indicates that he can as easily damn and destroy with his right hand as he can save and create. The combination of Creation and destruction is further suggested by the description of the void that precedes Creation with its unknowable darkness and emptiness:

Ne wæs her þa giet. nymþe heolstersceado.
wiht geworden. ac þes wida grund.
stod deop and dim. drihtne fremde.
idel and unnyt. on þone eagum wlat.
stiðfrihþ cining. and þa stowe beheold.
dreama lease. geseah deorc gesweorc.

commit bad counsel, to weave and to incite, when he spoke words, thirsting for malice, that he would win a home and high seat in the northern part of the kingdom of heaven.' *Gen.* 28b–34. As Doane notes, the placement of the rebellion in the north goes back to Is. XIV.12–13: 'How art thou fallen from heaven, O Lucifer, who didst rise in the morning? How art thou fallen to earth, that didst wound nations? 13. And thou saidst in thy heart: I will ascend into heaven, I will exalt my throne above the stars of God, I will sit in the mountain of the covenant, in the sides of the north.' See Doane, ed., *Genesis A*, p. 229.

14 Ohlgren ('Illustrations of the *Cædmonian Genesis*'; *Textual Illustration*, p. 89) identifies the angel above God in the middle register as Lucifer, but this is unlikely as there is no reason to depict Lucifer distributing palms of peace. It is far more likely that the scene represents the reestablishment of peace in heaven that is simultaneous with the Fall of the rebel angels. The image of the bound Satan is certainly based on contemporary images of the Harrowing of Hell, as on fol. 14 of the *c.* 1050 Tiberius Psalter (BL, Cotton Tiberius C. iv), a connection first made by Barbara Raw in her unpublished MA thesis, 'The Story of the Fall of Man and of the Angels in the MS Junius 11 and the Relationship of the Manuscript Illustrations to the Text' (University of London, 1953), 74. Ohlgren ('Illustrations of the *Cædmonian Genesis*', 211–12, n. 18) suggests the influence of Spanish Apocalypses on the Junius 11 page, though there is no concrete evidence for this.

semian sinnihte. sweart under roderum.
wonn and weste. oð þæt þeos woruldgesceaft.
þurh word geweard. wuldorcyninges.[15]

Only with the creation of the world of man will the brightness and beauty once held by Lucifer finally be restored.[16] And, like Lucifer, the earth itself and those that inhabit it will be both bright and beautiful, and dangerous and fallen. The relationship of entry (or creation) to expulsion, beginning to end, and birth to death is picked up in the details of the paradise landscape beneath the figure of God at the top of page 7 (pl. IIIb). Here, the small cross on the tree at the centre of the newly created world is a sign of the tree of life and the cross of the Crucifixion. The hart and pelican (if it is a pelican) are references to the psalms,[17] and may also be interpreted as figures of Christ, whose sacrifice will redeem the coming Fall of man.

In each of the three moments depicted in the drawings illustrating the Creation of the world, the artist has included a representation of light. The angels in the upper circle of the drawing on page 6 and the third circle of the drawing on page 7 hold bowls from which rays of light pour down from heaven towards earth. At the top of page 7, the mandorla that surrounds the figure of God suggests a similar manifestation of light. The association of divine light with Creation was traditional in the Early Christian church, and was taken up in England in the writings of both

15 'Here there was not yet anything but dark shadows existing, but the wide abyss stood deep and dim, separated from the Lord, idle and unprofitable. He looked on that with his eyes, the King strong in peace, and beheld that joyless place, he saw the darkness hovering in the perpetual night, black under the skies, dark and waste, until this world creation came into being through the word of the King of glory.' *Gen.* 103–11.

16 The void in heaven left by the Fall of the angels and the need to create man in order to fill it are commented on by Augustine (*Enchiridion* XXIX (CCSL 46), 65) and Ælfric (*The Homilies of the Anglo-Saxon Church*, ed. B. Thorpe, 2 vols. (London, 1844–6), I, 12 and *Exameron Anglice*, pp. 57–8). In his 'Sermo de Initio creaturae, ad Populum, Quando Volueris' (*Homilies*, ed. Thorpe, I, 12), Ælfric writes: 'Ða wolde God gefyllan and geinnian þone lyre þe forloren wæs of þam heofenlicum werode, and cwæð þæt he wolde wyrcan mannan of eorðan, þæt se eorðlica man sceolde geþeon and geearnian mid eadmodnysse þa wununga on heofenan rice, þe se deofel forwyrhte mid modignysse.' ('Then God wished to supply and make good the loss that had been suffered from the heavenly troop, and said that he would make man from earth, so that earthly man should prosper and earn with humility the dwellings in the heavenly kingdom which the devil had forfeited through his pride.')

17 The hart to Psalm XLI.1, and the pelican to Psalm CI.7.

Bede and Ælfric.[18] The unusual focus on light in these drawings of Junius 11 is, however, more likely due to the contrast between the light of heaven and divine Creation and the darkness of hell and damnation in the poem that they accompany. However individual interpretation of the images might vary,[19] they are clearly intended to be understood in conjunction with the words of the text written at the top of page 6:

folde wæs þa gyta.
græsungrene. garsecg þeahte.
sweart synnihte. side and wide.
wonne wægas.[20] þa wæs wuldortorht.
heofonweardes gast. ofer holm boren.
miclum spedum. metod engla heht.
lifes brytta. leoht forð cuman.
ofer rumne grund. raþe wæs gefylled.
heahcininges hæs. him wæs halig leoht.
ofer westenne. swa se wyrhta bebead.
þa gesundrode. sigora waldend.
ofer lagoflode. leoht wið þeostrum.
sceade wið sciman. sceop þa bam naman.
lifes brytta. leoht wæs ærest.
þurh drihtnes word. dæg genemned.
wlitebeorhte gescaft. wel licode.
frean æt frymðe. forþbæro tid.
dæg æresta. geseah deorc sceado.
sweart swiðrian. geond sidne grund .˙.[21]

[18] See Bede, *In Genesim* (CCSL 118A), 6; Doane, ed., *Genesis A*, p. 233; Ælfric, 'On the Old and New Testaments', in *Heptateuch*, ed. Crawford, p. 17.

[19] For the differing interpretations and arguments see P. Blum, 'The Cryptic Creation Cycle in MS Junius xi', *Gesta* 15 (1976), 211–26; Henderson, 'Programme', pp. 165–8; Raw, 'Probable Derivation', p. 136.

[20] This is spelled *wegas* in the manuscript.

[21] 'Then the earth was yet ungreen of grass. The ocean covered with the darkness of endless night, dark ways far and wide. Then was the glorious brightness, the spirit of the Guardian of heaven carried over the sea with great speed. The Lord of angels, the Giver of life, commanded light to come forth over the wide ground. Swiftly the High King's bidding was fulfilled. Holy light was over the waste, according to the Master's command. Then the Lord of victories divided light from darkness, shade from radiance, over the water. The Giver of Life then created names for both. The light was first named day through the word of the Lord, creation bright in beauty. That time of bringing forth the first day at the beginning well pleased the Lord. He saw the dark shadow withdraw black across the wide ground.' *Gen.* 116b–134.

Neither the text nor the illustrations of the Creation in the Old English Hexateuch place the same emphasis on light and the separation of light from darkness. The text of the Hexateuch closely follows the Vulgate, saying simply: 'God cwæð ða: Gewurðe leoht, and leoht wearð geworht. God geseah ða ðæt hit god wæs, and he todælde <þæt> leoht fram ðam ðystrum. And het ðæt leoht dæg and þa ðystru niht.'[22] The episode is not depicted but only implied in the image of the Fall of the angels, which was simultaneous with the creation of light.

The diagrammatic nature of the Junius 11 drawings of the Creation and their relationship to other images of the Creation from late Anglo-Saxon manuscripts has already been noted.[23] The idea of the Creation as the product of the Word, an idea which has its source in the writings of Augustine, was visualized in the three eleventh-century Anglo-Saxon images of the Creation whose iconography is unparalleled elsewhere in the early medieval world: the Tiberius Psalter (BL, Cotton Tiberius C. vi, 7v); the Royal Bible (BL, Royal I. E. VII, 1v) (pl. XLIVa); and the Bury Psalter (Biblioteca Apostolica, Reg. Lat. 12, 68v).[24] All three miniatures show the head of God above a circle containing a representation of the nascent world. From his mouth issue two long trumpets through which the word and the world will be born. In all three pictures God holds a balance in his right hand, and in the Tiberius Psalter and Royal Bible illustrations he also holds a compass (as well as a cross-shaft in the latter manuscript). These are the tools with which God will measure the waters and weigh the heavens, but they are not yet in use, as it is the word that comes first. This is Creation as annunciation, and the world, contained within the circle of God's body, is in the process of passing through the trumpets, as

22 'God said let there be light and light came into being. God saw that it was good and he separated light from darkness. And he called that light day. And he called the darkness night.' (The angled brackets denote missing or incorrect letters in the manuscript.) *Heptateuch*, ed. Crawford, p. 81.

23 For the influence of the Junius 11 drawings on later manuscript art see H. R. Broderick, 'The Influence of Anglo-Saxon Genesis Iconography on Later English Medieval Manuscript Art', in *The Preservation and Transmission of Anglo-Saxon Culture*, ed. P. E. Szarmach and J. T. Rosenthal (Kalamazoo, MI, 1997), pp. 211–39.

24 Temple, *Anglo-Saxon Manuscripts*, nos. 98, 102, and 84. See A. Heimann, 'Three Illustrations from the Bury St. Edmunds Psalter and their Prototypes', *JWCI* 29 (1966), 39–59. See also J. E. Rosenthal, 'Three Drawings in an Anglo-Saxon Pontifical: Anthropomorphic Trinity or Threefold Christ?' *Art Bull.* 43.4 (1981), 547–62.

the dove of the Holy Spirit prepares to take flight.[25] Together with the frontispiece, the Junius 11 images of the Creation document the process symbolized by the Royal Bible image and its parallels. All might be understood as deriving ultimately from such works as the diagrams showing the division and grouping of biblical books by Hilary, Jerome and Augustine in the Codex Amiatinus (Florence, Biblioteca Medicea Laurenziana Amiatinus 1, fols. 6r, 7r and 8r). In each of these diagrams,

[25] While all three drawings do have sources in the diagrams illustrating the division of scripture in earlier manuscripts, they have no exact parallels in either Early Christian or earlier Anglo-Saxon art. They may, however, have an immediate Anglo-Saxon source traceable to Wearmouth-Jarrow and the age of Bede. A collection of epigrams produced for Milred, bishop of Winchester from 745 to 775, preserves, along with a copy of Ceolfrith's dedication from the Codex Amiatinus, a pair of couplets linking the word of the Lord with that of Isaiah: 'Eloquium Domini quaecunque uolumnia fundunt,/ spiritus hoc sancto fudit ab ore Deus./Esias domini cecinit miracula uates/atque euangelicis concinit ore tubis.' ('Whatever volumes display the Lord's eloquence, God the spirit has poured forth from his holy mouth. Isaiah the prophet sang the Lord's miracles and sounded forth from his mouth with angelic trumpets.') Richard Marsden (*The Text of the Old Testament in Anglo-Saxon England*, CSASE 15 (Cambridge, 1995), pp. 96–8) has identified the manuscript from which the couplet was copied as 'Offa's Bible', one of the three great bible pandects produced at Wearmouth-Jarrow under Abbot Ceolfrith (689–716). It was acquired by Offa, king of Mercia, in the second half of the eighth century and subsequently presented to Tilhere, bishop of Worcester. The bible remained at Worcester until at least the eleventh century. Marsden has also suggested that the text of the Royal I. E. VII bible may have been produced at Worcester in the late tenth century. Whether the image of the Creation that prefaces Genesis was added there, or after its arrival at Christ Church, Canterbury in the mid-eleventh century (to which it has been assigned on purely stylistic grounds, though a Winchester provenance is also possible (*ibid.*, 327)) there is a possibility that the image was influenced by the Offa Bible couplet. Only the first couplet appears in Amiatinus at the top of the diagram showing the grouping of biblical books according to St Augustine on folio 8r, indicating that this would probably also have been its position in the Offa Bible. Marsden believes that both couplets have their origin in the *Codex grandior*, the sixth-century Cassiodoran bible likely to have been the pandect of the *uetusta translatio* from which the Wearmouth-Jarrow bibles were copied. He suggests further that the fact that the second couplet does not appear in the Codex Amiatinus is an indication that there were differences between Ceolfrith's three copies (*ibid.*, pp. 97 and 103; see also G. Henderson, 'Cassiodorus and Eadfrith Once Again', in *The Age of Migrating Ideas: Early Medieval Art in Northern Britain and Ireland* , ed. R. M. Spearman and J. Higgitt (Edinburgh, 1993), pp. 82–91). The frontispiece to Junius 11, which makes visual the same scriptural references in a different form, may be part of that tradition of 'unity in diversity' (Henderson, 'Cassiodorus and Eadfrith', p. 84).

circles representing the Old and New Testaments and different geometric shapes containing the names of the individual books of the bible are suspended from roundels with golden images of the Father (Hilary), Son (Jerome) and Holy Ghost (Augustine).[26] The image of the figure at once outside but part of the Creation is echoed in Junius 11 by the lightly sketched figure of a man in the upper right corner of page 7. It is far from certain, however, that the figure is contemporary with the production of the manuscript and, whatever the date of his addition, he is most probably to be interpreted as a reader or viewer rather than an active participant in the events depicted.[27]

EVE, ADAM AND PARADISE

According to Ælfric's homily on the Creation, man's purpose is to fill the void in heaven left by the fallen angels: 'Ða wolde God gefyllan and geinnian þone lyre þe forloren wæs of þam heofenlicum werode, and cwæð þæt he wolde wyrcan mannan of eorðan, þæt se eorðlica man sceolde geþeon and geearnian mid eadmodnysse þa wununga on heofenan rice, þe se deofol forwyrhte mid modignysse.'[28] It is therefore somewhat ironic that, as it comes down to us, the Creation of man and the story of his brief sojourn in paradise in Junius 11 begins with the creation of Eve (pl. IV), whose body the poet, but not, surprisingly, the artist, will repeatedly link with that of Lucifer.[29] Indeed the difference between the textual and pictorial treatments of Eve is one point at which we can see the process of visual representation as translation working most clearly. On the right-hand side of the drawing, God bends over the sleeping Adam holding the rib that he has just removed from his side. On the left-hand side of the drawing, God stands in a similar pose over the newly born Eve, who looks up at him with a gesture of prayer. Her animation is in marked contrast

26 See R. L. S. Bruce-Mitford, *The Art of the Codex Amiatinus*, Jarrow Lecture, Jarrow, 1967.

27 R. E. Finnegan, 'The Man in "Nowhere": A Previously Undiscovered Drawing in Bodleian MS Junius11', *English Studies* 79.1 (1998), 23–32; and see below, p. 101.

28 *Homilies*, ed. Thorpe, I, 12. 'Then would God fill and restore the loss that had been suffered from the heavenly host, and said that he would make man of earth, so that the earthly man should flourish and earn with humility those dwellings in the heavenly kingdom that the devil had forfeited through his pride.'

29 P. Belanoff, 'The Fall (?) of the Old English Female Poetic Image', *PMLA* 104 (1989), 822–31.

to the passive sleep of Adam, and is perhaps indicative of her more active role in the events that are to follow. Yet, as with so many of the drawings in this manuscript, this is not simply an illustration of a single event. In addition to the creation of woman, the artist has represented the reestablishment of peace in heaven and the filling of the void created by the Fall of the rebel angels. This is indicated quite literally by the return of the architectural frame signifying the order and stability of the kingdom of heaven, in contrast to the disorder and nebulous nature of hell, and serving here to unite the kingdoms of heaven and earth. It is also suggested more subtly by the way in which the ordered angels in heaven preside over paradise just as they presided over the Fall of Lucifer and his followers on page 3, and as they will preside over the second Fall of the angels on page 16 (pl. VIII).

Prominent amongst the heavenly figures are the archangel Michael standing in the open doorway and an angel who holds open the door with one hand and grasps a cross-key in the other. Together, the two prefigure the angel barring the door to paradise at the expulsion (pl. XX). The detail helps to establish visually the fact that the events that will lead to the loss of paradise begin here with the introduction of Eve into paradise, and serves to frame the story of the Fall with images of admission and exclusion. The figure of Michael, receiver of souls, and the iconographic relationship of the key-bearing angel with the figure of St Peter also suggests that the page is meant to evoke images of the Last Judgement where Peter serves as gate-keeper to heaven and Michael bears souls up to heaven. On folio 7 of the *c.* 1031 New Minster *Liber Vitae* (London, British Library, Stowe 944; pl. XLIVb) Peter with his key welcomes the saved to heaven in the upper register, and uses the key to club a demon in the middle register. In the lowest register an angel, presumably Michael, locks the door to hell with his right hand while holding a second key in his left. A learned Anglo-Saxon audience would have recognized Michael as the special protector of Israel and the guardian of Christian armies as well as the angel of the Last Judgement.[30] His figure may have served as an allusion to events to come in *Exodus*, *Daniel* and *Christ and Satan* as well as to the expulsion.

[30] Daniel XII.1. On Michael in Anglo-Saxon England see R. Johnson, 'Archangel in the Margins: St Michael in the Homilies of Cambridge, Corpus Christi College 41', *Traditio* 53 (1998), 63–91.

The newly created Adam and Eve resting in paradise are also *englum gelice*, 'like the angels' who look down on them from above, and this is emphasized by the placement of these words, the last on the page, directly above the angels. Augustine uses the metaphor of light to parallel the Creation of man with that of the angels.[31] The angels are the first light, but man is illuminated, like the angels and like God himself, through his intelligence. Intellectual light, the light of reason, sets men and women apart from the rest of Creation, a theme that was the subject of extensive comment both within Anglo-Saxon England and across early medieval Europe.[32] The familiarity of the subject would have helped to reinforce the contrast developed in the Junius 11 manuscript between the kingdom of God and his Creation, and the darkness of hell.

Heaven and earth are physically connected in this drawing by a ladder. The combination of the sleeping figure of Adam and the ladder leading towards heaven is most likely derived from depictions of Jacob's ladder.[33] The visual reference to Jacob's dream serves to connect Adam, as first father, not only to Jacob, whose 'seed shall be as the dust of the earth', but also to Abraham and Isaac, with whose story the Junius 11 *Genesis* now ends, and with the sons of Jacob (his seed) who will reappear in *Exodus*. Whether *Genesis* is complete or nearly complete as it comes down to us, or whether it would have continued through the story of Jacob, is impossible to determine. However, the question is not crucial to the interpretation of

31 *Gen Litt.* I.ii. 20 (CSEL 28).

32 *Ibid.*; F. Biggs, '"*Englum gelice*": *Elene* line 1320 and *Genesis A* line 185', *NM* 86 (1985), 447–52.

33 'And when he was come to a certain place, and would rest in it after sunset, he took of the stones that lay there, and putting under his head, slept in the same place. 12. And he saw in his sleep a ladder standing upon the earth, and the top thereof touching heaven: the angels also of God ascending and descending by it; 13. And the Lord leaning upon the ladder, saying to him: I am the Lord God of Abraham thy father, and the God of Isaac; the land wherein thou sleepest, I will give to thee and to thy seed. 14. And thy seed shall be as the dust of the earth: thou shalt spread abroad to the west, and to the east, and to the north, and to the south: and in thee and thy seed all the tribes of the earth shall be blessed. 15. And I will be thy keeper whithersoever thou goest, and will bring thee back into this land: neither will I leave thee, till I have accomplished all that I have said. 16. And when Jacob awaked out of sleep, he said: Indeed the Lord is in this place, and I knew *it* not. 17. And trembling he said: How terrible is this place! this is not other than the house of God, and the gate of heaven,' Gen XXVIII.11–17. See also Raw, 'Probable Derivation', p. 140.

this picture, as it, like so many of the Junius 11 drawings, functions intertextually and intervisually, that is it alludes to images and events typologically related to, but not contained in, the text of the poem. The reference is particularly apt because it is on the following page that God instructs Adam and Eve to fill the earth with their children, the first reference to the innumerability topos which recurs repeatedly throughout the manuscript and is implied in the allusion to Jacob.

It is also quite possible that the image of heaven here at the beginning of man's life on earth was designed to resonate with the description of the kingdom of heaven in lines 647–55 of *Christ and Satan*:

þær is geat gylden. gimmum gefrætewod.
wynnum bewunden. þæm þe in wuldres leoht.
gongan moten to godes rice.
and ymb þa weallas. wlitige scinað.
engla gastas. and eadige sawla.
þa ðe heonon ferað.
þær martiras. meotode cwemað.
and herigað hehfæder. halgum stefnum.
cyning in cestre.[34]

This description occurs at the end of the section of *Christ and Satan* that includes the Harrowing of Hell and Last Judgement, the moments at which the door to heaven will be opened to Adam and Eve, and the moment at which it will be opened to all the faithful.

Eve's pose is also complex, prefiguring both her fall and her ultimate redemption and also serving to unite her typologically with Mary, the new Eve. She looks up at the cross-nimbed Lord in a pose of prayer and adoration, while he bends over her and takes her by the hand. The composition is close to that of Anglo-Saxon representations of the Harrowing of Hell in which Christ bends over the mouth of hell while reaching down to Eve and Adam (pl. XLVa). In the Harrowing of Hell Eve appeals to Christ for release from her punishment because she is ultimately the mother of Mary, and thus of Christ himself. Her appeal appears in a number of late Anglo-Saxon texts including the Easter

[34] 'There is a golden gate adorned with gems, encircled with light, for those who in the light of glory might go into God's kingdom, and around the walls the spirits of angels and blessed souls, those who travel hence, shine beautifully. There martyrs serve the lord and praise the high father with holy voices, the king in the city.'

homilies, Junius 121 fols.148v–154v[35] and Blickling vii,[36] and *Christ and Satan* in which the poet tells us:

ræhte þa mid handum. to heofen cyninge.
bæd meotod miltse. þurh marian had.
hwæt þu fram minne dohtor.[37] drihten onwoce.
in middangeard. mannum to helpe.
nu is gesene. þæt ðu eart sylfa god.
ece ordfruma ealra gesceafta.[38]

In the drawing, the visual association of the figure of Eve with that of Mary is strengthened by the door to heaven, which will be closed by Eve with the Fall but reopened by Mary with the birth of Christ.[39] The

[35] 'Geara me, min Drihten, for þinre modor lufan of ðære ðu wære geeadmet þæt ðu menniscne lichaman underfenge. Heo onfeng flæsc of minum flæsce and ban of minum bane.' ('Have pity on me, my Lord, for love of your mother from whom you were humbled. So that you received a human body. She received flesh of my flesh and bone of my bone.') A. M. L. Fadda, '"De descensu Christi ad inferos": una inedita omelia anglosassone', *Studi medievale* 13 (1972), 989–1011, at 1006.

[36] 'Ic þe halsige nu, Drihten, for þinre þeowene Sancta Marian, þa þu mid heofonlicum wuldre geweorþodest; hire innoþ þu gefyldest nigon monaþ mid ealles middangeardes weorþe; þu wast þæt þu of minre dehter, Drihten, onwoce; and þæt hire flæsc is of minum flæsce, and hire ban of minum banum.' ('I entreat you now, Lord, for the sake of your servant St. Mary, whom you have honoured with heavenly glory. You filled her womb for nine months with all the earth's prize. You know that you, O Lord, were born from my daughter, and that her flesh is of my flesh, and her bone of my bones.') R. Morris, *The Blickling Homilies of the Tenth Century*, EETS 58, 63, 73 (London, 1874–80; reprinted in one vol. 1967), 89. See also M. Clayton, *The Cult of the Virgin Mary in Anglo-Saxon England*, CSASE 2 (Cambridge, 1990), 255–6.

[37] The manuscript reads *mire dohtor*.

[38] 'Then she reached with her hands to the Heavenly King, asked the Lord's mercy through the person of Mary: "Lo, from my daughter, Lord, you were born on earth to help men. Now it is seen that you are God Himself, and eternal author of all creation."' *Christ and Satan* 435–40. This passage may have been prefaced by a drawing of the Harrowing of Hell. See below, p. 206.

[39] See also the antiphon: 'O clavis David, et sceptrum domus Israel, qui aperis et nemo claudit; claudis et nemo aperit: veni et educ vinctum de domo carceris, sedentem in tenbris et unbra mortis.' ('O key of David and sceptre of the house of Israel; you who opens and no one closes; who closes and no one opens: come and lead out of the prison house the captive sitting in darkness and the shadow of death.') The antiphon was recited at Vespers during Advent, and combines the image of Christ as key of David and opener and closer of doors, with the Virgin of Advent. The antiphon is the inspiration for the second lyric of *Christ I* in the Exeter Book. For the text of the

iconography of this page, in its association of Eve with Mary and Adam with Abraham and Jacob (and by extension Christ), introduces the theme of motherhood and fatherhood into the illustrations at the same point at which it is introduced into the text of the poem:

þa gebletsode. bliðheort cyning.
metod alwihta. monna cynnes.
ða forman twa. fæder and moder.
wif and wæpned. he þa worde cwæð.
temað nu and wexað. tudre fyllað.
eorðan æl grene incre cynne.
sunum and dohtrum.[40]

A similar range of motifs and intervisual references is depicted on the *Liber generationis* page of the late-tenth-century Boulogne Gospels (Boulogne-sur-Mer, Bibliothèque Municipale 11, fol. 12) illuminated at St Bertin by an Anglo-Saxon artist.[41] Here, from a semi-circle above the 'L' of *Liber*, five angels preside over the Nativity and Annunciation to the shepherds. The page is prefaced by a two-page sequence of portrait busts depicting all of Christ's ancestors from Abraham to Jacob. Clearly, the genealogical connections between the Old and New Testaments, and between the biblical and contemporary eras, was a popular topic in late Anglo-Saxon England.

Eve's pose on page 9 may also be intended to refer forward to the vision of the Last Judgement, itself typologically related to the Harrowing of Hell, that Eve is granted at the moment of her fall. The pose is repeated on page 10, where both she and Adam stand in prayer before God (pl. V). A lion and a dragon (or basilisk) appear in the lower margins of the drawing, a reference to Psalm XC.13: 'Thou shalt walk upon the asp and the basilisk: thou shalt trample under foot the lion and the dragon.' This is a subject that has a long history in Anglo-Saxon art, going back to the images of Christ over the beasts on the Ruthwell and Bewcastle monuments which were begun, if not completed, in the eighth century.

antiphon see R.-J. Hesbert, ed., *Corpus Antiphonalium Officii*, vol. 3: *Invitatoria et Antiphonae* (Herder, 1968) no. 4010.

40 'Then the blithe-hearted King, the Lord of Creation, blessed the first two of the race of men, father and mother, woman and man. He then said: "be fruitful and multiply, fill the all-green earth with offspring, sons and daughters, your family".' *Gen.* 192–8.

41 See E. Temple, *Anglo-Saxon Manuscripts 900–1066*, Survey of Manuscripts Illuminated in the British Isles 2 (London, 1976), ill. 148.

The association of Christ trampling the beasts with the Harrowing of Hell was also current in tenth- and eleventh-century England. Kathleen Openshaw has shown the importance of the textual and visual links between the two scenes (and the Crucifixion) in the Tiberius Psalter,[42] and the association is also made in the Junius 121 homily.[43] Yet just as the beasts provide a visual link between God's first blessing of Adam and Eve and their redemption by Christ, between their birth in the physical world and their rebirth in heaven, they also provide a visual link to the Fall and Eve's guilt. Eve, pushed to the border of the architectural frame, stands with one foot on a lion who slinks off into the margins of the page with its tail between its legs – both it and Eve are simultaneously within and outside paradise. The transgression of space is further enhanced by the way in which the lion looks out at us rather than at God, a detail that helps to link the viewer with the fallibility of the first couple. The lion trampled by Christ represents sin, death and the devil, and like the devil is, as noted previously, responsible for stealing sheep from the fold. In the Junius 121 homily Adam associates himself with one of these lost sheep when he says to Christ, 'Ic dwolade swa swa þæt unwise sceap and forweard and losade.'[44] The motif of the dragon and lion as guardians of hell was popular in Anglo-Saxon England from at least the ninth century. A penitential prayer found in the ninth-century Book of Cerne (Cambridge, University Library, Ll. 1. 10, fols. 56–7v), in the eleventh-century Cambridge, Corpus Christi College 391, pp. 84–8, and in the eleventh-century Crowland Psalter (Oxford, Bodleian Library, Douce 296, 122v) reads:

> Te ergo supplico et deprecor sancte michael archangele qui ad animas accipiendas accepisti potestatem ut animam meam suscipere digneris quando de corpore meo erit egressa et libera eam de potestate inimici ut pertransire possit portas infernorum et vias tenebrarum ut non se deponat leo uel draco qui consuetus est animas in inferno recipere et ad aeterna tormenta perducere. Te deprecor sancte Petre princips apostolorum qui claues regni caelorum accipiendas accepisti potestatem ut portas paradysi michi aperire digneris.[45]

[42] K. M. Openshaw, 'Battle between Christ and Satan', p. 26.

[43] '*Super aspidem et basiliscum ambulabis et conculcabis leonem et draconem*, þæt is, "Ðæt tredst leon and dræcan".' Fadda, '"De descensu Christi"', p. 1002.

[44] 'I erred just as that unwise sheep and perished and was lost.' *Ibid.*, 1006.

[45] 'Therefore I appeal and pray to you, St Michael archangel, who has received the power to receive blessed souls, that you deign to take up my soul when it leaves my body, and

Read together, the details of the archangel Michael and the key-bearing angel in the door to heaven on page 9, and the lion and dragon at the edges of the frame on page 10, suggest the ultimate judgement of Adam and Eve and the fact that their souls, like those of their Anglo-Saxon readers, hang in the balance.

Pages 10 and 11 in the Junius manuscript are singletons, and both Raw and Doane have noted that something appears to be missing here, though again it is hard to say just what, as there is no break in the sense of the text.[46] Whatever material may or may not be missing between the pages, their compositions make it clear that they were meant to be understood in relation to each other. The frame of the drawing on page 10 overlaps the last words of the text on that page, God's statement *Inc hyrað eall* ('it all belongs to you', *Gen.* 205b), words which we see enacted on page 11. Such a literal combination of picture with the text to which it refers is not limited to Junius 11, but occurs also on folio 71r of the Harley Psalter (London, British Library, Harley 603). Here the artist has framed verse 8 of Psalm CXXXVIII, 'Si ascendero in caelum tu illa es si descendero in infernum ades',[47] with an open hell-mouth. Similarly, the picture on page 11 (pl. VI) is a very literal illustration both of the text on page 10, in which God gives Adam and Eve dominion over the animals, and of the three lines of manuscript text isolated above the figures:

þa sceawode. scyppend ure.
his weorca wlite. and his wæstma blæd.
niwra. gesceafta. neorxnawang stod.
god and gastlic. gifena gyfylled.[48]

free it from the power of the enemy so that it may pass over the gates of hell and the ways of darkness, and so that the lion may not destroy it, nor the dragon who is accustomed to receive souls in hell and lead them to eternal torments. I appeal to you St Peter, prince of apostles, who received the keys of the kingdom of heaven and power to receive souls, that you deign to open the gates of paradise to me.' The text is from CCCC 391 (A. Hughes, ed., *The Portiforium of Saint Wulstan* (London, 1960), pp. 3–4). See also, A. B. Kuypers, ed., *The Prayer Book of Aedelvald the Bishop, Commonly Called the Book of Cerne* (Cambridge 1902), pp. 111–14; K. Openshaw, 'Battle between Christ and Satan', p. 22.

46 Raw, 'Probable Derivation', p. 133, and 'Construction', p. 257; Doane, ed., *Genesis A*, p. 9, believes that around 130 lines of poetry are missing.

47 'If I ascend into heaven, you are there; if I descend into hell, you are there.'

48 'Then our Creator looked at the beauty of his works, and the fruit of his blessedness, his new creations. Paradise stood good and holy, filled with grace.' *Gen.* 206–9.

But the image is more than just an illustration of the text. As the drawing on page 10 contains a clear allusion to Psalm XC, so that on page 11 contains a clear allusion to Psalm VIII.8–10:

8. Thou hast subjected all things under his feet, all sheep and oxen: moreover the beasts also of the field.
9. The birds of the air, and the fishes of the sea, that pass through the paths of the sea.
10. O Lord our Lord how admirable is thy name in all the world.

Éamonn Ó Carragáin notes that the two psalms, and hence the two images, are related typologically. Psalm XC was sung each evening at compline, but was associated particularly with the reestablishing of paradise by Christ on Good Friday. Adam too was placed in paradise on a Friday.[49] These two drawings then link the establishment of paradise with the establishment of the New Paradise, and Adam with Christ, the second Adam and perfect man.[50] Within the manuscript, the themes of praise and creation referenced in Psalm VIII look backward to the call for praise with which the manuscript opens and forward to the Canticle of the three children in *Daniel*.[51] The themes of the two psalms are also brought together in *Christ and Satan*, which opens with an account of the Creation before turning to Christ's final triumph over the devil.

More specifically, the repetition of the details of the lion that looks out at us and the figure trampling on an animal establish a formal as well as an iconographic connection between the drawings on pages 10 and 11. On page 11, Adam stands on the left with his foot on a ram, a mirror-image of Eve's pose with the lion in the previous illustration. The ram may once again suggest Adam as the stolen sheep, but it is more likely that it appears here as a symbol of sacrifice used to establish a typological relationship between Adam, Abraham and the story of the sacrifice of Isaac, and perhaps beyond that to Christ, both at the Crucifixion and as prefigured in Psalm XC.[52] The description of the sacrifice of Isaac in

[49] See M. Walsh and D. Ó Cróinín, eds., *Cummian's Letter 'De Controversia Paschali' and the 'De Ratione Conputendi'* (Toronto, 1988), pp. 88–9.

[50] É. Ó Carragáin, personal communication; É. Ó Carragáin, *Liturgical Thought and the Dream of the Rood* (London, forthcoming).

[51] *Dan.* 362–408. For a discussion of the song in its manuscript context see below, pp. 104–6.

[52] See Clayton, *Cult of the Virgin Mary*, p. 168.

Exodus explicitly identifies Abraham as the founder of a new people who will inhabit a new land:

he að swereð. engla þeoden.
wyrda waldend. and wereda god.
soðfæst sigora. þurh his sylfes lif.
þæt þines cynnes. and cneowmaga.
randwiggendra. rim ne cunnon.
yldo ofer eorðan. ealle cræfte.
to gesecgenne. soðum wordum.
nymðe hwylc þæs snottor. in sefan weorðe.
þæt he ana mæge. ealle geriman.
stanas on eorðan. steorran on heofonum.
sæbeorga sand.[53] sealte yða.
ac hie gesittað. be sæm tweonum.
oð egipte. ingeðeode.[54]
land cananea. leode þine.
freobearn fæder. folca selost. ·~·[55]

The vertical arrangement of God, Adam and Abraham (signified by the ram) forms a patriarchal trinity: God the Father, Adam the first father, and Abraham the first of the biblical patriarchs. Related to the way in which the drawing provides a typological diagram of descent from Adam is the way in which it provides a metaphorical illustration of God's command to increase and multiply. Both Adam and Eve grasp the branches of trees whose flowers echo the shape of the male and female genitals, implying that they are themselves amongst the fruits of paradise. The word *wæstma*, here used in reference to creation in general, can mean both fruit and offspring, and is used in both senses throughout this poem in which the fertility of the land and its produce is repeatedly linked to

[53] The manuscript reads *sund*.

[54] The manuscript reads *incaðeode*.

[55] 'He swears an oath [to you], the Lord of angels, controller of fate, and God of hosts, trustworthy in victories, through his own life, that men over the earth, warriors, through all their skill in telling true words will not be able to count the number of your kinsmen, unless one should become so wise in heart that he alone may count the stones on earth, stars in heaven, sand of the sea cliffs, and salt waves; but they will occupy the land between the two seas as far as Egypt, your people, native people of the land of Canaan, the noble sons of the father, the best of peoples.' *Ex.* 432–46. See also J. R. Hall, 'Niwe Flodes: Old English "*Exodus*" 362', *N&Q* NS 22 (1975), 1243–4.

the fertility and prosperity of the human race – perhaps a reflection of the monastic ideal of the harmony between man and nature.

'Genesis B' begins on page 13 in the middle of God's prohibition. Clearly, something is missing from the manuscript at this point, but again we cannot be certain how much text or which illustrations, if any, might have been lost. Neither the scribe nor the artist treats this section of the manuscript as in any way distinct from *'Genesis A'* despite the arguments of modern scholars.[56] While such a distinction is of central concern to those interested in the sources of the poem, it is not necessary to an understanding of the textual narrative. For this, as Pasternack has stressed, 'Origin of the verses is not so significant as composition, and composition is not done by a single author, but through a process of shaping and reshaping previous performances and previous texts. Here, not minding the separate origins of these verses, the scribe gives the readers no option for considering these separate poems: the page directs readers simply to continue.'[57] In terms of the visual narrative, any missing material is largely irrelevant as here too the story of Adam and Eve continues without pause. They stand in plate VIIa pointing to the trees of life and death, while above, God, who had blessed them from an expansive heavenly kingdom in the preceding illustrations, turns from paradise to heaven, now reduced to a tiny mandorla shape at the centre of the architectural frame. In this instance, the drawing is a close visualization of the lines:

he let heo þæt land buan.
hwearf him þa to heofenum. halig drihten.
stiðferhð cyning. stod his handgeweorc.
samod on sande. nyston sorga wiht.
to begrornianne. butan heo godes willan.
lengest læsten. heo wæron leofe gode.
ðenden heo his halige word. healdan woldon.[58]

[56] For summaries of the different arguments see Doane, ed., *Genesis A*, pp. 38–58; Doane, ed., *Saxon Genesis*, pp. 28–42; Remley, *Biblical Verse*, pp. 94–8; Hall, 'Theological Unity'.

[57] Pasternack, *Textuality of Old English Poetry*, p. 182.

[58] 'He allowed them to dwell in that land. The holy Lord, the strong-minded King, turned then to heaven. His handiwork stood together on the ground, they knew nothing of sorrow to be lamented, but that they should fulfil God's will for the longest time. They were beloved to God so long as they were able to keep his holy word.' *Gen.* 239b–245.

In spite of the fact that Adam and Eve as yet know nothing of sorrow, the artist, echoing the slightly foreboding words of the poem, suggests the loss of paradise through the increasing separation of heaven and earth and the turning figure of the Lord. Moreover, just as the text directs the reader to continue, both the pose of the Lord and the leaf that sprouts from the column framing the right side of the drawing invite the viewer to turn the page and read again of the Fall of the rebel angels. The message is one of cyclical continuity rather than textual disruption.

Textually, the importance of the second Fall of the angels is indicated by the eight-line initial that begins the passage:

HÆFDE se ælwalda. engelcynna.
þurh handmægen. halig drihten.
tene getrimede. þæm he getruwode wel.
þæt hie his giongorscipe. fyligan wolden.
wyrcean his willan. forþon he him gewit forgeaf.
and mid his handum gesceop. halig drihten.[59]

The lowest beast-head bites fiercely at the *lig* of the word *halig*, a sign once again of the treachery and violence that is to come (pl. VIIb). This second and far more dramatic account of the Fall of the rebel angels leaves the reader in no doubt about the direct relationship between the Fall of the angels and that of the *englum gelice* Eve and Adam. Creation and Fall coexist within divine order, and perhaps, as Paul Ricoeur suggests, 'Creation continues to be a drama where the initial vulnerability to chaos allows us to anticipate the fragility of the created order.'[60] What is more, the second Fall presents us with a psychological portrait of Lucifer/Satan, complete with human motivations, desires and faults.[61] Lucifer is the Lord's retainer as Eve is Adam's, and both betray that relationship of homage, service and obedience which is of course at the heart of Anglo-Saxon as well as biblical social order. The poet tells us:

[59] 'The Ruler of the angels, the Lord, had through his mighty hand created ten [angels] in whom he trusted well that they would follow his allegiance, and work his will, because he gave them intelligence and created them with his hands, holy Lord.' *Gen.* 246–51.

[60] P. Ricoeur, 'Fides quaerens intellectum: Antécédents bibliques', *Archivo di Filosofia* 68 (1990), 19–42, at 36–7.

[61] See Doane's discussion of Satan in *Saxon Genesis*, pp. 116–38.

swa deð monna gehwilc
þe wið his waldend winnan ongynneð.
mid mane wið þone mæran drihten. þa wearð se mihtiga gebolgen.[62]

This is also the point at which Lucifer is given a new name, Satan, and evil begins to take on an identifiable, concrete presence prior to its entry into the world:

cwæð se hehsta. hatan sceolde.
satan siððan. het hine þære sweartan helle.
grundes gyman. nalles wið god winnan.[63]

The repetition of the Fall of the angels at this point allows both poet and artist to explore different nuances of the episode. The final repetition of the story in *Christ and Satan* will add even further to both the description and Satan's psychological portrait. The result of this sequential repetition is the creation of an increasingly complex picture of hell and its inhabitants, the latter becoming more and more real and individualized with each telling. It also has the effect of reinforcing the ever-present threat of hell and damnation in the minds and eyes of the manuscript's readers. If, as Augustine believed, eternity has no past or future, but only an 'eternal present' (*totum esse praesens*), then these events are always taking place and the sequential repetition, or layering, of image and story may be one way of documenting this phenomenon.[64]

The direct connection between biblical time and the contemporary order is also established in the illustrations that face each other on pages 16 and 17 (pls. VIII, IX). Here, the series of iconographic references with which the manuscript began, God/Christ in majesty, the Last Judgement, and the Harrowing of Hell, are combined in a single pair of images. God appears as ruler of heaven amongst the angels on the top of page 16 and flanked by seraphim at the top of page 17, an image of Creation and Judgement that mirrors that of the frontispiece. The framing wings of the angels and seraphim help to unite the two images of judgement past and

62 'So does each man who begins to struggle against his Lord, with evil against the great Lord. Then the Mighty One became enraged.' *Gen*. 297b–9. As Doane notes (*Saxon Genesis*, p. 126), it is difficult to believe that the poet is not deliberately equating social and divine order.

63 'The Highest One said that he should ever after be called Satan, then commanded him to take care of hell's dark abyss, not at all to strive against God'. *Gen*. 344–6.

64 Augustine, *Confessiones* (CSEL 33.1), xi. 13. For a discussion of the theoretical implications of this topic see Ricoeur, *Time and Narrative*, I, 25.

future. The beast-mouth of hell reinforces this historical continuum by establishing connections between this scene and contemporary images of the Harrowing and Last Judgement (pls. XLIVb, XLVa), as well as the biting beast-mouths of the decorated initial with which this episode begins. Satan too is the bound Satan of the Harrowing, and this combination of biblical and temporal references helps us to understand that Satan, like Christ, is a continuous presence in the world. In reference to this image of Satan Doane notes that, 'his binding in Hell, which is really a binding into the present, is a message that Adam and Eve are not historically remote either, but in the same position as the audience'.[65] The artist has further helped to drive home the relevance of the image to its audience by depicting Satan and his followers not as grotesque demons but as primarily human forms, in some cases complete with genitals and therefore sexuality. According to Ælfric, it is the body that distinguishes men from the angels: men have bodies, while angels do not. The acquisition of sexualized bodies makes the separation of fallen from heavenly angels[66] and the association of the former with Adam and Eve all the more obvious. While not commented on in the text, the depiction of these sexualized bodies also explicitly places male disobedience and fall before the fall of Eve.

Rather than striving against God directly, Satan now turns to battle against heaven through Adam and Eve. But his hatred of Adam also arises out of the very human emotion of jealousy – jealousy that Adam now possesses the exalted position that he once held:

þæt me is sorga mæst.
þæt adam sceal. þe wæs of eorðan geworht.
minne stronglican. stol behealdan.
wesan him on wynne. and we þis wite þolien.
hearm on þisse helle.[67]

[65] *Saxon Genesis*, p. 135.

[66] Ælfric says that God created the angels 'ealle lichamlease, leohte and strange, buton eallum synnum' ('all bodiless, light and strong and without any sin'). 'On the Old and New Testament', *Heptateuch*, ed. Crawford, p. 18, line 58. See also the homily *Natale Omnium Sanctorum* in *Homilies*, ed. Thorpe, I, 538: 'Englas sind gastas butan lichaman' ('angels are spirits without bodies'); and C. Lees, 'Engendering Religious Desire: Sex, Knowledge and Christian Identity in Anglo-Saxon England', *Jnl of Medieval and Early Modern Studies* 27.1 (1997), 17–45.

[67] 'It is the greatest sorrow to me that Adam, he who is made of earth, shall occupy my mighty throne, that he will be in bliss and we suffer these tortures, pain in this hell.' *Gen*. 364b–368.

This quite personal expression of hatred for Adam may be one of the reasons Satan sends his messenger to tempt Adam before Eve. In the battle between Satan and Adam, Eve is secondary, merely a tool through which the deception of Adam can be achieved. Satan's complaint about the darkness and suffering of hell and his desire that Adam and his descendants should also seek hell, and serve him rather than the Lord, is written on page 21, with the narrative of the Temptation and Fall beginning on page 22. The illustration on page 20 (pl. Xa), as noted above, provides a visual preface to and summary of the events that follow.[68]

Much has been written about the poem's version of the Fall and how it should be interpreted.[69] The exact form of the tempter when he approaches Adam is not clear in the text. The poet does state that he takes the form of a snake after entering paradise 'wearp hine þa on wyrmes lic. and wand him þa ymbutan. / þone deaðes beam. þurh doefles cræft.',[70] but Adam's reaction to him in the poem gives no indication that he retains this form during the Temptation. Indeed, along with the God of *Exodus*, and Christ in *Christ and Satan*, the messenger is one of the manuscript's great shape-shifters, changing from demon to serpent to false angel and back again. Adam responds to the tempter's words both with a logical argument and with the strength of his faith. He tells the tempter that he does not know whether or not he is truly the Lord's messenger, that he does not recognize the wisdom of his argument (*Gen.* 534), that he is unlike any angel he has ever seen (*Gen.* 538–9), and that without a sign (*tacen*, *Gen.* 540) that he has been sent by God he will not listen to him. In his approach to Eve the messenger turns Adam's words to his own good, playing not only on Eve's loyalty to Adam, but also revealing to her that Adam refused to believe in his angelic nature and

68 See above, p. 11.

69 R. Woolf, 'The Fall of Man in *Genesis B* and the *Mystère d'Adam*', in *Studies in Old English in Honor of Arthur G. Brodeur*, ed. S. B. Greenfield (Eugene, OR, 1963), pp. 187–99; K. Dubs, '*Genesis B*: A Study in Grace', *American Benedictine Review* 33 (1982), 47–64; A. Renoir, 'Eve's I.Q. Rating: Two Sexist Views of Genesis B', in *New Readings on Women in Old English Literature*, ed. H. Damico and A. H. Olsen (Bloomington, IN, 1990), pp. 262–72; G. Overing, 'On Reading Eve: *Genesis B* and the Reader's Desire', in *Speaking Two Languages: Traditional Disciplines and Contemporary Theory in Medieval Studies*, ed. A. J. Frantzen (Albany, NY, 1991), pp. 35–63.

70 'Then he cast himself into the body of the serpent and wound around the tree of death with devil's craft'. *Gen.* 491–2.

stressing that clearly she must as he does not look like a devil (*Gen.* 587). As a proof of the truth of his words and his good intentions he gives her the sign he did not give Adam, a vision of heaven that is not depicted for the viewer. The false sign given to Eve and the sign not offered to Adam contrast with the true sign of the covenant established between God and Abraham later in the poem. In the illustration that accompanies the Temptation of Eve (pl. XII), the posture of the messenger, whose body turns from Adam to Eve, and the apples he balances in each hand beautifully convey the difference between the two Temptations, and the transition from one to the other. The presence of Adam in this drawing, and the way in which Eve looks towards him, further serve to suggest the vision of the endangered husband that the messenger keeps firmly in Eve's mind throughout her Temptation. While at first glance it might seem possible to interpret the drawing as depicting a joint Temptation, and perhaps Fall, Adam does not hold the apple, and his open-palmed gesture is a conventional way of indicating restraint, or the physical attempt to ward something off.[71] The open palm and pointing finger turn the action back towards the tempter and Eve and contrast with Eve's hands, which close firmly around the fruit.

The actual eating of the apple is decentralized both by the dramatic central figure of the tempter and by the narrative motion of the illustration, yet this is the most dramatic moment in the poem. It is at this point that Eve assumes the traditional feminine role of peaceweaver while simultaneously transgressing it by assuming the active masculine role of lord which, according to the messenger, Adam refused to accept.[72] This is also the point at which the boundaries separating earth, heaven and hell are crossed and obscured – standing on earth, Eve is granted a vision of heaven by Satan in hell:

Heo þa þæs ofætes æt.   alwalden bræc.
word and willan.   þa meahte heo wide geseon.
þurh þæs laðan læn.   þe hie mid ligenum beswac.
dearnenga bedrog.   þe hire for his dædum com.
þæt hire þuhte hwitre.   heofon and eorðe.
and eall þeos woruld wlitigre.   and geweorc godes.
micel and mihtig.   þeah heo hit þurh monnes geþeaht.

[71] Dodwell, *Anglo-Saxon Gestures*, p. 45.

[72] See discussions in J. Chance, *Woman as Hero in Old English Literature* (Syracuse, NY, 1986), pp. 65–79; Overing, 'On Reading Eve'.

ne sceawode. ac se sceaða georne.
swicode ymb þa sawle. þe hire ær þa siene onlah.
þæt heo swa wide. wlitan meahte.
ofer heofonrice.[73]

It is significant that the vision is withheld from the viewer. The fact that we hear it only through Eve's words but cannot see it for ourselves is an indication of its false nature. In contrast, we have seen the true vision of God enthroned (a vision based on Isaiah and John) in the manuscript's frontispiece, a sight that will not be revealed to Eve until after her rescue from hell at the end of *Christ and Satan*. The deceptive character of the vision may be further highlighted by the bodies of Eve and the messenger who share the vision and help to direct the reader's eyes to its textual description, which appears on the facing page. Adam, to whom it is never revealed, turns his back to the page. The drama and danger of the moment are likely indicated by the dark acanthus frieze and claw-like projections of the architectural frame.

In eating the apple, the physical boundaries of the body are also transgressed and Eve's body becomes identified with the forbidden fruit. The poet tells us that when she approaches Adam,

Sum heo hire on handum bær. sum hire æt heortan læg.
æppel unsælga.[74]

In addition, by eating the apple Eve has gained the power of language, yet just as she has failed to read and interpret properly the signs offered her by the tempter, she now fails to recognize the false message conveyed in her own words.[75] Adam is in turn deceived by her words, an account of

[73] 'Then she ate that fruit, broke the word and the will of God. Then she could see far through the devil's gift, he who betrayed her with lies, secretly seduced her, that which came to her through his doings, so that heaven and earth seemed brighter to her and all this world more beautiful, and God's work great and mighty, although she did not look at it through human perception. But the enemy skilfully practised deceit around her soul, he who previously granted her the power of vision, so that she could look widely over heaven.' *Gen.* 599–609.

[74] 'A certain thing she carried in her hand, a certain thing lay at her heart, the unholy apple.' *Gen.* 636–37.

[75] According to Augustine the Fall of man was also a fall into language, and Eve would be guilty of misreading by accepting as true what a deceptive author knew to be false. See *De utilitate credendi*, iv.10, (PL 42.72). See also Stévanovitch, 'Envelope Patterns in *Genesis*'.

her false vision, and the danger of his situation is universalized by the poet, who warns:

bið þam men full wa.
þe hine ne warnað. þonne he his geweald hafað.[76]

As noted previously, the artist has suggested the dialogue that accompanies Eve's temptation of Adam by the physical contact between the two.[77] Eve's vision also helps to make her situation more real for the poem's audience through its sensuality and its first-person account of inner thought and bodily experience (qualities also captured in the artist's portrayal of her body):

Ic mæg heonon geseon.
hwær he sylf siteð. þæt is suð and east.
welan bewunden. se ðas woruld gesceop.
geseo ic him his englas. ymbe hweorfan.
mid feðerhaman. ealra folca mæst.
wereda wynsumast. hwa meahte me swelc gewit gifan.
gif hit gegnunga. god ne onsende.
heofones waldend. Gehyran mæg ic rume.
and swa wide geseon. on woruld ealle.
ofer þas sidan gesceaft. ic mæg sweglas gamen.
gehyran on heofnum. wearð me on hige leohte.
utan and innan. siþðan ic þæs ofætes onbat.[78]

The vision further serves to establish her fallen position and to unite this Old Testament event with the present and future. She sees God to the south and east, placing her in the north-west, a position associated with hell, and also the location of Lucifer's longed-for throne (*Gen.* 32). Yet for all its falseness her vision is also one of Redemption, of the Last Judgement, the time of Christ's final triumph over Satan. Its typological

[76] 'That man will be full of woe who does not maintain his guard while he has his power.' *Gen.* 634–5.

[77] See above, p. 42.

[78] 'I can see hence to where he himself sits, that is to the south and east, surrounded with wealth, he who created this world. I see his angels moving around him with wings, the greatest of all people, the most beautiful troop. Who could give me such understanding if God had not plainly sent it, the lord of heaven? I can hear widely and see far over all the world, over this vast creation. I can hear joyful music in heaven. My mind has been enlightened within and without since I tasted that fruit.' *Gen.* 666b–677. See Stévanovitch, 'Envelope Patterns', on the flawed language and logic of Eve's speech.

relationship to the Harrowing of Hell suggests that even at this moment of Fall, Redemption is in sight.

The lower register of the drawing depicts the reversal of fortune that comes with Adam and Eve's disobedience. They fall to the ground in despair where once they stood upright, their poses reversing the flow of the narrative from left to right and quite literally suggesting desire for the past and fear of the future. Their figures fulfil the desire of Satan and his messenger that they be *forweorpan, forlæran and forlæden* ('thrown down, mislead and corrupted', *Gen.* 691b–92). The messenger, his true demonic identity now revealed, spits at them with contempt as he prepares to return to hell. His gleeful attitude in this drawing again reflects the text of the poem which tells us that *hloh þa and plegode boda bitre gehugod* ('the bitter-minded messenger then laughed and played') at the sight of Adam's fall (*Gen.* 724b–725).[79]

Before revealing the Lord's judgement on Adam and Eve, the poet describes the couple's remorse and presents us with a series of first-person speeches and dialogues, beginning with the boasts of the messenger and his personal account of the Fall of the angels (*Gen.* 740b–50). This is the third account of the Fall of the angels in this poem, and the second to make explicit the causal link between their Fall and that of Adam and Eve. It also now reveals the similarities of their fates: the angels were driven into hell as Adam and Eve will be driven out of paradise.[80]

unc wearð god yrre.
forþon wit him noldon. on heofonrice.
hnigan mid heafdum. halgum drihtne.
þurh geongordom. ac unc gegenge ne wæs.
þæt wit him on þegnscipe. þeowian wolden.
forþon unc waldend wearð. wrað on mode.
on hyge hearde. and us on helle bedraf.

[79] See Doane, ed., *Genesis A*, p. 229; P. Salmon, 'The Site of Lucifer's Throne', *Anglia* 81 (1963), 118–23; T. D. Hill, 'Some Remarks on "the Site of Lucifer's Throne"', *Anglia* 87 (1969), 303–11.

[80] 'God became angry with us because in heaven we were not willing to bow our heads in vassalage to the Holy Lord; but it was not our fate that we would serve him in thaneship. Therefore the Lord became angry in his mind with us, hard in his spirit, and drove us into hell, cast down the greatest of hosts into that fire, and with his hands restored again the heavenly thrones and granted that kingdom to mankind.' *Gen.* 740b–750.

on þæt fyr fylde. folca mæste.
and mid handum his. eft on heofonrice.
rihte rodorstolas. and þæt rice forgeaf.
monna cynne.

Two full-page drawings (pls. XI, XV) and one half-page drawing (pl. XVI) are devoted to this section of the poem, which in textual terms is lacking in visual drama. The artist shows us Adam and Eve contemplating the consequences of their actions, both together and apart, in five separate scenes. The purpose of these drawings is certainly to convey the turmoil of the couple, and the poet emphasizes once again that they are a couple, a married pair.[81] The drawings are all used to stress moments of separation and despair. On pages 34 and 39 (pls. XIV, XVI) Adam and Eve stand together in the top panel and separated amongst the trees in the bottom panel. Isolated at the top of the full-page illustration on page 34 are the words 'nu hie wordcwyde his lare forleton·⁄' ('now they have relinquished his command and his counsel', *Gen.* 730b–1). The finality of this loss is reinforced by the emphatic punctuation at the end of the line. A similar dramatic union of text, punctuation and illustration can be seen on page 36 where the text reads, 'sceolde he þa bradan ligas. / secan helle gehliðo. þær his hearra læg·⁄' ('he had to seek the broad flames, the abyss of hell, where his master lay', *Gen.* 763b–4). The line is followed by a *punctus elevatus* and the illustration of the tempter's return to hell. The journey down to hell is of course one that Adam and Eve too will now have to make, and this is suggested visually by the artist's depiction of hell as an ominous black shape looming threateningly up at the couple. In fact, Adam's right foot is positioned just within its entrance.

The Judgement of the Lord begins on page 41 (pl. XVII). At the bottom of the page Adam and Eve hide their bodies with leaves. The text on page 40 ends with Adam's confession to God: 'Ic eom eall eall nacod' ('I am entirely all naked', *Gen.* 871b). The words are aligned with his head on the facing page and are directed visually to God through Adam's upturned head and the gesture of his hand. The enormity of Adam and Eve's crime is also indicated graphically by the fact that the beginning of God's questioning of Adam on page 42 has been picked out with a seven-line decorated initial that includes three fierce biting heads, one of which

81 The phrases used are *sinhiwan somed* ('married couple together'), *Gen.* 778; and *sinhiwan twa* ('the married couple, the two'), *Gen.* 789.

snaps at the text.[82] The arrangement of the figures of Adam, Eve and the Lord on the page further suggests the dialogue of confession and blame contained in the poem, but does not emphasize Eve's guilt over Adam's. It is true that Adam and God gesture towards each other in a conversation that seems to exclude Eve, yet it is over her figure, not Adam's, that the Lord stands. When compared to the same scene in the Hexateuch, where Eve lies beneath Adam turning away from both him and God (pl. XLVIa), or to Bishop Bernward's doors at Hildesheim, where everything including the tree points an accusing finger at Eve, this and the following image of judgement (pl. XVIII) are models of restraint. As has been noted previously, Eve's words at this point are also unusual.[83] While Adam puts the blame firmly on Eve,[84] Eve acknowledges her own guilt and takes responsibility for her actions:

> Me nædre beswac. and me neodlice.
> to forsceape scyhte. and to scyldfrece.
> fah wyrm þurh fægir word. oð þæt ic fracoðlice.
> feondræs gefremede. fæhðe geworhte.
> and þa reafode. swa hit riht ne wæs.
> beam on bearwe. and þa blæda æt.[85]

Her speech does reveal that she was urged on to sin by the serpent, but rather than simply serving to shift the blame it is also an affirmation of a newly gained subjectivity and human understanding: *I* performed a wicked deed, took the apple and ate it.

Eve's ability to recognize the true nature of her actions, as well as those of Adam and the serpent, may be reinforced by her use of the word *fah* (*Gen.* 899), meaning hostile or guilty but also beautiful or decorated in variegated colouring. The serpent is *fah*, like the Anglo-Saxon sword which the word is frequently used to describe,[86] both beautiful and

82 See above, p. 32.

83 Belanoff, 'Fall (?) of the Old English Female Poetic Image', p. 829.

84 'me ðа blæda on hand. bryd gesealde. / freolucu fæmne. freadrihten min. / ðe ic þe on teonan geþah. [*ic* added over line by scribe]' 'The woman, the beautiful woman, gave the fruit into my hand, which I took as an insult to you.' *Gen.* 883–5.

85 'The snake deceived me and eagerly urged me to sin and to greediness, the beautiful deadly serpent through his fair words, until I wickedly carried out a hostile attack, performed a wicked deed, took from the tree in the wood as it was not right to do, and ate the fruit.' *Gen.* 897–902.

86 See, for example, *Beowulf*, lines 1459 (*atertanum fah*, 'deocrated with poisonous stripes') and 2671 (*fyrwylmum fah*, 'shining with surges of fire').

deadly, and it is Eve who first recognizes and speaks this fact. It is confirmed by both the narrator and the Lord who use the same word to describe the serpent within the space of twelve lines.[87] This threefold repetition links the perception of Eve to that of both God and the poem's authorial voice, and suggests that her former false vision has been replaced by true insight. The Lord's judgement on the serpent is depicted in the upper half of plate XVII, where the serpent crawls off into the foliate scroll of a marginal column, symbolic of the marginal wilds it is henceforth doomed to inhabit.

God's separate judgement of Adam and Eve is illustrated on page 44 (pl. XVIII). Here the artist has mirrored the narrative flow of the poem by depicting God twice, first passing judgement on Eve to the left, and then turning to judge Adam on the right. The gestures of the figures serve to unite the sequence of judgement on this page with its continuation on the facing page (pl. XIX). The sentence at the top of page 45 further relates the sin of Adam and Eve and their punishment directly to the experience of the poem's audience:

> Hwæt we nu gehyrað:　　hwær us hearmstafas.
> wraðe onwocan.　　and woruldyrmðo.[88]

The importance of this sentence is flagged graphically by the small capital with which it begins and the colon following the word *gehyrað*. The poem then goes on to relate how the Lord clothed Adam and Eve and expelled them from paradise. In the drawing below the text, the first of two illustrating the Expulsion, Adam and Eve are dressed in the garments of contemporary Anglo-Saxon men and women, rather than the simple robes more common in Genesis illustrations.[89] The objects they carry are also those that would have been used by contemporary Anglo-Saxons. While Adam's agricultural tools, here a spade and bag of seeds, are traditional, the spindle that Eve carries at her breast is not. If Eve carries anything in early medieval Expulsions, it is usually a distaff.[90] The shape of the

[87] *fagum wyrme* (*Gen.* 904b), *fah mid fotum sinum* (*Gen.* 913).

[88] 'Listen, now we shall hear where trouble for us, evil and world-miseries, awoke'. *Gen.* 939.

[89] See H. L. Kessler, *The Illustrated Bibles from Tours* (Princeton, NJ, 1977), pls. 1, 3 and 4; Weitzmann and Kessler, *Cotton Genesis*, figs. 60–4.

[90] See Weitzmann and Kessler, *Cotton Genesis*, figs. 60–4; Kessler, *Illustrated Bibles*, pls. 1–5 and figs. 29–33.

spindle on this page repeats that of the apple the poem tells us has lodged itself in her breast, but it is possible that it also served to equate Eve with Anglo-Saxon women, who were renowned for their textile production.[91] More importantly, it helps to maintain the typological relationship between Eve and Mary established at Eve's creation. The spindle was an object associated with Mary and is sometimes shown as her attribute in early medieval depictions of the Annunciation. Both in the Annunciation panel from the *c.* 550 throne of Archbishop Maximian in Ravenna, and on the Anglo-Saxon influenced Genoels-Elderen ivory book cover (Brussels, Musées royaux d'Art et d'Histoire) she holds both a distaff and a spindle.[92] It has been suggested that Mary also holds a spindle in the annunciation scenes on both the Hovingham shrine slab and the Ruthwell 'cross', but this is highly debatable and both are now so worn that it is difficult to be sure of any such details.[93] Although she does not appear with a spindle in any surviving Anglo-Saxon manuscript, she is shown with what has been interpreted as a shuttle in the annunciation scene from the Benedictional of Æthelwold (BL, Add. 49598, 5v).[94] The likelihood that the detail was meant to associate Eve with Mary is strengthened by the fact that Sarah holds an identical spindle in the illustration on page 88 (pl. XLIIIb). As previously noted, Eve, Sarah and Mary thus form a matriarchal trinity paralleling the patriarchal trinity of Adam, Abraham and God.

91 G. R. Owen-Crocker, *Dress in Anglo-Saxon England* (Manchester, 1986), ch. 9.

92 On the latter see C. Neuman de Vegvar, 'The Origin of the Genoels-Elderen Ivories', *Gesta* 29.1 (1990), 8–24. See also Weitzmann and Kessler, *Cotton Genesis*, 37.

93 For Hovingham see J. Hawkes, 'Mary and the Cycle of Resurrection: the Iconography of the Hovingham Panel', in *The Age of Migrating Ideas*, ed. R. M. Spearman and J. Higgitt (Edinburgh and Stroud, 1993), pp. 254–60. Hawkes identifies the object at Mary's feet as a basket of wool with a strand of wool rising out of it connecting to a now lost spindle, but James Lang has identified the same object as a vase with a lily (*York and Eastern Yorkshire*, vol. III of *Corpus of Anglo-Saxon Stone Sculpture* (Oxford, 1991), 148). For Ruthwell see G. Henderson, *Vision and Image in Early Christian England* (Cambridge, 1999), p. 139. Henderson is the only scholar who has made this identification, and it seems highly unlikely.

94 For a discussion of this miniature and its Carolingian parallels see Deshman, *Benedictional*, pp. 9–17, pl. 8, and fig. 1. See also Chance, *Woman as Hero*, pp. 77–9.

EXILE

The land to which Adam and Eve are exiled does not resemble either that in which they appear in other early medieval Genesis cycles or that suggested by the harsh words of God's punishment. Rather than a joyless land in which they wander naked and destitute,[95] the pair cross a fertile landscape to reach a comfortable and well-appointed dwelling (pls. XX, XXI). The roof of clouds and the flowering landscape beneath their feet on page 46 may be a reference to the unusual words of the poem immediately following the Expulsion:

> No hwæðre ælmihtig. ealra wolde.
> adame and euan. arna ofteon.
> fæder æt frymðe. þeah þe he him from swice.
> Ac he him to frofre. let hwæðere forð wesan.
> hyrstedne hrof. halgum tunglum.
> and him grundwelan. ginne sealde.
> het þam sinhiwum sæs and eorðan
> tuddorteondra. teohha gehwilcre.[96]
> to woruldnytte. wæstmas fedan.[97]

Adam turns to gaze wistfully back at the door to paradise and the angel who now guards it, in a possible reference to man's ultimate return to paradise at the Last Judgement.[98] For an Anglo-Saxon audience this was a theme that went back to the very origins of Christianity. The allegory of the sparrow that figures so significantly in Bede's account of the conversion of King Edwin juxtaposes the transitory nature of an earthly paradise with the vastness of eternity, and man's desire for knowledge of the hereafter.[99] The theme was also prominent in the homilies of Ælfric,[100]

[95] 'þu scealt oðerne eðel secean. / wynleasran wic. and on wræc hweorfan. / nacod niedwædla. neorxnawanges. / dugeðum bedæled.' ('You shall seek another homeland, a more joyless dwelling, and wander in exile, naked and destitute, deprived of the gifts of paradise'.) *Gen.* 927–30.

[96] The manuscript reads *gehilcre*.

[97] 'The Almighty did not yet wish to take all favours from Adam and Eve, the Father at the beginning, although they had rebelled against him. But as a comfort to them he allowed to continue in being a roof decorated with holy stars, and gave them broad earthly wealth. He commanded each fruitful species of the sea and land to bring forth fruit for the worldly needs of the married pair.' *Gen.* 952–60.

[98] Cf. Hebrews XIII.14.

[99] *HE* II.13.

[100] Gatch, *Preaching and Theology*, pp. 66–8.

for whom life was a period of exile during which man awaited his return to the kingdom of God. The angel in the doorway, often identified as Michael, looks both forward to the Last Judgement and backward to the creation of Eve, where Michael stood in the doorway to heaven (pl. IV). In a sense the Expulsion from paradise represents a rebirth into a new mortal life and the beginning of a new order of creation and procreation. The artist signals the change in order through his depiction of Eve who does not turn back like her husband, but strides confidently forward.

The drawing of the birth of Abel on page 47 is one of the most unusual in the manuscript (pl. XXI). Rather than depicting Adam tilling the soil and Eve nursing Cain or Abel, subjects that traditionally appear at this point,[101] the artist has depicted the birth of Abel, with the infant Cain and an enthroned Adam witnessing the event. Eve's labour takes precedence over Adam's, which appears only as a small scene in the upper left corner of the illustration devoted primarily to the story of Cain and Abel on page 49 (pl. XXII). Iconographically, the illustration of Eve's labour is also unusual. Early medieval illustrated Genesis cycles typically depict Eve nursing her children either outdoors or in a crude hut or bower. The Junius 11 illustration departs from this tradition and is clearly related to contemporary Anglo-Saxon images of the Nativity, such as that in the tenth-century Benedictional of St Æthelwold (pl. XLVIIa), or the naming of Christ on folio 22v of the same manuscript.[102] The artist has not, however, copied his source exactly (whatever specific image it might have been), as the stable in which the Nativity takes place has been changed into a comfortable Anglo-Saxon interior. The association between Eve and Mary established in earlier illustrations is here strengthened by the fact that it is the birth of Abel, who prefigures Christ, that we see. Moreover, Abel's death, like Christ's, is here explicitly foreshadowed in his birth, as the text above the illustration records the story of Cain's murder of his innocent brother.

The use of space in this illustration is also suggestive. The enthroned Adam, his arms open to receive his sons, is confined within the smallest of

[101] See Kessler, *Illustrated Bibles*, esp. figs. 1–5, 29 and 33. In the Hexateuch (BL, Claudius B. iv, 7v) Adam and Eve are both shown working the soil, Adam with a spade and Eve with a pickaxe, and the birth of Cain and Abel is not depicted.

[102] See Deshman, *Benedictional*, pl. 16. See also Boulogne-sur-Mer, Bibliothèque Municipale, 11, fol. 12.

the three arches, while the bed in which Eve reclines takes up two thirds of the picture, suggesting woman's dominant role in the process of procreation. It is now the bodies of Eve and her descendants that will bring forth new life, most particularly sons and heirs. Cain floats alone, cut off from both parents in the middle of the illustration. In fact, his peculiar location draws our eyes to him. Here too is a foreshadowing of his future exile from family and homeland, a future that is foretold in the text of the poem above his head:

cwealmdreore swealh.
þæs middangeard. monnes swate.
æfter wælswenge. wea wæs aræred.
tregena tuddor. of ðam twige siððan.
ludon laðwende. leng swa swiðor.
reðe wæstme.[103]

The imagery of the tree and fruit that reappear in this passage serve to unite Cain's crime to his mother's crime, and to reinforce the connection between the fruit of the tree of death that Eve carried inside her after the Fall and her son, the fruit of her body. The poet explicitly unites the two (and the biblical figures with their contemporary readers) in the lines at the bottom of page 47 and top of page 48:

ræhton wide.
geond werþeoda. wrohtes telgan.
hrinon hearmtanas. hearde and sare.
drihta bearnum. doð gieta swa.
Of þam brad blado. bealwa gehwilces
sprytan ongunnon. we þæt spell magon.
wælgrimme wyrd. wope cwiðan.
nales holunge. ac us hearde sceod.
freolecu fæmne. þurh forman gylt.
þe wið metod æfre. men gefremeden.[104]

[103] 'The earth swallowed the blood of the slaughtered one, man's blood, after the deadly blow. Woe was raised, the fruit of pain. From that branch afterwards grew evil, more intensely the longer it went on, a horrible fruit.' *Gen.* 985b–990.

[104] 'The twig of harm reached widely throughout peoples, the branches of sorrow, hard and painful, touched mankind. They do so still. Each of evils from that broad leaf began to sprout. We may mourn that story, that cruel event, with weeping, not at all without cause. But that noble woman harmed us severely through the first crime which man ever performed against the Lord.' *Gen.* 990b–999.

The passage also looks forward to the genealogical tree, the descendants of Cain, whose members appear in the following pages.

The story of Cain and Abel is depicted on page 49 (pl. XXII) where the pictorial narrative complements that of the text, the recapitulation of Cain's actions on the facing page. Cain appears to the upper left, behind his father, harvesting the fruits of the earth which he offers to God alongside his brother to the upper right. The murder of Abel and the earth's swallowing of his blood are depicted to the lower right, while Abel's blood crying out to the Lord appears at bottom left. Cain's confession is contained in the text above the drawing. The picture continues the imagery of fruit and tree with Abel's blood watering the ground from which his brother's crops grow, while his body rises up out of the same earth to cry out to the Lord.[105] The earth that was once fruitful for Cain will henceforth be barren, and there is a marked contrast between the productive earth tilled by Adam and Cain and grazed by Abel's flocks (the earth from which both Cain and Abel bring their offerings in the top half of the picture), and the barren earth beneath the body of Abel in the lower half of this picture and that beneath the feet of Cain on page 51 (pl. XXIII). The images of death and rebirth on this page recall both the return of the messenger into the earth (hell) after the fall of Adam and the introduction of death into the world, and the creation of Eve with Adam born of the earth and Eve raising her hands in prayer to the Lord, in a pose echoed by that of Abel in this picture.

GENEALOGY AND SOCIAL ORDER

Three full-page illustrations are devoted to the descendants of Cain, beginning with the depiction of his receiving his mark and undertaking his journey into exile on page 51. The narrative starts at the top of the page where Cain is decisively separated from the Lord by a jagged line. The text on the opposite page tells us that this is the point at which God places a mark upon him as both an indication of his status as outcast and exile, and a sign that he should not be slain. The two beast-heads that appear in the corners of the upper border may also function as a mark of

[105] For an important discussion of this episode see C. D. Wright, 'The Blood of Abel and the Branches of Sin: *Genesis A*, *Maxims I* and Aldhelm's *Carmen de uirginitate*', *ASE* 25 (1996), 7–19.

Cain and his family's outcast status. Formally they are reminiscent of the beast-head in the border of the drawing depicting God's judgement on the serpent, and may serve as signs of Cain's animal-like nature as well as his exile. Yet neither the text nor the illustrations of Cain's descendants down to his slayer Lamech portray them as obvious outcasts. The poet describes them as princes or nobles (*æðelings*, *Gen.* 1059), swordbearers (*sweordberende*, *Gen.* 1060), distributors of treasure (*Mathusal magumdælde*, *Gen.* 1069), and inheritors of wealth (*Lameh onfeng . . . botlgestreonum*, *Gen.* 1073b–1075). In the illustrations, both men and women are shown seated on chairs or benches with elegantly patterned cushions (pl. XXIVa). Even Lamech's sons, Iabal the harpist and Tubel-Cain the smith, are shown practising their crafts in an architectural setting (pl. XXIVb). The illustrations of the genealogy of Cain in the Hexateuch show similar settings, though neither the architecture nor the furnishings are as elaborate as those in Junius 11.[106] The most likely reason for the somewhat unusual iconography of Junius 11 is that the men and women pictured are meant to reflect the world of their Anglo-Saxon audience. The architectural settings of these drawings are not as elaborate as those used for the genealogy of Seth, and Cain and his descendants are not shown with the attributes of power that will appear with them, so the artist does make a distinction between the true and false, or clearly noble and less noble, branches of the genealogical tree. The descent from Cain ends with Lamech's sons, who are workers: the harpist, the smith and the herdsman/ploughman, Jubal (who is not mentioned in the poem but is shown in the illustration on page 54). It is possible that the descendants of Cain are meant to reflect the workers, one of the three orders of society elaborated in the writings of Alfred and Ælfric. In his 'On the Old and New Testament', Ælfric writes, 'Se cinestol stynt on þisum þrim stelum: LABORATORES, BELLATORES, ORATORES. LABORATORES sind þe us bigleofan tiliað, yrðlingas and æhte men to þam anum betæhte'.[107] For both Alfred and Ælfric all three orders were necessary to the maintenance of the kingdom,[108] and each was based not on wealth but on occupa-

[106] See BL, Claudius B. iv, fols. 9–10.

[107] 'The throne stands upon these three pillars: Laboratores, Bellatores, Oratores. Laboratores are ploughmen and husbandmen, whose only pursuit is to is to supply us with sustenance.' *Heptateuch*, ed. Crawford, p. 71.

[108] 'On þisum þrim stelum stynt se cynestol, and gif an bið forud, he fylð adun sona þam oðrum stelum to unþearfe gewiss.' ('On these three pillars stands the throne; and if

tion,[109] a distinction which also seems to apply to the labouring descendants of Cain in Junius 11.

The Bellatores (warriors) and Oratores (clergy), on the other hand, are represented as being amongst the descendants of Seth, all depicted with attributes of power and Anglo-Saxon kingship. Seth holds a spear (pl. XXV); Cainan, with crown and staff, sits on an elaborate throne, his well-armed band of retainers behind him (pl. XXVI); Malaleel stands before an altar (pl. XXVII); Enoch has a book and halo (pl. XXIX); Mathusael is accompanied by his comitatus (pl. XXXI); Noah, with crown and staff, is shown instructing both his people and his sons (pl. XXXII).[110] Beginning with Seth, they are also seedbearers (*sædberendes Sethes lice*, *Gen.* 1145) and fathers described as 'strewing' or 'generating' (*strienan*) their descendants,[111] a poetic formula that continues the motif of male creation, here literally generation, and contrasts the blessed fruitfulness of the line of Seth with the ultimate barrenness of that of Cain, whose descendants must work the land. Moreover, at least one illustration is devoted solely to each of these leaders and their families, while the lineage of Cain is compressed into a total of three illustrations. In addition to being noble these men are just (*soðfæst*, *Gen.* 1106) and blessed (*eadig*, *Gen.* 1107 and *gesælig*, *Gen.* 1138); they invoke God (*se nemde god*, *Gen.* 1135), are wise (*gleawferhð*, *Gen.* 1152) and are leaders (*aldordema*, *Gen.* 1156). The language is important, and it is reflected in the illustrations. These generations are blessed because, like the readers of this text, they praise God where the generations of Cain do not. The artist seems to have made a deliberate effort to convey this visually in the depictions of both Malaleel (pls. XXVII, XXVIII) and Enoch (pls. XXIX, XXX). The drawings of Enoch are complex and have been partially discussed

one of them is decayed it falls down and at once the other pillars become useless.') *Ibid.*, p. 72.

109 See M. Godden, 'Money, Power and Morality in late Anglo-Saxon England', *ASE* 19 (1990), 41–65; see also, Ælfric, *Homilies*, ed. Thorpe, II xix.

110 Gollancz (*Cædmon Manuscript*, pp. xliv–xlv) connects Noah's pose, which he describes as one of 'handshaking', to the biblical etymology of his name. See Gen. V.29: 'And he called his name Noe, saying: This same shall comfort us from the works and labours of our hands on the earth, which the Lord hath cursed.'

111 See J. W. Butcher, 'Formulaic Invention in the Genealogies of the Old English *Genesis A*', in *Comparative Research on Oral Traditions: A Memorial for Milman Perry*, ed. J. M. Foley (Columbus, OH, 1985), pp. 73–92. The word is used for both Cain and Seth's lines in Claudius B. iv.

already;[112] however, there seems no reason for showing Malaleel before an altar other than to indicate his praise of God.[113] The altar and Malaleel's pose of prayer also remind us of other images of offering and establish a relationship between him and Abel (pl. XXII), Enoch, Noah (pls. XXXVII, XXXVIII) and ultimately Abraham. In death, Malaleel is represented almost as a type of Christ or Mary, with three mourning women on one side and a group led by a man swinging a censor on the other. Presumably these are his children, but the composition recalls Byzantine and Ottonian representations of the Dormition of the Virgin.[114] While women accompany the death of several of the Sethite fathers in Claudius B. iv, they simply raise a hand to their faces in a conventional gesture of mourning. The grief of the women in Junius 11 is closer to that of the women surrounding the dying Mary in the Benedictional of Æthelwold (BL, Add. 49598, 102v) than it is to the Hexateuch illustrations.

Even more unusual than the amount of space devoted to Seth and his successors is the amount of space devoted to their wives. In contrast to both the Vulgate and the text of the Hexateuch, where fathers beget sons, the text of the Junius 11 *Genesis* mentions the role of their wives. Adam does not simply beget Seth, he is born to Adam and Eve,[115] Seth takes a wife and begets Enos,[116] Enos begets Cainan through marriage or

[112] See pp. 9–10 above; see also p. 87 below.

[113] The list of Hebrew names in Luke in the Book of Kells (Dublin, Trinity College Library A. I. 6) records: 'Maalelehel laudatus dei uel laudeus deum.' See P. McGurk, 'An Edition of the Abbreviated and Selective Set of Hebrew Names found in the Book of Kells', in *The Book of Kells: Proceedings of a Conference at Trinity College, Dublin 6–9 September 1992* (Aldershot, 1999), pp. 102–32, at p. 125.

[114] E.g. the cover of Munich, Bayerische Staatsbibliothek, Clm 4453 (Gospels of Otto III) and Clm. 4452, 161v (Pericopes of Henry II).

[115] 'soðfæst sunu. þam wæs seth noma. / se wæs eadig. and his. yldrum ðah. / freolic to frofre. fæder and meder. / adames and euan. wæs abeles gield. / on woruldrice.' ('A just son who was named Seth. He was blessed, a noble comfort to his parents, his father and mother, Adam and Eve. He was Abel's replacement in the world'.) *Gen.* 1106b–10. Compare Claudius B. iv: 'Eft Adam gestrynde sunu ðone he nemde Seth, and ðus cwæð: Drihten me sealde ðisne sunu for Abel, ðe Cain ofsloh' ('Again Adam begat a son who he named Seth, and said, "The Lord gave me this son for Abel, who Cain slew".' *Heptateuch*, ed. Crawford, pp. 94–5).

[116] 'him on laste seth. leof weardode. / eafora æfter yldrum. eþelstol heold. / and wif begeat. wintra hæfde. / fif and hunteontig. þa heo furðum ongan. / his mægburge. men geicean. / sunum and dohtrum. sedes eafora. / se yldesta wæs. enos haten.'

legitimate sexual intercourse (*gebedscipe*),[117] Malaleel receives Jared from his wife,[118] and Jared's wife brings Enoch into the world.[119] As in the depiction of the birth of Cain and Abel (pl. XXI), these women are given a prominent, though admittedly separate, space in the illustrations. They are shown either in childbed, emphasizing their role in the birth of their sons, or enthroned with their children. The model for both types of depiction is Mary. The addition of the midwives in the drawings depicting the birth of Mathusael and Noah with his three sons (pls. XXXI, XXXII) indicates that these illustrations are modelled even more closely on the Nativity than was the depiction of the birth of Cain and Abel, and they are particularly close to the depiction of the Nativity on

('After him Seth guarded the dear [people], the son after his elders. He held the country and took a wife. He had 105 winters when he began to increase his lineage with sons and daughters. The eldest of Seth's sons was called Enos'.) *Gen*. 1128–34. Compare Claudius B. iv: 'Seth gestrynde sunu and nemde hine Enos. Se Enos ongan ærest clypian Drihtnes Naman, . . . Seth wæs <*hundwintre and .v.*> ða he gestrynde Enos. Ymb seofan and hundeahtatigwintre æfter ðam he gestrynde suna and dohtra' ('Seth begat a son and named him Enos. Enos began first to call upon the name of the Lord . . . Seth was 105 when he begat Enos. About 87 winters after that he begat other sons and daughters.' *Heptateuch*, ed. Crawford, pp. 95–6).

117 'he wæs leof gode. and lifde her. / wintra hundnigontig. ær he be wife her. / þurh gebedscipe. bearn astrynde. / him þa cenned wearð. cainan ærest. / eafora on eðle.' ('He was beloved by God and lived here 90 years before he begat children by his wife through marriage. Then to him Cainan was brought forth first, a son in the homeland.') *Gen*. 1146–50. Compare Claudius B. iv: 'Enos gestrynde Cainan, ða he wæs hundnigontigwintre' ('Enos begat Cainan when he was 90 years old.') *Heptateuch*, ed. Crawford, p. 96).

118 'Him on laste heold. land and yrfe. / malalehel. siððan missera worn. / se frumgara. fif and sixtig. / wintra hæfde. þa he be wife ongann. / bearna strynan. him bryd sunu. / meowle to monnum brohte.' ('After him Malelahel held land and inheritance a multitude of half-years. The leader had 65 winters when he, by his wife, began to beget children. His bride to him, woman to man, brought a son.') *Gen*. 1167–72. Compare Claudius B. iv: 'Witodlice Malaleel gestrynde Iared, ða he wæs fif and sixtigwintre.' ('Truly Malaleel begat Iared when he was 65 years old.') *Heptateuch*, ed. Crawford, p. 97.

119 'þa seo sæl gewearð. / þæt his wif sunu. on woruld brohte. / se eafora wæs. enoc haten. / freolic frumbearn.' ('When it came about that his wife brought forth a son into the world. The son was called Enoch, noble first-born.') *Gen*. 1186b–9. Compare Claudius B. iv: 'Iared gestrynde Enoch, ða he wæs hundwintre twa and syxtig' ('Iared begat Enoch when he was 126 years old.') *Heptateuch*, ed. Crawford, p. 97.

folio 44 of the Boulogne Gospels, discussed above.[120] Since Noah, like Abel, prefigures Christ, the iconography is clearly appropriate. Cainan's wife enthroned with her son Malaleel (pl. XXVI) is more likely based on the Adoration of the Magi (pl. XLVIIb). Ultimately, the same iconographic sources are used for the depictions of the mothers of the generations of Cain although, as with the men, there are subtle differences. Cain's wife (pl. XXIII) is not dressed as lavishly as Seth's (pl. XXV), nor is the architectural setting in which she appears as grand. The foliate patterns decorating the hall or town in which Seth, his wife and son appear may refer to their more fertile and fruitful line. Iared's wife (pl. XXIVa, top) is not shown in childbed but tending her cradled infant, an iconography not associated with Mary, but possibly modelled on images of the midwives bathing the Christ child.[121] Maviael's wife (pl. XXIVa, middle) sits on a throne, but neither it nor the setting is as lavish as those in the drawings of Eve with Seth or Cainan's wife with Malaleel (pls. XXV, XXVI). The wives of the Sethites, on the other hand, display their symbols of power – their fertile bodies, sons and female attendants – as a complement to the weapons and retainers, images of male power, displayed by their husbands. While the images do play on the traditional association of women with the body and domestic space, and do limit female power to the ability to produce male heirs, they also reflect the very real way in which Anglo-Saxon queens attained and manipulated power, shaping their own histories through their bodies and their sons.[122]

The portrayal of Enoch in Junius 11 is both controversial and typologically complex, and thus merits special attention. Enoch is a type of Christ, and the illustrations in Junius 11 elucidate the typology in a way that those in the Hexateuch do not.[123] The poet tells us that because of his loyalty to God:

[120] Boulogne-sur-Mer, Bibliothèque Municipale, 11. See Temple, *Anglo-Saxon Manuscripts*, pl. 148.

[121] See, for example, Oxford, Bodleian Library, Rawlinson B. 484, 85r. In Claudius B. iv midwives are shown bathing Ishmael (fol. 28r), the sons of Lot's daughters (fol. 34r), Isaac (fol. 35r), Jacob and Esau (fol. 40v), and one of the children of Tamar (fol. 57r). It must be added however, that on fol. 93r of the Bury Psalter (Vatican, Biblioteca Apostolica, Reg. lat. 12) both Joseph and Mary are shown tending their child.

[122] See Karkov, 'Anglo-Saxon Genesis'; and below, pp. 150–2.

[123] In Claudius B. iv Enoch simply climbs a ladder towards heaven and God (fol. 11v).

se rinc heonon.
on lichoman. lisse sohte.
drihtnes duguðe. nales deaðe swealt.
middangeardes. swa her men doþ.
geonge and ealde. þone him god heora.
æhta and ætwist. eorðan gestreona.
on genimeð. and heora aldor somed.
Ac he cwic gewat. mid cyning engla.
of þyssum lænan. life frean.
on þam gearwum. þe his gast onfeng.
ær hine to monnum modor brohte.[124]

The linking of Enoch's birth to his death, or ascension, repeats the linking of beginnings and ends that forms a recurring pattern throughout the Junius manuscript. It also links him specifically to Christ, whose death is always present in his birth, and the poet's statement that Enoch's mother 'brought him to men', as Mary brought Christ to men, helps to establish Enoch as a figure of Christ in birth as well as in death. Enoch's return to the kingdom of heaven 'with the king of angels' looks both backwards and forwards in time, suggesting the kingdom of heaven established at the beginning of Creation (and the poem), and also the final journey to the kingdom of heaven at the Last Judgement. The latter is also the time at which Enoch will return with Elias to earth before his second and final journey to heaven.[125] As Carol Farr points out, the idea 'that they remain in some zone between the ordinary world and heaven, preaching in the present time, is an important one for it endows them with the potential for reference to past, present and future'.[126] She goes on to note that both men are frequently understood in relation to the structuring of history. In

124 'The man sought joy hence while still in his body, the salvation of the Lord; not at all did he die an earthly death, as men do here, young and old, when God takes away their possessions and goods, earth treasures, and their lives also. But he, living, went with the king of angels from this transitory life, the lord, in those clothes which his spirit received before his mother brought him to men.' *Gen.* 1203b–1213.

125 As has already been noted (see above, p. 9), the dragon, open book and halo serve to relate the portrait of Enoch in plate XXIX to scenes of the Harrowing of Hell and the Last Judgement. As mentioned above (p. 9), the dragon is particularly important because, as a symbol of the Antichrist, it recalls Enoch's return to earth, his battle and second death and resurrection. Ælfric describes Enoch's return and death, relating them to the death and resurrection of all men. See above, p. 10, n. 37.

126 C. Farr, *The Book of Kells: Its Function and Audience* (London, 1997), p. 114.

De schematibus et tropis, for example, Bede identifies Enoch, the seventh son of Adam, as an anagogical figure of the heavenly bliss of the elect at the Last Judgement, the end of the seventh age of the world.[127] The motif of ascent further serves to link the death of Enoch with the Harrowing of Hell through its compositional similarities with the Ascension of Christ. The Blickling homilist relates that it is after having rescued Adam, Eve and the patriarchs from hell that Christ 'raþe he lifgende ut eode of his byrgenne mid his agenre mihte aweht, & eft mid his unwemmum lichoman hine gegyrede' ('immediately went living from the tomb, raised by his own power, and afterwards clothed himself with his unspotted body').[128] In the illustrations on pages 60 and 61, the artist has managed to convey visually this complex set of typological relationships. The actual ascension (pl. XXX) is clearly modelled on Anglo-Saxon versions of the Ascension of Christ,[129] with the twelve men who surround Enoch at the bottom of the drawing, presumably his sons, based on the twelve apostles who witness Christ's Ascension.[130] The repetition of the two angels grasping Enoch at the bottom and top of the page conveys the idea that he is carried bodily from earth to the kingdom of the angels.[131]

127 *Ibid.*, p. 115.

128 Morris, *Blickling Homilies*, pp. 88–9.

129 The classic treatment of the subject is still M. Schapiro, 'The Image of the Disappearing Christ: the Ascension in English Art around the Year 1000', *Gazette des Beaux-Arts* Series 6 (March 1943), 135–52; repr. in his *Late Antique, Early Christian and Medieval Art: Selected Papers* (New York, 1979), pp. 267–87.

130 See also *Christ II* in the Exeter Book, lines 491–9: 'Ða wearð semninga sweg on lyfte / hlud gehyred. Heofonengla þreat, / weorud wlitescyne, wuldres aras, / cwomun on corðre. Cyning ure gewat / þurh þæs temples hrof þær hy to segun / þa þe leofes þa gen last weardedum / on þam þingstede, þegnas gecorene. / Gesegon hi on heahþu hlaford stigan, / godbearn of grundum.' ('Then suddenly a loud harmony was heard in the air. A host of angels, a beautiful troop, heaven's angels came in a throng. Our king departed through the roof of the temple while they looked on, those who yet watched the footsteps of the Beloved in that meeting-place, the chosen servants. They saw the Lord, the Son of God, ascend to the heights from the earth.')

131 The fact that Enoch must be carried to heaven separates his ascension from that of Christ, who is able to ascend under his own power. See Gregory, *Homilies in Evangelia*, Liber II, hom. 29 (PL LXXVI, cols. 1216, 1217); and Schapiro, 'Disappearing Christ', p. 271.

NOAH AND REBIRTH

The Sethite genealogy ends with the naming and depiction of Noah's three sons, Sem, Cham and Japheth on page 63 (pl. XXXII). Noah's wife, accompanied by a midwife, lies in childbed at the left of the picture. She and her husband are the only couple not depicted facing each other, perhaps reflecting the primacy of Noah as father and creator, and the rebirth of the earth that his story initiates. It is through him that life will be preserved in and reborn from the ark. The turn in the poetic narrative is signalled by the four-line beast-headed initial 'O' that begins the account of the intermarriage of the children of God and the daughters of Cain, and God's ensuing wrath and punishment upon them.

The story of Noah returns to an extended consideration of the themes of Creation, Fall, Judgement and Redemption that are at the heart of the poet's treatment of the story of Adam and Eve. The ark that God commands Noah to build contains all life within it as God contained all life within himself at the beginning of the poem. The artist indexes this connection through the addition of two seraphim flanking the ark (pl. XXXIV) as it is about to set sail. They recall the two seraphim that flank God in the frontispiece to the manuscript (pl. I), and are mentioned neither in the poem nor in the Vulgate text. As the depiction of the Creation in Anglo-Saxon art makes clear (pls. IIIa, IIIb, XLIVa), order, balance and measurement were characteristic of both Creator and Creation. The careful recording of the God-given measurements according to which Noah constructs the ark are evidence of the divine order that binds together both moments of creation,[132] as well as a reminder that creation is again the product of the Word. As God's hands figured prominently in the story of the Creation, so too they figure prominently in the story of Noah. Both poem and illustrations follow the text of the bible in indicating that it is God who closes and, in the illustration, opens the door to the ark with his own hands (pls. XXXV, XXXVI). God also seals the door with a sign, an episode that, as Doane notes, is considerably elaborated in the poem:[133]

[132] Doane, ed., *Genesis A*, p. 260.

[133] *Ibid.*, p. 264.

Him on hoh beleac. heofonrices weard.
merehuses muð. mundum sinum.
sigora waldend. and segnade
earce innan. agenum spedum.
nergend usser.[134]

The depiction of God closing and opening the ark is unusual. It does not appear in the Hexateuch, and is extremely rare in medieval art in general. This is another instance in which the text and illustration present a unified vision of narrative action, in this case one that stresses God's presence and protection throughout the episode.

The ark, like the earth, is a divinely created house of the living, and a prefiguration of the church, while its steersman, Noah, is a prefiguration of Christ, a typology developed in the writings of Ambrose, Augustine and Bede.[135] In the illustration on page 66 Noah has literally become the steersman, while the ark itself is composed of a church-like structure within a Viking-inspired ship. The levels within the architectural centre of the ark are described in both the Vulgate and the text of the poem, and are frequently depicted in early medieval illustrations of the scene,[136] but the Junius 11 artist has added a tower capped with a weathercock to either side of the central structure, enhancing its ecclesiastical appearance. Weathercocks do appear crowning what are intended to be images of contemporary Anglo-Saxon churches in a number of manuscripts,[137] as

134 'The Lord of heaven closed the ark's door behind him with his hands, the lord of victories, and blessed the ark within with his power, our Saviour.' *Gen*. 1363–7.

135 Ambrose, *De Noe et arca*, ed. K. Schenkl, CSEL 32.1 (Vienna, 1897), pp. 613–97; Augustine, *De civitate Dei*, xv. 26; Bede, *In Genesim* (CCSL 118A), vi, 13–18. See also Doane, ed., *Genesis A*, p. 259; Crawford, ed., *Heptateuch*, p. 24; the *Andreas* poem in the Vercelli Book, lines 66–95 (ASPR II, 4–5); J. Danielou, *From Shadows to Reality: Studies in the Biblical Typology of the Fathers* (Westminster, MD, 1960), pp. 85–102.

136 E.g. BL, Claudius B. iv, fols. 14–15v; Vienna, Nationalbibliothek, Cod. Theol. gr. 31, pp. 3–4; Girona, Museu de la Catedral de Girona, Num. Inv. 7 (11), fols. 102v–103. See also M. McC. Gatch, 'Noah's Raven in *Genesis A* and the Illustrated Old English Hexatuech', *Gesta* 14.2 (1975), 3–15.

137 See fol. 118v of the *c.* 970 Bendictional of Æethelwold (BL Add. 49598) and fol. 2v of the Lanalet Pontifical (Rouen, Bibliothèque Municipale A 27 (368)), dated to the second quarter of the eleventh century. The *Narratio Metrica de S. Swithuno*, written at Winchester *c.* 992–4, describes a golden weathercock capping the tower of Winchester Cathedral (Deshman, *Benedictional*, p. 140). Whether it was intended to

well as the *c.* 1155 seal of Christ Church, Canterbury, and it is certainly possible that the detail was meant to draw the connection between church past and church present, the journey of Noah and that of the Anglo-Saxons.[138]

The story of the Flood is also one of destruction and linked as firmly to the Last Judgement as it is to the Creation.[139] The seraphim that flank the ark in plate XXXIV and the Creator in plate I are similar to the seraphim or angels that flank Christ in Anglo-Saxon versions of the Last Judgement (pl. XLIVb). The order and proportions of the ark, and the Creation before it, are also in marked contrast to the disorder and unknown proportions of hell. *Christ and Satan* contrasts the divine order of heaven and the kingdom of the saved measured by God's hands, to the kingdom of hell that Satan is forced to measure unsuccessfully with his hands. While God knows all, Satan has no knowledge of the extent of his kingdom:

> wast þu þonne þe geornor. þæt þu wið god wunne.
> Seoððan þu þonne hafast. handum ametene.
> hu heh and deop. hell inneweard seo.
> grim græfhus.[140]

In a broader context, both Ælfric and Wulfstan compared the Flood with

represent a specifically Anglo-Saxon church or not, the motif does seem to have been a general way of identifying an ecclesiastical structure (*ibid.*, n. 201).

138 See *English Romanesque Art 1066–1200*, eds. G. Zarnecki, J. Holt and T. Holland (London, 1984), no. 358; see also the plan of the waterworks of Christ Church in the Eadwine Psalter (Cambridge, Trinity College R. 17. 1, fol. 285).

139 1 Peter III.19–21 introduces the parallels between the Flood, baptism and the Harrowing of Hell, itself a type of judgement: 'In which also coming he preached to those spirits that were in prison: which had been some time incredulous, when they waited for the patience of God in the days of Noe, when the ark was a building: wherein a few, that is, eight souls were saved by water. Whereunto baptism being of the like form, now saveth you also: not the putting away of the filth of the flesh, but the examination of a good conscience towards God by the resurrection of Jesus Christ.' Bede elaborates on the text of Peter and expands his commentary to connect the era of the patriarchs with that of his readers, a simultaneity that is also characteristic of the Junius manuscript. See Bede, *In primam ep. Petri* (PL 93.59). See also J. J. Campbell, 'To Hell and Back: Latin Tradition and Literary use of the "Descensus ad Inferno" in Old English', *Viator* 13 (1982), 107–58, at p. 121.

140 *Christ and Satan* 704–7. 'Be glad then that you struggled against God after you have measured with hands how high and deep hell is within, grim house of the dead.'

the fire of Doomsday,[141] and the fact that the Last Judgement could come at any time and was likely to come very soon was a recurring theme in both their writings. The virtuous Noah's salvation from the Flood therefore became a model for contemporary men and women seeking salvation.[142] Its centrality in the liturgy of Lent ensured that the destruction of the sinful was as much in the thoughts of those participating in the mass as the salvation of the blessed. Lent was a time of penance as well as baptism; from Ash Wednesday to Maundy Thursday sinners were publicly rebuked and humiliated with expulsion from the church, the kingdom of the sacred.[143] The relevance of this particular version of the Noah story to the manuscript's Anglo-Saxon audience was reinforced by specific details such as the portrayal of the ark as a structure reminiscent of the contemporary church, and the poet's direct addressing of his readers (*nergend usser, scyppend usser*).[144]

The illustration on page 73 ushers in both a new artist and a new world (pl. XXXVI). God holds open the door of the ark while Noah and his three sons step out onto land, their wives preparing to follow them out of the doorway. The shape of the ark in this illustration has been a source of controversy. Gatch has documented the fact that there are two major traditions behind the depiction of the ark, one which shows a stepped or architectural structure, and a second that depicts the ark as a tub or sarcophagus.[145] It may be that the new artist was drawing on this second tradition, either because he was using a different model or because he wanted to emphasize a slightly different aspect of the story of the Flood. Whatever the model, Noah's journey is a type of baptism, and baptism and death are closely related, in part because baptism represents the death of one's former life outside the church as much as it represents a rebirth

141 Ælfric, *Sermo de dei Iudicii*, in *Homilies*, ed. Pope, II, 60–85; Wulfstan, *Secundum Lucam*: 'And witodlice ealswa flod com hwilum ær for synnum, swa cumð eac for synnum fyr ofer mancynn, and ðærto hit nealæcð nu swyðe georne.' ('And truly just as the Flood came before on account of sins, so will fire come over mankind also on account of sins, and for that purpose it will approach very eagerly.') D. Bethurum, ed., *The Homilies of Wulfstan* (Oxford, 1952), III, 7–9. See also Gatch, *Preaching and Theology*, pp. 89–90 and 109.

142 A point also made by Doane (*Genesis A*, p. 258).

143 A. J. Frantzen, *The Literature of Penance in Anglo-Saxon England* (New Brunswick, NJ, 1983), pp. 157–9.

144 'Our Lord', 'our Creator', *Gen.* 1367 and 1391. See Doane, *Genesis A*, p. 265.

145 Gatch, 'Noah's Raven'.

into new life within the church. The baptismal font was referred to as both a grave and a womb from which men and women would be reborn.[146] In this context the iconography of either tub or sarcophagus would be appropriate.[147] If the first two depictions of the ark suggested the former pictorial tradition, it is possible that this picture, and perhaps the incomplete illustration on page 70, suggest the latter. Like Christ resurrected from the tomb, or the dead rising from their graves at the Last Judgement, Noah and his family emerge from the narrow confinement of their ship:

> holm wæs heononweard. hæleð langode.
> wægliðende. swilce wif heora.
> hwonne hie of nearwe. ofer nægledbord.
> ofer streamstaðe. stæppan mosten.
> and of enge ut. æhta lædan.[148]

The last line above the scene of disembarkation eerily calls to our attention the threat of death and judgement at the same time as it suggests great joy:

> He fremede swa. and frean hyrde.
> stah ofer streamweall. swa him seo stefn bebead.
> lustum miclum. and alædde þa.
> of wægþele. wraðra lafe.[149]

One might also note that the curved, vaguely circular shape of the ark in the accompanying illustration links this moment of new creation to the spheres of the Creation at the beginning of the poem (pls. IIIa, IIIb).[150]

146 O. B. Hardison, *Christian Rite and Christian Drama in the Middle Ages* (Baltimore, MD, 1965), p. 153.

147 Gatch, 'Noah's Raven', p. 4. See Luke XVIII.26–31, and Ælfric, *Sermo de dei Iudicii*, in *Homilies*, ed Pope, II, 60–4.

148 'The sea was departing. The men yearned, the seafarers, and their wives also, [for the time] when they from that narrow place over the nail-studded deck, over the shore, might step and lead their possessions out from that confined space.' *Gen.* 1431–5.

149 'He did so and obeyed the Lord, went up over the shore, and led them, as the voice commanded him with great joy. From the ark [came] the leavings of the evil ones.' *Gen.* 1493–6. Doane (*Genesis A*, p. 274) notes the awkwardness of the last line, but believes that its sense is clear: 'Noe and his family are not themselves wicked, but are the surviving members of the race of the men who were otherwise the race of *wraðra*.'

150 It also echoes the womb-like shape of hell (pl. XV), already established as a dark and chaotic *hof* (line 44) in contrast to the orderly and precisely built *hof* (lines 1345, 1393, 1489) of the ark. See below, p 161.

Plate XXXVII depicts Noah's offering to God and God's blessing on Noah and his three sons, both episodes recounted in the text below the picture. The hart standing at Noah's feet recalls the hart beneath Adam's feet in plate V, and helps to unite the idea of the Creation with that of new creation, and paradise with that of the newly fertile earth, as well as the two moments of blessing. Like Adam, Noah is here told to be fruitful and multiply, and is given dominion over the creatures that inhabit his new paradise:

> Tymað nu and tiedrað.   tines brucað.
> mid gefean fryðo.   fyllað eorðan.
> eall geiceað.   eow is eðelstol.
> holmes hlæst.   and heofonfuglas.[151]
> and wildu deor.   on geweald geseald.
> eorðe ælgrene.   and eacen feoh.[152]

The poet's use of the phrase *nergend usser* (our Lord) in line 1505 again serves to remind readers that they, like Noah, should praise and make offerings to the Lord, and that the Lord's blessing is upon them, the descendants of Noah, as it was upon Noah and his sons. God's covenant with Noah may have had particular significance in at least some areas of Anglo-Saxon England. The inscription over the south porticus of the church at Breamore, Hampshire, reads: 'HER SWUTELAÐ SE GECWYDRAEDNES ÐE' ('Here the covenant is made manifest to you'). Richard Gameson suggests that the arrangement of this phrase over an arch might have reminded Anglo-Saxon viewers of the *arcus*, the symbol of God's covenant with Noah.[153]

Noah's wife and daughters-in-law are not depicted in the drawing though they are mentioned in the poem (*and heora feower wif*, *Gen.* 1546). Doane comments on the fact that this particular passage seems to have been of special interest to readers from the time in which the manuscript was produced, citing the very worn state of page 75 on which the line occurs, the addition of a gloss consisting of the four apocryphal names of

151 The manuscript reads *heofonfugla*.

152 'Be fruitful now and multiply, enjoy glory with joy and peace; fill the earth, increase all. Into your control is given a native land, and the fish, and birds, and wild animals, the all-green earth, and increase of cattle.' *Gen.* 1512–17.

153 Gameson, *Role of Art*, p. 73; R. and F. Gameson, 'The Anglo-Saxon Inscription at St Mary's Church, Breamore, Hampshire', *ASSAH* 6 (1993), 1–10.

the women, and subsequent scholarly debate over the meaning and metre of the text at this point.[154] The interest in the line and the addition of the gloss are in keeping with the persistent presence of women in general in both the text and the programme of illustrations in Junius 11. Claudius B. iv provides evidence of a similar interest in the female members of Noah's family, as the artist of that manuscript has shown them both assisting their husbands in the vineyard and receiving, or at least witnessing, God's blessing on the family.[155]

The meaning of the illustrations on pages 76–8 (pls. XXXVIII – XL), and their relationship to the poetic narrative have already been discussed;[156] whether the unusual pairing of illustrations on pages 76 and 77 was deliberate or not, the obvious harmony between text and illustration is restored on page 78. Coming at the end of the story of Noah's drunkenness and Cham's disrespect for his father, the picture recapitulates what we have just read in the poem. Yet it also serves as a fitting preface to the story of the lineage of Noah that follows. As noted previously, the actual depiction of Noah's uncovered genitals is unusual in early medieval art. It suggests the fertility of the human race, also evoked by the poet's reference to Noah as *sunu Lamehes* ('son of Lamech', *Gen.* 1589) at the top of this page and by the account of his sons' progeny on the facing page. Noah's nakedness, like the land itself; emphasizes the fact that the human race will indeed be fruitful and multiply, and that fertility is further suggested by the unusually luxuriant vegetation that grows over Noah's bed. Obviously, these vines are meant to represent the vineyard, but they are not usually shown attached to the bed, and the motif may in this case be meant to echo the vines and beasts that curl up and around the pillar behind Mathusael and his tribe in the depiction of the birth of Lamech (pl. XXXI), a visual echo of the genealogical reference in the text. Similar ideas lie behind the later depiction of the Tree of Jesse, a figural diagram of Christ's royal ancestry, though clearly there can be no unequivocal reference to images of this subject at such an early date.

The drawing on page 81 (pl. XLI) illustrates the story of Nimrod recounted in the poem on pages 80 and 81. At the bottom, Nimrod leads

154 Doane, *Genesis A*, pp. 276–7; Gollancz, *Cædmon Genesis*, pp. lxiii–lxvii. Both Gollancz and Doane speculate on an Irish source for the names.

155 BL, Claudius B. iv, fols. 16v–17.

156 See above, p. 14.

his people and their cattle to their new home in Babylon,[157] while at the top, Nimrod and his men prepare to build the tower of Babel. The upward gaze of a number of the figures in this illustration suggests the idea of raising the tower. It also directs the reader's eyes to the text at the top of the page where the curious breaking of the word *meahte* between *meah* on the last line of page 80 and *te* on the first line of page 81 might possibly be intended to suggest the breaking up of language that will result from their efforts.[158] The poet's use of the word *hlædræ* ('ladder', *Gen.* 1675) in his description of the tower built by these sons of Adam (*Adames eaforan*, *Gen.* 1682) contrasts the folly of the man-made ladder, and the vain attempt to reach heaven, with the divine ladder that connected heaven with paradise during the creation of Eve (pl. IV).[159] The crenellated wall of the town in which Nimrod and his men stand gazing upwards also echoes the crenellated walls of hell from which Satan and his demons gaze upwards (pls. VIII, IX), indicating that Satan's attempt to establish his greatness in heaven was as futile as Nimrod's attempt to establish his kingdom on earth. Moreover, just as Satan's speech after the second Fall of the angels is characterized by disruptive language, the result of his fall, so human speech will be disrupted as a result of Nimrod's fall.

God's punishment is depicted on the following page (pl. XLIIa) where four groups scatter in different directions. The man and woman who lead the group in the lower register of the drawing recall the figures of Adam and Eve departing from paradise (pl. XIX) and help to link the two events typologically. At the upper right two men work aimlessly on the unfinished tower, one futilely chopping at a bit of foliage that sprouts from the border of the illustration. Visually, the motif may relate back to the rich foliage suggestive of the fruitfulness of Noah and his sons in the scene of the drunkenness of Noah (pl. XL). It may further be used to

157 Illustrating *Gen.* 1649–50: 'gewiton him þa eastan æhta læden. / feoh and feorme.' ('They departed then from the east taking their possessions, cattle and goods.')

158 Such awkward word divisions occur in only three other places in the poem, pages 30 (*heo-foncyninges*) and 37 (*ge-weald*), both part of the story of the Fall, and page 93 (*to-geanes*) in the account of the wars of Abraham.

159 See Augustine on Nimrod's work as a challenge to God, *De civitate Dei*, xvi.4 (CCSL 47–8). God appears on a ladder watching the construction of the tower on fol. 19 of Claudius B. iv, but the text refers to the tower as *steple* and does not mention the ladder at all.

remind us of the family of Seth that put out shoots (*wriðade*, *Gen.* 1702) culminating in the birth of Abraham, whose story begins on this page.

ABRAHAM

The story of Abraham opens with the poet's careful establishment of a relationship between Abraham and Lot's lives on earth and their lives in heaven:

> ða magorincas.   metode geþungon.
> abraham and loth.   unforcuðlice.
> swa him from yldrum   æðelu wæron.
> on woruldrice.   forðon hie wide nu.
> dugeðum demað.   drihta bearnum.[160]

The lines also look forward to the Harrowing of Hell as described in *Christ and Satan*, at which time Abraham and his descendants are taken up into heaven by Christ.[161] The simultaneity of the two events as presented here again serves to incorporate the Anglo-Saxon present into the biblical past and future. The reader's identification with the narrative was reinforced by the prominence of both Abraham and the Harrowing of Hell in the liturgy of the Anglo-Saxon church.[162] The poet himself reminds his readers of this fact when he indicates the textual source of his knowledge of Sarah's name:

> seo fæmne wæs.[163]
> sarra haten.   þæs þe us secgeað. bec.[164]

The last three illustrations to be completed depict God's words to Abraham and Abraham's journey out of Haran (pl. XLIIb), Abraham giving thanks to God (pl. XLIIIa), and Abraham and Sarah approaching Egypt (pl. XLIIIb). The first is a very literal illustration of the events

160 'The men prospered with the Lord, Abraham and Lot, nobly, as they were from the lineage of leaders in the world; therefore they now widely judge with the hosts the sons of multitudes.' *Gen.* 1714–18.

161 'hofon hine mid him. handum halige. / witigan up to eðle. abrahames cynn.' ('They took him with their holy hands up to their ancestral homeland, Abraham's race.') *Christ and Satan* 458–9.

162 Fadda, '"De descensu Christi ad inferos"'; Gatch, *Preaching and Theology*, 57; Openshaw, 'Weapons in the Daily Battle'.

163 The word *wæs* was added above the line by the scribe.

164 *Gen.* 1722b–3. 'The woman was called Sarah, so the books tell us.'

described by the poet. At the top, God orders Abraham to leave Haran, while two figures, presumably Sarah and Lot, look on from within the gate of the city; in the middle register, Abraham leads Sarah and his people towards Canaan. The joined hands of Abraham and Sarah, a sign of their marriage, may also be meant to recall the joined hands of Noah and God (pl. XXXVIII), the latter a sign of their covenant. In the bottom register, God once again appears to Abraham, promising him that the fertile land into which he travels will belong to his descendants. The use of the word *ælgrene* (*Gen.* 1751 and 1787) provides yet another reference back to Noah and the new *ælgrene* land that he and his sons established (*Gen.* 1517), as well as to the *ælgrene* earthly paradise (*Gen.* 197). On each of the four occasions in which the word is used it accompanies either God's order to be fruitful and multiply (to Adam, Eve and Noah) or his promise of blessed and numerous progeny (to Abraham), and links the fertility of the earth with that of the human race.[165]

Abraham's thanks and reverence are depicted in plate XLIIIa where, at the top of the illustration, he stands between two buildings and prepares to build an altar. The two-towered structure, cruciform windows and curtained doorway of the building on the right may refer to the temple and the church and certainly help to establish visually the deeply religious nature of the scene.[166] Moreover, the building of this altar looks forward to the altar Abraham will build for the sacrifice of Isaac, traditionally thought to be the site on which Solomon would build his temple.[167] Doane notes further that Ambrose, amongst other commentators, equated Abraham's leaving Haran with the Christian's rejection of the life of the flesh for life within the church,[168] a significance which the Junius 11 artist may well be articulating. Directly beneath the church-like structure, Abraham makes his offering of a pot of incense, while at lower left he

165 For further discussion see below, p. 127.

166 Cruciform windows also appear in the drawings on pages 82 and 88, but there are no towers or curtains and the structures are clearly less church-like. In the mosaic of the parting of Lot and Abraham in the church of S. Maria Maggiore, Rome (*c.* 432–40) the parted curtains of the temple behind Abraham and Isaac are contrasted with the open city gates behind Lot and his daughters, details which help to mark the former as blessed.

167 This theme will be picked up in *Exodus* 389–98. See below, p. 146.

168 Doane, ed., *Genesis A*, p. 288; Ambrose, *De Abraham* II.i.2 (ed. K. Schenkl, CSEL 32.1 (Vienna, 1897), pp. 501–638).

once again receives God's blessing. In the poem, Abraham builds two altars and makes two offerings, and in both episodes the poet reminds us of God's blessing. After the first offering we are told that Abraham remembered God's holy words,[169] and during the second we are reminded of God the Creator and Measurer of heaven and earth by the term *metend* ('measuring one') in line 1809b. The drawing serves as an appropriate illustration to either or both of these episodes. It is, after all, possible that the two buildings are meant to represent the two altars and that we are dealing with a pictorial conflation of the separate episodes.

After the second offering, Abraham departs with Sarah for Egypt (pl. XLIIIb), and as they approach the land he warns her that for his sake and because of her beauty she must say that she is his sister rather than his wife. Sarah of course obeys. In the drawing on page 88 Abraham leads her and their retinue towards the gabled halls of the high city of Egypt (*hornsele hwite and heahyrig*, *Gen.* 1821). Sarah walks obediently behind Abraham, as Eve followed Adam out of paradise (pl. XIX), and the Babylonian woman followed her husband out of Babel (pl. XLIIa). As already mentioned, the spindle she clutches near her breast mirrors the spindle held by Eve, linking them both as mothers of prefigurations of Christ (Abel and Isaac), but also establishing a contrast. Eve, by her inability to see the truth, disobeyed the Lord and deceived Adam through false loyalty; but Sarah's loyalty is true and she obeys the words of her lord, Abraham, despite his apparently dishonest behaviour and the resulting threat to her honour.

It is evident from this analysis of the completed drawings and their relationship to the text of the poem that the 'illustrations' function in a variety of ways. Some, such as the drawing of God closing and opening Noah's ark (pls. XXXV, XXXVI) are close to literal illustrations of the words of the poet; others, such as the manuscript's frontispiece (pl. I), are designed to function both intra- and intervisually, establishing connections between a number of different drawings and the events they portray; while still others, the drawing of the messenger leaving hell on page 20, for example (pl. Xa), are clearly translations of the text into a pictorial

169 'lisse gemunde. / heofonweardes gehat. þa him þurh halig word. / sigora self cyning. soð gecyðde.' ([He] remembered with joy God's promise which the King of victories himself had truly declared to him through his holy word.') *Gen.* 1795b–1797.

language that conveys ideas, or elaborates on the action, in a way that the poetic narrative alone cannot or does not do. Moreover, as indicated by the lack of a representation of Eve's vision, the absence of the image, like the notion of silence in a text, can be as significant, and as much a part of narrative technique, as its presence.[170] It remains now to extend this analysis to the rest of the manuscript, with the important caveat that all suggestions as to what might or might not have been intended for the unfinished drawings must remain hypothetical. Nevertheless, by using a thematic approach it is possible to identify points at which images and ideas established in the completed illustrations recur or are echoed in the poetic texts (and might possibly have been picked out in the illustrations planned for the rest of the manuscript), and these have much to reveal about the overall unity of the manuscript. With this in mind we turn now to a consideration of some of the major themes and motifs that can be identified in each of the four poems.

170 On representation and that which cannot be represented see M. Bal, 'Textuality and Realism', in *Reading 'Rembrandt': Beyond the Word–Image Opposition* (Cambridge, 1991), pp. 216–46, esp. pp. 227–30 and 237–42.

4

Word, sign and reader

The main theme of the four Junius 11 poems is undoubtedly the cycle of Fall and Redemption that runs uninterruptedly from the Creation to the Last Judgement, and within which the manuscript's audience was and is specifically located. But the Junius 11 poems are more than just paraphrases of biblical material; their authors (or compilers) have structured their material so that the theme of the book, its writing and proper interpretation, becomes central to the manuscript. Related to the theme of the word and the written text is that of vision and dreaming, the image that, like a text, calls for proper interpretation. Cassiodorus described chronicles as *imagines historiarum* – images, likenesses, or pictures of history.[1] While Junius 11 is not a chronicle *per se*, it does both record and construct an historical picture. We can thus extend the analysis of word and sign within the poem to include the very writing of the poems and drawing of the illustrations, and the voice and vision of the poets and artists.

Robert Finnegan's recent discovery of the figure of a man outside the arcs of Creation on page 7 (pl. IIIb) has interesting implications for any understanding of the act of reading in Junius 11.[2] The figure is lightly drawn in the upper right-hand corner of the page and gazes down intently at the nimbed figure of God. Finnegan identifies him as the work of the second artist but, while possible, the comparative evidence he cites is not conclusive.[3] Whether drawn by the second artist or not, the man is clearly

1 Cassiodorus, *An Introduction to Divine and Human Readings*, trans. L. W. Jones (New York, 1946), p. 116; G. Spiegel, *The Past as Text* (Baltimore, MD, 1997), p. 101.

2 Finnegan, 'The Man in "Nowhere"'.

3 *Ibid.*, p. 26.

a later addition to the page and therefore becomes an apt image of the reader situated at one remove from the events depicted, and of the act of reading. This paralleling of acts of creation across time and space is typical of the Junius 11 manuscript. Here, as Finnegan explains:

> The first artist has drawn God in the act of primal creation, the depiction being a re-creation literally; the second artist's creation watches both the first artist's rendering of the re-created Genesis story, and the action of the story itself. Thus we have an arresting movement of 'creativities' from the fact of primal creation, through its re-creation by the first artist, to a figure created by the second artist, but not part of the main Genesis action, that measures not only the quality of the first artist's recreation, but, perhaps, the substance of the action he illustrates, the Genesis myth itself.[4]

This cycle of creativities can also be extended to the readers, for whom the figure acts as a mirror, since we too are engaged in the act of recreating the story. The page becomes a delightfully witty and multivalent model for the book and its audience.

THE WORD IN THE BOOK

The book, a creation of words, is both a mirror of and vehicle for God's Creation through the Word. Words, both spoken and written, are thus a critical element within both the text and the drawings in the manuscript, though no words actually appear in any of the drawings. There are no images framed by words as in the Red Book of Darley (pl. XLVIIIb),[5] no words of dialogue included within the picture space as in the donor portrait in St Dunstan's class-book,[6] and no scrolls indicating either dialogue or the passing of words or text from one figure to another, as in the portrait of John in the Eadui Codex, or the frontispiece to Ælfric's *Grammar*.[7] Nevertheless, dialogue is suggested through the poses and gestures of the figures, which give most of the drawings a pronounced narrative content (whether they are understood primarily as illustrations of the accompanying text or not). In a couple of instances dialogue is suggested more literally than in others. The blood of Abel crying out to

[4] *Ibid.*, pp. 31–2. [5] See above, p. 47.

[6] Oxford, Bodleian Library, Auct. F. 4. 32, 1r (in E. Temple, *Anglo-Saxon Manuscripts 900–1066* (London, 1976) ill. 41).

[7] Hannover, Kestner Museum WM XXIa 36, 147v (Temple, ill. 227); Durham, Cathedral Library, B. III. 32, 56v (Temple, ill. 315).

the Lord is represented in the drawing on page 49 by the bust of Abel dramatically emerging from the ground, his arms raised towards God (pl. XXII). The mouths of Satan and his messenger are depicted as open on pages 20 and 36 (pls. Xa, XV) in the illustrations of the messenger's departure from hell and his recounting of his success, respectively. These are the only two drawings in the manuscript where this is the case, and the detail may be intended to differentiate the false words and faulty reasoning of their language from the true words of God. Visually the open mouths of the two connect them with the open mouth of hell itself, again reflecting the problematic and dangerous nature of their language. Words and language may also have been the topic of the pictures planned for pages 172 (possibly a portrait of Daniel writing), 176–7 (possibly the three children learning the Chaldean language and entering Nabuchodonosor's service) and 212 (possibly Daniel interpreting the writing on the wall), though naturally that must remain a hypothesis.

The word is also present in the poems in the form of Christ as the Word, and the idea of the Creation as the manifestation of the Word of God – the act of Creation as an act of speaking. All was darkness and waste until the world came into being through the Word of God.[8] To a certain degree the images we see are all reflections of the Word at work in the world. Both *Exodus* and *Christ and Satan* open with summaries of the Creation of the world, echoing the Creation story from *Genesis* and suggesting a connection between the Creation through the Word and the creation of the poems through the words of the poets.[9] The writing and

[8] 'wonn and weste. oðþæt þeos woruldgesceaft. / þurh word gewearð. wuldorcyninges.' *Gen*. 110–11.

[9] 'ða wæs forma sið. / þæt hine weroda god. wordum nægde. / þær he him gesægde. soðwundra fela. / hu þas woruld worhte. witig drihten. / eorðan ymbhwyrft. ond uprodor. / gesette sigerice. ond his sylfes naman. / ðone yldo bearn. ær ne cuðon. / frod fædera cyn. þeah hie fela wiston.' ('That was the first time that the God of hosts addressed him [Abraham] with words: there he told him of many true wonders, the wise Lord, how this world was made, the circuit of the earth and the heavens, the victorious kingdom established, and his own name, which the children of men previously knew not, the race of wise fathers, though they knew much.') *Ex*. 22b–29. 'Þæt wearð underne. eorðbuendum. / þæt meotod hæfde. miht and strengðo. / ða he gefestnade. foldan sceatas. / seolfa he gesette. sunnan and monan. / stanas and eorðan. stream ut on sæ. / wæter and wolcn. ðurh his wundra miht. / deopne ymblyt. [MS *ybmlyt*] clene ymbhaldeð. / meotod on mihtum. and alne middangeard. / he self mæg. sæ geondwlitan. / grundas in heofene. godes agen bearn. / and he ariman mæg. rægnas scuran. /

reading of Anglo-Saxon poetry thus become a mirror for divine Creation, a typological relationship which has its origins for the Anglo-Saxons in Bede's story of Cædmon and the birth of Anglo-Saxon poetry through Cædmon's divinely inspired song of Creation.[10] *Daniel* does not open with the story of the Creation, but the poem may have been intended simply to continue the narrative from the point at which *Exodus* left off. There is little sense of a break in narrative flow between the two poems, though there are certainly differences in the styles of the two poets. However, *Daniel* does include a reference to the Creation in Nabuchodonosor's first dream, and also includes the canticle of the three children, in which God is praised by his creations:

Ðe Gebletsige. bylywit fæder.
woruldcræfta wlite. and weorca gehwilc.
heofonas and englas. and hluttor wæter.
þa ðe of roderum. on rihtne gesceaft.
wuniað in wuldre. ða þec wurðiað.
and þec ælmihtig. ealle gesceafte.
rodorbeorhtan tunglu. þa þe ryne healdað.
sunna and mona. sundor anra gehwilc.
herige in hade. and heofonsteorran.
deaw and deor scur. ða ðec domige.
and þec mihtig god. gastas lofige.
byrnende fyr. and beorht sumor.

dropena gehwelcne. daga enderim. / Seolua he gesette. þurh his soðan miht. / swa se wyrhta. þurh his wuldres gast. / serede and sette. on six dagum. / eorðan dæles. up on heofonum. / and heanne [Finnegan emends to *heaum*] holme. Hwa is þæt ðe cunne. / orðonc clene. nymðe ece god. / dreamas he gedelde, duguðe and geþeode, / Adam ærest. and þæt æðele cyn. / engla ordfruman. þæt þe eft forwarð.' ('It became revealed to earthdwellers, that the Creator had power and strength when he established the corners of the earth. He himself set the sun and the moon, the stones and the earth, the streams out in the sea, water and clouds, through the power of his wonders. The Creator in his might entirely encompasses the deep expanse, and all the earth. He himself, God's own Son, can look over the sea, the bottom of the ocean, and he can count each of the drops in a rain shower. He himself set the total number of days through his true power. So the maker, through his Holy Spirit, planned and set in six days the region of the earth, the upper heavens, and the high sea. Who is it that knows such skill entirely except eternal God? He allotted joys to men and nations, first Adam and that noble race, the Creator of angels, those who he afterwards destroyed.') *Christ and Satan* 1–21.

[10] *HE* iv.24, and see below, p. 187.

nergend hergað. niht somod and dæg.
and þec landa gehwilc. leoht and þeostro.
herige on hade. somod hat and ceald.
and þec frea mihtig. forstas and snawas.
winterbiter weder. and wolcenfaru.
lofige on lyfte. and þec ligetu.
blace berhtmhwate. þa þec bletsige.
eall eorðan grund. ece drihten.
hyllas and hrusan. and hea beorgas.
sealte sæwegas. soðfæst metod.
eastream yða. and upcyme.
wætersprync wylla. ða ðec wurðiað.
hwalas ðec herigað. and hefonfugolas.
lyftlacende. þa ðe lagostreamas.
wæterscipe wecgað. and wildu deor.
and neata gehwilc. naman bletsie.
and manna bearn. modum lufiað.
and þec israela. æhta scyppend.
herigað in hade. heran þinne.[11]
and þec haligra. heortan cræftas.
soðfæstra gehwæs. sawle and gastas.
lofiað liffrean. lean sellende.
eallum, ece drihten.[12]

[11] The manuscript reads *herran*. Farrell emends to *heran* and translates as 'servants'.

[12] 'Let the beauty of the world and each work praise you, gracious Father. Let heaven and angels and the clear waters of heaven, which dwell, in proper order, in glory, praise you. And let all Creation, the heaven-bright stars which hold their course, the sun and the moon, each apart, praise you, Almighty, in their degree. And let the stars, dew and heavy showers praise you. And let the spirits praise you, Mighty God. Let burning fire and bright summer praise you, Saviour. Let night and day together, and each land, light and dark, hot and cold together, praise you, mighty Lord, in their degree. And let frost and snow, winter-bitter weather and driving clouds in the air praise you, Lord almighty. And let bright, momentary lightning praise you. Let all earth's ground, hills and plains and high mountains, salt seaways, rising waves and welling springs praise you, true Lord. Let whales and flying birds praise you. Let rivers, moving waters, wild animals, and all cattle praise your name. And let each of the children of men who love you in their hearts, and Israel, your servants, praise you, Creator of lands, in their degree. And let the holy, excellent in heart, and each true soul and spirit love you, Lord of life, eternal Lord, who gives reward to all.' *Dan*. 368–96.

This song of praise reminds readers once again of the call to honour God with words of praise in the opening lines of *Genesis*. While the language of the song in *Daniel* differs from that of the Vulgate, it would still have been familiar to Anglo-Saxon readers from the *Benedicite omnia opera* (Daniel III.57–89), the canticle sung at Sunday lauds.[13] The words of the poem and the words of praise directed to God by his Creation, the product of his Word, would then have been united with the words of the readers, themselves a part of Creation. Such a complex layering of speech and speech-acts, artwork and viewer, is also found on the Ruthwell 'cross', where the first-person voice of the monument is echoed in both the act of reading and the liturgical texts through which the 'cross', its images and inscriptions, would have been explained and interpreted. Meaning there, and here, was forever in the process of being created between the voices of the work and those of the people who saw and used it.[14] In terms of narrative time the result is to unite the object and the audience in a new type of 'narrative present', a moment in which a series of distinctly separate times are brought together in and through voice.

In *Christ and Satan*, Satan describes an equally complex layering of word and voice as part of the speech in which he acknowledges his loss and fate:

> hwæt, we in wuldres wlite.[15]   wunian moston.
> þær we halgan gode.   heran woldon.
> and him sang ymb seld.   secgan sceoldon.
> þusendmælum.   þa we þær wæron.[16]

[13] P. Pulsiano, 'Psalters', *The Liturgical Books of Anglo-Saxon England*, ed. R. W. Pfaff, *OEN* Subsidia 23 (Kalamazoo, MI, 1995), pp. 61–85, at pp. 80–1; Remley, *Biblical Verse*, pp. 370–413. Remley notes that the text draws on 'the readings of a characteristically Anglo-Saxon text of *Canticum trium puerorum*' (p. 404).

[14] É. Ó Carragáin, 'Rome, Ruthwell, Vercelli: "The Dream of the Rood" and the Italian Connection', in *Vercelli tra Oriente ed Occidente tra Tarda Antichità e Medioevo: atti delle Giornate di studio: Vercelli 10–11 aprile 1997, 24 novembre 1997*, ed. V. D. Corazza (Alessandria, 1999), pp. 59–99; É. Ó Carragáin, 'The Ruthwell Crucifixion Poem in its Iconographic and Liturgical Contexts', *Peritia* 6–7 (1987–8), 1–71; É. Ó Carragáin, 'Crucifixion as Annunciation: The Relation of the *Dream of the Rood* to the Liturgy Reconsidered', *English Studies* 63 (1982), 487–505; C. E. Karkov, 'Naming and Renaming: the Inscription of Gender in Anglo-Saxon England', *Theorizing Anglo-Saxon Sculpture*, ed. C. E. Karkov and F. Orton (Morgantown, WV, forthcoming).

[15] In the manuscript, *in* is added above the line.

[16] The word *wæron* and the point are added above the line.

wunodon on wynnum. geherdon wuldres sweg.
beman stefne. byrhtword aras.
engla ordfruma. and to þæm æþelan.
hnigan him sanctas. sigetorht aras.
ece drihten. ofer us gestod.
and gebletsode. bilewitne heap.
dogra gehwilcne. and his se deora sunu.
gasta scyppend.[17]

In this passage, the songs of praise are silent, words that only might have been had the angels not rebelled. In hell, a sort of world turned upside down, words are used in lament rather than in praise. Nevertheless, the words that might have been now present to us an absent mirror of the songs of praise sung by the poet, angels and readers, a recurring theme within the manuscript. Moreover, the voices of the heavenly hosts are here joined by music, the voice of the trumpet, an instrument that appears frequently in *Exodus*, and one that is also associated with both the Creation and the Last Judgement. In Anglo-Saxon art, as we have seen, God speaks the Creation into being through two trumpets that issue from his mouth (pl. XLIVa), and the trumpeting evangelist symbols found in early manuscripts such as the Lindisfarne Gospels (London, British Library, Cotton Nero D. IV) are also metaphors of the creative process, divine inspiration becoming word. In this passage from *Christ and Satan* the voice of the trumpet announces the birth of *Christ*, the *Byrhtword* (Bright Word), who is in turn the 'author of angels', present within the Father, outside of time and before Creation, and ultimate victor over Satan in this poem.[18] The distinction between Father and Son in the passage is admittedly difficult.[19] However, although the poet may seem to confuse Father and Son, the identification of Christ as the Creative Word has

[17] 'Lo, we might have dwelled in the beauty of glory, where we would have obeyed holy God, and sung him songs of praise in thousands around the throne. When we were there we dwelled in joys, heard the music of glory, the voice of the trumpet. Christ (*Byrhtword*) arose, the Author of angels, and the saints bowed down to the noble One. The eternal Lord arose, the one bright in victory, and stood over us, and blessed the guiltless company each day, and his dear Son, the Creator of spirits.' *Christ and Satan* 231–42.

[18] See T. D. Hill, '"Byrhtword" and "Hælendes Heafod": Christological Allusion in the Old English *Christ and Satan*', *ELN* 8 (1970), 6–9.

[19] See Finnegan, *Christ and Satan*, pp. 100–1. Finnegan emends *his* to *þe* and translates line 241b as 'and this [was] the dear Son'.

already been suggested in *Genesis*.[20] A similar, though slightly less awkward union of the first two persons of the Trinity occurs in the opening lines of *Christ and Satan*, which move from the act of Creation to God's embrace of his Creation – recalling the drawings of the Creation in both this manuscript and the Royal Bible (pls. IIIa, IIIb, XLIVa) – and to the omnipotent Christ (*godes agen bearn*, *Christ and Satan* 10b). The union and indivisibility of Father and Son is likely to be related to the anti-heretical and specifically anti-Arian tenor of much of late Anglo-Saxon culture. The clearest instance of this in art is the portrait of John in the Eadui Codex (Kestner Museum WM XXIa 36, 147v), in which John and the eternal Word defeat Arius and his denial of the Word.[21]

Equally difficult to identify is the narrative voice of *Christ and Satan*. Christ is undeniably the poem's protagonist, and Finnegan has suggested that he is in fact the poem's narrator.[22] Finnegan argues that the narrator's extensive knowledge of, and implication that he was present at, the events he describes, indicate that he can only be Christ. However, as Finnegan himself acknowledges, there are problems with this position. For example, the narrator does not witness, but 'hears tell' (*gefregen*, line 224) of some events, speaks of himself in the third person (e.g. line 194), and suggests that he, like the poem's audience, is still awaiting the journey to the heavenly kingdom.[23] Moreover the *Daniel* poet also says that he heard and saw the events about which he writes.[24] While this does not suggest that the narrator of *Daniel* is either Christ or omnipotent, it does add to the poem's eschatological character and looks forward to both the themes and the voice of *Christ and Satan*.[25] But, narrator or not, Christ's extended

[20] See above, p. 47.

[21] As hell becomes a type of world turned upside down in Junius 11, so Eadui literally turns Arius and his words upside down in his gospel book. Arius lies beneath John's feet holding an upside-down scroll with the words *Erat tempus quando non erat* ('There was a time when he was not'). John's scroll is inscribed with the beginning of his gospel: 'In principio erat verbum. Et Verbum erat apud deum. Et deus erat verbum. Hoc erat in principio.'

[22] R. Finnegan, 'Christ as Narrator in the Old English *Christ and Satan*', *English Studies* 75.1 (1994), 2–16.

[23] 'neoman us to wynne. weoroda drihten. / uppe [MS *upne*] ecne gefean. engla waldend.' ('Take us to joy, up to eternal joy, Lord of hosts, Lord of angels.') *Christ and Satan* 197–8.

[24] E.g. lines 1 (*gefrægn ic*), 22 (*geseah ic*), 57 (*þa ic eðan gefrægn*).

[25] On the eschatological character of *Daniel* see P. Portnoy, '"Remnant" and "Ritual": The

monologues in *Christ and Satan* are evidence of a strong voice and help, as would any illustrations that might have been planned, to establish his active presence in the narrative.

Similarly God's presence in the manuscript is established through a combination of voice and repeated image. Eric Jager notes that in '*Genesis B*', 'God's teaching and authority are correlative with his vocal presence and not just with his abstracted "word", which can be reported, or subverted, or even entirely fabricated at "second-hand"'.[26] This is true not just of '*Genesis B*', but of the whole of the *Genesis* poem, as well as of *Christ and Satan*.[27] Jager adds: 'The Augustinian notion of an inheritance through Adam's "seed" entails the audience's corporate participation in the narrated events of the Fall, and the narrative's frequent reminders of their status as heirs invokes their collective presence at the recounted events. This aural presence of the audience complements the vocal presence of God.'[28] The presence of the voice, rather than just the words, of God is reinforced by the active narrative of the drawings, in which we see images of the conversations we overhear. It is not just the aural presence of the audience, but the visual, bodily one as well that both poet and artist invoke. We are placed before God, listening to or participating in his words and the historical narrative of the poem. The narrator's frequent direct addresses to the reader and the artist's modernizing of clothes and setting help to bridge the gap between biblical history and the Anglo-Saxon present. Poet and artist thus become mediators between word and reader, eye and image, a role embodied within the manuscript by the little figure on page 7.

VISIONS

Theoretically and semantically, exactly what separates a vision from a dream or from a sign is debatable. When it comes to dreams and visions, one could argue that a dreamer is asleep while a visionary is not, though both dreams and visions are frequently described or portrayed as blurring

Place of Daniel and *Christ and Satan* in the Junius Epic', *English Studies* 75.5 (1994), 408–21, at 413–17.

26 E. Jager, 'Invoking/Revoking God's Word: The *Vox Dei* in *Genesis B*', *English Studies* 71.4 (1990), 307–21, at p. 310.

27 In *Exodus* and *Daniel*, angels are the vehicles for the voice of God.

28 Jager, 'Invoking/Revoking', p. 321.

the boundaries between sleeping and waking. In the Early Christian world, however, a dream was understood as a product of the dreamer's mind, while a vision could only come from God – whether the person experiencing the vision was awake or asleep.[29] Since all the dreams in Junius 11 are the work of God rather than the will of the dreamer, and one of the visions is produced by Satan, the distinction cannot be valid within the context of this manuscript. Dreams and visions will, therefore, be considered here as basically the same phenomenon. The definition of what constitutes a 'sign' (as opposed to a symbol, icon or index) is more complex. Applying either the definition of signs developed by Augustine, or any of the numerous definitions coined by contemporary semioticians, to Junius 11 would be a huge undertaking.[30] Instead, we will focus on those things the poets designate as 'signs' by their choice of language. One thing that we can say unites dreams, visions and signs in the three Old Testament poems is that all look forward to the revelation of Christ triumphant in the New Testament poem, *Christ and Satan*. The end referred to in the beginning of the manuscript is continually kept before our eyes like a vision as we progress through its narratives.

The theme of true and false vision, what is revealed and what is concealed, is one of the strongest links between the four poems in the Junius 11 manuscript. The manuscript opens with an image (pl. I), a vision of God revealed to us, the readers, who offer him praise. As with this opening image, voice and the aural are as significant a part of the manuscript's dreams and visions as the visual. Eve's vision, as noted previously, is not depicted, and we therefore participate in it only secondarily. It is a false vision, and we know this not only from the

[29] On the terminology of sleeping and dreaming in Old English poetry see A. Harbus, 'Old English *swefn* and *Genesis B* line 720', in *Studies in English Language and Literature*, ed. M. J. Toswell and E. M. Tyler (London and New York, 1996), pp. 157–74. See also P. E. Dutton, *The Politics of Dreaming in the Carolingian Empire* (Lincoln, NB, and London, 1994), pp. 33–4; M. Kessels, 'Ancient Systems of Dream Classification', *Mnemosyne* 4th ser. 22 (1969), 389–424; M. Dulaey, *La rêve dans la vie et la pensée de Saint Augustin* (Paris, 1973), esp. pp. 49–55; and S. Kruger, *Dreaming in the Middle Ages* (Cambridge, 1992).

[30] Augustine somewhat loosely defined signs as things used to signify something. See *De doctrina christiana* II.vii (PL 34, col. 39). For a range of contemporary definitions see the collected essays in C. Marmo, ed., *Vestiga, Imagines, Verba: Semiotics and Logic in Medieval Theological Texts (XIIth–XIVth century)* (Turnhout, 1997); R. Innis, *Semiotics: An Introductory Anthology* (Bloomington, IN, 1985).

narrative context, but also by the fact that it is reported to us not through the voice of the poet, but by Eve, whose words and readings we cannot trust. In fact we do not even hear the details of the vision at the moment of its occurrence, but only after the event, as she describes it to Adam – a delay that distinguishes Eve's vision from every other dream or vision in the manuscript. At the moment of the vision we are told only that after eating the fruit the earth appeared bright and more beautiful to her, and that through the power of Satan's messenger she could see far over the heavenly kingdom. Indeed, the poet tells us that she does not see with her own vision, but through the messenger's skilful deceit.[31]

We do, however, hear the voice of the messenger. He reinforces her belief in the truth of the vision by telling her that she does not need to be told what he tells her, because she can see the truth with her own eyes, a clever bit of word-play that helps to conjure the false vision for both Eve and the reader:

> þu meaht nu þe self geseon.   swa ic hit þe secgan ne þearf.
> eue seo gode.   þæt þe is ungelic.
> wlite and wæstmas.   siððan þu minum wordum getruwodest.
> læstes mine lare.   nu scineð þe leoht fore.
> glædlic ongean.   þæt ic from gode brohte.
> hwit of heofonum.   nu þu his hrinan meaht.
> sæge adame.   hwilc þu gesihðe hæfst.
> þurh minne cime cræfta[32]

The messenger's words are as false as the vision. Eve cannot see for herself, nor can she, or does she, touch the vision. As the messenger tells her quite clearly, this vision is his work (*Gen.* 618a) and the result of her foolishly believing his words (*Gen.* 613).[33] The theme was a fairly common one in late Anglo-Saxon England. It is taken up in the references to the *psychomachia* in the Tiberius Psalter,[34] as well as in the homily 'On the Seven Gifts of the Holy Spirit' originally attributed to Wulfstan, where

[31] *Gen.* 600-9. See above, p. 71.

[32] There is no point after *cræfta*. 'Now you can see for yourself, so I do not need to tell you, Eve the good, that beauty and forms are not the same to you since you believed in my words, carried out my counsel. Now light shines before you, bright towards you, that I brought from God, white from heaven. Now you can touch it. Tell Adam what power of vision you have through my coming.' *Gen.* 611–18a.

[33] Jager, 'Invoking/Revoking', p. 316.

[34] Openshaw, 'Weapons in the Daily Battle', p. 20.

the *ungifa* (literally 'ungifts') of Satan are contrasted with the true gifts of God.[35]

The illustrations on pages 28 and 31 frame the text of Eve's fall and show us only the passing of words and fruit between the messenger, Eve and Adam. The only possible visual clue to the nature of the vision might be the blackness and claw-like shapes above the messenger on page 28 (pl. XII). However, the dark shapes may simply refer to the false image of the messenger himself. He is not a beautiful angel come from God as he claims, but is simply disguised as one, and Eve fails to see through his disguise as she fails to see through his deceit. In fact she tells Adam that she recognizes the angel by his outward appearance, his dress:

[35] Bethurum, *Homilies of Wulfstan*, 185–91 (lines 18–26 and 56–67): 'Be ðam seofanfealdan Godes gyfan Isaias se witega awrat on his witegunge be ðam halgan gaste and be his .vii. fealdum gifum. Þa seofonfealdan gyfa synd þus genamode: *sapientia* on Leden, þæt is wisdom on English; *intellectus* on Leden, andgyt on Englisc; *consilium* on Leden, þæt is rædgeðeht on Englisc; *fortitudo* on Leden, modes strengð on Englisc; *scientia* on Leden, god ingehyd on Englisc; *pietas* on Leden, arfæstnyss on Englisc; *timor Domini* on Leden, Godes ege on Englisc . . .

'Nu hæfð se yfele gast and se ungesawenlica feond herongean seofonfealde ungifa þæt syn unþearfa manegra manna and ða syndan wiðerræde mid ealle on ælce wisan þyssum godum Godes gyfum, þe we herbeforan ymbe sædan, and ða he dælð dæghwamlice þam mannum þe ungesalice him gehyrsumiað and Godes gyfa ne gymað ne Godes ege nabbað ne Godes læge healdað, ac fyligeað heora luste and idelum gewille. And þa yfelan ungifa þæs arleasan deofles syndan þus genamode on Ledengereorde: *insipientia*, þæt is unwisdom; *stultitia*, þæt is stuntnys; *inprouidentia*, þæt is receleasnys; *ignauia*, þæt is wacmodnys; *ignorantia*, þæt is nytennys; *impietas*, þæt is arleasnys; *temeritas*, þæt is dyrstignys.' ('Concerning the seven-fold gifts of God Isaiah the prophet wrote in his prophecy on the Holy Ghost and on his seven-fold gifts. The seven-fold gifts are thus named: *sapientia* in Latin, that is wisdom in English; *intellectus* in Latin, that is understanding in English; *consilium* in Latin, that is deliberation in English; *fortitudo* in Latin, strength of mind in English; *scientia* in Latin, good conscience in English; *pietas* in Latin, piety in English; *timor Domini* in Latin, fear of God in English . . .

'Now the evil spirit and the invisible enemy has seven-fold contrary ungifts that are hurtful to many men and that are the opposite of each and every instruction in God's good gifts, which we talked about previously, and which he shares daily with the unhappy men who obey him and do not have the care nor the fear of God, nor hold God's law, but follow their lust and idle will. And the evil ungifts of the wicked devil are thus named in the Latin language: *insapientia*, that is folly; *stultitia*, that is stupidity; *inprouidentia*, that is recklessness; *ignauia*, that is cowardice; *ignorantia*, that is ignorance; *impietas*, that is wickedness; *temeritas*, that is arrogance.') The homily also deals with the constant metamorphosis of the devil and the need for continual vigilance and true spiritual wisdom on the part of men and women.

ic on his gearwan geseo.
þæt he is ærendsecg.   uncres hearran.[36]

Like the bad reader or listener, she is taken in by surface appearances and cannot see things for what they really are. The artist shows us exactly what Eve really claims to see, a figure that looks like an angel, and nothing more. As a parallel to Eve's failure to see the true nature of the demonic messenger, Satan will be unable to recognize the truth of Christ's divinity within his 'disguise' as a man in *Christ and Satan*. Like Eve, Satan is incapable of putting word and image together. In this latter episode too, we are shown all that Satan is shown by the poet, and possibly by the artist, if an illustration was planned, yet we recognize Christ in both his natures.[37]

For an Anglo-Saxon audience, Eve's encounter with the angelic messenger and her resulting 'vision' may well have resonated with some of the traditional themes of Anglo-Saxon history and hagiography. In Bede's *Historia ecclesaistica* the cowherd poet, Cædmon, finds his voice after a vision and sings in praise of God's Creation. So too, Eve finds a voice after her vision, and speaks for the first time in the poem. Cædmon's words, though divinely inspired, are his own (according to Bede). Bede says that Cædmon 'began to sing verses he had never heard before' ('Quo accepto responso, statim ipse coepit cantare in laudem Dei Conditoris uersus quos numquam audierat').[38] Eve's words, on the contrary, are not her own, though they are spoken in her voice. The poet tells us that Eve was corrupted with 'lying words' and spoke under the will of the 'hellish enemy':

hwæt, se hellsceaða
gearwe wiste.   þæt hie godes yrre.
habban sceoldon.   and hellgeþwing.[39]
þone nearwan nið.   niede onfon.
siððan hie gebod godes.   forbrocen hæfdon.
þa he forlærde.   mid ligenwordum.
to þam unræde.   idese sciene.
wifa wlitegost.   þæt heo on his willan spræc.
wæs hine[40] on helpe.   handweorc godes. to forlæranne.[41]

[36] 'I see by his dress that he is the messenger of our Lord.' *Gen.* 657b–8.

[37] See below, p. 206..   [38] *HE* iv.24, p. 416.

[39] The manuscript reads *hellgeþwin*. Sievers, Doane and other editors suggest 'g' erased after 'n'.

[40] Manuscript reads *hire*.

[41] 'Lo, the hellish enemy knew well that they should have God's ire and hell-torture, of

But sight and image play a role in this manuscript that they do not in Bede's unillustrated history.

We do not see, as Adam does not see, the vision of God enthroned surrounded by his angels, nor do we, or Adam, hear the joyful music of heaven. We hear and see only Eve's words.[42] At this point, Adam becomes the bad reader, failing to recognize the source of the words spoken in his wife's voice, and trusting in a vision that remains invisible, like the devil with his 'ungifts' in the homily cited above. The whole story of Temptation and Fall in *Genesis* is characterized by a web of false images, deceitful voices, and flawed reading which the reader/viewer must also negotiate.[43]

Similarly, the false angel himself forms an interesting contrast to the truly angelic messengers of so many saints' lives. St Fursa is granted a vision of the angels and hears their songs of praise,[44] while St Guthlac receives an angelic visitor sent by God who reveals divine mysteries to him.[45] In both cases, the true inner vision of the saint results in genuine revelation, while Eve's flawed vision results only in deceit. Yet for all its falseness, the vision she describes does look forward to the Last Judgement and to her, and Adam's, eventual entry into heaven.

needs receive that oppressive torment after they had broken God's commandment, when he corrupted to folly with his lying words that lovely woman, most beautiful of women, so that she spoke under his will and was a help to him in deceiving God's handiwork.' *Gen*. 694b–703.

42 See above, p. 72.

43 A point noted by Stévanovitch ('Envelope Patterns') in her analysis of the various speeches that make up the narrative of the Fall.

44 'Ubi quadam infirmitate corporis arreptus, angelica meruit uisione perfrui, in qua admonitus est coepto Verbi ministerio sedulus insistere.' ('Once when he was suffering from an illness, he was counted worthy to enjoy a vision of angels, in which he was directed to maintain diligently the task that he had undertaken of ministering the Word.') *HE* iii.19, pp. 270–1.

45 'A secundo etenim anno, quo hanc heremum habitare coeperam, mane vespereque semper angelum consolationis meae ad meum colloquium Dominus mittebat, qui mihi misteria quae non licet homini narrare, monstrabat, qui duritiam laboris mei caelestibus oraculis sublevabat, qui absentia mihi monstrando ut praesentia praesentabat.' ('From the second year that I began to inhabit this desert place, every morning and evening the Lord has sent an angel to talk with me for my consolation, who showed me mysteries which it is not lawful for man to utter, who relieved the hardness of my toil with heavenly oracles, and who revealed to me things which were absent as though they were present.') B. Colgrave, ed., *Felix's Life of Saint Guthlac* (Cambridge, 1956), pp. 156-7.

Other visions in the poem *are* truly the work of God, and *are* likely to have been represented in the drawings. In these cases the reader witnesses the vision along with the men and women within the narrative. In *Exodus*, the Israelites are guided on their journey by the pillars of cloud and fire, which the poet appears to have conceived of as a semi-architectural canopy:

bælce oferbrædde. byrnendne heofon.
halgan nette. hatwendne lyft.
hæfde wederwolcen. swidum fæðmum.
erðan on uprodor. efne gedæled.
lædde leodwerod. ligfyr adranc.
hate heofontorht. hæleð wafedon.
drihta gedrymost. dægsceldes hleo.
wand over wolcnum.[46]

This is a truly multivalent vision, associated by the poet with a ship,[47] the tabernacle, the paschal candle (*heofoncandel*, *Ex.* 115), and the cross.[48] It was also traditionally identified as a sign of the incarnation and divinity of Christ.[49] In this instance we are dealing not with disguises but with an image that is genuinely many things at once. Given the distribution of the spaces left for drawings, it is hard to imagine that the vision would not have been included in the illustrations – in some form.[50] Moreover, these pictures would have had a special relevance to their Anglo-Saxon audience, who saw themselves as the chosen people, the direct descendants of Abraham. The journey of the Israelites, guided by the sign of the cross,

46 '[He] covered burning heaven with a ceiling, the hot air with a holy net. A cloud with its wide embraces evenly divided earth and heaven, led the people, and quenched the flaming sun hot heavenly brightness. Men looked on in amazement, the most joyful of troops. The protection of the day-shield wound over the sky.' *Ex.* 73–80a. Lucas, (*Exodus*, pp. 88–9) notes that the word *bælce* is a reference to the central beam or ceiling of the tabernacle, and that the term *nette* is therefore likely to refer to the curtain that hung from the cross-beams of the tabernacle.

47 It is a 'sailyard' (*seglerode*, *Ex.* 83a), its 'sail' (*segl*, *Ex.* 81b) covers the sun, and its 'holy sails' (*halige seglas*, *Ex.* 89b) tower in the air.

48 Lucas, *Exodus*, pp. 93–4.

49 '*In columna nubis et ignis* [XIII.21] .i. significat Christi incarnacionem ad diuinitatem eius.' ('In a pillar of cloud . . . and fire [XIII.21]: that is it signifies the incarnation of Christ and his divinity.') B. Bischoff and M. Lapidge, *Biblical Commentaries from the Canterbury School of Theodore and Hadrian*, CSASE 10 (Cambridge, 1994), pp. 346–7.

50 Lucas suggests that the pillar of cloud was the subject of the drawings intended for pages 147 and 152. See appendix, p. 204.

was hence their journey.[51] One might also speculate as to whether an Anglo-Saxon audience might have identified the triumph of the Israelites under the sign of the cross with the triumph of Oswald under the sign of the cross at Heavenfield, which, though occurring in the early days of the English church, had an enduring religious and iconographic influence.[52] Ælfric wrote a life of St Oswald based on Bede's account of the king and his cult. Both authors noted that with Christ's help Oswald and his little army[53] defeated the superior force of the pagan Cadwalla, as Moses and the Israelites triumphed over pharoah and his troops.

The most interesting aspect of the vision in *Exodus* is the way in which the two pillars shift and defy shape in the poem. They become like a sail hanging from a yardarm or cross-beam (*seglrode*, *Ex.* 83),[54] in an allusion to Noah's ark and the ship of the church. Yet in contrast to Adam and Eve's inability to recognize the shape-shifting messenger and his sign in *Genesis*, the people of Israel are able to recognize the Lord in all his shifting forms.[55]

fyrd eall geseah.
hu þær hlifedon. halige seglas.
lyftwundor leoht. leode ongeton.
dugoð israhela. þæt þær drihten cwom.
weroda drihten. wicsteal metan.[56]

51 See N. Howe, *Migration and Mythmaking in Anglo-Saxon England* (New Haven, CT, and London, 1989).

52 *HE* iii.2. Bede calls the cross the *signum sanctae crucis* ('sign of the holy cross'). The site of the battle of Heavenfield became a place of veneration, pilgrimage and miracles, and a special focus of devotion for the monks of Hexham, who built a church on the site. See also the essays in C. Stancliffe and E. Cambridge, eds., *Oswald: Northumbrian King to European Saint* (Stamford, 1995), particularly A. Thacker, 'Membra Disjecta: the Diffusion of the Body and the Diffusion of the Cult', pp. 97–127, esp. p. 108; and for the later cult D. Ó Riain-Raedel, 'Edith, Judith, Matilda: the Role of Royal Ladies in the Propagation of the Continental Cult', pp. 210–29, esp. p. 221.

53 Bede: 'parus exercitu, sed fide Christi munitio' (*HE* iii.2, p. 214); Ælfric: 'mid lytlum werode. Ac his geleafe hin getrymde' (*Ælfric's Lives of the Saints*, ed. W. W. Skeat, 2 vols., EETS OS 94 and 114 (London, 1966), II, 126).

54 In his gloss on this line Lucas notes that the compound *seglrode* consists of the words for sail and cross, and is otherwise unrecorded.

55 For a consideration of this theme in Anglo-Saxon art see Rosenthal, 'Three Drawings'.

56 'The army all saw how holy sails towered there, light-miracles of the air, the people, the troop of Israel perceived that their Lord had come to mark out a camping place.' *Ex.* 88b–92.

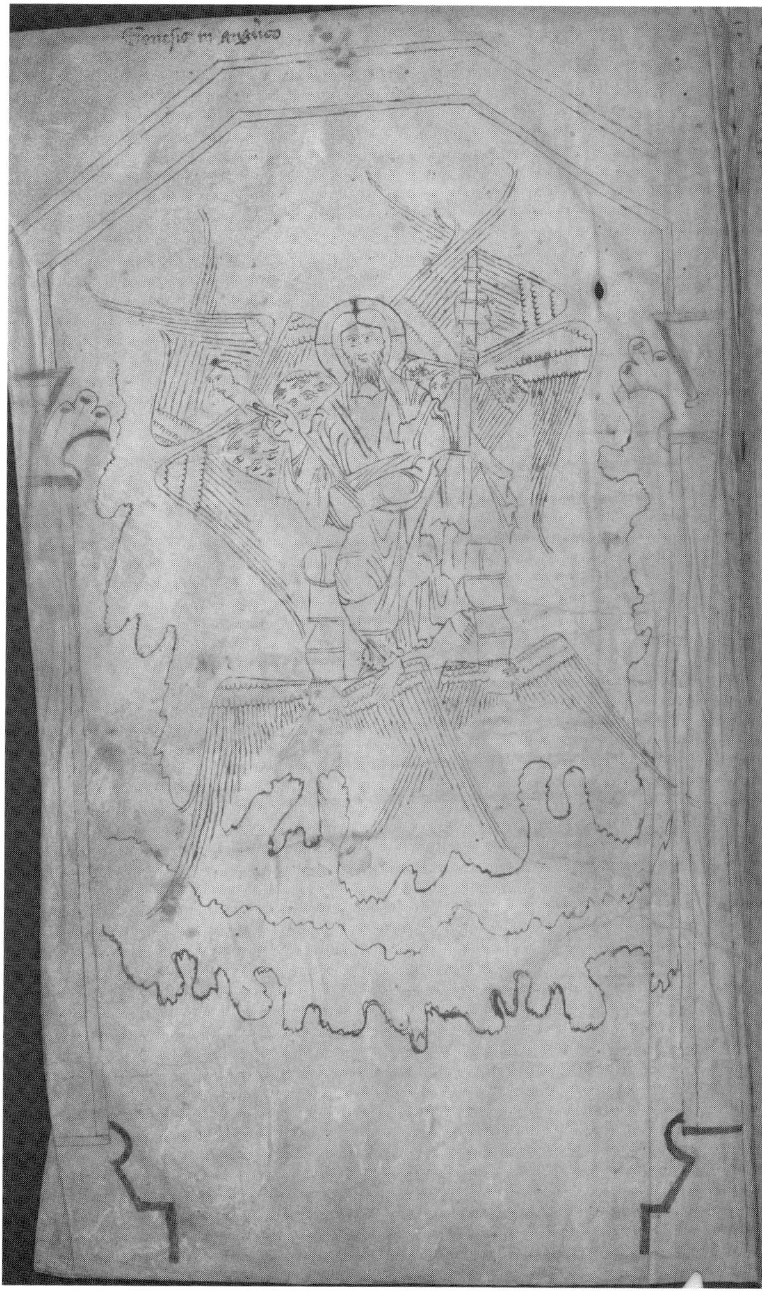

PLATE I Oxford, Bodleian Library, Junius 11, p. ii: God enthroned

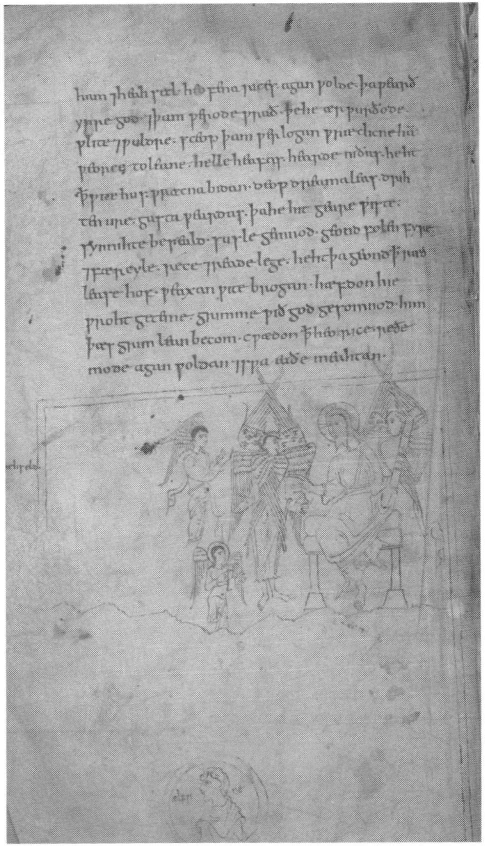

PLATE 11a Oxford, Bodleian Library, Junius 11, p. 2: God enthroned

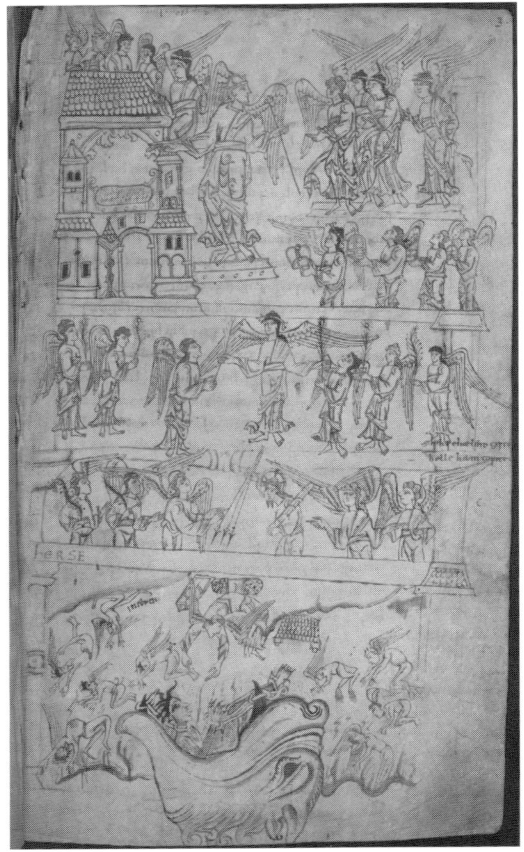

PLATE 11b Oxford, Bodleian Library, Junius 11, p. 3: Fall of the rebel angels

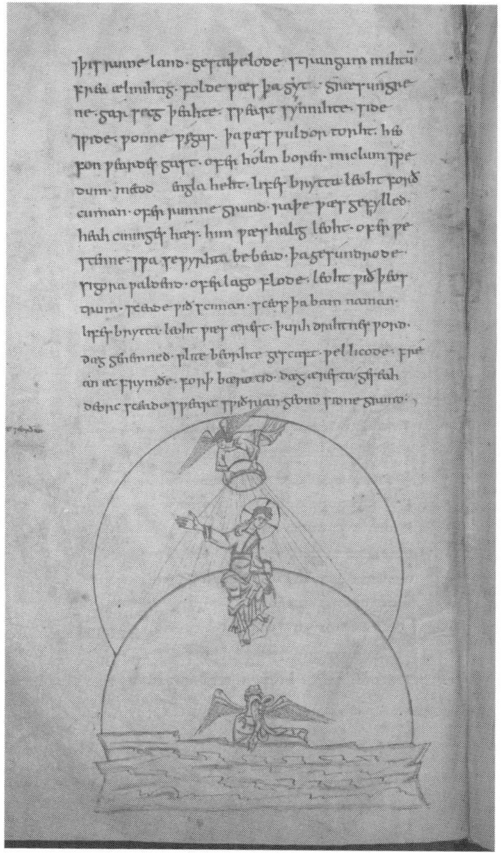

PLATE IIIa Oxford, Bodleian Library, Junius 11, p. 6: Creation

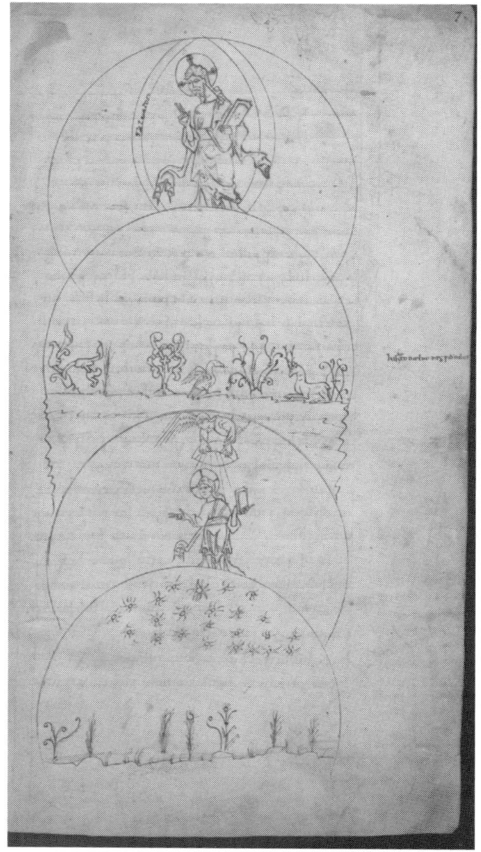

PLATE IIIb Oxford, Bodleian Library, Junius 11, p. 7: Creation

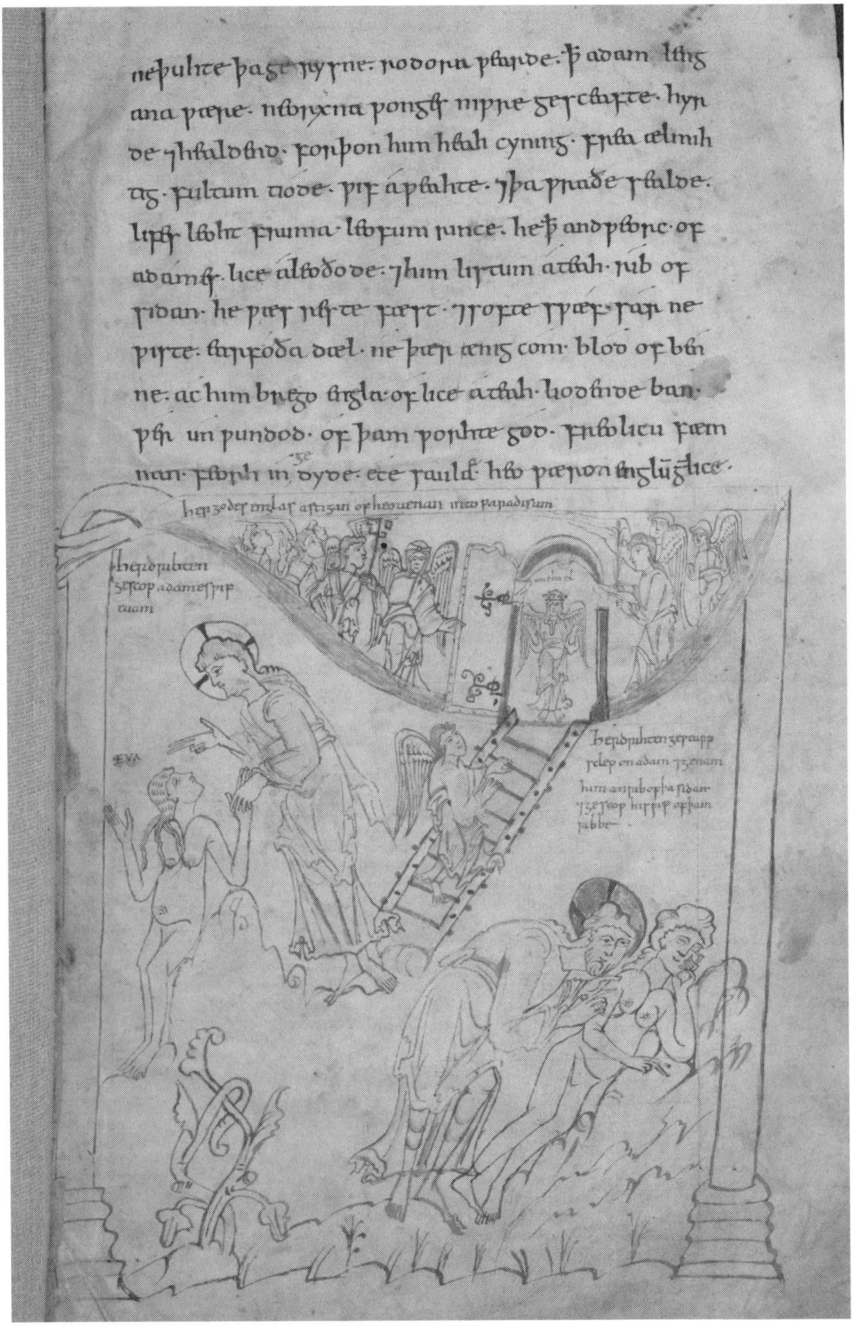

PLATE IV Oxford, Bodleian Library, Junius 11, p. 9: Creation of Eve

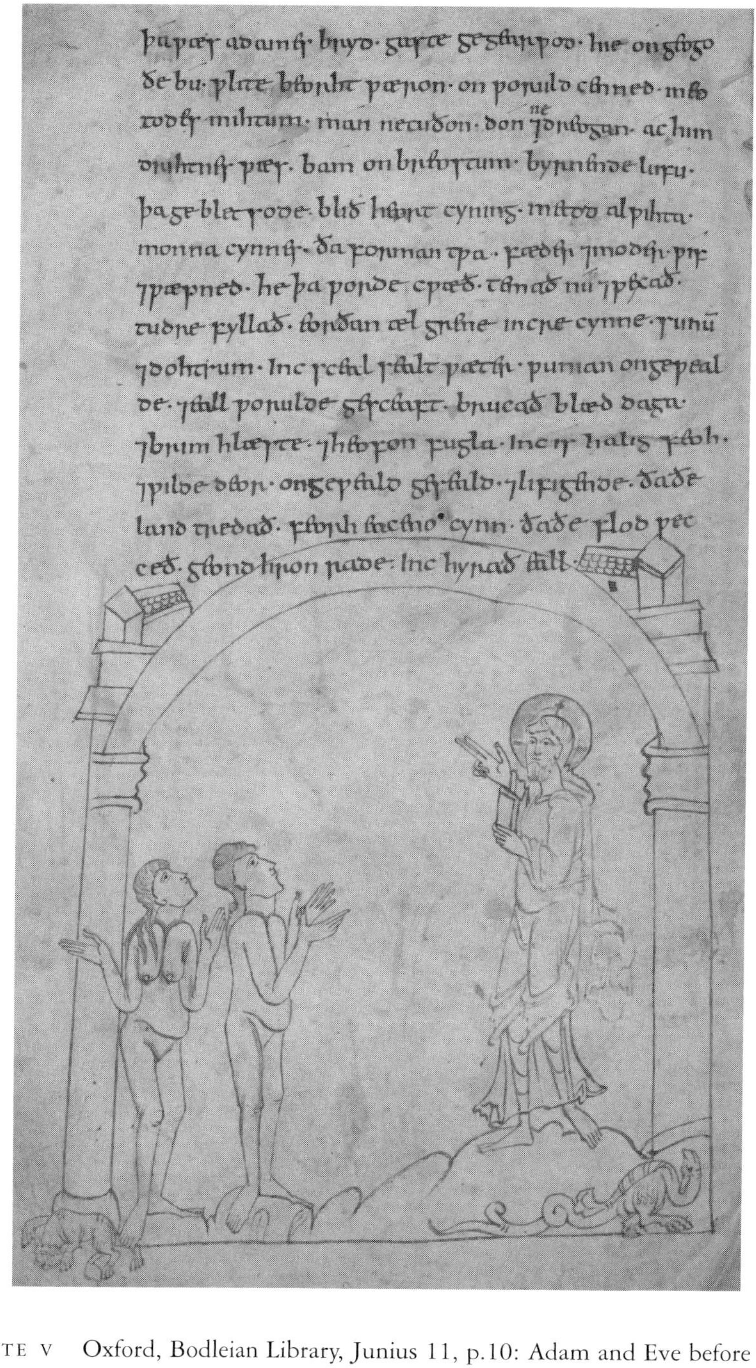

PLATE V Oxford, Bodleian Library, Junius 11, p.10: Adam and Eve before God

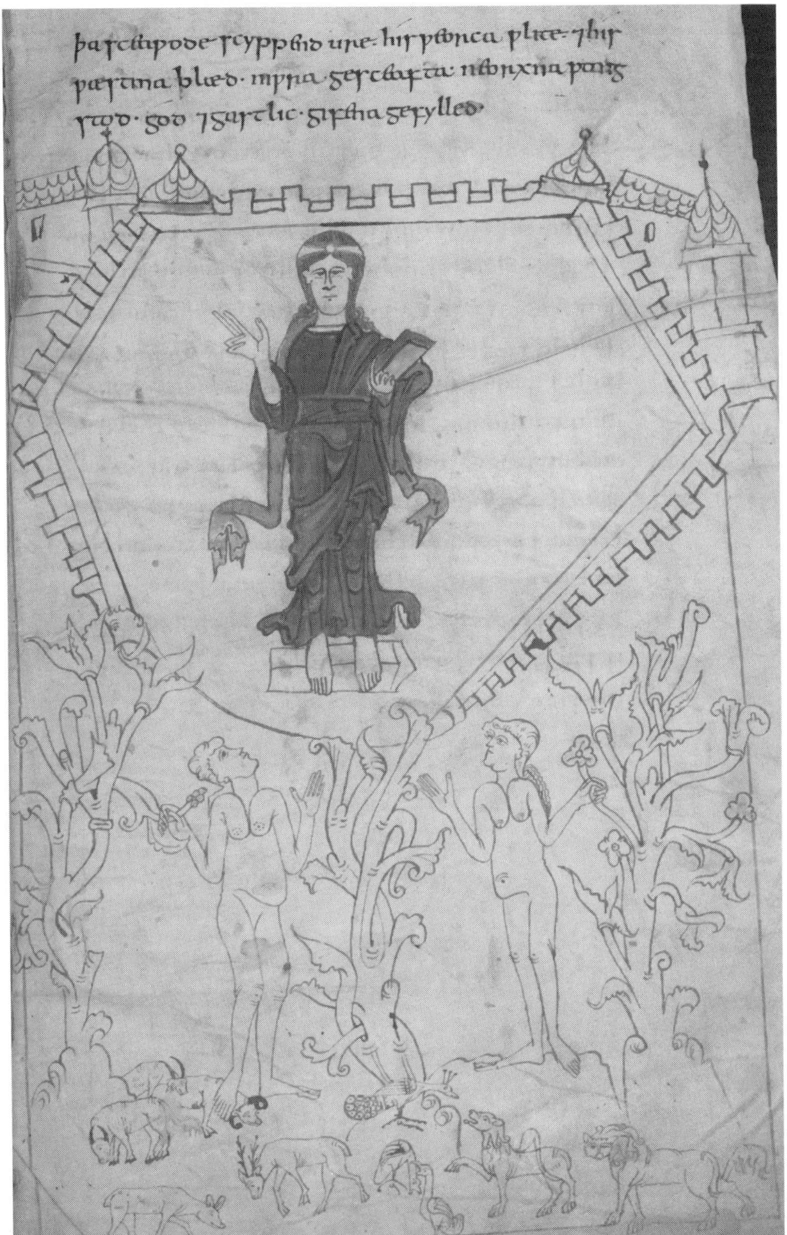

PLATE VI Oxford, Bodleian Library, Junius 11, p. 11: Adam and Eve in Paradise

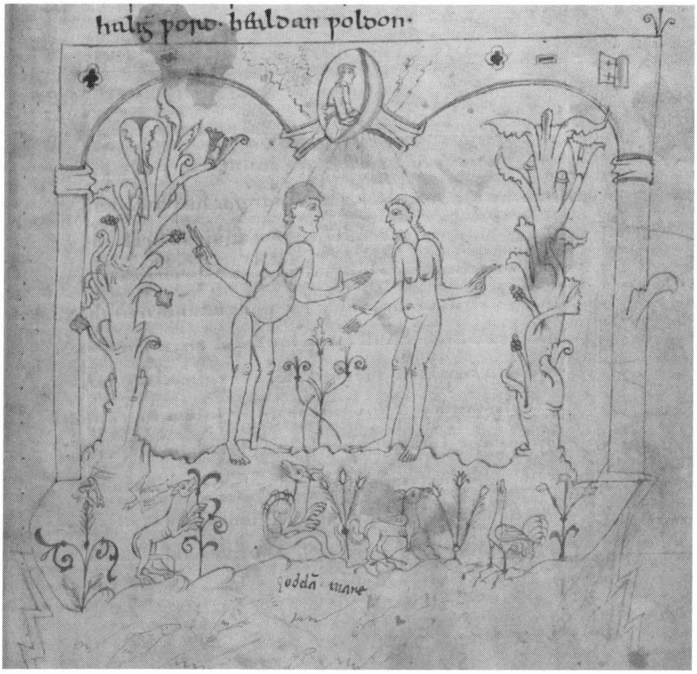

PLATE VIIa Oxford, Bodleian Library, Junius 11, p. 13: Adam and Eve in Paradise

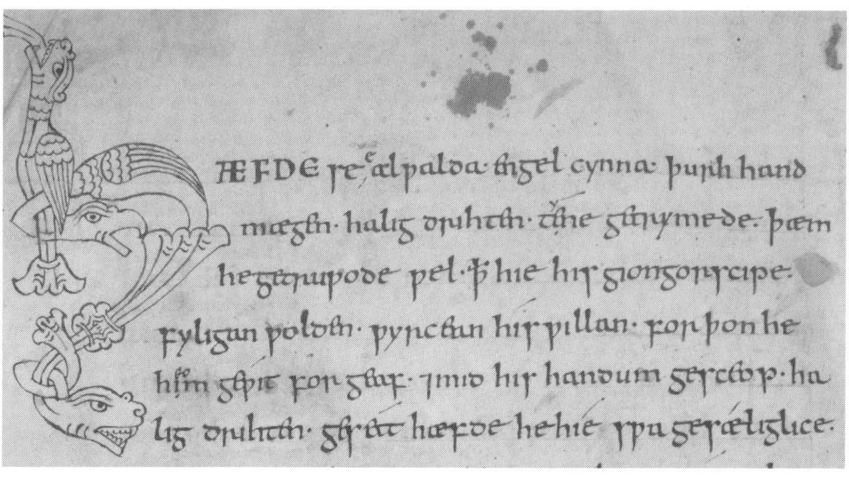

PLATE VIIb Oxford, Bodleian Library, Junius 11, p. 14: Initial 'H'

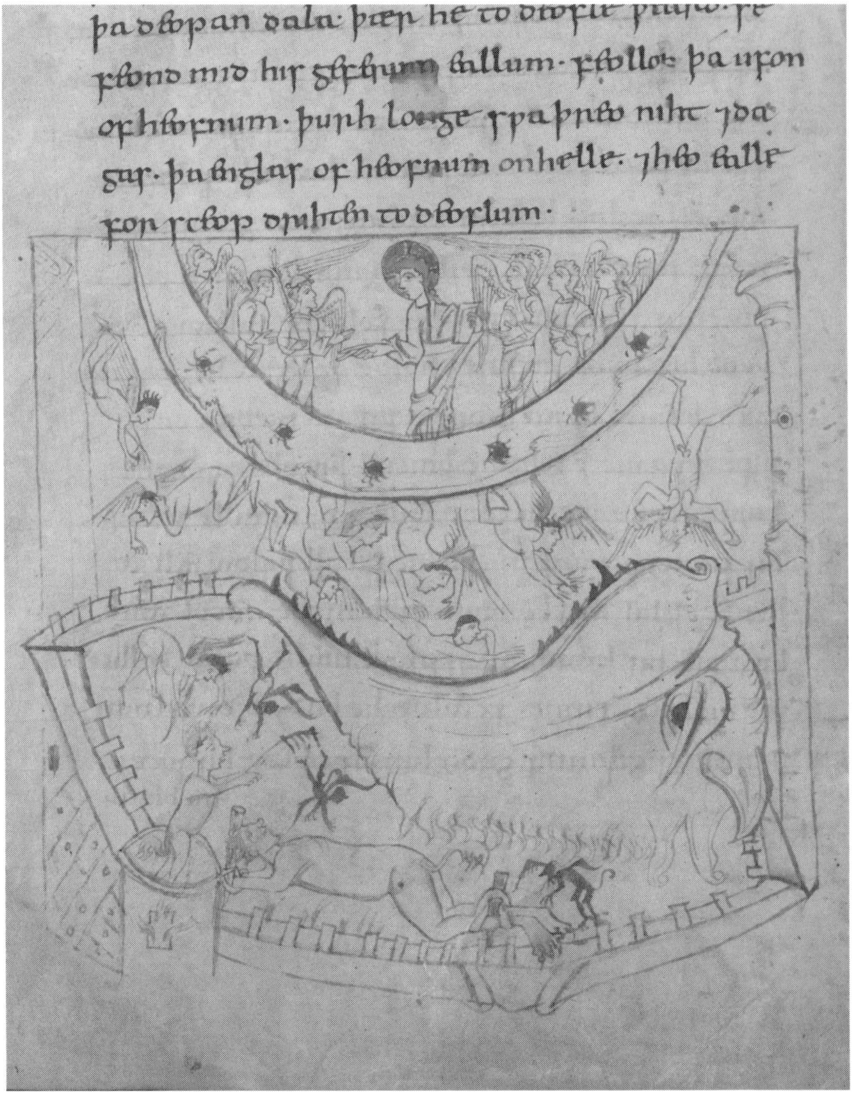

PLATE VIII Oxford, Bodleian Library, Junius 11, p. 16: Fall of the rebel angels

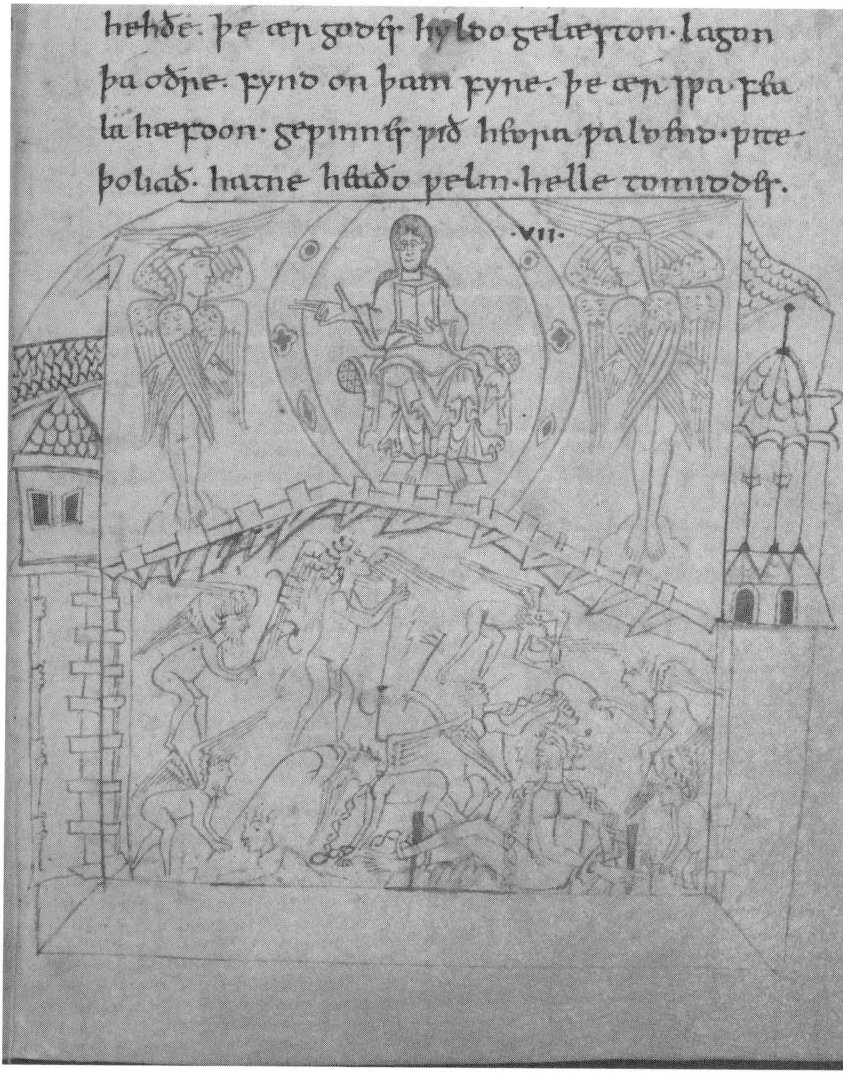

PLATE IX Oxford, Bodleian Library, Junius 11, p. 17: Satan in hell

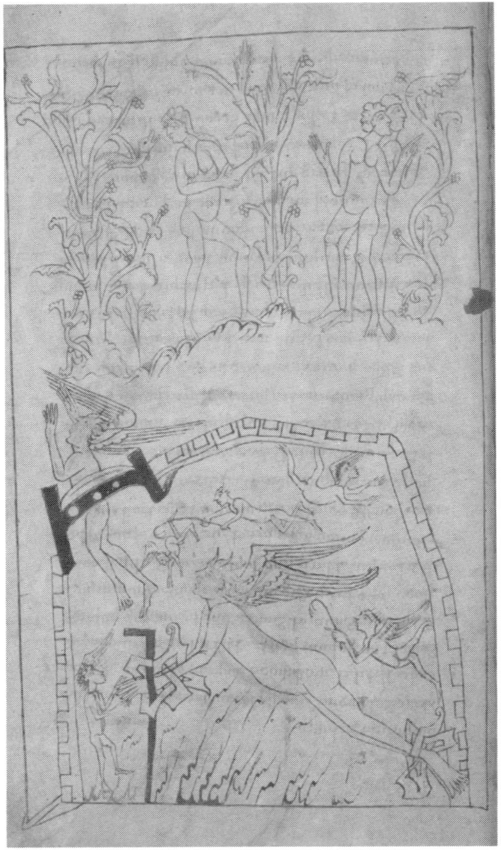

PLATE Xa Oxford, Bodleian Library, Junius 11, p. 20: Satan's messenger leaves hell

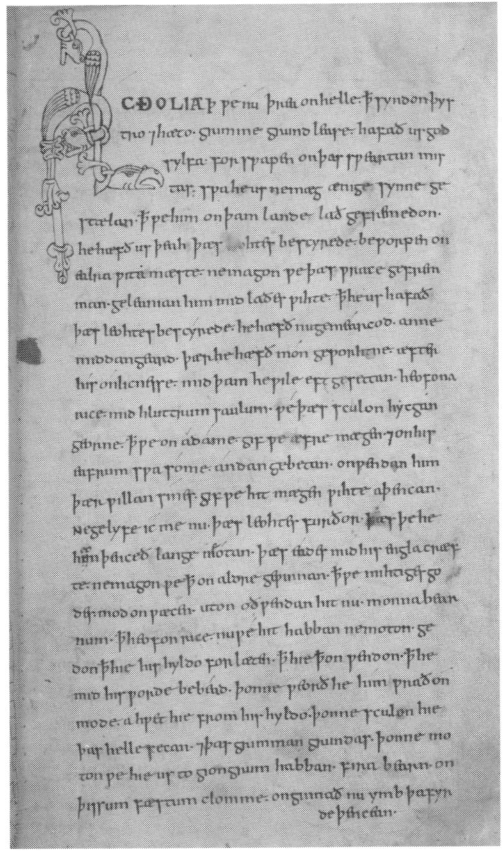

PLATE Xb Oxford, Bodleian Library, Junius 11, p. 21: Initial 'A'

NGAN hine þa gyrwan godes andsaca.
fus on frætwum. hæfde fæcne hyge.
hæleð helm on heafod asette. ⁊ þone full
hearde geband. spenn mid spangum.
wiste him spræca fela wora worda: wand him up

PLATE XIa Oxford, Bodleian Library, Junius 11, p. 23: Initial 'A'

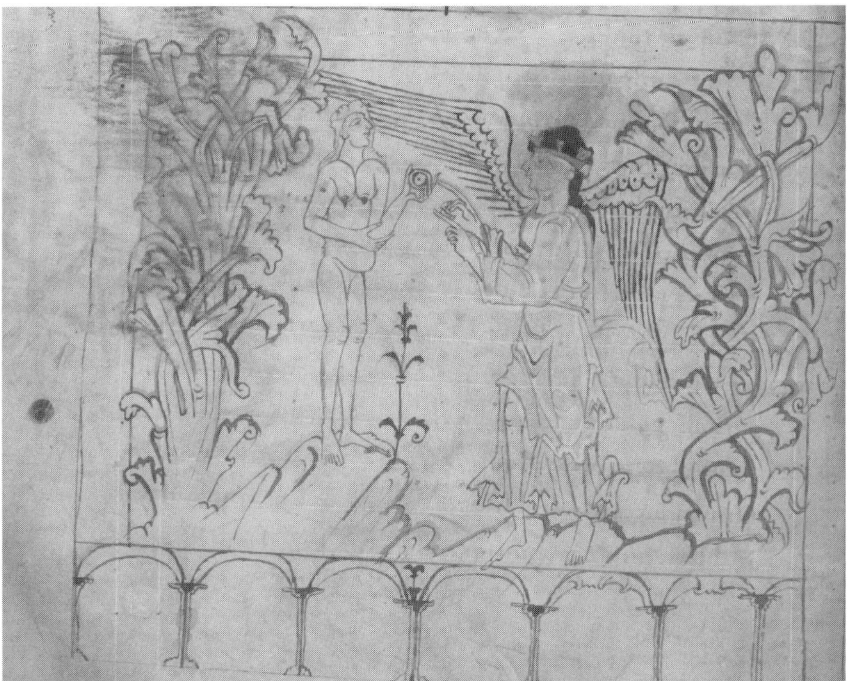

PLATE XIb Oxford, Bodleian Library, Junius 11, p. 24: Temptation of Adam

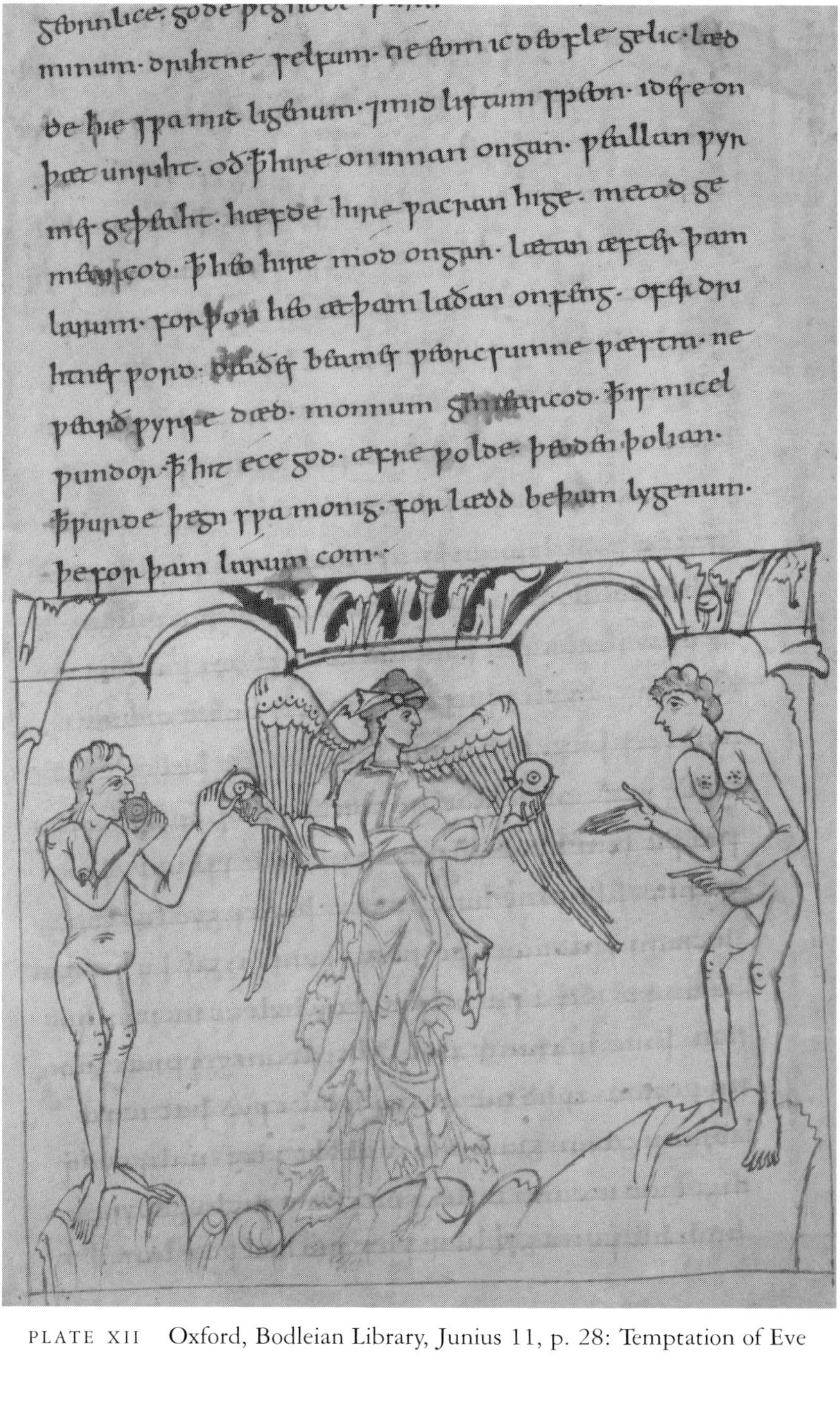

PLATE XII Oxford, Bodleian Library, Junius 11, p. 28: Temptation of Eve

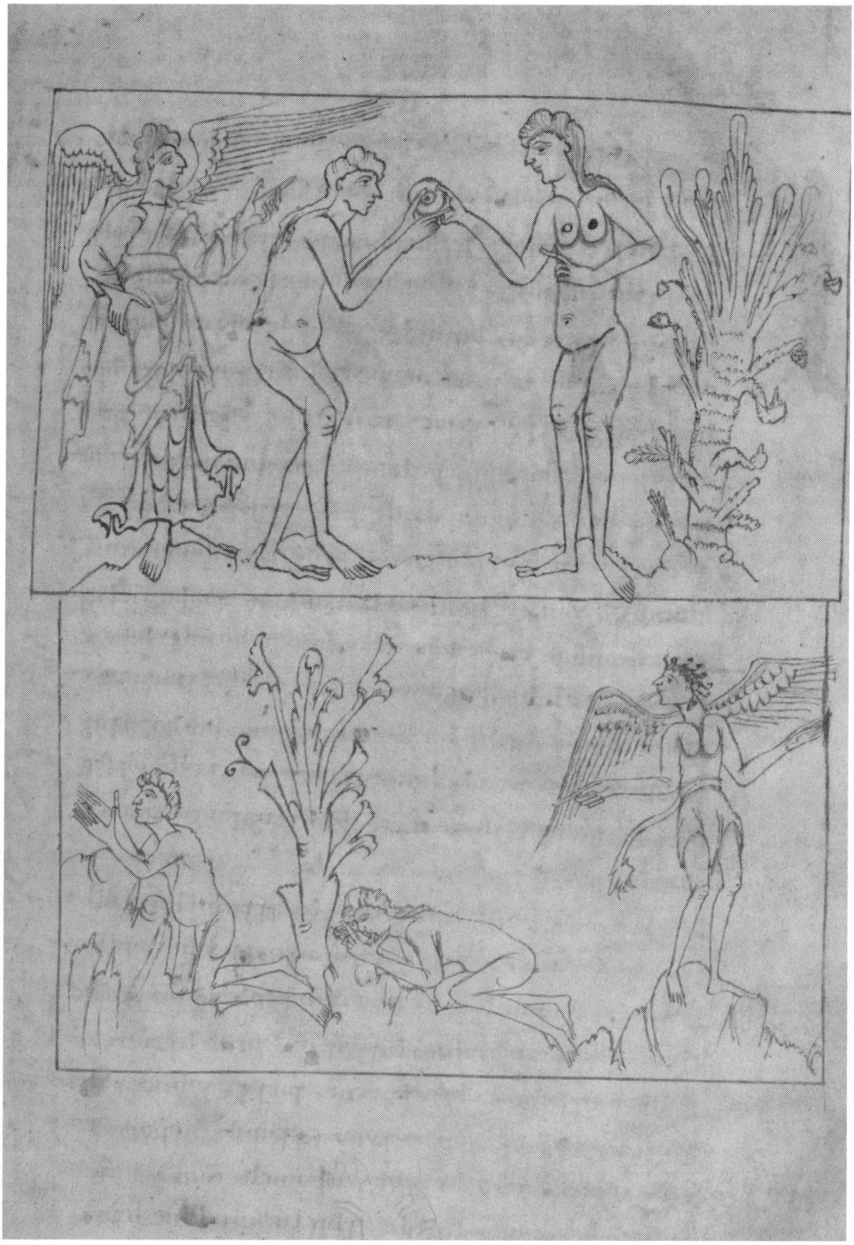

PLATE XIII Oxford, Bodleian Library, Junius 11, p. 31: Eve tempts Adam

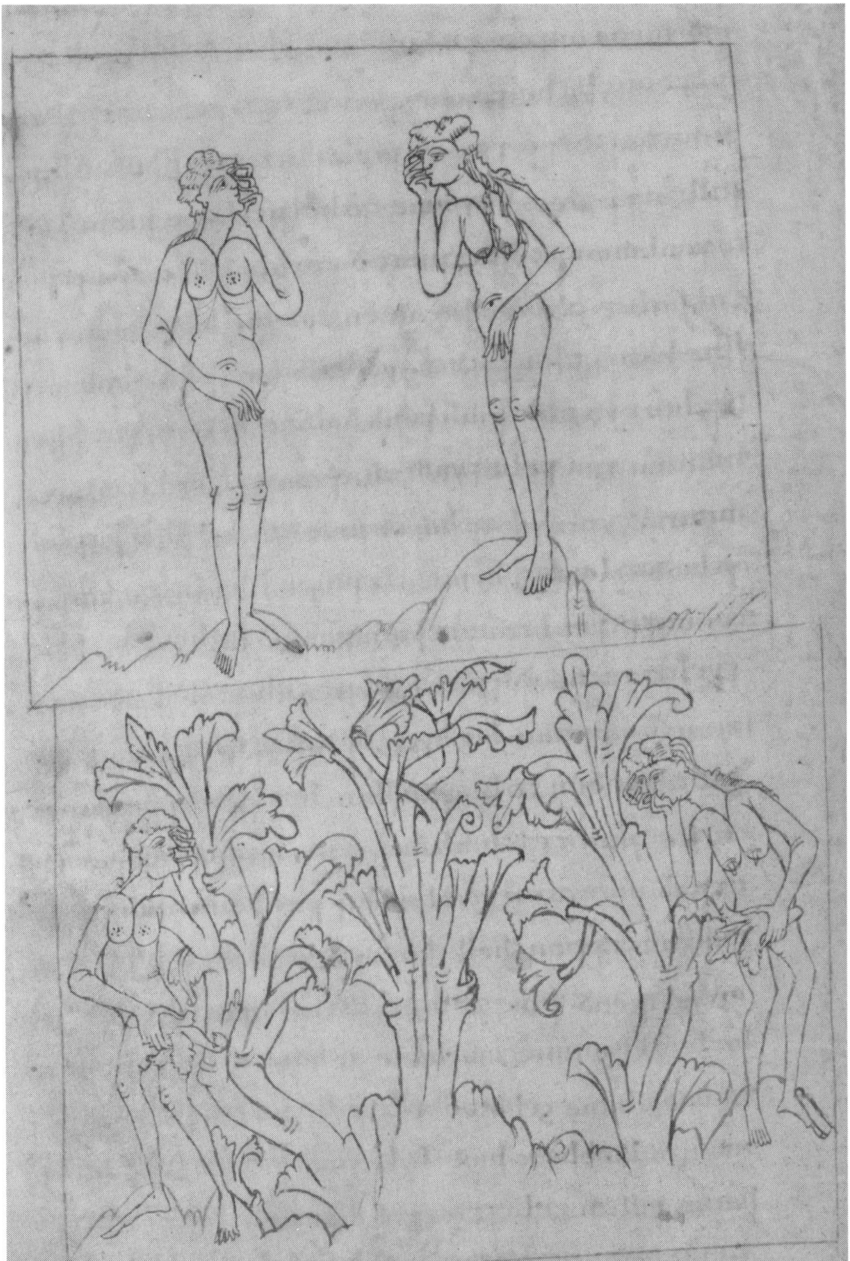

PLATE XIV Oxford, Bodleian Library, Junius 11, p. 34: Adam and Eve knowing nakedness

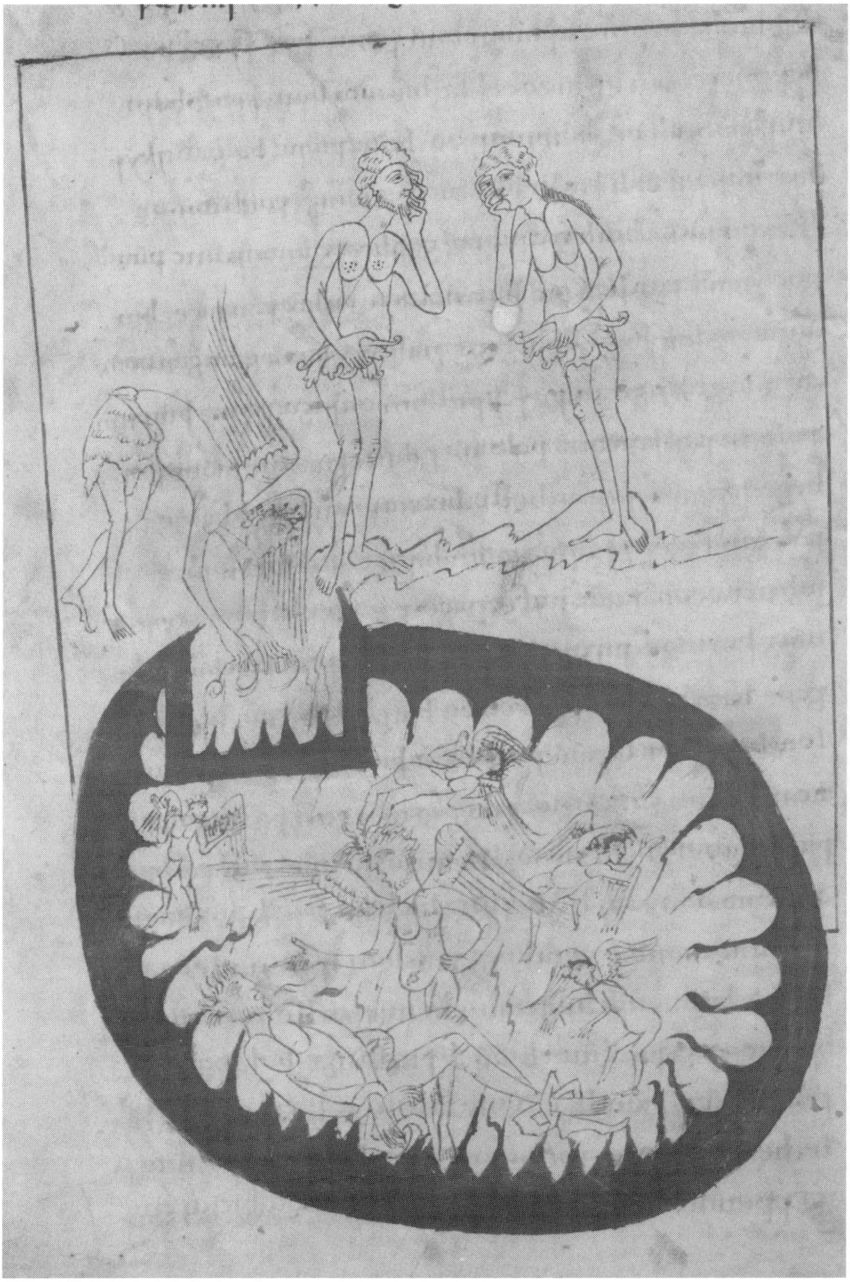

PLATE XV Oxford, Bodleian Library, Junius 11, p. 36: Messenger returns to hell

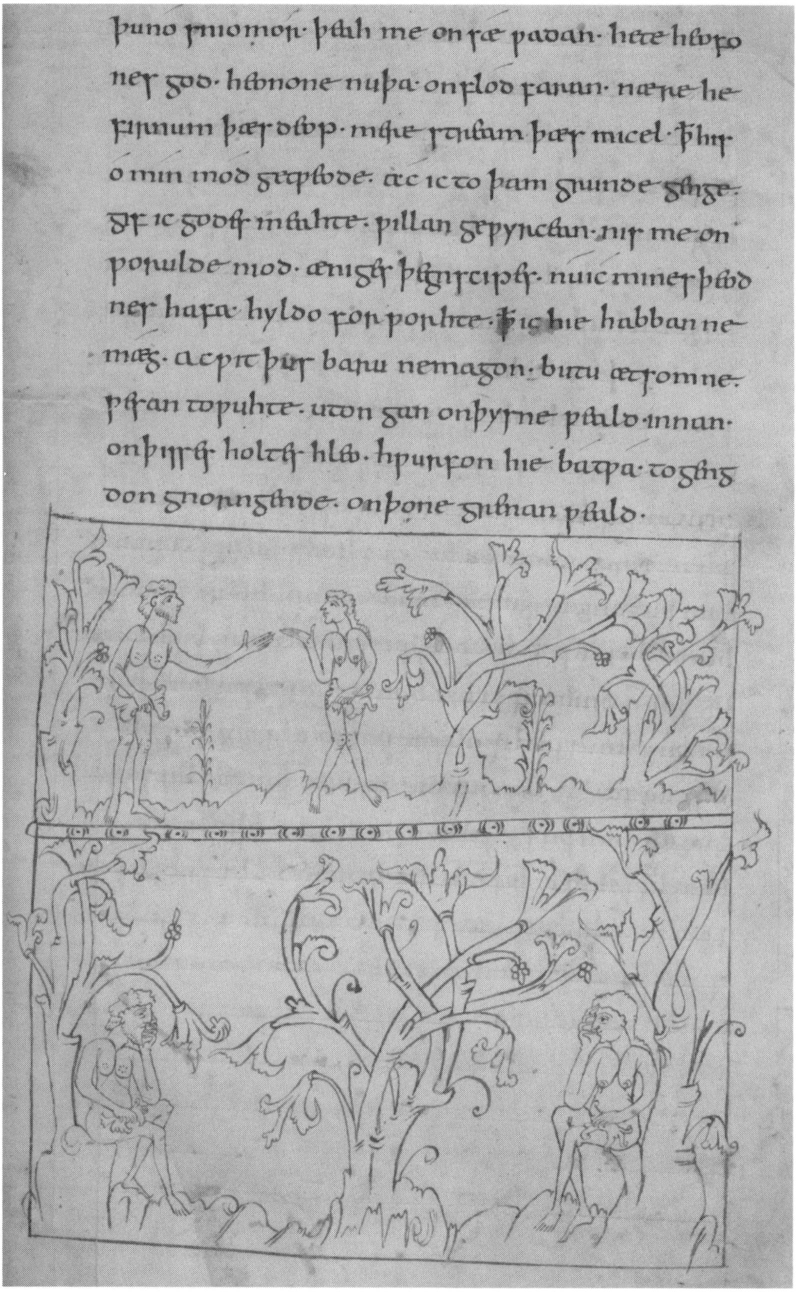

PLATE XVI Oxford, Bodleian Library, Junius 11, p. 39: Adam and Eve's remorse

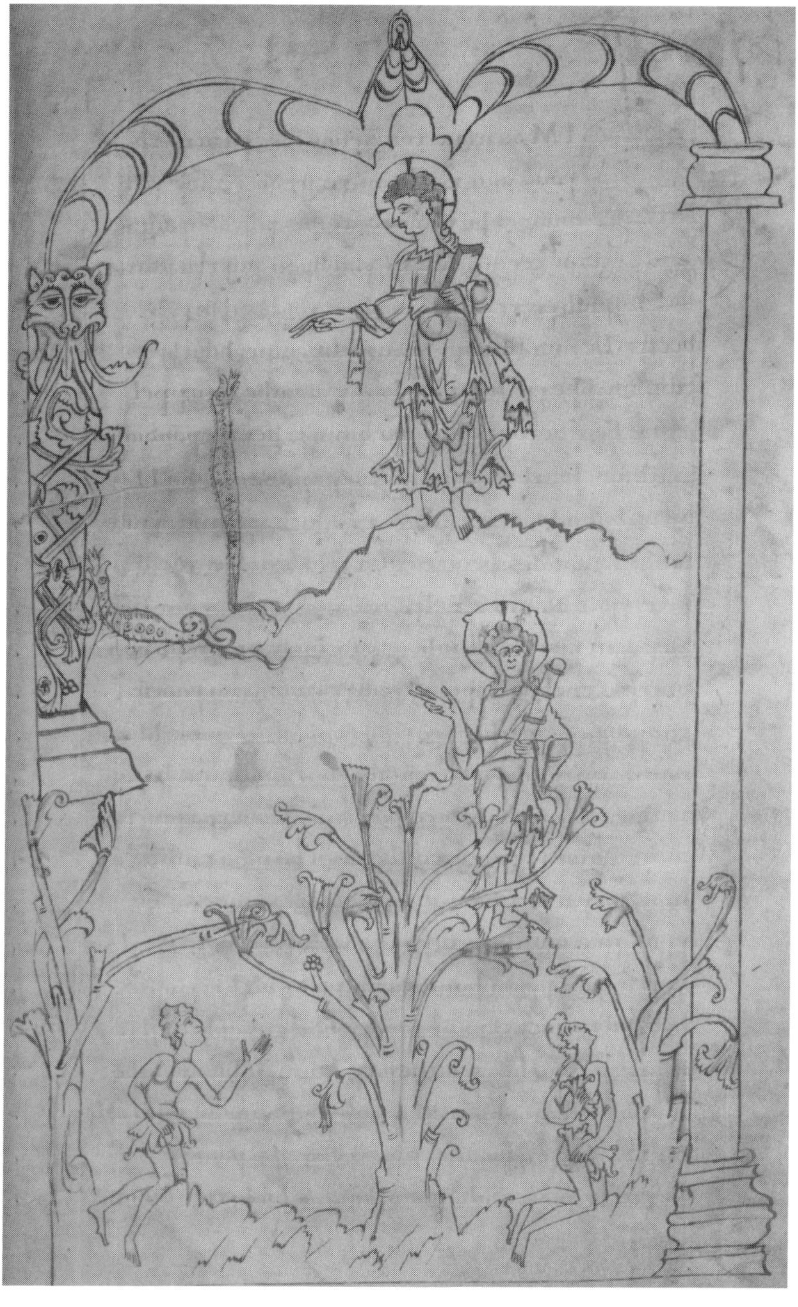

PLATE XVII Oxford, Bodleian Library, Junius 11, p. 41: Judgement of God on serpent

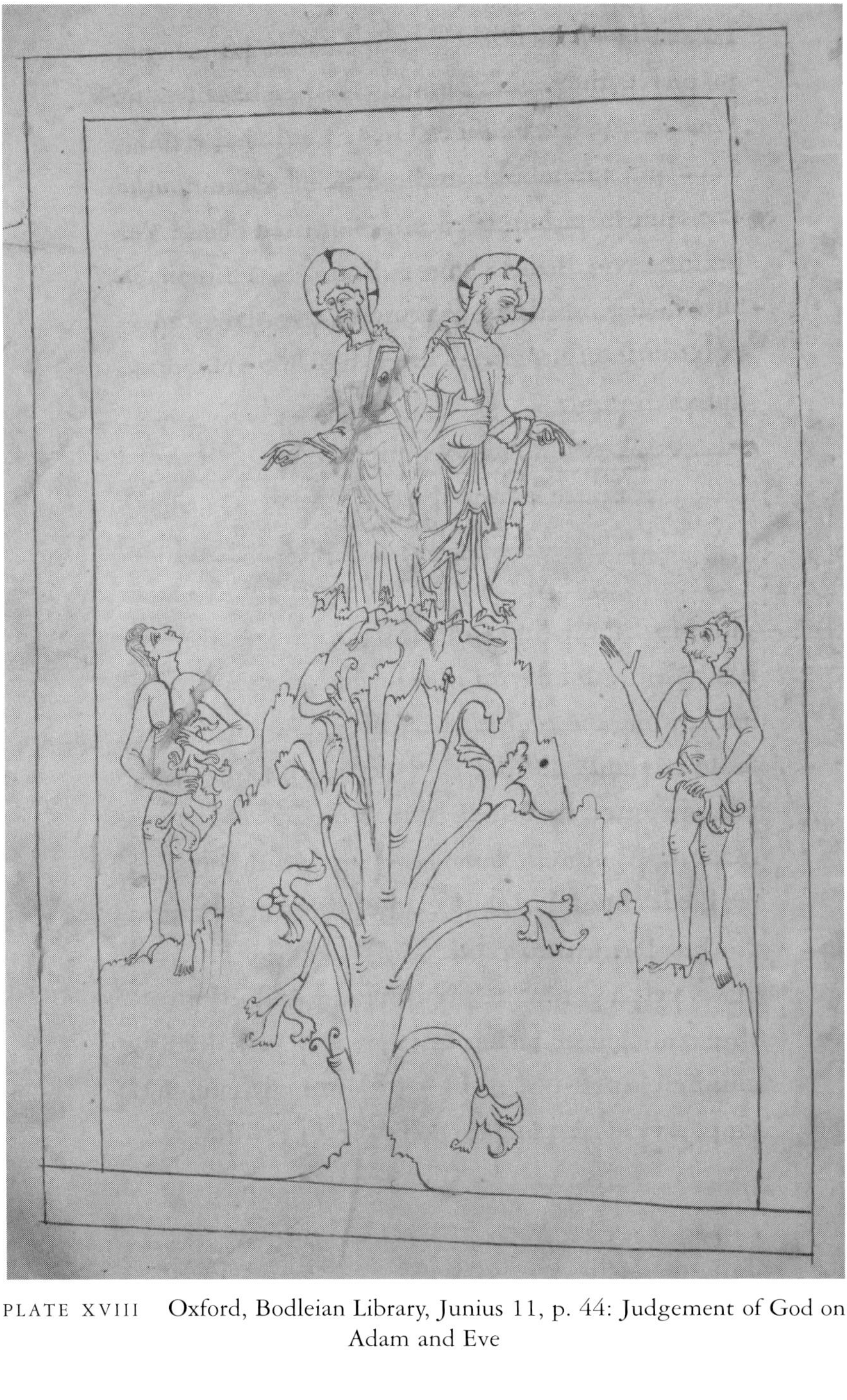

PLATE XVIII Oxford, Bodleian Library, Junius 11, p. 44: Judgement of God on Adam and Eve

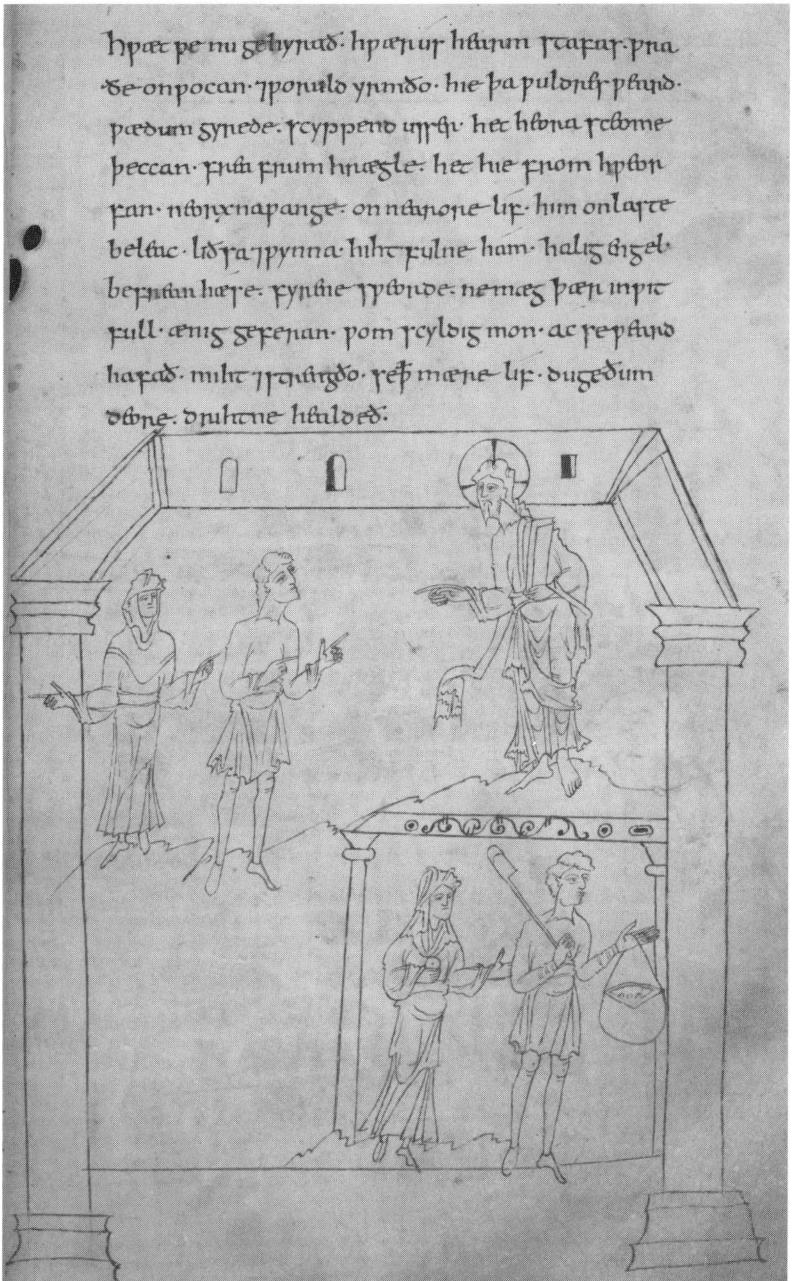

hwæt we nu gehyrað hwær us hearmstafas wra
ðe onwocan ⁊ woruldyrmðo. hie þa wuldres weard
wædum gyrede. scyppend usser. het heora sceome
þeccan. frea frum hrægle. het hie from hweor
fan. neorxnawange. on nearone lif. him on laste
beleac. liðsa ⁊ wynna hihtfulne ham. halig engel
be frean hæse. fyrene sweorde. ne mæg þær inwit
full. ænig geferan. wom scyldig mon. ac se weard
hafað. miht ⁊ strengo. se þæm mære lif. dugeðum
deore. drihtne healdeð.

PLATE XIX Oxford, Bodleian Library, Junius 11, p. 45: Expulsion

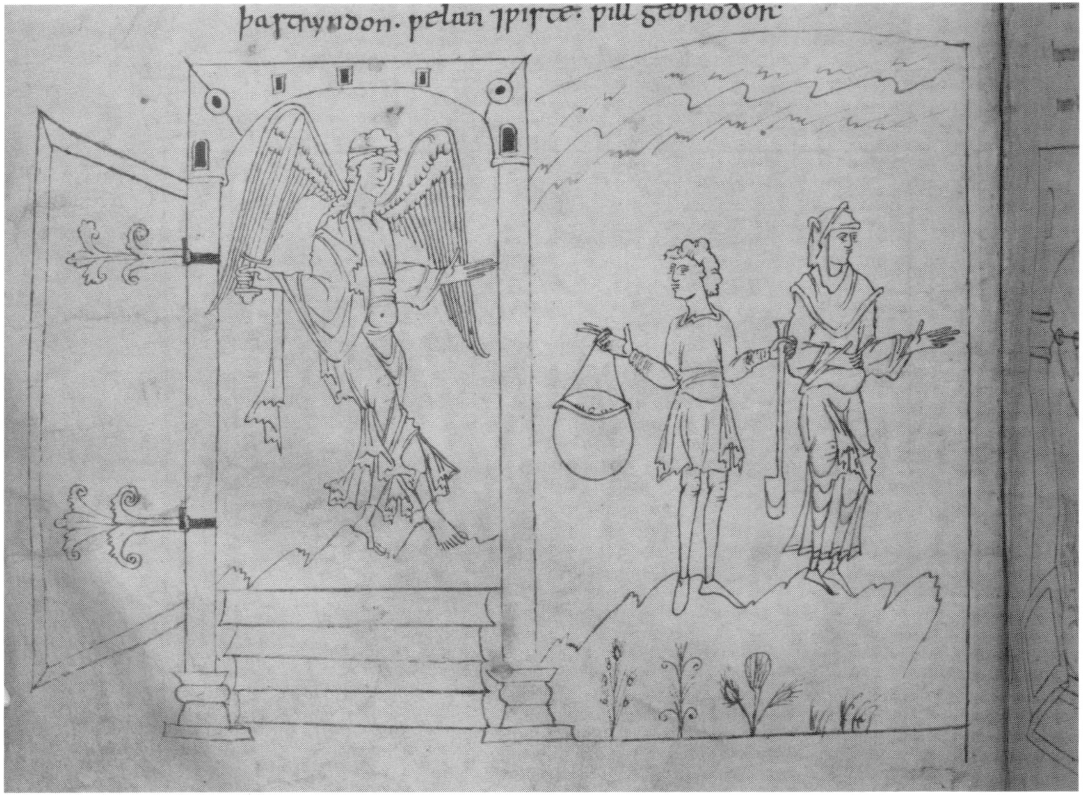

PLATE XX Oxford, Bodleian Library, Junius 11, p. 46: Expulsion

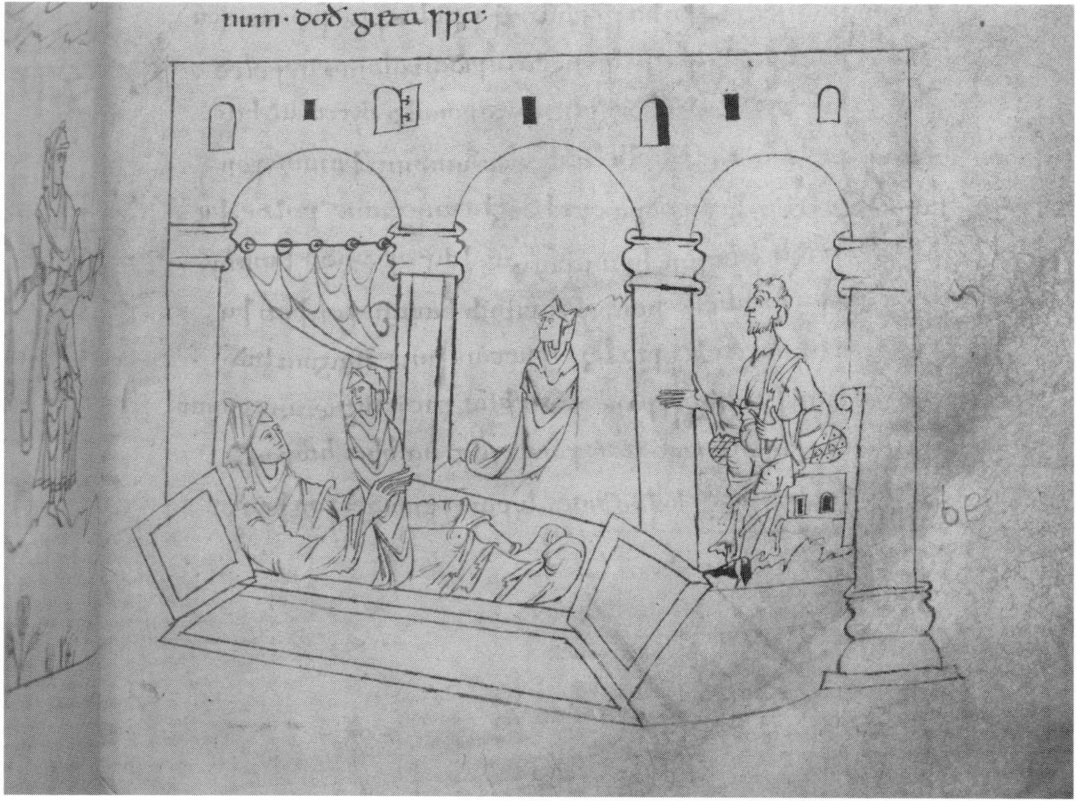

PLATE XXI Oxford, Bodleian Library, Junius 11, p. 47: Birth of Abel

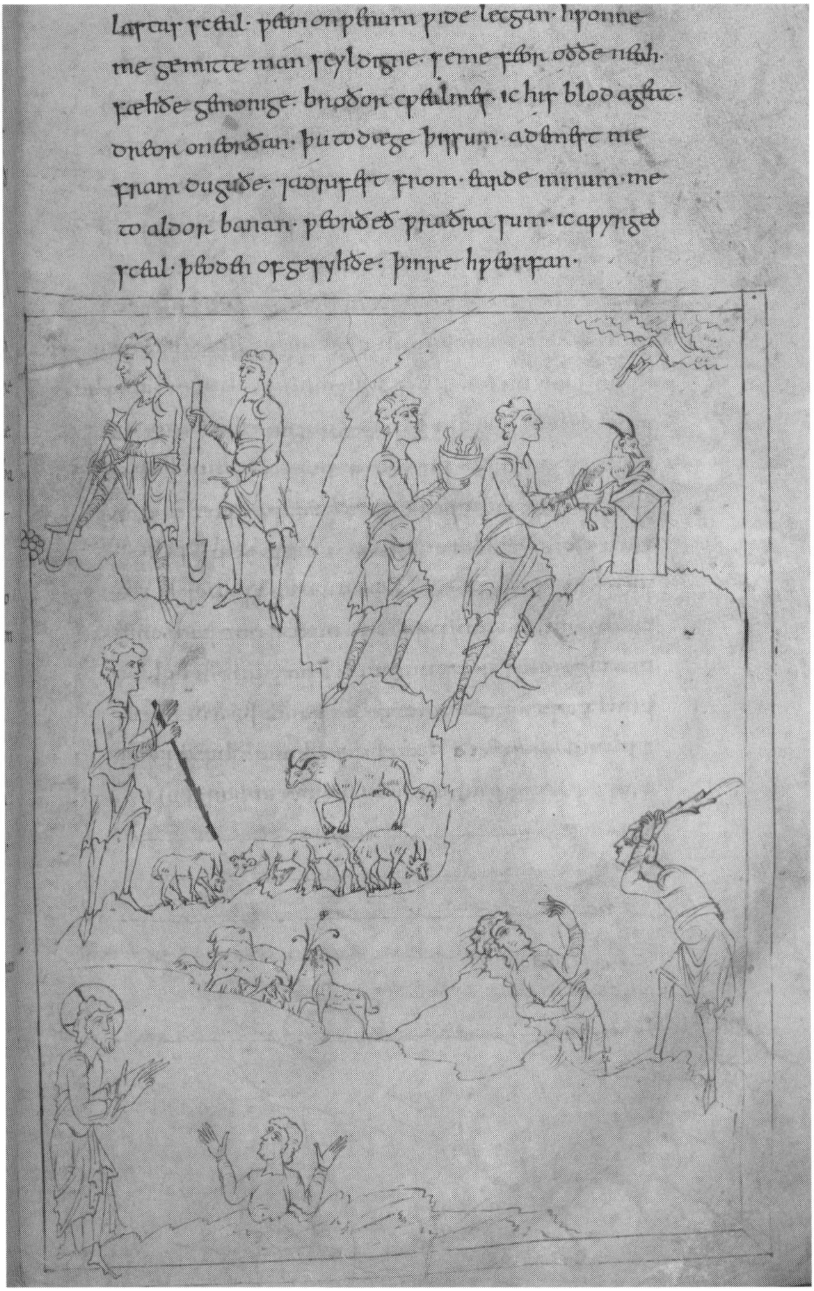
lastas sceal. wean onwealh wide lecgan. hwonne
me gemitte man scyldigne. se me feor oððe neah.
fæhðe gemonige. broðor cwealmes. ic his blod ageat.
dreor on eorðan. þu to dæge þissum. ademdest me
fram duguðe. and adrifest from. earde minum. me
to aldor banan. weorðeð wraðra sum. ic awyrged
sceal. þeoden of gesyhðe. þinre hweorfan.

PLATE XXII Oxford, Bodleian Library, Junius 11, p. 49: Cain and Abel

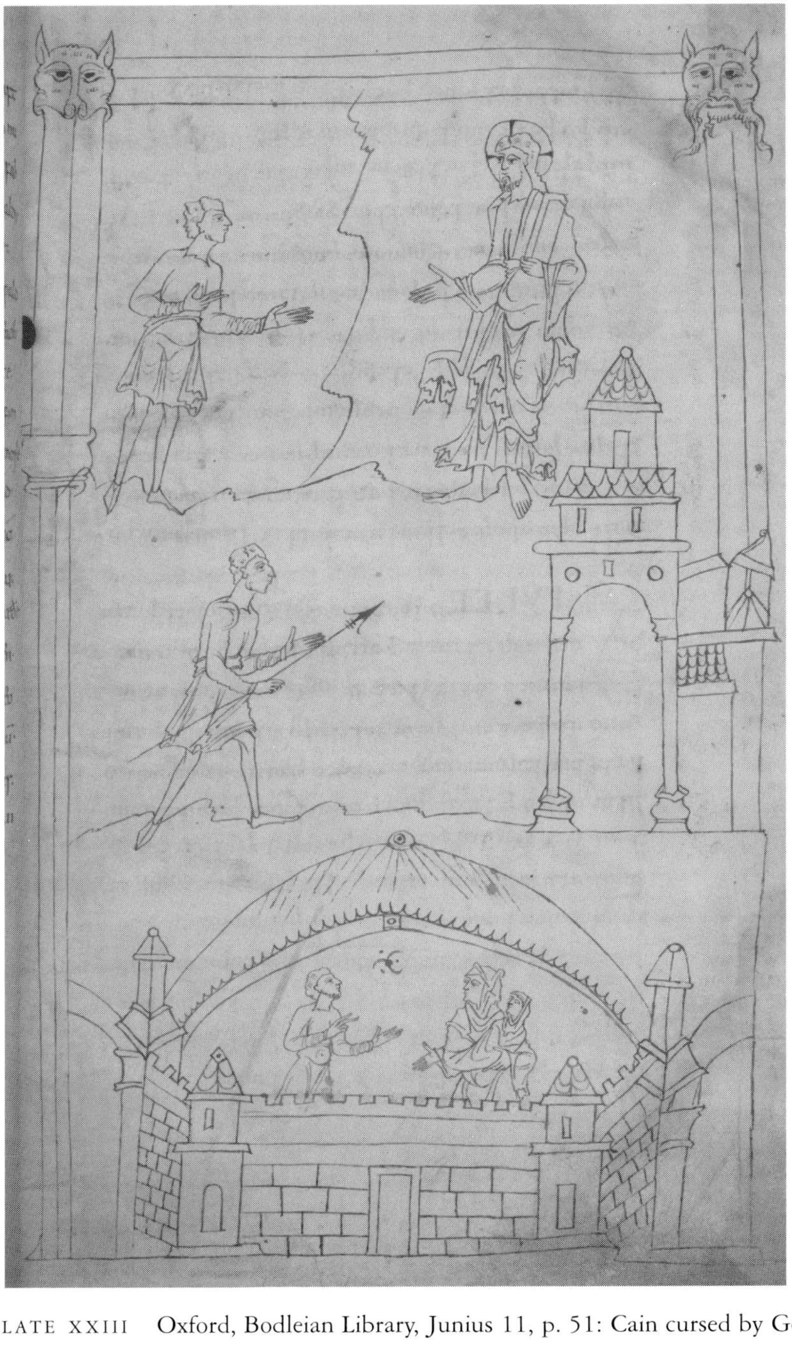

PLATE XXIII Oxford, Bodleian Library, Junius 11, p. 51: Cain cursed by God

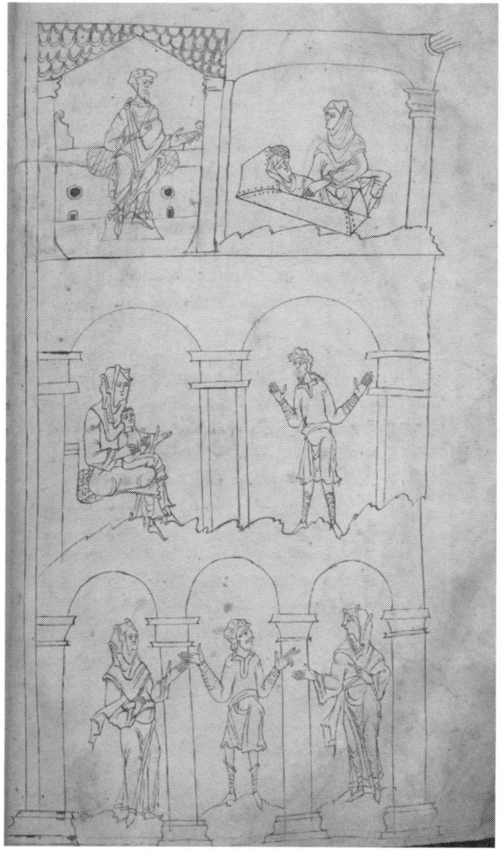

PLATE XXIVa Oxford, Bodleian Library, Junius 11, p. 53: Descent from Cain

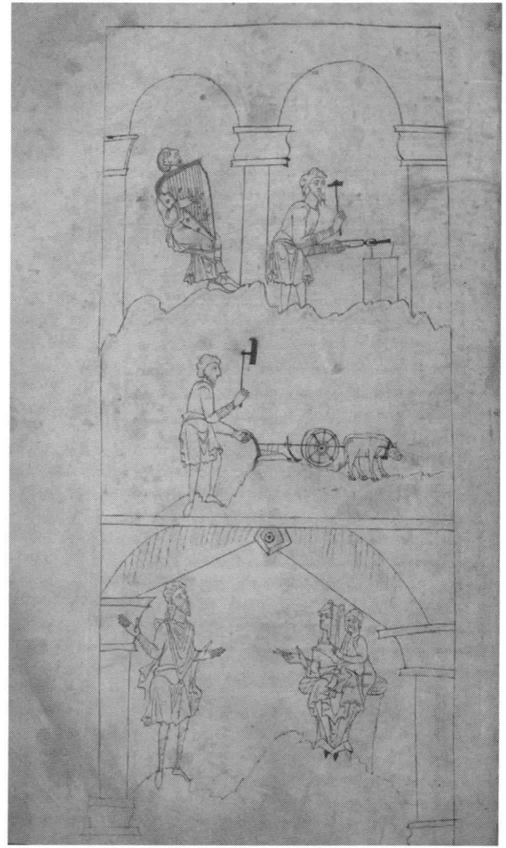

PLATE XXIVb Oxford, Bodleian Library, Junius 11, p. 54: Iared, Iubal and Tubal-Cain

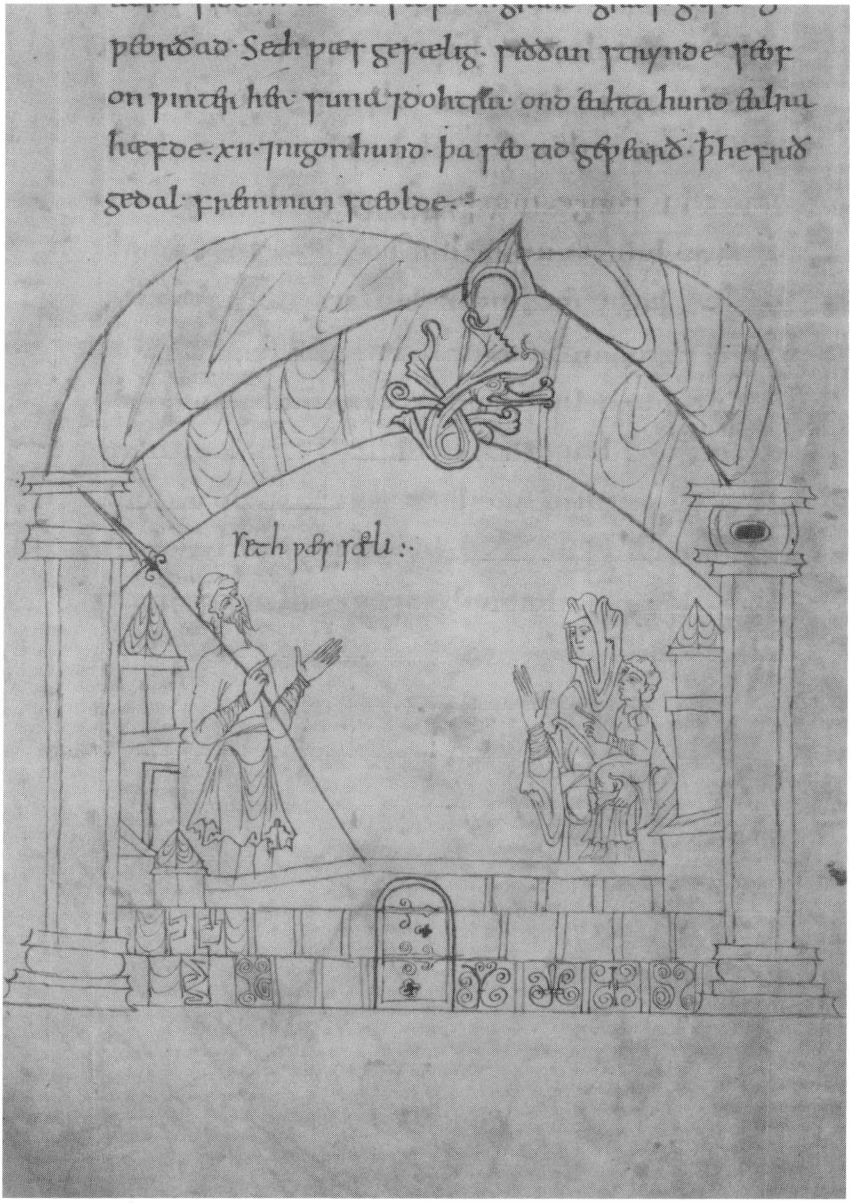

PLATE XXV Oxford, Bodleian Library, Junius 11, p. 56: Seth

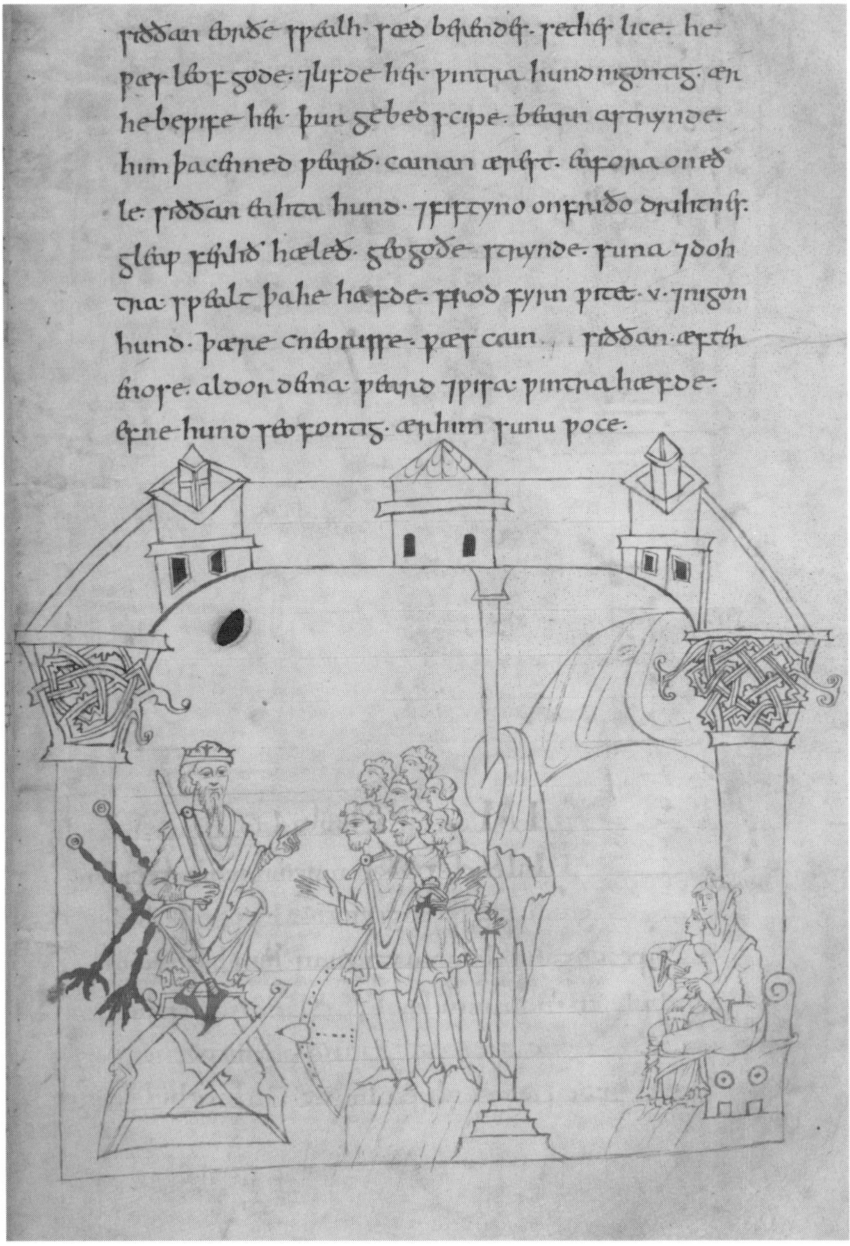

PLATE XXVI Oxford, Bodleian Library, Junius 11, p. 57: Cainan

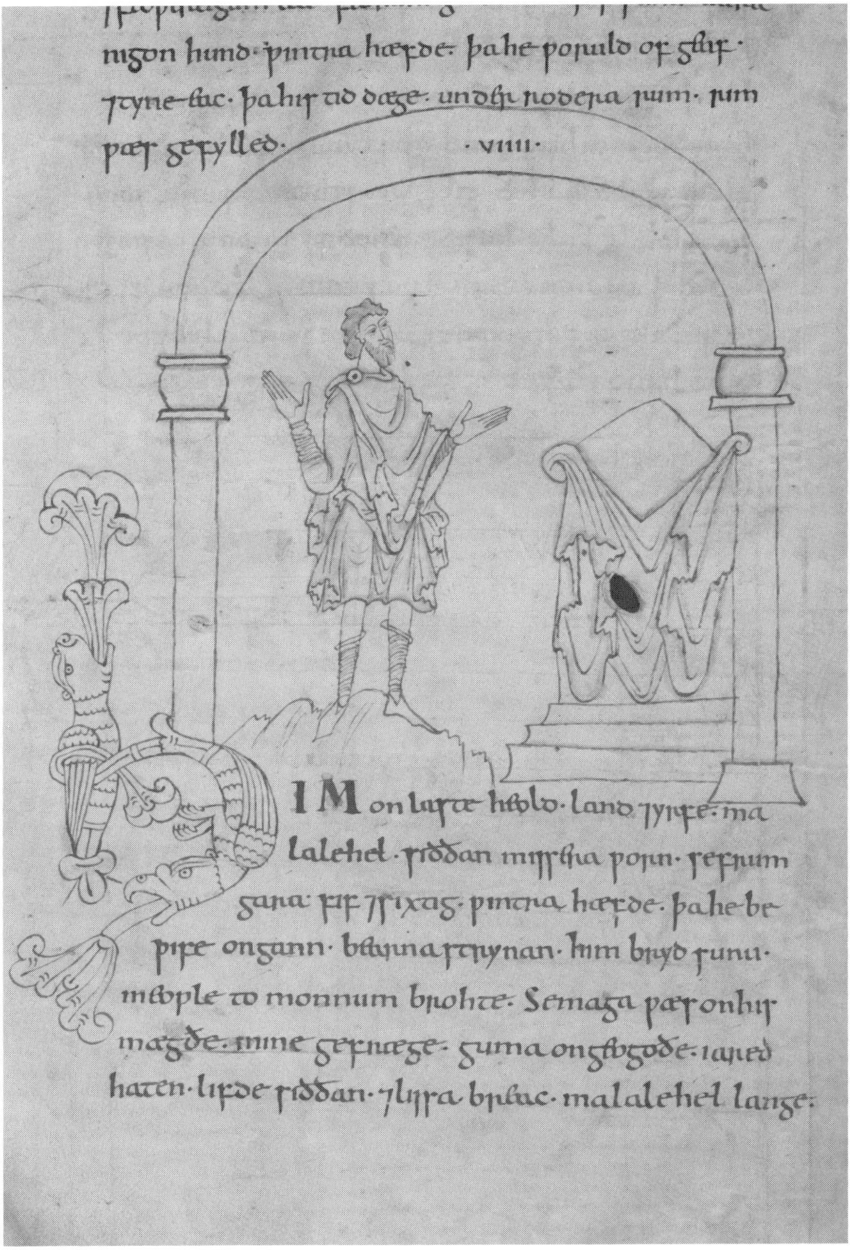

PLATE XXVII Oxford, Bodleian Library, Junius 11, p. 58: Malaleel

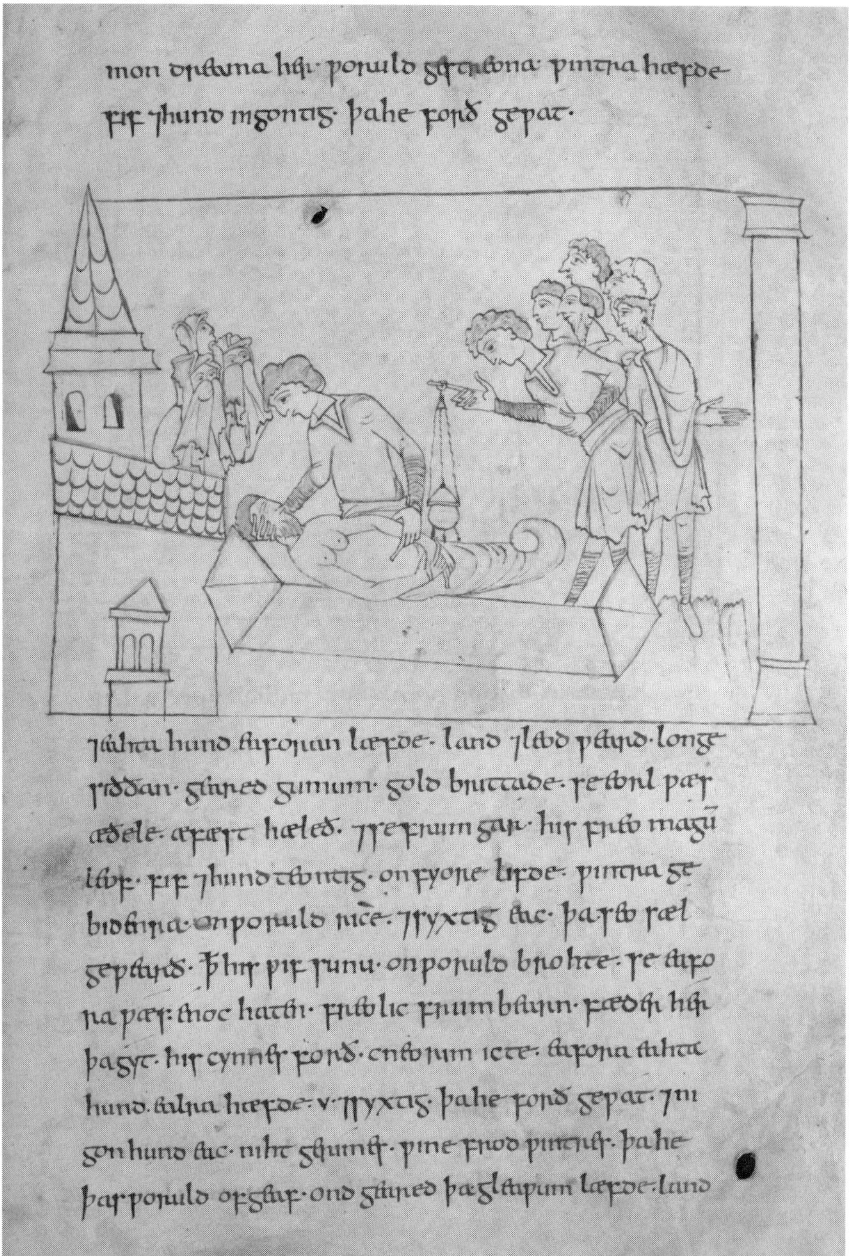

PLATE XXVIII Oxford, Bodleian Library, Junius 11, p. 59: Death of Malaleel

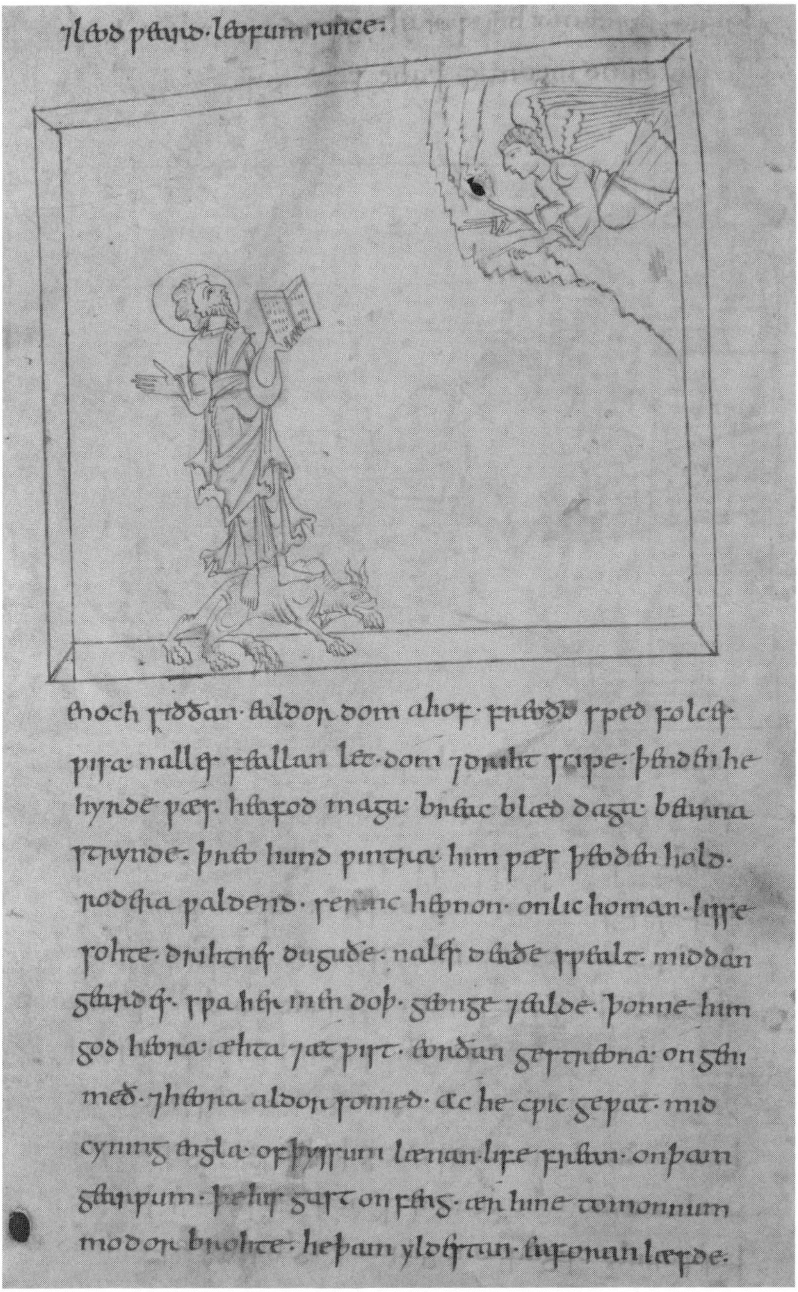

PLATE XXIX Oxford, Bodleian Library, Junius 11, p. 61: Enoch

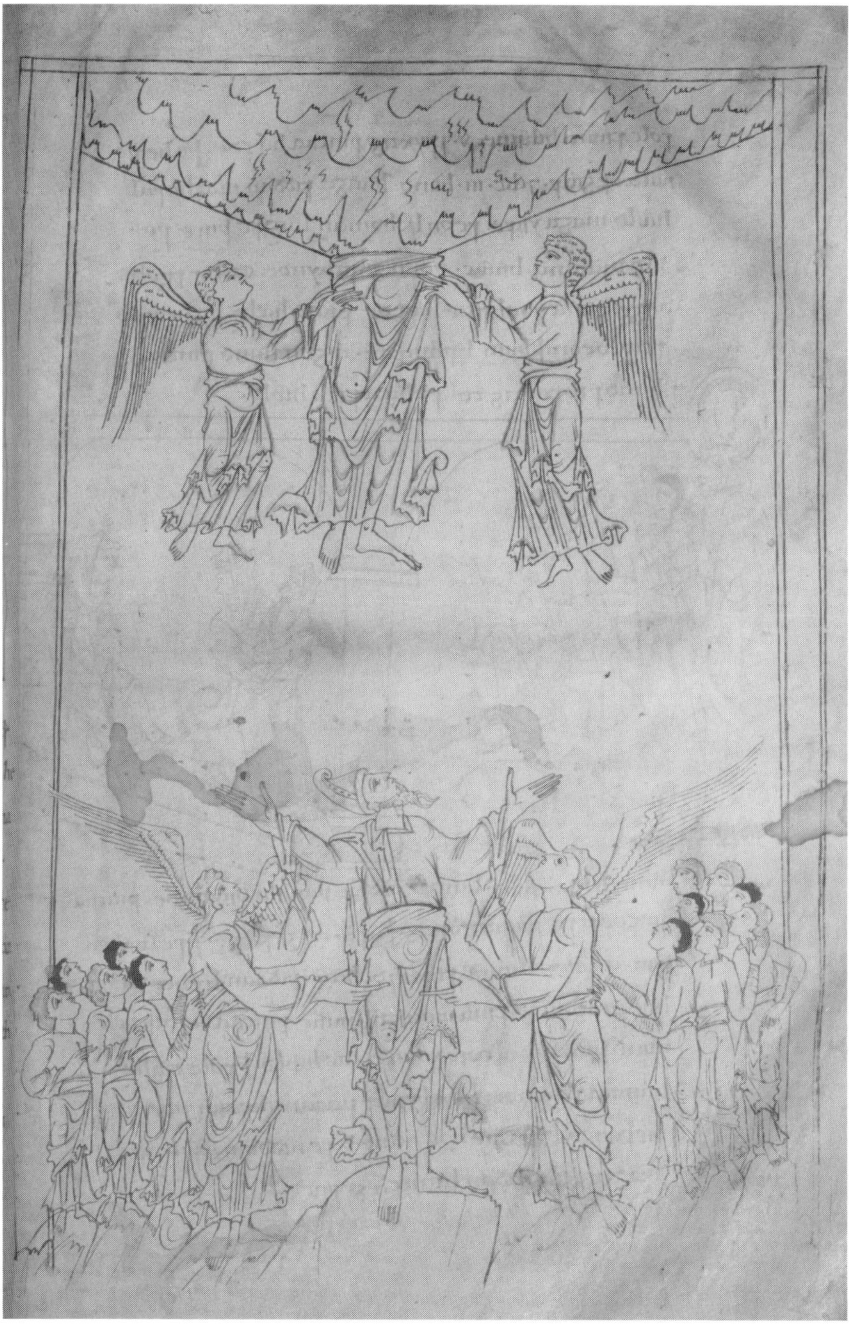

PLATE XXX Oxford, Bodleian Library, Junius 11, p. 61: Ascension of Enoch

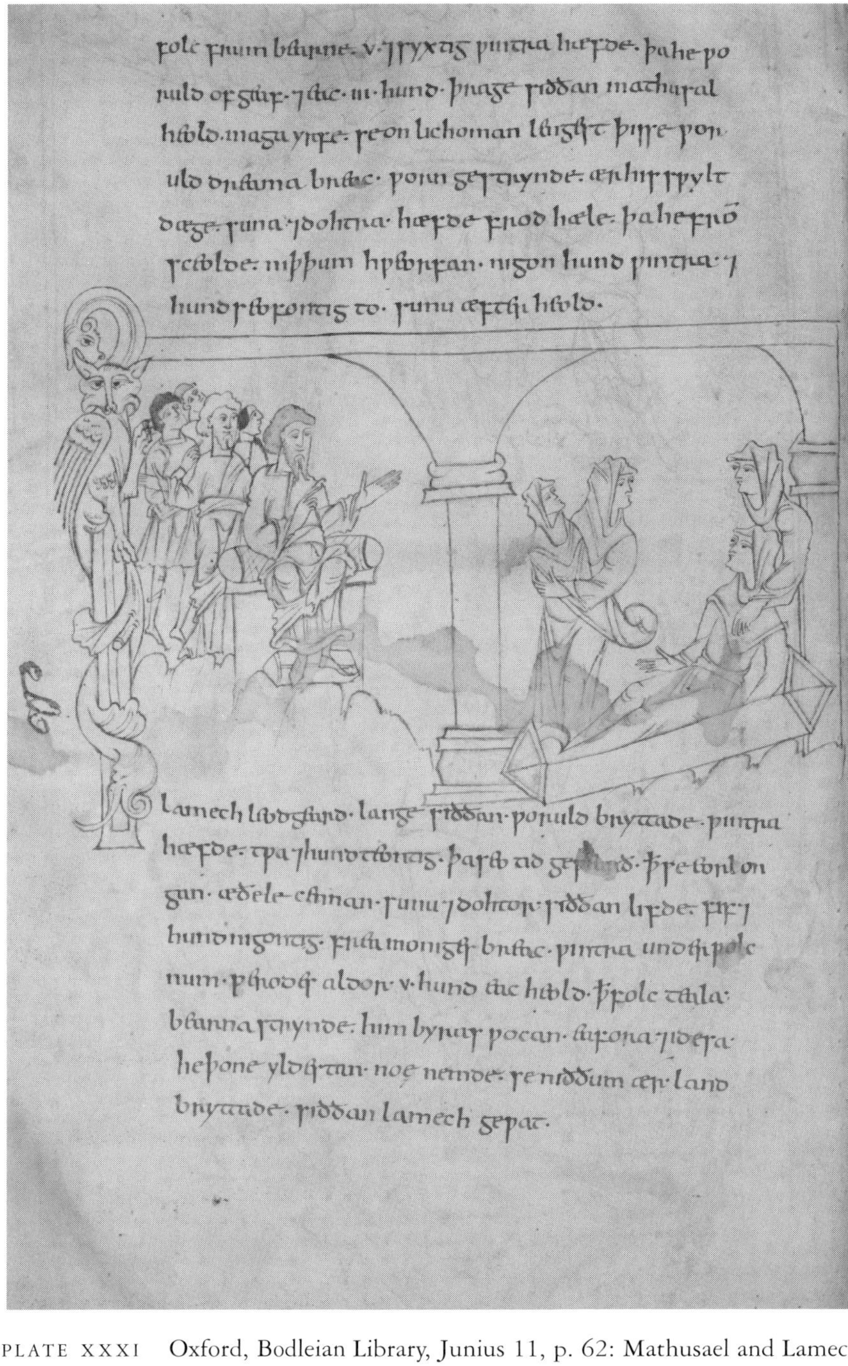

PLATE XXXI Oxford, Bodleian Library, Junius 11, p. 62: Mathusael and Lamech

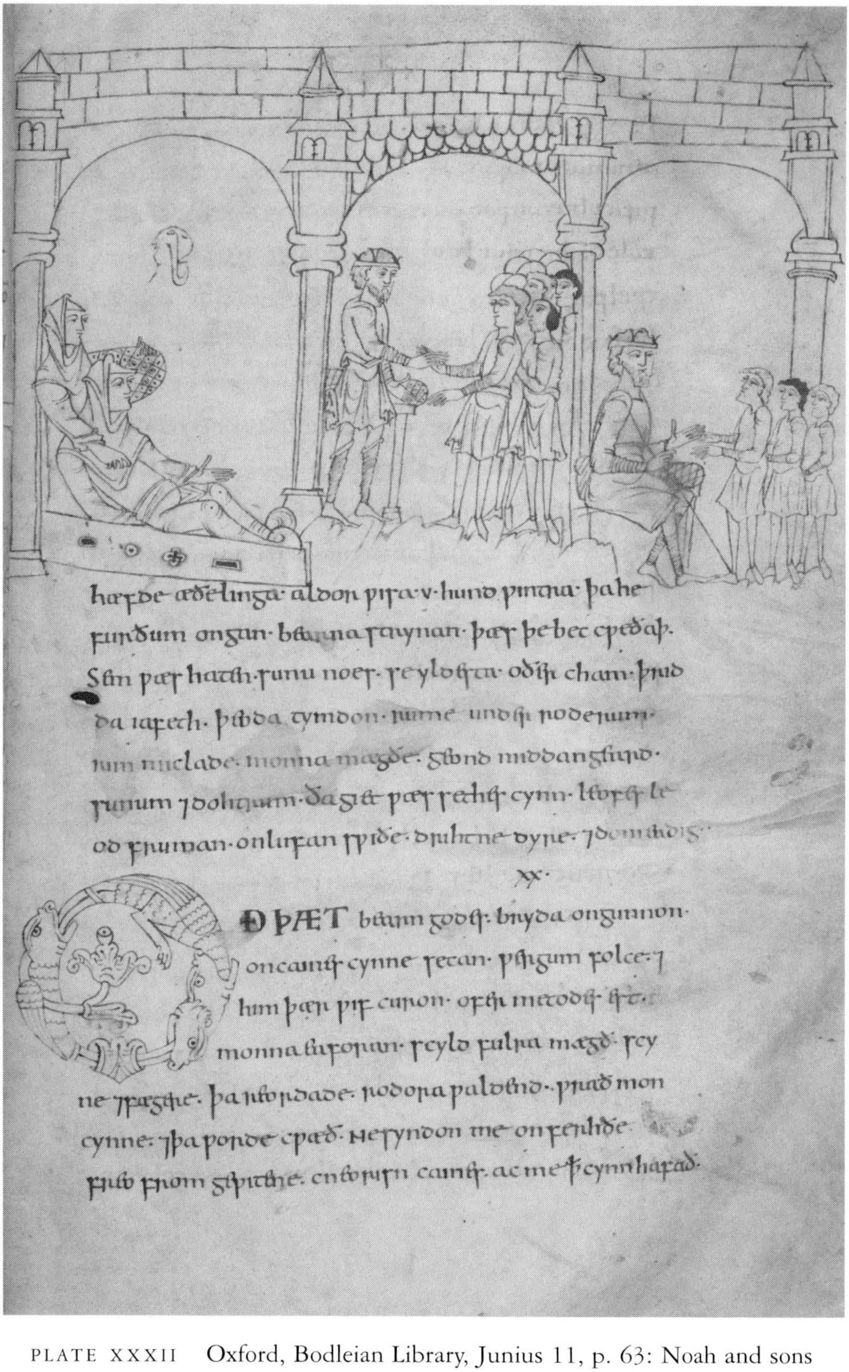

PLATE XXXII Oxford, Bodleian Library, Junius 11, p. 63: Noah and sons

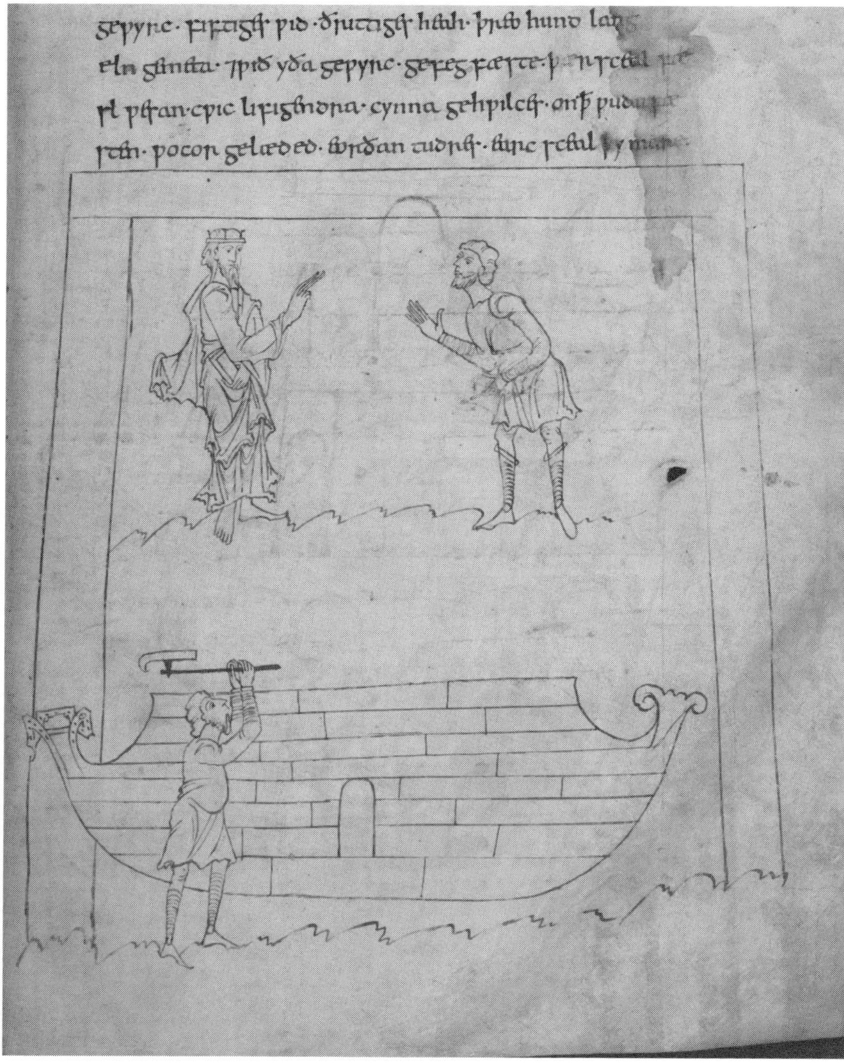

PLATE XXXIII Oxford, Bodleian Library, Junius 11, p. 65: Noah commanded to build ark

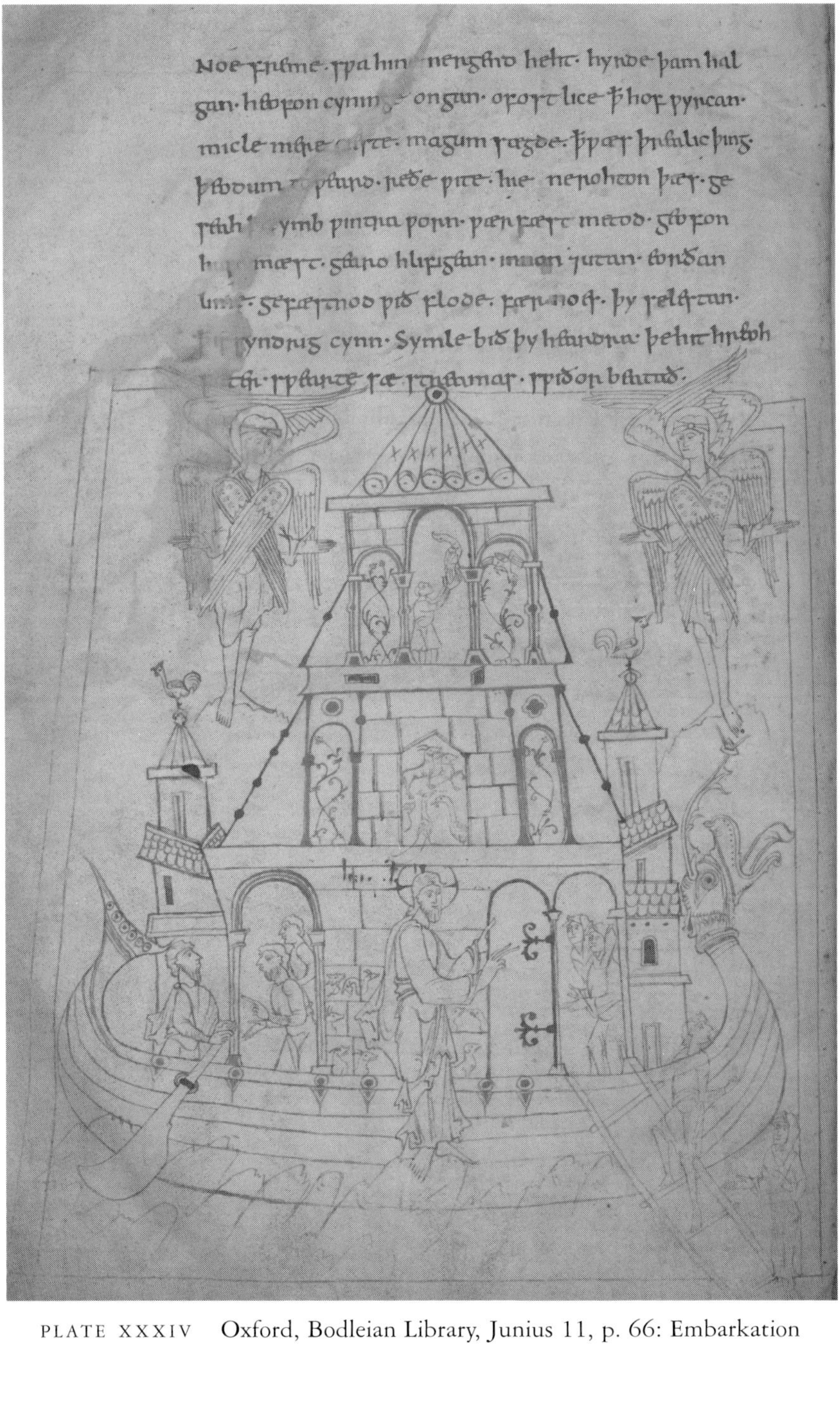

PLATE XXXIV Oxford, Bodleian Library, Junius 11, p. 66: Embarkation

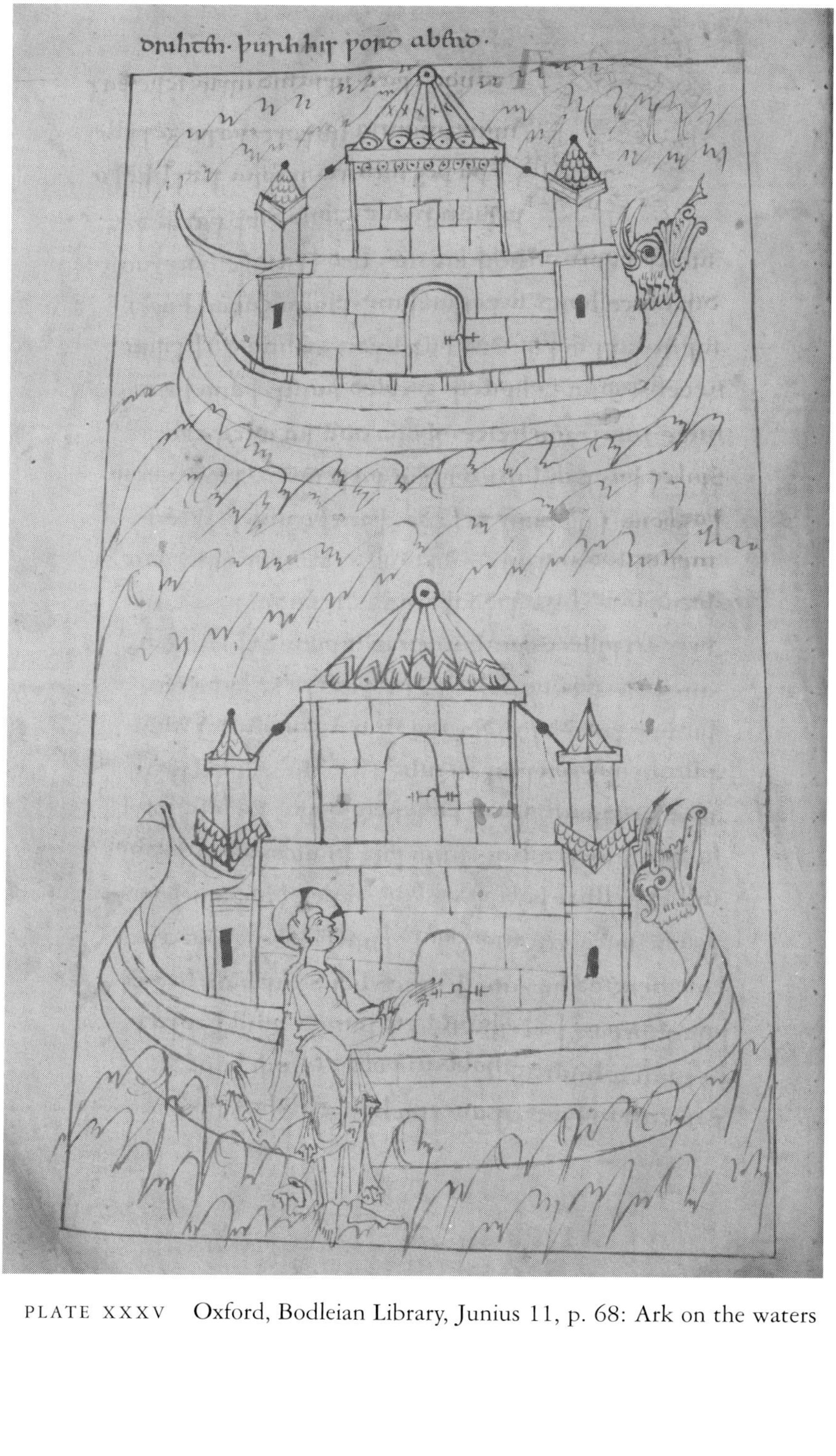

PLATE XXXV Oxford, Bodleian Library, Junius 11, p. 68: Ark on the waters

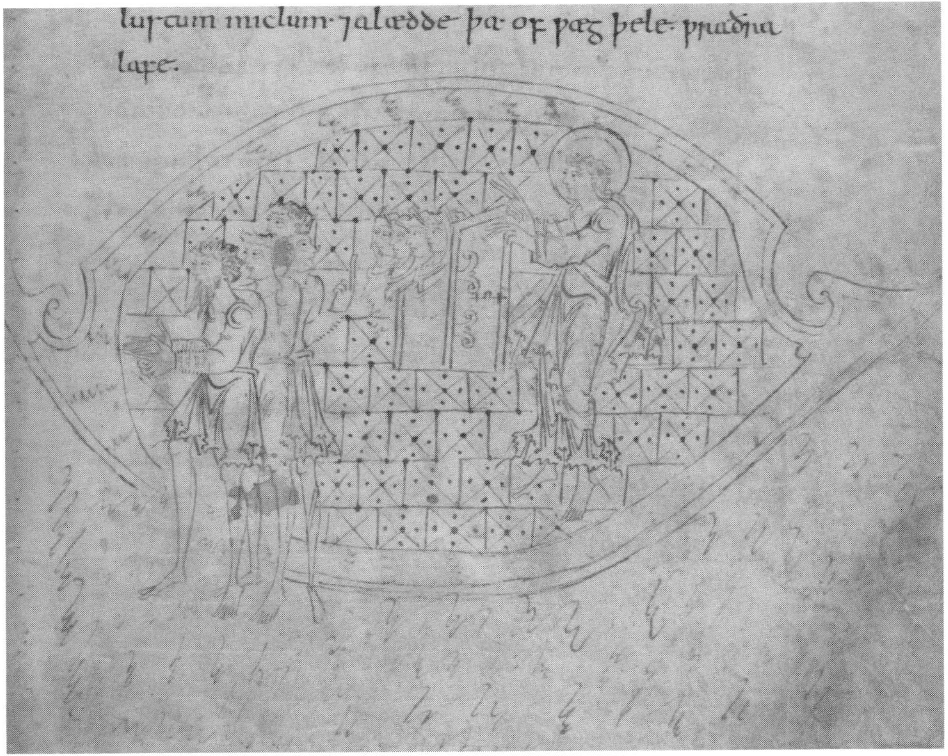

PLATE XXXVI Oxford, Bodleian Library, Junius 11, p. 73: Disembarkation

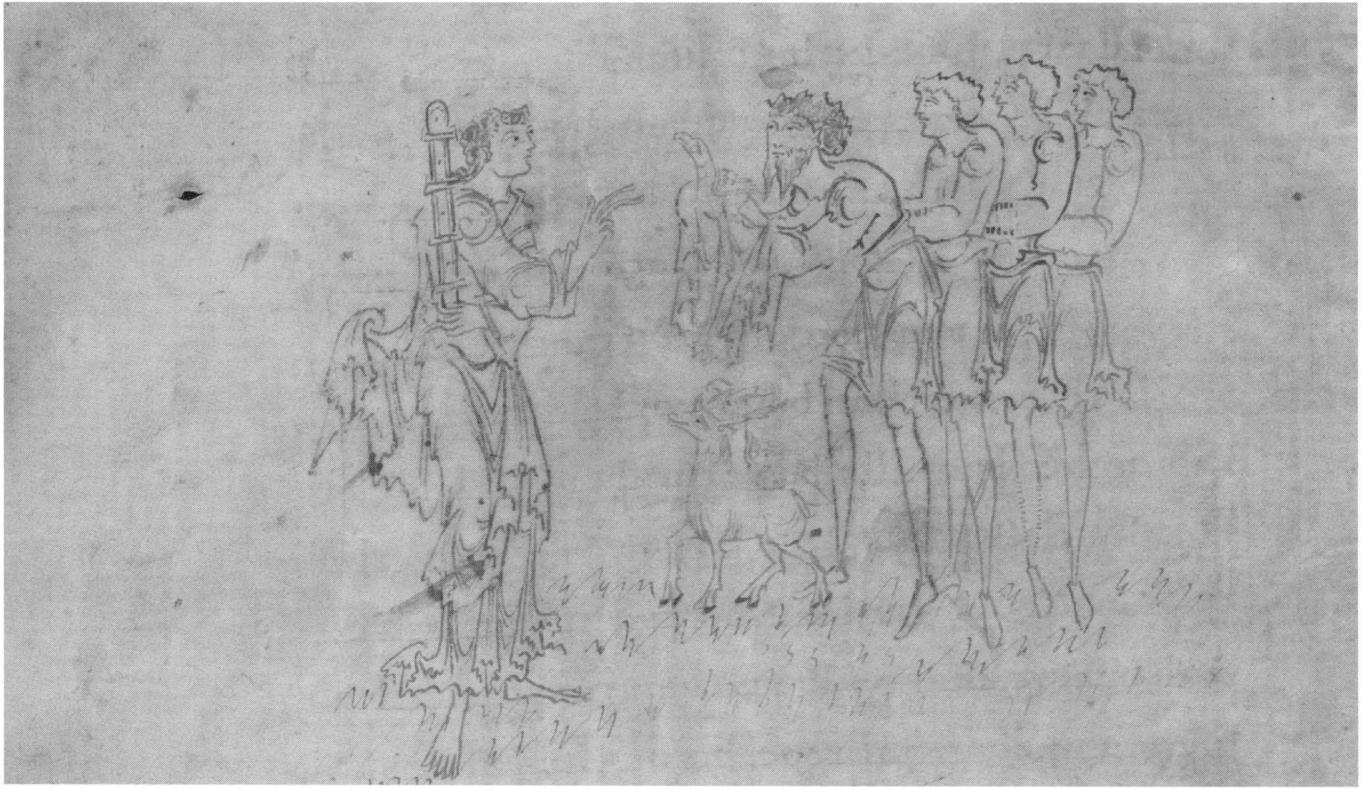

PLATE XXXVII Oxford, Bodleian Library, Junius 11, p. 74: Noah offers sacrifice

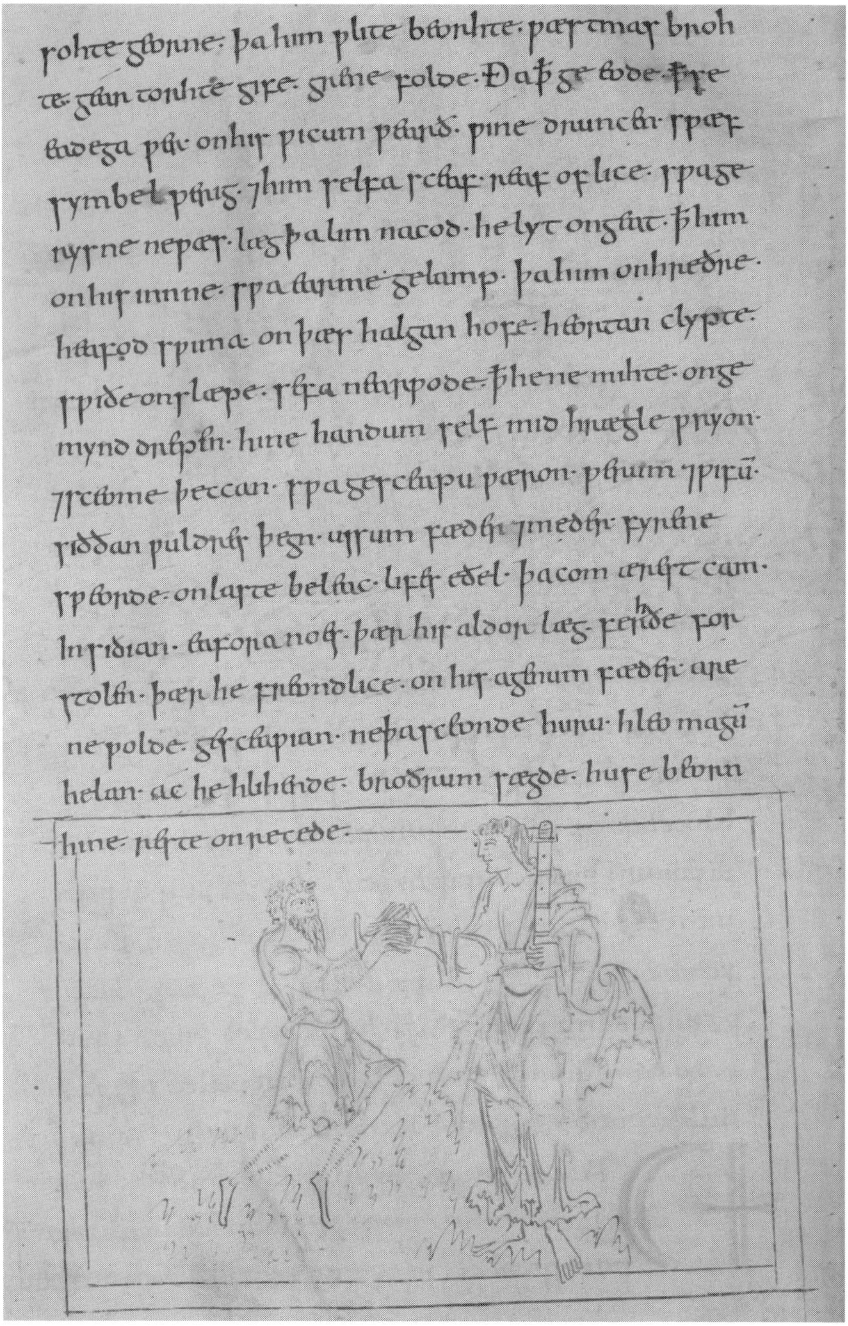

wohte geornne· þa him wlite beorhte· wæstmas brohte· geartorhte gife· grene wolde· Ða þæt geeode· þæt se eadega wer· on his wicum wearð· wine druncen· swæf symbel werig· 7 him selfa sceaf· reaf of lice· swa gerysne ne wæs· læg þa limnacod· he lyt ongeat· þæt him on his inne· swa earme gelamp· þa him on hreðre· heafodswima· on þæs halgan hofe· heortan clypte· swiðe on slæpe· sefa nearwode· þæt he ne mihte· ongemynd drepen· hine handum self· mid hrægle wryon· 7 sceome þeccan· swa gesceapu wæron· werum 7 wifum· siððan wuldres þegn· ussum fæder 7 meder· fyrene sweorde· on laste beleac· lifes eðel· þa com ærest cam· in siðian· eafora noes· þær his aldor læg· ferhðe forstolen· þær he freondlice· on his agenum fæder· are ne wolde· gesceawian· ne þa sceonde huru· hleo magum helan· ac he hlihhende· broðrum sægde· hu se beorn hine reste on recede·

PLATE XXXVIII Oxford, Bodleian Library, Junius 11, p. 76: Covenant with Noah

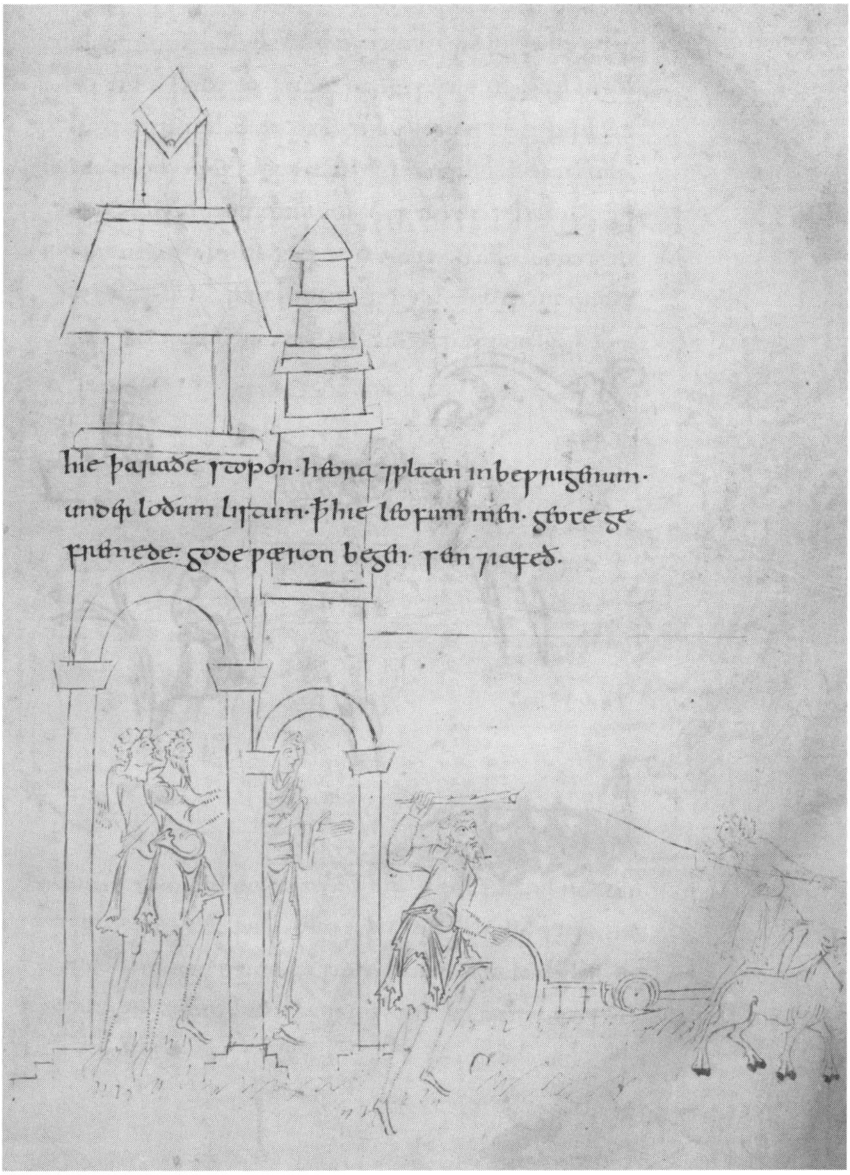

PLATE XXXIX Oxford, Bodleian Library, Junius 11, p. 77: Noah ploughing

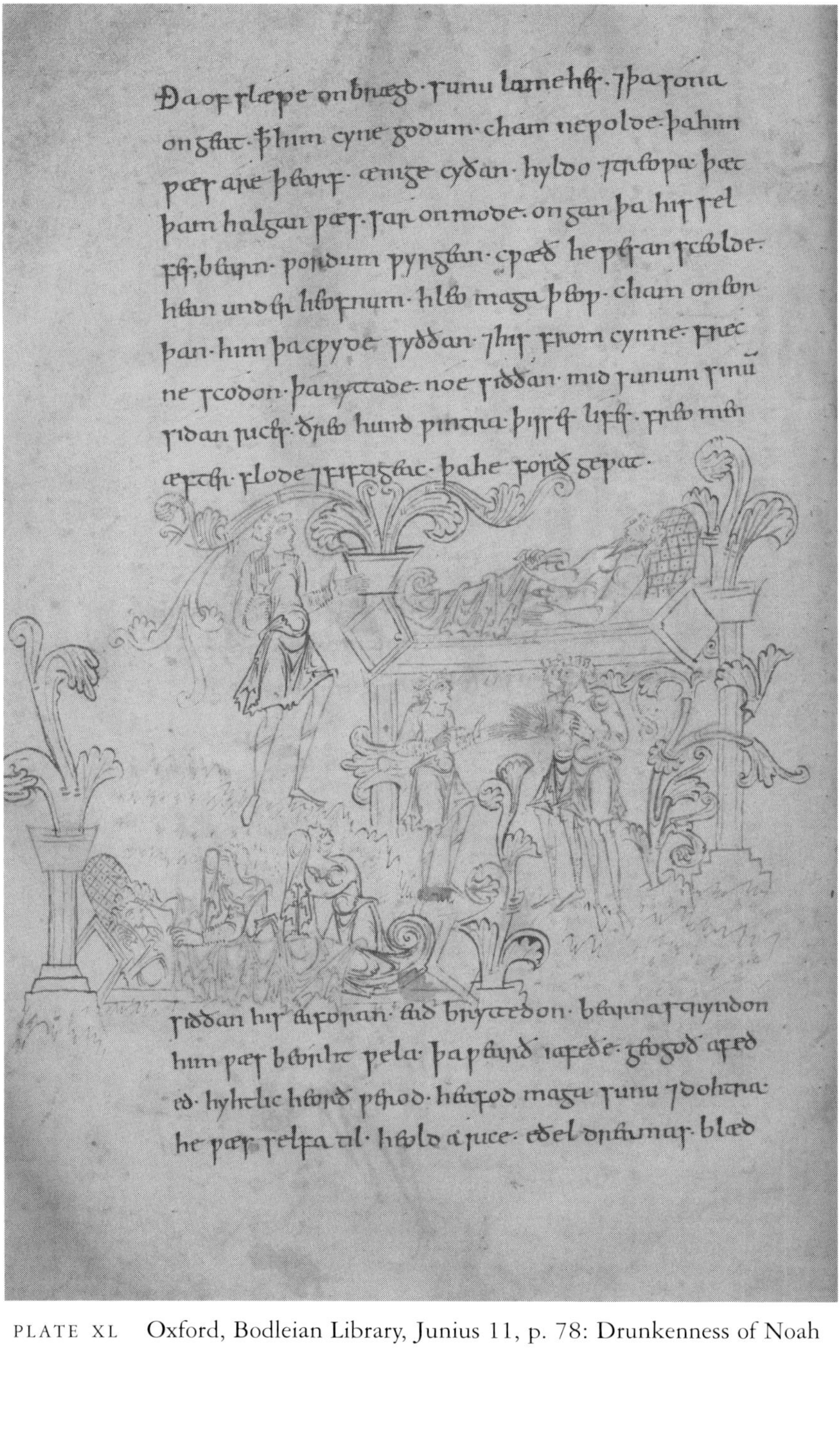

PLATE XL Oxford, Bodleian Library, Junius 11, p. 78: Drunkenness of Noah

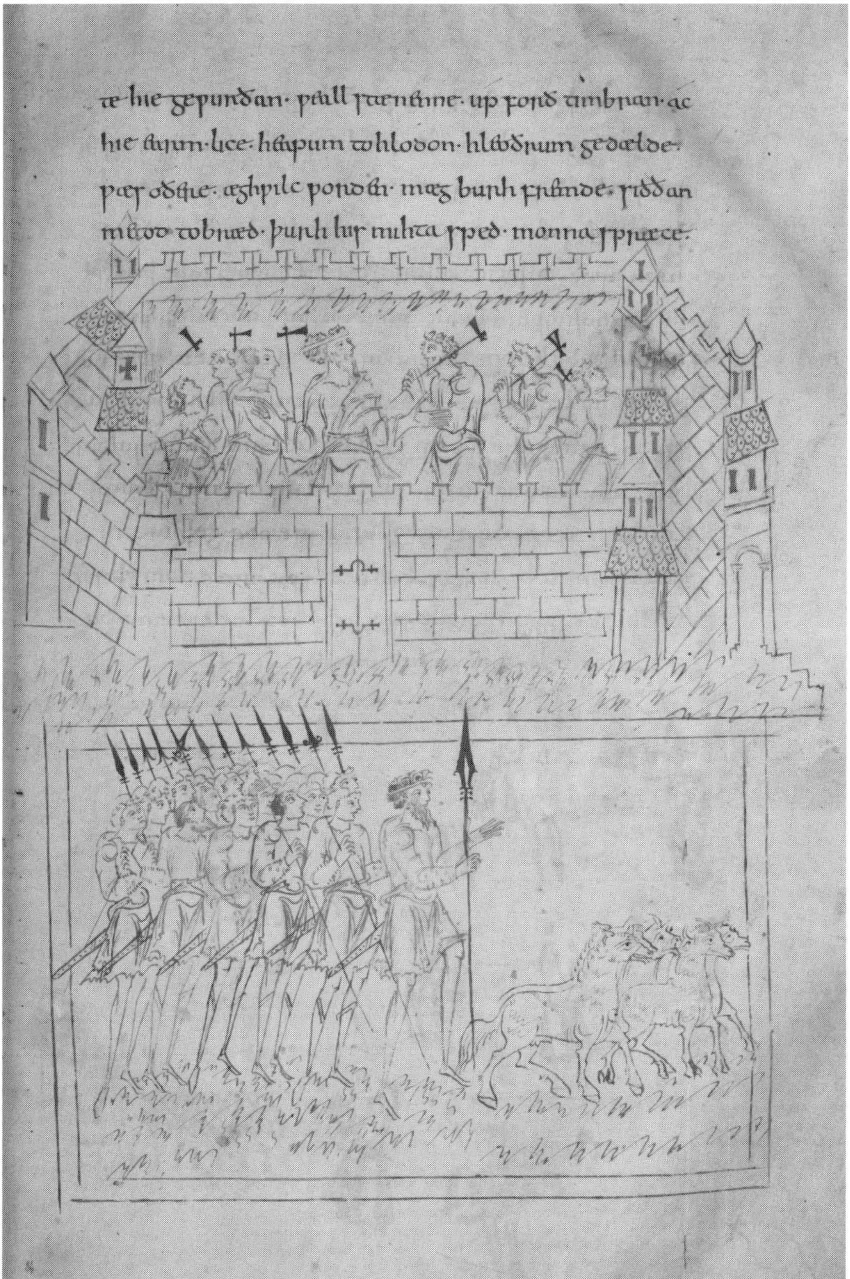

PLATE XLI Oxford, Bodleian Library, Junius 11, p. 81: Nimrod

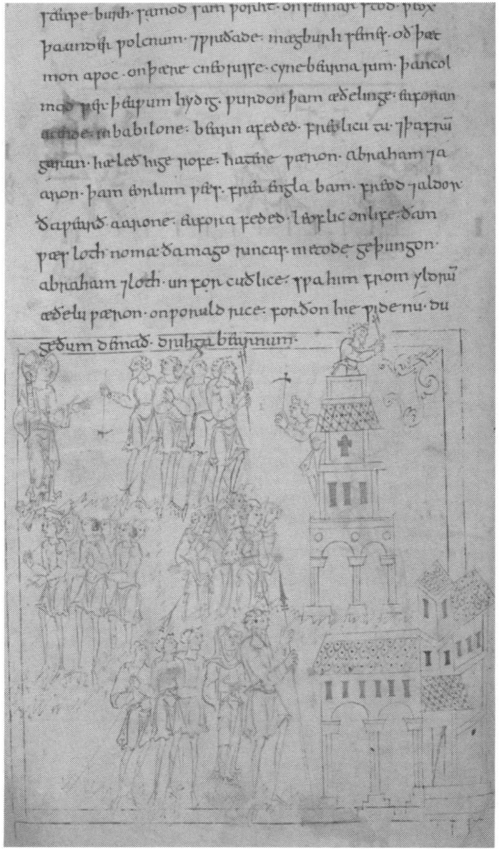

PLATE XLIIa Oxford, Bodleian Library, Junius 11, p. 82: Tower of Babel

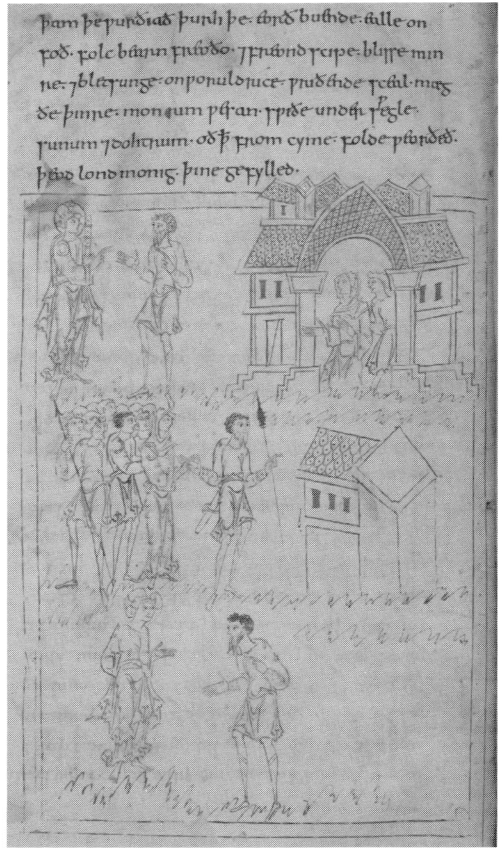

PLATE XLIIb Oxford, Bodleian Library, Junius 11, p. 84: Abraham with God

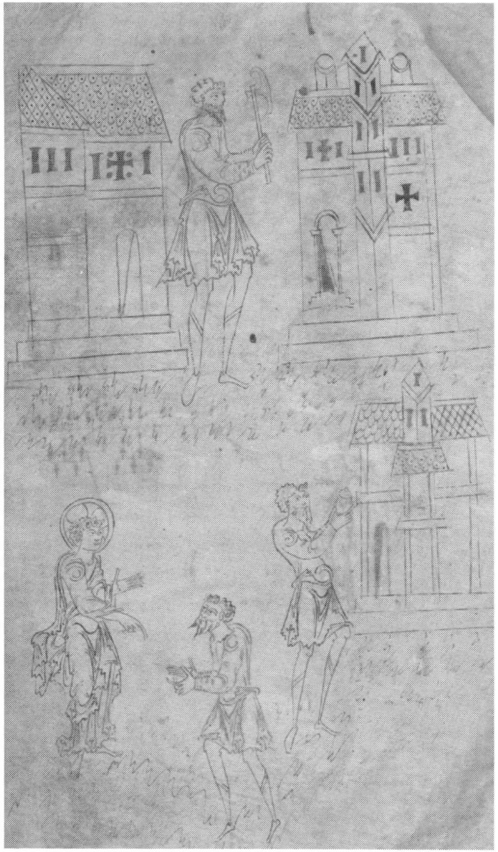

PLATE XLIIIa Oxford, Bodleian Library, Junius 11, p. 87: Abraham builds altar

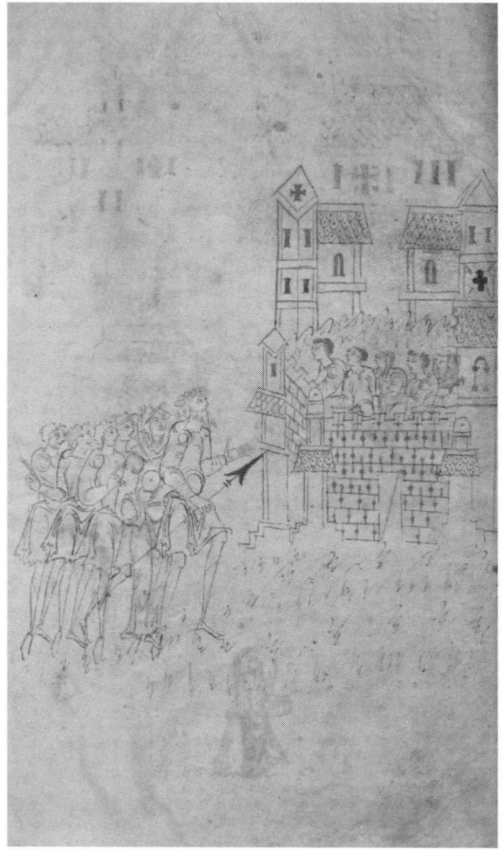

PLATE XLIIb Oxford, Bodleian Library, Junius 11, p. 88: Abraham's approach to Egypt

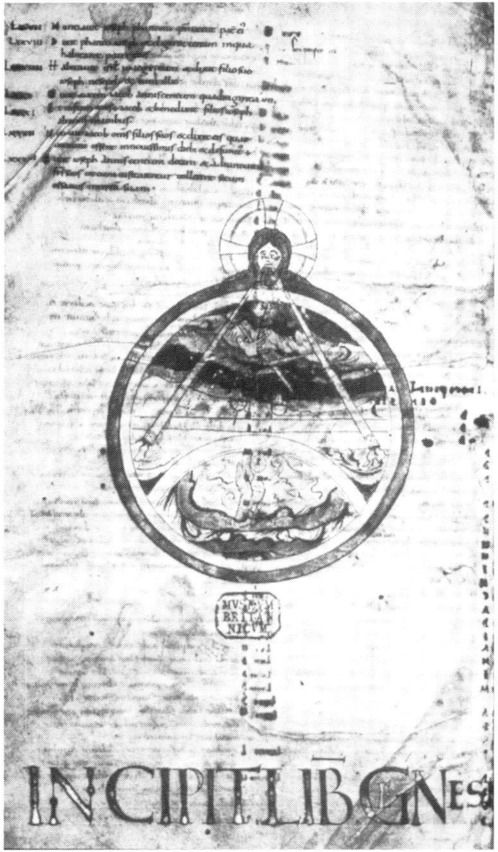

PLATE XLIVa London, British Library, Royal I.E VII (Royal Bible), fol. 1v: Creation

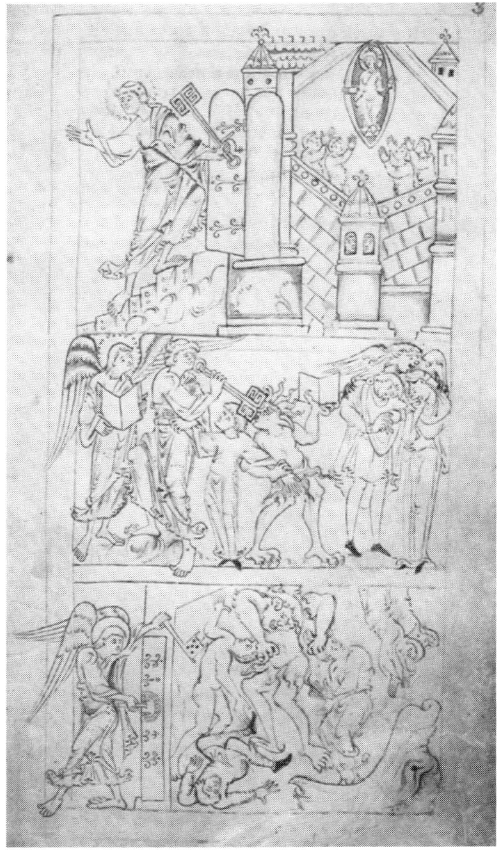

PLATE XLIVb London, British Library, Stowe 944 (New Minster Liber Vitae), fol. 7r: Last Judgement

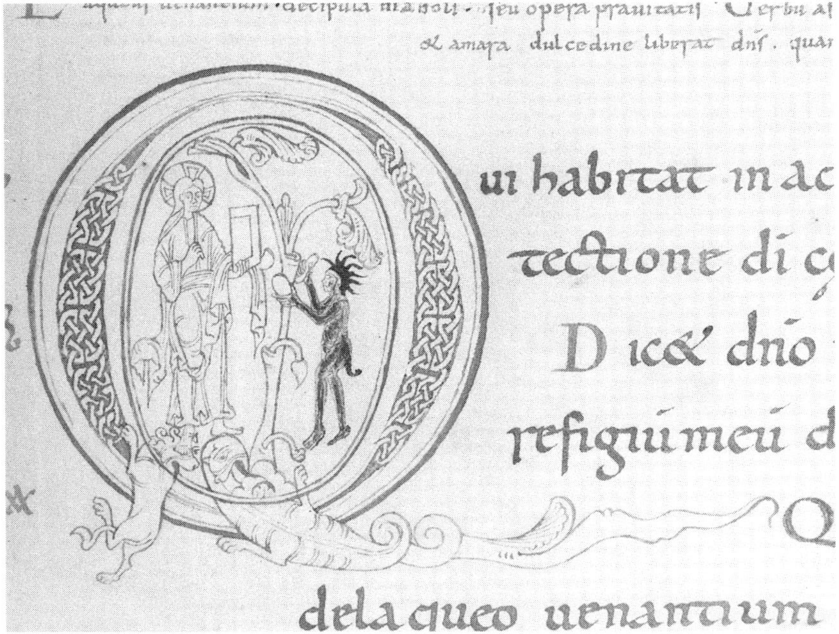

PLATE XLVb Boulogne-sur-Mer, Bibliothèque Municipale, 20 (Odbert Psalter), fol. 101: Temptation of Christ

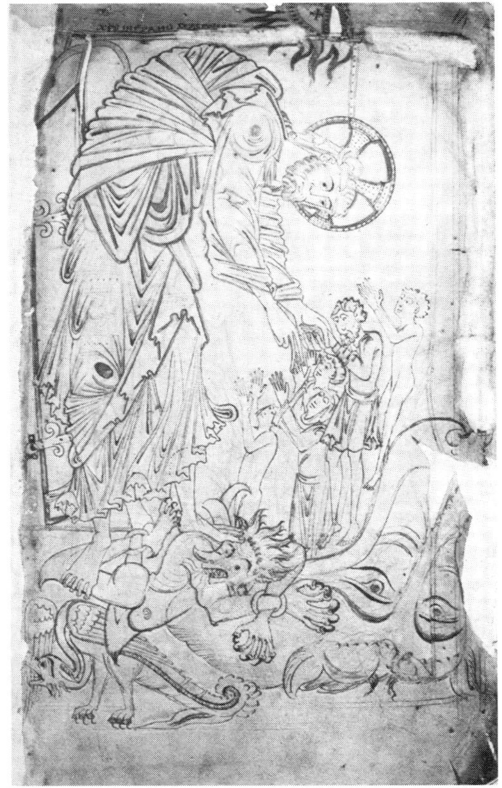

PLATE XLVa London, British Library, Cotton Tiberius C. vi (Tiberius Psalter), fol. 14: Harrowing of Hell

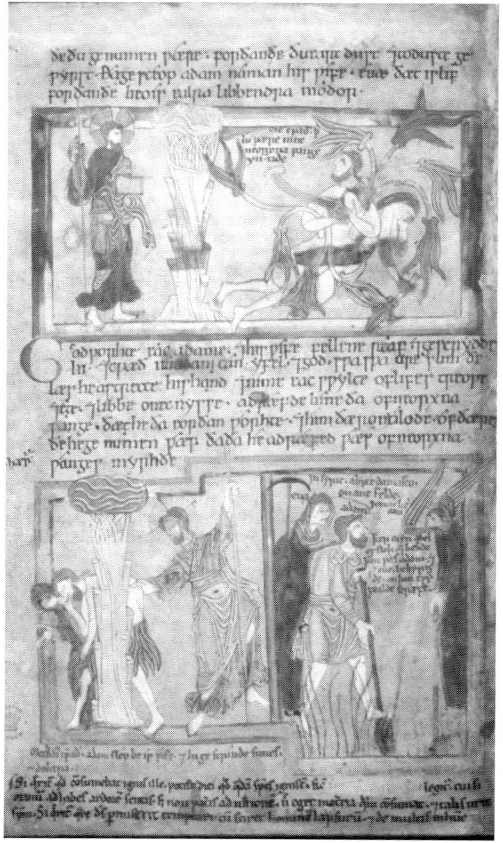

PLATE XLVIa London, British Library, Cotton Claudius B. iv (Hexateuch), fol. 7v: God's Judgement on Adam and Eve

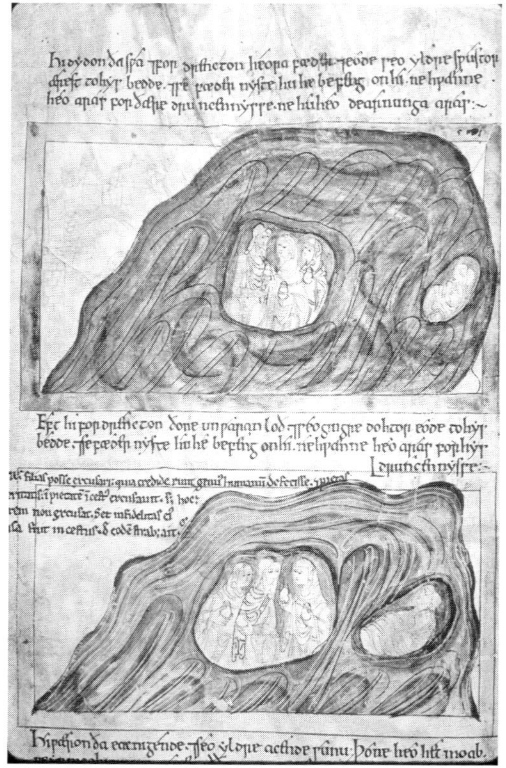

PLATE XLVIb London, British Library, Cotton Claudius B. iv (Hexateuch), fol. 33v: Lot and his daughters

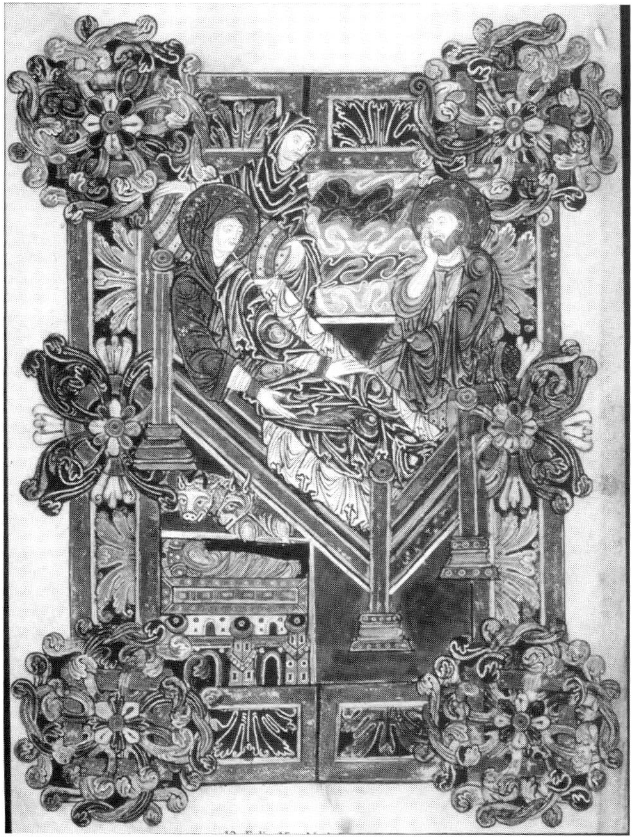

PLATE XLVIIa London, British Library, Additional 49598 (Benedictional of Æthelwold), fol. 15v: Nativity

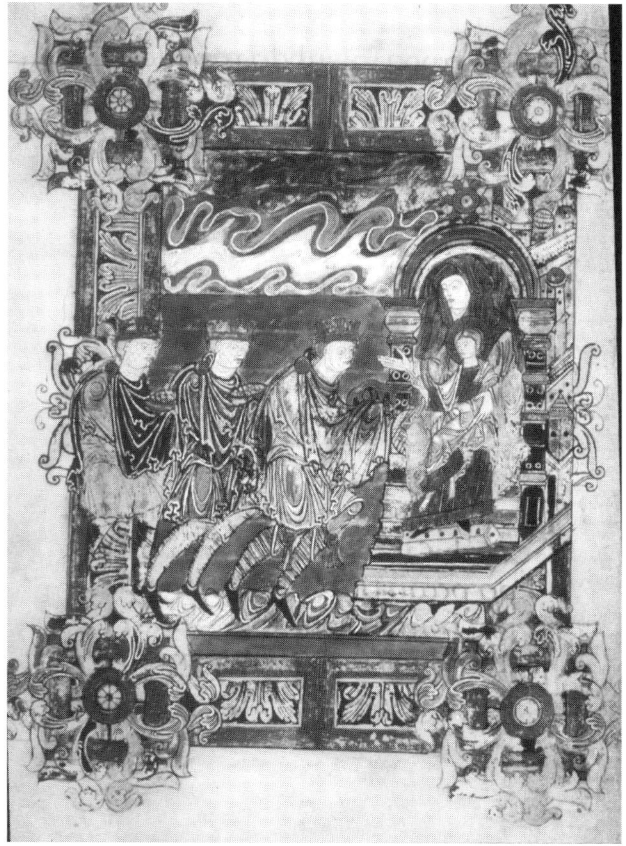

PLATE XLVIIb London, British Library, Additional 49598 (Benedictional of Æthelwold), fol. 24v: Adoration of the Magi

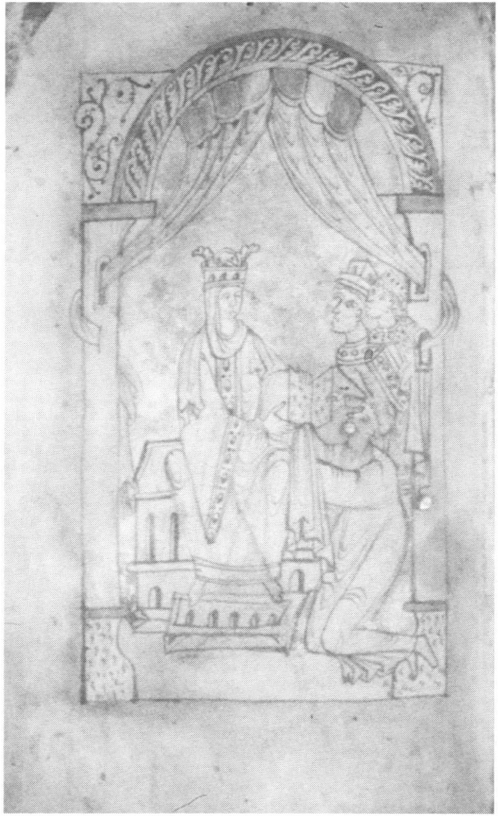

PLATE XLVIIIa London, British Library, Additional 33241 (*Encomium Emmae*), fol. 1v: Emma enthroned

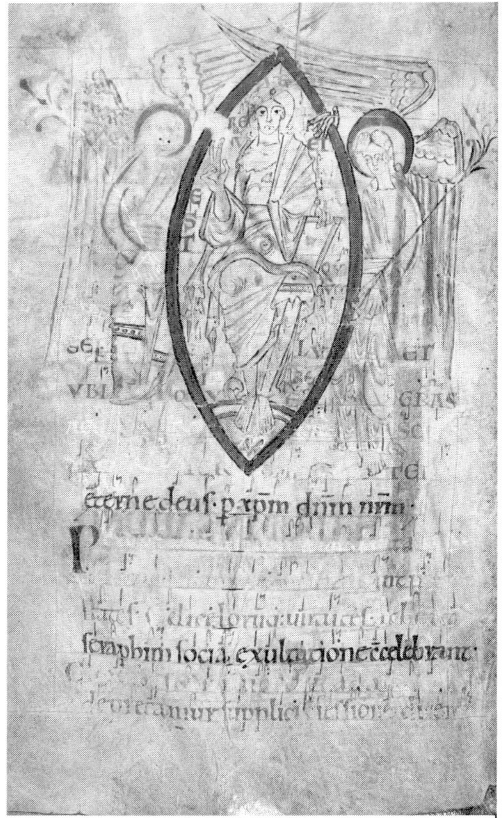

PLATE XLVIIIb Cambridge, Corpus Christi College, 422 (Red Book of Darley), p. 52: Christ in Majesty

The poet also develops the motif of the two pillars into a complex allusion to the cross.[57] It is a mast made up of two beams (*Ex.* 94) as it leads the Israelites, and when they have safely crossed the Red Sea it is explicitly identified as the cross:

folc wæs on lande.
hæfde wuldres beam. werud gelæded.
halige heapas. on hild godes.[58]

The image is particularly appropriate here, as the journey through the Red Sea was a type of baptism and an episode invoked in the Anglo-Saxon baptismal liturgy, and the vision recalls the sign of the cross made at baptism.[59] Ellen Martin notes that, on a structural level, the guiding image of the ship (or cross) in the sky can also be read as a symbol of the literary work, adding yet another facet to its relevance for a contemporary reader.[60] It is impossible to say whether or not this moment in the vision of the cross would have been illustrated, but nevertheless the words of the poet and the image they conjure resonate with one of the most powerful and enduring of all images in Anglo-Saxon culture, the triumphal cross. The phrase 'folc wæs on lande' echoes the parallel phrase 'Christ wæs on rode' of the Ruthwell 'cross' poem and the *Dream of the Rood*, and unites the saving of the Israelites with the moment of mankind's salvation in Christ's Crucifixion.[61] Moreover, it is by the vision of the cross that the Israelites are led to salvation, as is the dreamer in the *Dream of the Rood*, and the audience of, and figures represented on, the Ruthwell 'cross'. The cross in the

[57] P. J. Lucas, 'Old English Christian Poetry: the Cross in *Exodus*', in *Famulus Christi: Essays in Commemoration of the Thirteenth Centenary of the Birth of the Venerable Bede*, ed. G. Bonner (London, 1976), pp. 193–209.

[58] 'The people was on the land. The cross of glory led the troop, the holy troop, in the protection of God.' *Ex.* 567–9.

[59] Christian exegetes regularly interpreted the column of fire as Christ, who illumines the way to salvation through baptism. See Tertullian, *De baptismo* (CCSL 1), IX.1; Ambrose, *De sacramentis* (CSEL 73), I.vi.22; Danielou, *From Shadow to Reality*, pp. 178–201.

[60] E. E. Martin, 'Allegory and the African Woman in the Old English *Exodus*', *JEGP* 81 (1982), 1–15, at p. 6.

[61] The formula 'noun *wæs on* noun' occurs only three other times in Anglo-Saxon poetry: *Judgement Day*, line 57 (*se sceaða wæs on rode*, 'the warrior was on the cross'), *Beowulf*, line 210 (*flota wæs on yðum*, 'the ship was on the waves'), and (less exactly) *Beowulf*, line 1108 (*betst beadorinca wæs on bæl gearu*, 'the best of warriors was on the funeral pyre').

Dream is 'on lyft lædan leahte bewunden',[62] while the cross composed by the pillars in *Exodus* is 'lyftwundor leoht'.[63] The former is the 'beama beorhtost',[64] the latter 'in beorhtroder, beamas twegn'.[65] Both visions are identified by their respective poets and audiences as the tree of glory and both fill the sky with their splendour.[66] The Ruthwell 'cross', monumental and originally brightly painted, might have been perceived in a similar manner by its Anglo-Saxon audience.[67]

Perhaps the most important link between the visionary crosses is their role as both a means to and a sign of victory. The cross in the *Dream of the Rood* tells the dreamer that it is able to save all those who are in awe of it, and that it has opened up the true path of life to mankind:

ond ic hælen mæg
æghwylcne anra, þara þe him bið egesa to me.[68]

The Crucifixion in the *Dream of the Rood* is couched in heroic language with Christ as a warrior (*beorn*, *Dream of the Rood* 42) doing battle with the aid of the cross to redeem man's sins. In *Exodus*, God, made manifest in the vision of the cross, defeats the Egyptians and saves the Israelites. The *Exodus* poet, somewhat confusingly, recounts this spiritual battle in terms of an actual battle,[69] casting the Israelites as warriors for Christ. At Ruthwell, the monastic community for whom the cross was erected

62 *Dream of the Rood* 5, 'raised up on high, encircled with light'.

63 *Ex.* 90, 'a light wonder of the air'.

64 *Dream of the Rood* 6, 'brightest of beams'.

65 *Ex.* 94, 'two beams in the bright sky'.

66 *Wuldres treo* (*Dream of the Rood* 14b); *wuldres beam* (*Ex.* 568a).

67 A great deal of controversy has developed recently over the date and nature of the Ruthwell 'cross'. It has been suggested that the monument might originally have been a pillar or obelisk, with the cross-head added at a later date, and that the inscriptions too might have been added later. See F. Orton, 'Rethinking the Ruthwell Monument: Fragments and Critique; Tradition and History; Tongues and Sockets', *Art History* 21 (1998), 65–106; F. Orton, 'Northumbrian Sculpture (the Ruthwell and Bewcastle Monuments): Questions of Difference', in *Northumbria's Golden Age*, ed. J. Hawkes and S. Mills (Stroud, 1999), pp. 216–26; and the collected essays in C. E. Karkov and F. Orton, eds., *Theorizing Anglo-Saxon Sculpture* (forthcoming).

68 'And I may save each one of those who are in awe of me.' *Dream of the Rood* 85b–89.

69 On the nature of the battle in *Exodus* see Lucas, *Exodus*, 101–3; J. F. Vickrey, '*Exodus* and the Battle in the Sea', *Traditio* 28 (1972), 119–40; J. W. Earl, 'Christian Traditions and the Old English *Exodus*', *NM* 71 (1970), 541–70.

consisted of just such warriors, their daily struggle and triumph reflected in the cross's inscriptions and figural panels.[70]

But there is also a difference between the cross in *Exodus* and those at Ruthwell and in the *Dream of the Rood*. The former is silent, while the latter two have powerful voices. This may be due, at least in part, to the anachronistic presence of the cross of Christ in a poem dealing with Old Testament events. For the Israelites, this is still a vision whose ultimate fulfilment is far in the future, while for the dreamer and those who beheld the Ruthwell monument, all of whom lived in expectation of an imminent Last Judgement, the vision had a more immediate import. Moreover, the Israelites are quite precisely situated within the cycle of Fall and Redemption. The treasure they gather on the shores of the Red Sea, a sign of their immediate triumph in the final lines of the poem, will be taken from them because of their pride and forsaking of the Lord in *Daniel*. For the readers of the poem the crossing of the Red Sea was also a type for the Harrowing of Hell and the Last Judgement,[71] and thus a formal prefiguration of events to come in *Christ and Satan*, as well as an allusion to events still to come in their own lives. Ælfric's description of the *heofonlice tacn þære halig rode* as 'our banner' (*guðfana*) in the fight against the devil in his homily on 'The Exaltation of the Cross',[72] moves this imagery of battle and triumph from the realm of literary metaphor to that of daily experience.[73]

[70] Ó Carragáin, 'Ruthwell Crucifixion Poem'; Ó Carragáin, *City of Rome*; É. Ó Carragáin, 'Seeing, Reading, Singing the Ruthwell Cross: Vernacular Poem, Old English Liturgy and Implied Audience', *Art and Symbolism*, pre-printed papers 7, Medieval Europe: Conference on Medieval Archaeology (York, 1992), pp. 91–6; Karkov, 'Naming and Renaming'.

[71] G. Shepherd, 'Scriptural Poetry', in *Continuations and Beginnings*, ed. E. G. Stanley (London, 1966), pp. 1–36, at. p. 31; R. M. Trask, 'Doomsday Imagery in the Old English *Exodus*', *Neophilologus* 57 (1973), 295–7; Lucas, 'Old English Christian Poetry', p. 194; Earl, 'Christian Tradition', p. 566; J. P. Hermann, *Allegories of War: Language and Violence in Old English Poetry* (Ann Arbor, MI, 1989), ch. 3.

[72] *Ælfric's Lives of the Saints*, ed. W. W. Skeat, 2 vols., EETS 94 and 114 (Oxford, 1966), II, 153, lines 147–50.

[73] See also Openshaw, 'Weapons in the Daily Battle'.

DREAMS

While theoretically it is difficult to separate the visions from the dreams in Junius 11, there are some practical differences.[74] We are told that the dreamers are in bed and asleep in each case, and in each case the dreamer, if not the dream, was probably to have been included in the drawings. A further difference is that the dreams all include the words of God or his angels as spoken to the dreamer, while the visions are silent and related to us only by the poet or visionary. The Lord speaks to Abimelech in a dream, revealing to him that Sarah is Abraham's wife, and reassuring the reader that Abraham is good and wise despite the fact that his lie has endangered Sarah's honour.[75] Three blank spaces for drawings frame the dialogue between God and Abimelech, and it seems likely that at least one would have shown Abimelech asleep in bed, if not the Lord appearing to him. The scene is illustrated on folio 34v of Claudius B. iv.

The two dreams of Nabuchodonosor and their interpretation are central to *Daniel*, a poem that may have been framed by images of writing and reading, placing both a visual and textual emphasis on Daniel as interpreter.[76] The role of Daniel the prophet within the poem is mirrored by that of the poet in his transformation of his sources. Remley notes that the poet's exegesis of the opening verses of the biblical Daniel in lines 33–103 of the poem is 'one of the most remarkable surviving witnesses to scriptural *ruminatio* in Old English poetry'.[77] Nabuchodonosor's first dream is of a new Creation endangered by the cruelty of the earthly kingdoms.

siððan to reste gehwearf. rice þeoden.
com on sefan hwurfan. swefnes woma.
hu woruld wære. wundrum geteod.
ungelic yldum. oð edsceafte.
wearð him on slæpe. soð gecyðed.
þætte rices gehwæs. reðe sceolde gelimpan.
eorðan dreamas. ende wurðan.[78]

74 See also Harbus, 'Old English *swefn*'.

75 See Doane's comments on lines 1836–41 (*Genesis A*, p. 290).

76 Lucas suggests that the poem was prefaced by a drawing of Daniel writing and closed by a drawing of the prophet interpreting the writing on the wall. See appendix p. 205.

77 Remley, *Biblical Verse*, p. 259. See also Remley's discussion of the poem and its sources on pp. 259–73.

78 'After the mighty leader had turned to rest a terrible dream came into his mind, how

The Vulgate gives no clue to the content of the king's dream prior to its interpretation, and the description here, though brief, could be intended to echo the Creation narratives with which *Genesis* and *Exodus* begin.[79] The king is unable to understand his dream, that is, he is unable to read or interpret it properly. In this respect he is like Eve. He is also like Eve in his desire to acquire knowledge rather than impart learning, and here the poem differs significantly from the biblical account.[80] Unlike Eve, Nabuchodonosor does not attempt to understand the dream himself, but calls for a revelation of its meaning. The illustration at the bottom of page 177 may have shown the king in the process of dreaming, though as the details of the dream are so vague it is doubtful that it showed any more than that. Nebuchodonosor's magicians are unable to help him. They are *deofolwitgan* (literally 'devil-prophets', *Dan.* 128), the implication of the word being that their knowledge, like Eve's vision, comes from Satan. Daniel's, on the other hand, comes from God, mediated through the voice of an angel (this is a poem that is all about translation):

þæt him engel godes. eall asægde.
swa his mandrihten. gemæted wearð.[81]

The most interesting aspect of this first dream is, of course, that its exact contents are never revealed to us. We are told only that Daniel revealed the dream to the king so that he understood it from beginning to end:

Ða eode daniel. þa dæg lyhte.
swefen reccan. sinum frean.
sægde him wislice. wereda gesceafte.
þætte sona ongeat. swiðmod cyning.
ord and ende. þæs þe him ywed wæs.[82]

the world was made with wonders unlike the new creation of men. The truth was revealed to him in sleep, that in each reign should take place a cruel end to the joys of the earth.' *Dan.* 108–15.

79 While the exact sources for the different parts of the poem remain problematic, few would now disagree that it is a carefully structured poem. The content of the poem may owe much to Old Latin and Greek sources; however, it is clear that the material either fitted the desired content and structure of Junius 11, or was adapted to do so. See Remley, *Biblical Verse*, ch. 4; E. R. Anderson, 'Style and Theme in the Old English *Daniel*', *English Studies* 68 (1987), 1–23.

80 G. Overing, 'Nebuchadnezzar's Conversion in the Old English *Daniel*: A Psychological Portrait', *Papers on Language & Literature* 20.1 (1984), 1–14, at p. 4.

81 'An angel of God told him all as his lord had dreamed it.' *Dan.* 156–7.

82 'Then Daniel went at daylight to explain the dream to his lord; he told him wisely of

The reasons for this are unclear, though it may be that focusing on Daniel's God-given ability to interpret and translate correctly was deemed more important than the details of the dream itself.[83] Alternatively, the poet's brief description of the content of the dream has already revealed its meaning to us, so there is no longer any need for the lengthy account of the visionary statue found in the biblical sources. It may also be significant that these images of creation and the fall of kingdoms evoked by the poet's words echo those of Eve's vision. She saw an image of the Last Judgement while still within God's newly created paradise, and her vision was both part and symbol of her own fall and the loss of the kingdom of paradise. Likewise, Nabuchodonosor at the height of his power receives a dream which foretells the loss of earthly kingdoms. And, like Eve's vision, Nabuchodonosor's dream is apocalyptic, not only revealing the destruction of earthly kingdoms, but also referring ultimately to the establishment of the eternal kingdom.

Perhaps because he was drunk, Nabuchodonosor cannot recall his first dream on waking; the second, however, he does remember, though that makes it no less terrifying than the first. The poet unveils the content of this dream to us as the king dreams it, and it may also have been illustrated in the spaces left for drawings on pages 199 and 200. The poet's description of the tree expands on that of the biblical verses so that the tree not only fills the heavens, but its branches reach from sea to sea, and it is entirely encircled by chains.[84]

þuhte him þæt on foldan. fægre stode.
wudubeam wlitig. se wæs wyrtum fæst.
beorht on blædum. næs he bearwe gelic.
ac he hlifode. to heofontuglum.
swilce he oferfæðmde. foldan sceatas.
ealne middangeard. oð merestreamas.
twigum and telgum. ðær he to geseah.
þuhte him þæt se wudubeam. wilddeor scylde.
ane æte. eallum heolde.
swylce fuglas eac. heora feorhnere.

the destiny of nations, so that the proud king at once understood from beginning to end, that which had been shown to him.' *Dan*. 158–62.

83 N. D. Isaacs, *Structural Principles in Old English Poetry* (Knoxville, TN, 1968), p. 146; Remley, *Biblical Verse*, pp. 253 and 274–6.

84 Remley, *Biblical Verse*, p. 281.

on þæs beames. bledum name.
Ðuhte him þæt engel. ufan. of roderum.
stigan cwome. and stefne abead.
torhtan reorde. het þæt treow ceorfan.
and þa wildeor on weg. fleon.
swylce eac þa fugolas. þonne his fyll come.
het þonne besnædan. seolfes blædum.
twigum and telgum. and þeh tacen wesan.
wunian wyrtrumam. þæs wudubeames.
eorðan fæstne. oðþæt eft cyme.
grene bleda. þonne god sylle.
het eac gebindan. beam þone miclan.
ærenum clammum. and isernum.
and gesæledne. in susl don.
þæt his mod wite. þæt migtigra
wite. wealdeð. þonne he him wið mæge.[85]

On one level the tree is, as Daniel explains, a sign of Nabuchodonosor's fortunes, of his suffering, but also of the redemption that will come when he finally sees the truth and comes to believe in God. But this tree that encompasses all the earth and nurtures all creatures is also an allusion to the tree of life and beyond that to the cross as the tree of life. The opening lines of Nabuchodonosor's dream recall the opening lines of the *Dream of the Rood*:

Þuhte me þæt ic gesawe syllicre treow
on lyft lædan leohte bewunden,
beama beorhtost. Eall þæt beacen wæs
begoten mid golde. Gimmas stodon

[85] 'It seemed to him that a lovely tree stood beautiful on the earth, its roots were fast and it was bright with fruit. There was not a similar tree in a grove, but it reached to the stars in heaven and it spread over the earth's surfaces, the whole earth, to the sea-waves, with its twigs and branches. It seemed to him that he saw that the tree sheltered wild beasts, the one held food for all, and birds also took their sustenance from the fruit of the tree. It seemed to him that an angel descended from the heavens above and commanded with clear words. He ordered the tree to be cut down, and the wild animals to flee, and also the birds, and then its fall should come. He ordered then the fruits, twigs and branches to be cut off, and that the roots of that tree should remain, fast in the earth, as a sign, until green shoots should again come, when God granted it. And he ordered also that the great tree be bound with brass and iron fetters, and bound to be in torture, that his mind might know that a mightier one had the power of torture than he could prevail against.' *Dan.* 497–522.

fagere æt foldan sceatum, swylce þær fife wæron
uppe on þam eaxlegespanne. Beheolden þær engel dryhtnes ealle,
fægere þurh forðgesceaft. Ne wæs ðær huru fracodes gealga,
ac hine þær beheoldon halige gastas,
men ofer moldan and eall þeos mære gesceaft.[86]

This is not to say that the *Dream of the Rood* was in any way a source for *Daniel* (or vice versa), but simply to say that the two use similar language to express related themes. Although the parallels are not exact, nevertheless both cross and tree are tortured, bound, and ultimately rediscovered (or regrown), as signs of faith and salvation. Nabuchodonosor's exile amongst the wild beasts for seven years is also a type of man's exile from, and return to, paradise in the seventh age of the world.

The meaning of Nabuchodonosor's second dream again relates to the theme of creation, judgement, and the loss of kingdom that characterized both his first dream and Eve's vision. The imagery of the cross as tree is picked up in the drawing of the Creation on page 7 (pl. IIIb), in which a small tree with a cross at its centre is accompanied by a bird and beast.[87] The rich visual description may well have been reflected in the details of the drawing intended to accompany the king's dream of the tree. Related images of the cross as instrument of salvation are, as we have seen, echoed in the heavenly vision that leads the Israelites out of Egypt in *Exodus*, and in the account (and possible illustration) of the Crucifixion in *Christ and*

[86] 'It seemed to me that I saw a most wonderful tree raised up in the air, encircled with light, the brightest of trees. That sign was all covered with gold, gems stood fair at the surfaces of the earth, and there were five up on that shoulder-beam. All beheld there the angel of the Lord, fair throughout Creation. That was certainly not the gallows of a criminal, but holy souls, men over the earth, and all this glorious creation beheld it there.' *Dream of the Rood* 4–12.

[87] This type of imagery was extremely common in Anglo-Saxon art in the form of the inhabited vinescroll, one of the most popular types of decoration on the sculpted monuments and fittings of the early church. See, for example, the eighth-century Ruthwell and Bewcastle monuments, or the fragments of architectural sculpture from Jarrow. For Ruthwell see R. N. Bailey and R. Cramp, eds., *Cumberland, Westmorland and Lancashire North-of-the-Sands*, vol. II of *Corpus of Anglo-Saxon Stone Sculpture* (Oxford, 1988), ills. 682 and 685–7; for Bewcastle see *ibid*., ills. 91, 17; for Jarrow see R. Cramp, ed., *County Durham and Northumberland*, vol. I of *Corpus of Anglo-Saxon Stone Sculpture* (Oxford, 1984), ills. 545–6. The addition of the little watching figure outside the arcs in which the Creation is taking place on page 7 of the Junius 11 manuscript provides an interesting contrast to the passive sleeper watching creation and destruction in his dream.

Satan.[88] The poet's unprecedented portrayal of Nabuchodonosor as a type of evangelist preaching a gospel message to men can then be understood in the context of these interrelated visions of judgement and salvation and the sign of the cross that he is granted.[89] Perhaps too the lines would have elicited from the poem's audience images of their own gospel books typically covered with the sign of the cross.

SIGNS

One thing that distinguishes a sign from a vision or a dream in the Junius 11 manuscript is permanence. While dreams and visions may have eternal meaning, they themselves are ephemeral. Signs, on the other hand – God's covenant with Abraham and his people, the sign of circumcision, or blessing – are either eternal themselves or enacted and reenacted eternally, they are in effect signs that unite past, present and future. Ælfric states that the spiritual sign, the 'significance of the cross', remains always with God no matter how fragmented and dispersed the actual wood might be.[90] Like the Word itself, the cross was also perceived as present, or at least prefigured, from the moment of Creation. In Book X of Prudentius' *Peristephanon*, a well-known text in late Anglo-Saxon England, the martyr Romanus tells his executioners:

> Crux ista Christi, quam nouellam dicitis,
> nascente mundo factus ut primum est homo,
> expressa signis, expedita est litteris:
>
> aduentus eius mille per miracula
> praenuntiatus ore uatum consono.[91]

[88] See *Christ and Satan* 502–11, 545–54.

[89] See Remley, *Biblical Verse*, p. 283. See also M. Godden, 'Biblical Literature'. Godden notes (p. 223) that Ælfric identified Nabuchodonosor as 'one of the few pagans granted a perception of Christ' prior to his incarnation.

[90] 'Is swa þeah to witenne þæt heo is wide todæled . mid gelomlicum ofcyrfum to lande gehwilcum . ac seo gastlice getacnung is mid gode æfre a unbrosnigendlic . þeah þe se beam beo tocoruen.' ('It is however, we should note, that it is widely distributed through frequent division to each land. But the spiritual sign is always with God, ever incorruptible although the tree be cut to pieces'.) 'The Exaltation of the Holy Cross', 143–6, in *Lives of the Saints*, II, 153.

[91] ('This cross of Christ that you call new, at the world's birth when man was first created, was revealed by signs and narrated in writings, and its coming was foretold in a

The cross is arguably one image that appears in Junius 11 as both vision and sign. It is alluded to in the vision of *Exodus* and the second dream of Nebuchodonosor, but it also appears literally as a sign in the form of the tree of life (pl. IIIb), the cross-keys of the angel on page 9 (pl. IV), or the staff of Christ, and metaphorically as a sign of triumph and the church.

There are four primary words used for 'sign' in Junius 11: *beacen*, *tacen*, *segn*, and *gebletsian* ('to bless or make the sign of the cross'). Compounds and other forms of these words – e.g. *friðotacen* (*Gen.* 2371), *heofonbeacen* (*Ex.* 107), or *gesegnian* (*Christ and Satan* 359) – also appear. There does seem to be a difference in the way the words are used within the individual poems. In *Genesis*, *gebletsian* is used only three times to describe God's blessing at significant points within the poem: his blessing of Adam and Eve (*Gen.* 192), his blessing of Noah and his sons after the flood (*Gen.* 1505), and his blessing of Abraham (*Gen.* 1752). In each case the blessing is also depicted in the accompanying drawings (pls. V, VI, XXXVII, XLIIIa).[92] While it might be argued that the verb cannot possibly entail making the sign of the cross in an Old Testament context, the image of God with his hand raised in blessing at each point suggests that an Anglo-Saxon audience would have envisioned the act, completing the sign of the cross themselves from memory, just as their eyes frequently made the sign of the cross in reading images or inscriptions.[93] In his homily on the Exaltation of the Cross, Ælfric told his audience in no uncertain terms:

> Þeah þe man wafige wundorlice mid handa ne bið hit þeah bletsung buta he wyrce tacn þære halgan rode.[94]

thousand miracles by the united voice of the prophets.') *Aurelii Prudentii Clementis Carmina*, ed. M. P. Cunningham (CCSL 126), p. 351, lines 621–5.

92 In line 2359 God tells Abraham that he will bless (*bletsian*) Ismael, though the actual act of blessing is not described in the text and there is no indication that it was to have been illustrated.

93 The inscription on the crown of the Coppergate Helmet, for example, reads: 'IN NOMINE:DNI:NOSTRI:IHV:SCS:SPS:DI:ET:OMNIBVS:DECEMVS:AMEN:OSHERE:XPI' (from nose to nape of neck), 'IN NOMINE : DNI : NOSTRI : IHV : SCS : SPS' (from crown to left ear) and 'DI : ET : OMNIBVS : DECEMVS : AMEN : OSHER[E] : XPI' (from crown to right ear). See E. Okasha, 'The Inscriptions', in *The Anglian Helmet from Coppergate*, ed. D. Tweddle, The Archaeology of York, The Small Finds 17/8 (London, 1992), 1012–16.

94 'Though a man wave wonderfully with his hands, it is nevertheless not a blessing unless he makes the sign of the holy cross.' *Lives of the Saints*, II, 154.

Interestingly, each of the three blessings in *Genesis* is accompanied by a reference to the fruitfulness of the land these blessed people inhabit. The blessing on Adam and Eve precedes God's command to increase and multiply, and to fill the *ælgrene* earth with sons and daughters:

þa gebletsode. bliðheort cyning.
metod alwihta. monna cynnes.
ða forman twa. fæder and moder.
wif and wæpned. he þa worde cwæð.
temað nu and wexað. tudre fyllað.
eorðan ælgrene incre cynne.
sunum and dohtrum.[95]

The blessing on Noah and his sons precedes God's similar words to them as they inherit a new *ælgrene* earth after the flood:[96]

þa he noe
gebletsade. and his bearn somed.
þæt he þæt gyld on þanc. agifen hæfde.
and on geogoðhade. godum dædum.
ær geearnod. þa him ealra wæs.
ara este. ælmihtig god.
domfæst dugeþa. þa gyt drihten cwæð.
wuldres. aldor. word to noe.
Tymað nu and tiedrað. tires brucað.
mid gefean fryðo. fyllað eorðan.
eall geiceað. eow is eðelstol.
holmes hlæst. and heofonfuglas.[97]
and wildu deor. on geweald geseald.
eorðe ælgrene. and eacen feoh.[98]

95 'Then the blithe-hearted King, the Lord of Creation, blessed the first two of the race of men, father and mother, female and male. He said these words: "Multiply now and grow, fill the all-green earth with your offspring, your family, sons and daughters."' *Gen*. 192–8a.

96 See Ambrose, *De Noe et arca*.

97 The manuscript reads *heafonfula*. Doane and other editors emend to *heofonfuglas*.

98 'Then he blessed Noah and his sons together, because he had given that sacrifice in thanks, and had done good deeds in youth, had previously deserved all that almighty God, liberal in honours, powerful in gifts, had given him. Then the Lord, the Prince of glory, said words to Noah: "Be fruitful now and multiply, enjoy glory with the joy of peace, fill the earth, increase all. Into your power is given a homeland, and the fish in the sea, and the sky-birds, and wild animals, the all-green earth and increase of cattle."' *Gen*. 1504b–17.

Abraham too receives both a blessing and an all-green earth:

Ða se halga spræc. heofonrices weard.
to abrahame. ece drihten.
gewit þu nu feran. and þine fare lædan.
ceapas to cnosle. carram ofgif.
fæder eðelstol. far swa ic þe hate.
monna leofost. and þu minum wel.
larum hyre. and þæt land gesec.
þe ic þe ælgrene. ywan wille.
brade foldan. þu gebletsad scealt.
on mundbyrde. minre lifigan.[99]

The blessing can be extended to the poem's Anglo-Saxon readers for whom the words *crescite et multiplicamini* would have been a familiar part of the Quinquagesima and Sexagesima liturgies.[100] In *Genesis* the verb *gebletsian* implies more than the simple act of blessing, referring also to the fertility and prosperity of both man and earth.[101] In each case, the blessing and the sign of the cross that accompanies it, reveal a new earthly paradise in which man and nature, at least for a time, live in harmony in a newly all-green world.[102] There are only ten other recorded uses of the word *ælgrene* (*ealgrene*) in Old English, and in each case it is used in a similar context,[103] so that the word itself becomes a sign of blessing and renewal. The interrelationship of verbal and visual signs in these passages

[99] 'Then the Lord, the Guardian of Heaven, the eternal Lord, spoke to Abraham: "Go now and take your movables, breeding stock. Leave Haran, your father's homeland. Travel as I command you, dearest of men, and obey well my advice, and seek that all-green land that I will show you, broad earth. You shall be blessed and live in my protection."' *Gen*. 1744–53.

[100] Remley, *Biblical Verse*, pp. 147–8.

[101] The association is continued in late Anglo-Saxon England in the rituals and texts used in blessing agricultural land. See K. L. Jolly, *Popular Religion in Late Saxon England: Elf Charms in Context* (Chapel Hill, NC, 1996), ch. 1.

[102] The only other use of the word *ælgrene* in *Genesis* is in line 1787, the point at which Abraham sees the land promised to him in lines 1746–51.

[103] *Christ in Judgement* 1128, in which the all-green earth participates in Christ's suffering at the Crucifixion; *Andreas* 798, in which the corpses of Abraham, Isaac and Jacob are commanded to reveal the wonders of God's Creation; *Metres* 20, line 78a, in reference to the waters and fertile earth of the Creation; and three times in the psalter in glosses to 'novella' in Psalm CXXVII.3: 'uxor tua sicut vitis abundans in lateribus domus tuae filii tui sicut novella olivarum in circuitu mensae tuae' ('Thy wife as a fruitful vine, on the sides of the house. Thy children as olive plants round about thy table').

may have its source in Augustine, who wrote of fertility in Genesis and nature:

In his omnibus nanciscimur multitidines et ubertates et incrementa; sed quod ita crescat et multiplicetur, ut una res multis modis enuntietur et una enuntiatio multis modis intellegatur, non inuenimus nisi in signis corporealiter editis et rebus intellegibiliter excogitatis.[104]

It is tempting to link the sign of blessing and its accompanying reference to the colour green with Moses' *grene tacn* in *Exodus*, a prefiguration of the cross of Christ,[105] but the cross as a sign of renewal might have had too broad a baptismal significance to support such a narrow reading. On a general level, the salvation gained by the Israelites in *Exodus*, and the successive earthly paradises inhabited by Adam and Eve, Noah, and Abraham all look forward to our return to Christ, the living tree, at the end of time.[106] The theme was particularly popular with Ælfric, who turned to it on several occasions, most notably in the *Hexameron*.[107] Moreover, in the temporal world this particular use of cross as sign had a long history in England, as evidenced by the late seventh- or early eighth-century cross slab from Jarrow inscribed with the words 'IN HOC SINGULARI SIGNO VITA REDDITUR MUNDO' ('In this unique sign life is returned to the world').[108]

104 'In all these cases we find multitudes, fertility and increase. But as to what might increase or multiply in such a manner that a single thing might be stated in many ways and a single statement might be understood in many ways, this we discover only in signs corporeally expressed and in things intelligibly conceived'. Augustine, *Confessiones* III.24.

105 Hermann, *Allegories of War*, p. 60; T. N. Hall, 'The Cross as Green Tree in the *Vindicta Salvatoris* and the Green Rod of Moses in *Exodus*', *English Studies* 72.4 (1971), 297–307; M. Luria, 'Why Moses' Rod is Green', *ELN* 17 (1980), 161–3.

106 Hall, 'Cross as Green Tree', p. 303.

107 'And he of deaðe aras on ðam ðriddan dæge and awende ðæt swurd of ðam wæge mid ealle ðæt we inn moton gaan to ðam upplican paradise to ðam lifes treowe, ðæt is se leofa Hælend ðe ðæt ece lif forgifð ðam ðe hine lufiað.' ('And he arose from death on the third day and removed the sword entirely from the way so that we might go up into paradise to that tree of life that is the beloved Lord, he who grants eternal life to those that love him'.) *Exameron Anglice*, ed. Crawford, pp. 71–2, lines 510–14.

108 Cramp, *Durham and Northumberland*, part I, pp. 112–3l; part II, Pls. 95, no. 518; 96; 97, no. 521. The inscribed portion of the slab (Jarrow 17) is now built into the east wall of the north porch of the church at Jarrow.

While rare in *Genesis*, both *gebletsian* and *bletsian* are altogether absent from *Exodus*. In both *Daniel* and *Christ and Satan* the verbs *gebletsian* and *gesegnian* are used interchangeably.[109]

Although *beacen* and *tacen* are collocations,[110] that is they can have similar meanings, there is a distinction in the way they are used in *Genesis*. *Tacen* is used only for marks made on the body: the mark of Cain (line 1022),[111] and the mark of circumcision (2313, 2322, 2326, 2371 (*friðotacen*) and 2377).[112] The circumcisions of Ismael and Isaac are distinguished by the use of the word *segn* (*Gen*. 2372) for Ismael and *beacen* (*Gen*. 2769) for Isaac. *Segn* is not used elsewhere in *Genesis*, and the only other use of *beacen* is in reference to the tower of Babel (*Gen*. 1666 and 1680). However, throughout the manuscript *beacen* and its compounds are used to describe striking spectacles, miracles, or signs witnessed by large groups of people. In *Exodus* the word is used for the pillar of flame (*Ex*. 107), the trumpet signal to the Israelites (*Ex*. 219),[113] the golden Lion of Judah (*Ex*. 320), and the sunrise during the Israelites' passage through the Red Sea (*Ex*. 345); in *Daniel* the term is used to refer to Nabuchodonosor's idol (*Dan*. 191), the three Hebrew children in the furnace (*Dan*. 487), and the writing on the wall (*Dan*. 729). The word may be used for Isaac's circumcision in *Genesis* to mark him as a type of Christ and a sign of salvation for his people. The pillar of flame, Lion of Judah, and three children are also

109 *Daniel*: *bletsian*, lines 358, 389 and 399; *gebletsian*, line 362; *Christ and Satan*: *gebletsian*, line 240; *gesegnian*, lines 349 and 614.

110 E. Okasha, '"Beacen" in Old English Poetry', *N&Q* 23 (1976), 200–7.

111 The mark is also called a *freoðobeacen* ('sign of peace') in line 1045.

112 *Tacen* is also the word used by Ælfric in his homily on the circumcision of Christ. See *Ælfric's Homilies the First Series*, ed. P. Clemoes, EETS SS 117 (Oxford, 1997), 224–31; Lees, *Tradition and Belief*, p. 117. See also A. W. Astell, 'Holofernes Head: *Tacen* and Teaching in the Old English *Judith*', *ASE* 18 (1989), 117–33.

113 The use of *beacen* in reference to sound is unusual in Old English poetry. However, it has been suggested that OE *beacen* derives from Latin *bucina*/*buchum* ('trumpet/sound of a trumpet') (see Okasha, 'Beacen', p. 200). The word is used in a mid-eleventh-century Pontifical (Cambridge, Corpus Christi College 44, fol. 1r) in the first sentence of a text on the spiritual significance of church bells: 'Her ys amearcud be þam beacnum þe we beað to cyricean mid gesamnude' ('Here it is marked by that sign [bell] that we are summoned to church'). See Budny, *Catalogue*, p. 683.

symbols or types of Christ,[114] as is the sunrise, God's light come from the east.[115]

The *tacen* that Satan's messenger fails to offer Adam (*Gen.* 540) but does offer Eve (*Gen.* 653) is also marked on the body. It is ultimately unclear whether the *tacen* is the fruit or the vision or both – we are told only that he showed her a *tacen* (*iewde hire tacen*, *Gen.* 653) and that she showed a *tacen* to Adam:

worhte mid þam wordum. þe heo þam were swelce.
tacen oðiewde. and treowe gehet.[116]

But Eve shows Adam both the apple and her vision, the latter portrayed vividly to him through her words. The confusion continues after the Fall. Eve implies that the vision is the *tacen* in her lament at its disappearance:

þæt wif gnornode.
hof hreowigmod. hæfde hyldo godes.
lare forlæten. þa heo þæt leoht geseah.
ellor scriðan. þæt hire þurh untreowa.
tacen iewde. se him þone teonan geræd.[117]

Adam, however, laments that he carries the mark (*tacen*) of the apple and his disobedience on him still:

me ða blæda on hand. bryd gesealde.
freolucu fæmne. freahdrihten min.
ðe ic þe on teonan geþah. nu ic þæs tacen wege.[118]
sweotol on me selfum.[119]

114 On the subject of the Lion of Judah, Lucas (*Exodus*, p. 119) states: 'This interpretation is encouraged in the present context by the use of *segn* and *beacen*, words already employed to refer to the pillar or the pillar as Cross: like the Lion of Judah the Cross was a symbol of Christ'. See also, Lucas, 'Old English Christian Poetry'; S. Dleéani-Nigoul, 'L'utilization des modèles bibliques du martyre par les écrivains du IIIe siècle', in *Le monde latin antique*, ed. J. Fontaine and C. Pietri (Paris, 1985), II, 334–8.

115 Cf. *Beowulf*: 569b–70 'Leoht eastan com / beorht beacen Godes' ('the light come from the east, the bright sign of God').

116 '[She] brought it about with words because she showed such a token and promised good faith.' *Gen.* 713–14.

117 'That woman grieved, sadly lamented in her heart that she had lost God's favour and relinquished his counsel. Then she saw that radiance pass away elsewhere, that sign he who counselled wrong showed her through her faithlessness.' *Gen.* 770b–4.

118 The *ic* is added above the line.

119 'The bride gave the fruit into my hand, the beautiful woman, my Lord, which I took as an insult to you. Now I carry the clear mark of it on myself.' *Gen.* 883–6a. One

Unlike the sign of blessing, the *tacen* is generally not depicted, its presence on the body, particularly in the form of circumcision, perhaps precluding its presence in the illustrations. The one exception to this general rule is the apple. We do see the apple offered to Adam and Eve, and we may well see the mark of the Fall on Adam in the beard that becomes a sign of his gender.

Tacen is also the word used by Satan to describe his Fall from heaven in *Christ and Satan* (line 89), an event that most certainly left a mark on his body in his change from Lucifer to Satan, angel to devil, bodilessness to embodied form.[120] The change is vividly depicted in the illustrations of the Fall of the angels in *Genesis* (pls. IIb, VIII) in which the angels lose their robes and are transformed into demonic bodies, complete with genitals in some instances. Elsewhere in Junius 11 *tacen* carries a more varied meaning. In *Exodus* it is used only to describe the green rod of Moses.

hwæt, ge nu eagum to   on lociað.
folca leofost.   færwundra sum.
hu ic sylfa sloh.   and þeos swiðre hand.
grene tacne.   garsecges deop.[121]

As noted above, the rod of Moses is a sign of both salvation and the living cross. The emphasis placed on seeing the rod in this passage suggests that it would have been included in the illustration on page 157, and it is unfortunate that we cannot now know what shape it would have taken.[122]

problem is that Adam claims that he is not offered the *tacen* by the messenger ('ne þu me oðiewdest ænig tacen', *Gen.* 540), even though he is offered the apple: 'genam þær þæs ofætes. and wende him eft þanon. / þær he wiste hadgeweorc. heofoncyninges. / ongan hine þa frinan. forman worde. / se laða mid ligenum. langað þa awuht. / adam up to gode. ic eom on ærende hider. / feorran gefered. ne þæt nu fyrn ne wæs. / þæt ic wið hine sylfne sæt. þa het he me on þysne sið faran. / het þæt þu þisses ofætes æte.' ('He took from there that fruit and went back again to where he perceived the handiwork of the heavenly King. He began to question him first with words, the hateful one, with lies: Do you long for anything from God, Adam? I am come hither on his errand, [and] have journeyed far. It was not long ago that I sat with him. Then he commanded me to travel on this journey, commanded that you eat this fruit'.) *Gen.* 493–500.

120 See above, p. 68.

121 'Lo, look now with your eyes, dearest of people, at a certain miracle, how I have struck the ocean depths with the green rod in this right hand.' *Ex.* 278–81.

122 See appendix, p. 204.

Both the three Hebrew boys in the fiery furnace and the writing on the wall in *Daniel* are referred to as *tacen* and *beacen*. *Daniel* is particularly interesting because it provides a contrast to *Genesis* in that angels as the bearers of true words and true signs replace Satan and his messengers, the bearers of false words and false signs in the earlier poem. Daniel, as we have seen, receives his understanding of Nabuchodonosor's first dream from an angel, while both the miracle of the three boys in the fire and the writing on the wall are the work of angels.[123]

The miracle of the three boys in the fiery furnace is a sign in several senses of the word, and not simply because it is identified as such in the poem. The poet says:

> Swa wordum spræc. werodes ræswa.
> babilone weard. siððan he beacen onget.
> swutol tacen godes.[124]

Lucas suggests that no fewer than five drawings may have been devoted to the story of the three boys and their ordeal, making it one of the most heavily illustrated single episodes in the manuscript. Text and illustration would no doubt have complemented each other, but it is likely that they would also have referred intertextually and intervisually to themes within and beyond the manuscript. The story is a type of baptism, the Harrowing of Hell and the Last Judgement, and thus combines themes already explored in *Exodus* with those yet to be narrated in *Christ and Satan*.[125] The episode of the three boys in the fire is also an antitype of the Fall of the rebel angels and the image of Satan in hell, with the figure of the descending and ascending angel helping to link its various meanings.[126] As such, it serves as a bridge between the Fall of the angels in *Genesis* and the same story in *Christ and Satan*. The three boys remain faithful and obedient to God, unlike Satan and his followers, and, with the aid of a true angel, walk unharmed through the fire. In contrast, Satan is chained

[123] Farrell, ed., *Daniel*, pp. 27–8.

[124] 'So the nation's leader, the guardian of Babylon spoke words after he understood that sign, God's clear sign.' *Dan*. 486–8a.

[125] Augustine, *Ennarrationes in Psalmos*, Psalm CI (PL 36, 1313–14); Jerome, *Commentarii in Danielem* (CCSL 75A), I, 808; Alcuin, *De fide sanctae et individuae Trinitatis*, III (PL 101, 11–58).

[126] Farrell (*Daniel*, p. 129) notes that the angel ascends back into heaven as does Christ after the Harrowing. But the angel can also be contrasted with Satan's messenger in *Genesis*, who journeys in exactly the opposite direction.

and burns eternally in the fires of hell. As it is almost certain that a drawing of the three in the furnace was planned, the freedom of the boys within the flames would no doubt have been emphasized, providing a striking visual contrast to the repeated images of the bound Satan.[127] Moreover, while in the midst of the flames the three direct clear and ordered words of praise to God, in contrast to the confused and fragmented boasts and laments of Satan in *Genesis*. In this respect too, the episode becomes a bridge between *Genesis* and *Christ and Satan*; in both the true words of praise sung in heaven and elicited from the reader are opposed to the treacherous words of Satan and his messenger.[128]

The song of Azarias (*Dan*. 283–332) also notes the similarity between the Israelites, the fallen angels, and the fallen Adam and Eve. Like Satan, the Israelites are guilty of the sin of pride (*oferhygdum*, *Dan*. 297; cf. *Gen*. 22 and 29). Like Eve (and Adam), they have broken their promise to God (*bræcon bebodo*, *Dan*. 298; cf. *Gen*. 599b–600a). Like all three, they are exiles:

for oferhygdum.
bræcon bebodo. burhsittendum.
had oferhogedon. halgan lifes.
siendon we towrecene. geond widne grund.
heapum tohworfene. hyldelease.
is user lif. geond landa fela.
fracoð and gefræge. folca manegum.
þa us ec bewræcon. to þæs wyrrestan.
Eorðcyninga. æhta gewealde.
on hæft heorugrimra. and we nu hæðenra.
þeowned þoliað.[129]

[127] Cf., for example, the illustrations of the Hebrews in the furnace in the Spanish Bible of 960 (León, Real Col. De San Isidoro, fol. 318) and the Morgan Beatus of *c*. 940–5 (New York, Pierpont Morgan Library, 644, 248v).

[128] For an excellent discussion of obedience and language in the story of the Hebrew children see J. W. Kirkland and C. E. Modlin, 'The Art of *Azarias*', *MÆ* 41 (1972), 9–15.

[129] 'They broke the commandments for dwellers in cities out of pride, the nation despised holy life. We are scattered throughout the wide ground, scattered in crowds, without mercy. Our life is despised and notorious throughout many lands to many people. We are also banished into the controlling power of the worst of earthly kings, in the captivity of savages, and we now endure the slavery of heathens.' *Dan*. 297b–307a.

The poet's language both reinforces the theme of obedience,[130] and places the three boys and the Hebrew people directly between the Fall and exile of *Genesis*, and the redemption offered in the Harrowing of Hell in *Christ and Satan*.

The language of the song uses formulaic variation to invoke God in a number of roles.[131] He is the *metod alwihta* ('Measurer of all things', *Dan.* 283a), *rodora waldend* ('Lord of the heavens', *Dan.* 290b), *gasta scyppend* ('Creator of spirits', *Dan.* 291b and 314b), *halig drihten* ('holy Lord', *Dan.* 292b), *wereda wuldorcyning* ('God of hosts', *Dan.* 308a), *ece drihten* ('eternal Lord', *Dan.* 309b and 330b), *weroda waldend* ('Lord of hosts', *Dan.* 331a), *woruldgesceafta* ('world-Creator', *Dan.* 331b), *sigora settend* ('Maker of victories', *Dan.* 332a), and *soðfæst metod* ('righteous Lord', *Dan.* 332b).[132] He has no one name, title or shape, like the pillars of cloud and fire in *Exodus* or the cross in the *Dream of the Rood*. The verbal play highlights his omnipotence and omnipresence, but also his unknowable nature. God is here present through the signs of the angel, the miracle, the words of the song and the creation it describes, but he himself is absent from the text. We do not hear his voice as we do in *Genesis* and *Christ and Satan*, nor do we see his image as we do in *Genesis* (and may have done in *Christ and Satan*).

The unknowability of God and its expression through verbal parallels and variations is also the subject of the late Anglo-Saxon poem *Prayer*.[133] Sarah Keefer has explored the ways in which language is used in that poem to create a text which incorporates the three orders of the Christian church: the church militant, the church triumphant and the heavenly host.[134] The variation in the song of the three children may, at least in

130 Kirkland and Modlin, 'Art of *Azarias*', p. 11.

131 *Ibid.*, p. 10.

132 There are parallels here with Cædmon's 'Hymn' in which God is the Guardian of heaven, the Measurer, glorious Father, eternal Lord, Holy Shaper, Guardian of mankind, and Lord almighty.

133 London, BL Cotton Julius A. II, fols. 136–44; E. V. K. Dobbie, *The Anglo-Saxon Minor Poems*, ASPR VI (New York and London, 1942), 94–6.

134 S. L. Keefer, 'Respect for the Book: A Reconsideration of "Form", "Content" and "Context" in Two Vernacular Poems', *New Approaches to Editing Old English Verse*, ed. S. L. Keefer and K. O'Brien O'Keeffe (Cambridge, 1998), pp. 21–44, at p. 42. For art historical parallels see Rosenthal, 'Three Drawings'; and J. Rosenthal, 'The Pontifical of St Dunstan', in *St Dunstan: His Life, Times and Cult*, ed. N. Ramsay, M. Sparks and T. Tatton-Brown (Woodbridge, 1992), pp. 143–63.

part, be intended to do the same: (1) it identifies God as *weroda waldend*, *rodera waldend* and *gasta scyppend*, and heaven as home of the *engel ælbeorht*;[135] (2) it makes reference to earthly *werðeode* and those *lifgende . . . onworulde*;[136] and (3) it mentions the Lord of Abraham, Isaac and Jacob.[137] The account of the Crucifixion and the Ascension in lines 545–66 of *Christ and Satan*, with its description of Christ's leading us from captivity to salvation and Christ's own return to the heavenly home, can be understood in the same way.[138] It might be possible to extend this structure to the manuscript as a whole so that *Exodus*, *Daniel* and *Christ and Satan* are understood as incorporating the church militant, the church triumphant and the heavenly host respectively, though that is not my purpose here.

The double descent of the angel into the furnace in *Daniel* (paralleling the double fall of Lucifer in *Genesis*) may be a further way of suggesting the eternal presence of God combined with a sense of his physical absence. The angel appears first in line 237, where he is sent directly from God:

halige him þær help geteode.   sende him of hean rodere.
god gumena weard.   gast þone halgan.
engel in þone ofn   innan becwom.
þær hie þæt aglac drugon.
freobearn faðmum beþeahte.   under þam fyrenan hrofe.[139]

But at the end of Azarias's song we are also told:

ða of roderum wæs.
engel ælbeorht.   ufan onsended.
wlitescyne wer.   on his wuldorhaman.[140]

This second appearance of the angel and the repetition of his protective

[135] *Dan.* 331, 290–1, 314 and 336.

[136] *Dan.* 285 and 295–6.

[137] *Dan.* 313–14. The Canterbury glosses note: 'Sed isti tres meliores caeteris patribus fuerunt obseruando pactum circumcisiones.' ('These three were better than other patriarchs by observing the contract of the circumcision.') Bischoff and Lapidge, *Biblical Commentaries*, pp. 390–1, 17.

[138] Hall, 'Old English Book of Salvation History', p. 228.

[139] 'The Holy one made a help for them there. God, Lord of men sent to them from high heaven, the holy spirit. The angel came into the oven, there where they endured that torment, covered the noble youths with protection under that fiery roof.' *Dan.* 235–9.

[140] 'Then from heaven the all-bright angel was sent from above, the beautiful man in his glorious dress.' *Dan.* 335b–7.

powers is followed by the canticle of the three children, a cycle that suggests that God (or salvation) and words of praise evoke each other. Azarias sings because of his faith in God and is granted salvation, which results in another song of praise. The miracles and the praise multiply before our eyes. But the second song is also different in that it is sung with a communal voice, and its words invoke all of Creation to join in the praise of God:

bæden bletsian. bearn isræla.
eall landgesceaft. ecne drihten.
ðeoda waldend. swa hie þry cwædon.
modum horsce. þurh gemæne word.[141]

What begins as one voice thus becomes many, culminating in the voices of all Creation. The voices of the manuscript's readers, who are a part of this Creation, are here joined with those of the three boys at each reading. On a more literal level, the canticle was sung during Sunday lauds, so that past and present, as well as all Creation, met in a single voice within the space of the church.[142] Within the context of the manuscript, the unified voices of praise here also provide a contrast to the breaking up of language and understanding that resulted from the building of the tower of Babel (Babylon being the narrative setting for both events). While the Hebrews, the Chaldeans, and the Anglo-Saxons do not speak the same language, they can be united through faith and obedience, and their voices can then be as one. The creation of harmony out of variety is reinforced by the boys' identification of God as *frea folca gehwæs* ('Lord of each people', *Dan.* 400a), and *lifes leohtfruma, ofer landa gehwilc* ('Lord of life over each land', *Dan.* 408), phrases that do not appear in the biblical source but do help to establish the presence of the church militant in this poem. It is after hearing the song and witnessing the miracle that many of Nabuchodonosor's people come to believe in God, though the king himself will not be converted until after his own exile.

The three-in-one voice of the boys also becomes a type of the three-in-

141 'The children of Israel entreated all Creation to bless the eternal Lord, the Ruler of nations. So the three, wise in their minds, said through a common voice.' *Dan.* 358–61.

142 Patrick Conner points out that the song also accompanied the *ordo* for the Ember Days in the Leofric Missal (Bodleian Library, 579, fol. 6). See P. W. Conner, *Anglo-Saxon Exeter: A Tenth-Century Cultural History* (Woodbridge and Rochester, NY, 1993), p. 189.

one nature of the Trinity, which is anachronistically praised near the end of the song:

we þec bletsiað.
frea folca gehwæs. fæder ælmihtig.
soð sunu metodes. sawla nergend.
hæleða helpend. and þec halig gast.
wurðiað in wuldra.[143] witig drihten.[144]

Within the context of the manuscript as a whole, the episode may have served to link beginning and end. The manuscript opens with a request for the readers' words of praise, while the final poem, *Christ and Satan*, repeatedly calls for the same. In addition, the repetition of God's haloed figure three times in the drawings of the Creation on pages 6 and 7 in *Genesis* (pls. IIIa, IIIb) becomes a sign of the Trinity present in and before the Creation; while *Christ and Satan* opens with a brief summary of the Creation which explicitly includes God the Father (*meotod*, *Christ and Satan* 2a), the Son (*godes agen bearn*, *Christ and Satan* 10b), and the Holy Spirit (*wuldres gast*, *Christ and Satan* 14b).[145] Similarly, while the image of the three boys in the fire and their song is an antitype of the lament of Satan in hell, the episode is also a type of the Harrowing of Hell. The Harrowing is described (and was possibly to be illustrated) in *Christ and Satan*, and is repeatedly indexed by the image of the bound Satan in *Genesis* (pls. IIb, VIII, IX, Xa, XV).

The struggle against sin and temptation, and the desire for true knowledge and judgement are brought to a climax in the final passages of *Daniel*. This last Old Testament poem ends with Baltasar's feast and the writing on the wall, a metaphor for the triumph of the church, the Harrowing of Hell, and also a potent reference to each Christian's struggle against sin and the devil, and each Christian's hope for salvation. As such the allusions to the Harrowing that recur throughout the manuscript become an effective means of linking passages and episodes both in terms of their poetic structure within the manuscript and in terms of their theological meaning within the larger context of the Christian church.

143 The manuscript reads *wurðað in wuldre*.

144 'We adore you Lord of each people, Father almighty, true Son of the Lord, Saviour of souls, Helper of men, and you Holy Spirit, honoured in glory, wise Lord.' *Dan*. 399b–403.

145 See above, p. 47.

Whether *Daniel* is complete as it survives or not, the story does provide an appropriate culmination for the acts of seeing and interpretation that make up the poem. According to the biblical book of Daniel (V.24–8) the writing on the wall read *mane, thecel, fares* ('he has numbered, has weighed and has divided'), acts associated with the God of Creation. But Daniel is also apocalyptic and thus provides a fitting introduction to *Christ and Satan*. The writing on the wall, a sign of judgement and doom, looks forward to the book of life and the Last Judgement. In addition, Baltasar and the Shinarites try to tempt Daniel into revealing his knowledge in exchange for gifts, just as the devil will try to tempt Christ with the wealth of the world at the end of *Christ and Satan*. Like Christ, Daniel cannot be tempted and, like Christ, he is the only one fully able to understand and judge what has been written. Christ's first words to Satan during his Temptation are:

wendest þu, awyrgda. þæt awriten nære.
nymþe me ænne[146]

while Daniel refers to Baltasar's courtiers as *ge deoflu* (*Dan.* 749a), and hence void of understanding. Like Satan, Baltasar challenges the power and authority of God, and divine judgement is the result:

ða wearð bliðemod. burga aldor.
gealp gramlice. gode on andan.
cwæð þæt his hergas. hyrran wæron.
and mihtigran mannum to friðe.
þonne isræla. ece drihten.
him þæt tacen wearð. þær he to starude.
egeslic for eorlum. innan healle.
þæt he for leodum. ligeword gecwæð.
þa þær in egesan. engel drihtnes.
let his hand cuman. in þæt hea seld.
wrat þa in wage. worda gerynu.
baswe bocstafas. burhsittendum.
ða wearð folctoga. forht on mode.
acul for þam egesan. geseah he engles hand.
in sele writan. sennera wite.[147]

[146] *Christ and Satan* 674–5a. 'Did you imagine, accursed one, that it was not written, except by me alone'. There is apparently something missing after line 675a.

[147] 'Then the town-leader was glad at heart, boasted fiercely to God in his rage and said that his armies were stronger and mightier as a protection to men than Israel's eternal

The letters in *Daniel* are truly a sign, a trace of God's Judgement that looks forward to its enactment, not described in the Old English poem. They are also likely to have been the subject of the illustrations planned for page 211, and possibly also page 212.[148] The reader is by this means located alongside Baltasar and Daniel looking at the letters. Whether they would have been intelligible within the drawing is an interesting but unanswerable question. If they were not, we would have been left, like Baltasar, unable to read the Judgement for ourselves; if they were, we would have been given the choice between ignorance and knowledge, depending on whether or not we were able to interpret them properly. The Judgement itself is, significantly, not revealed, but left in the balance awaiting the final Judgement of *Christ and Satan*. Daniel says only that Baltasar has been judged by God because of his insolence, his pride, and his misuse of the sacred vessels of the Israelites. The poem ends with Daniel's invocation of Nabuchodonosor's conversion and true belief, providing a contrast to Baltasar's denial of God:

> ac þæt oftor gecwæð.   aldor ðeoda.
> soðum wordum.   ofer sin mægen.
> siððan him wuldres weard.   wundor gecyðde.
> þæt he wære ana.   ealra gesceafta.
> drihten and waldend.   se him dom forgeaf.
> unscyndne blæd.   eorðan rices.
> and þu lignest nu.   þæt sie lifgende.
> se ofer deoflum   dugeþum wealdeð.[149]

The withholding of Judgement situates both Baltasar and his people, and the poem's Anglo-Saxon audience, amongst those waiting to be judged. The mysterious letters then become a sign pointing towards the revelation of Judgement in *Christ and Satan*, which opens with the line 'Þæt wearð

Lord. A sign appeared to him, as he stared there, terrible for men in that hall, because he spoke falsely to the people. Then with terror an angel of the Lord let his hand come there into that high hall, wrote mysterious words in scarlet letters on that wall for the town-dwellers. Then the leader became afraid in his mind, fearful because of the terror. He saw the hand of the angel write in the hall the torture of the Shinnarites.' *Dan.* 712–26.

148 See appendix, p. 206.

149 'But the lord of nations more often said true words before his people after the Lord of glory made known wonders to him, that he was the single God of all Creation, Lord and Ruler, who gave him judgement, blameless glory in earth's kingdom. And you now deny that he is living, he who holds power over devils.' *Dan.* 757–64.

underne eorðbuendum'.[150] The last line of *Daniel*, with its ominous foreboding of Judgement to come, is echoed by the final words of *Christ and Satan*: 'la, þus beo nu on yfele! noldæs ær teala!'[151] While the anachronistic structure of *Christ and Satan* has been the subject of much comment, it does not present a problem in terms of the manuscript's larger themes and structure. In his *Confessiones* (VI.8) Augustine contrasts the eternal Word of God with the ephemeral human voice that has both beginning and end. While not claiming divinity, the authors and artists of the Junius 11 poems have managed to mirror the *Verbum* in the *verba*. The negating or displacing of what we have come to define as 'endings' keeps the human voices alive. As long as the book (admittedly an ephemeral object) survives, we are eternally repeating the words and imagining our own endings for the poems in an ongoing cycle that is mirrored by the repetition of episodes and images within the manuscript. Most importantly, beginnings mirror ends and ends bring us back to beginnings. We, the readers, awaiting our final Judgement, are left waiting and scrutinizing our thoughts and actions. The openness of the ending leaves us forever within the cycle of Fall and Redemption, good and bad reading, true and false understanding, until the coming of the Last Judgement and the end of the earthly book and its audience.

150 'It is revealed to the earth dwellers.'

151 'Lo, thus may evil be upon you! You would not ever before do rightly!' *Christ and Satan* 729.

5

The book and the body

The bible has come to be seen as one of the great narrative plots of history, serving as the structural model for a host of historical and fictional narratives through the centuries. According to this model, the beginning of a book is about the beginning and the end of a book is about the end, mirroring the biblical progression from Genesis to Apocalypse.[1] One would expect that a manuscript composed of biblical poetry would adhere to such a structure, but Junius 11 does not. The beginning simultaneously invokes the beginning, the end, the here and now, and the question of what existed before Creation, while the end circles back to the theme of Temptation and Fall with which the manuscript began. The result is a continuum in which the human and the divine are paralleled, interwoven, contrasted and combined in what might best be termed a narrative or eternal present. But Genesis and the Apocalypse also centre on the body, its creation, procreation, failings and destruction, themes which are explored in a number of different ways throughout the Junius 11 poems. Moreover, the book these poems constitute can itself be considered a sort of body. It was once flesh, it still has a voice, it describes in words the Word as creative force, and it interacted – and continues to interact – with the bodies of its creators and its readers. Riddles, particularly *Riddle* 26 from the Exeter Book, played on just this transformation from living being to speaking object[2] and indicate that, theoretical issues aside, the Anglo-Saxons, like any manuscript-producing culture, were keenly aware

[1] P. Ricoeur, *Time and Narrative*, trans. K. McLaughlin and D. Pellauer, 3 vols. (Chicago, IL, 1984–8) II, 23–6; F. Kermode, *The Sense of an Ending: Studies in the Theory of Fiction* (New York, 1966).

[2] See B. J. Muir, *The Exeter Anthology of Old English Poetry* (Exeter, 1994), p. 309.

of the levels of body and voice indexed by the book. This chapter will examine five specific subjects relating to the body that are central to the Junius 11 poems: the creative and procreative body, the outcast body, bodiliness, the body of Christ, and the body of the book and its audience.

CREATION, PROCREATION AND GENEALOGY

Genesis is by definition about creation, especially the creation of the body. It is hardly controversial to say that this creation is almost exclusively patriarchal: God creates man, and from man creates woman. The ensuing story is a patrilineal narrative that focuses on the rise and fall of peoples and kingdoms, creating history out of procreation. The *Genesis* poem can be divided into four sections, each dealing with the creation of a people or dynasty by God, Adam, Noah and Abraham respectively. The creation of a new people by the three Old Testament fathers, Adam, Noah and Abraham, mirrors the creation of humankind by God the Father. As Gabrielle Spiegel stresses, the biblical story of Creation becomes both the model for and the divine origin of the social order,[3] as well as historical change.[4] This is played out in a number of ways within the manuscript. As each of the patriarchs receives God's blessing he inherits a revitalized *ælgrene* earth,[5] linking the prosperity of the individual leader to the collective good of his people, and reflecting the paradise created for Adam and Eve at the beginning of the poem.[6] The genealogical sections of *Genesis*, particularly those dealing with the generations from Adam to Noah, have also been greatly expanded from their biblical sources, as we have already seen. The distribution of pictures in *Genesis* keeps the viewer's eyes firmly on the procreative body by emphasizing the images of

[3] G. Spiegel, 'Genealogy: Form and Function in Medieval Historical Narrative', *History and Theory* 22.1 (1983), 43–53, at pp. 51–2.

[4] G. Spiegel, 'History, Historicism, and the Social Logic of the Text in the Middle Ages', *Speculum* 65.1 (1990), 59–86, at p. 80.

[5] See above, p. 98.

[6] See also Byrhtferth's *Enchiridion* in which the names (Byrhtferth calls them signs, *tacna*) of Adam and Deus are linked to the physical universe and its workings in much the same way as the images of God and Christ will be in later medieval art. Byrhtferth, *Enchiridion*, pp. 146–7 and 374; cf. the image of the relationship between man and the universe in Hildegard von Bingen's *Liber divinorum operum* (Lucca, Bibliotheca Statale, Cod. Lat. 1942, 9r) written *c.* 1170–71 and illustrated in the early thirteenth century.

patriarchs and matriarchs at the expense, perhaps, of the 'more dramatic' battle scenes. These men and women thus create not only the generations described in the text, but the narrative fabric of the text itself. The illustrations focus our attention on men as protectors or leaders of their people, sitting on thrones, carrying swords or spears, and addressing their retainers or families. While women may be unusually prominent in *Genesis*, the linear progression from poem to poem is effected through the male body and genealogy. The references back to Noah and Abraham embedded in *Exodus* and *Daniel* serve in part to establish a genealogical and biological line running from the Creation to the Last Judgement and ultimately expanding to incorporate the audience of the manuscript. The Israelites are identified at the opening of *Exodus* as *Abrahames sunum* ('sons of Abraham', *Ex*. 18), linking both poems and generations. More specifically, the sacrifice of Isaac, Abraham's favoured son and heir, at the end of *Genesis* is repeated in *Exodus* at one of the moments of greatest drama, the moment just before the destruction of Pharoah's troops. As Abraham and Isaac were tried in *Genesis*, the Israelites will be tried in *Exodus*, and they will all triumph. If, as seems likely, the last few drawings in *Genesis* were to have been devoted to the sacrifice of Isaac, and the first two drawings of *Exodus* were to have depicted the slaying of the first-born and the departure of the Israelites, the pictures would clearly have helped to reinforce this connection.

The genealogical theme appears again as the Israelites enter the Red Sea. The poet describes them as marching tribe by tribe across the sea-bed observing both kinship and rank within kinship: 'cynn æfter cynne. cuðe æghwilc/mægburge riht.'[7] As they move forwards, their genealogy projects backwards to their origins in the patriarchs Noah and Abraham.

him wæs an fæder.
leof leodfruma. landriht geþah.
frod on ferhðe. freomagum leof.
cende cneowsibbe. cenra manna.
heahfædra sum. halige þeode.
israela cyn. onriht godes.
swa þæt orþancum. ealde reccað.
þa þe mægburge. mæst gefrunon.

[7] 'Tribe after tribe. Each knew the right of the tribes.' *Ex*. 351–2.

frumcyn feora. fæderæðelo gehwæs.
niwe flodas. noe oferlað.
þrymfæst þeoden. mid his þrim sunum.
þone deopestan drencefloda.[8]
þara ðe gewurde. on woruldrice.
hæfde him on hreðre. halige treowa.
forþon he gelædde. ofer lagustreamas.
maðmhorda mæst. mine gefræge.[9]
on feorhgebeorh. foldan hæfde.
eallum eorðcynne. ece lafe.
frumcneow gehawæs.[10] fæder and moder.
tuddorteondra. geteled rime.
mismicelra [or missenlicra].[11] þonne men cunnon.
snottor sæleoda. eac þon sæda gehwilc.
on bearm scipes. beornas feredon.
þara þe under heofonum hæleð bryttigað.
Swa þæt wise men. wordum secgað.
þæt from noe. nigoða wære.
fæder abrahames. on folctale.
þæt is se abraham. se him engla god.
naman niwan asceop. eac þon neah. and feor
halige haeapas. in gehyld bebead.
werþeoda geweald. he on wræce lifde.[12]

[8] Manuscript reads *drenfloda*.

[9] Manuscript reads *fr frage*.

[10] Manuscript reads *gehæs*.

[11] Manuscript reads *mismicelra*.

[12] 'They had one father, beloved leader, who held the landright, wise in mind, beloved kinsman. One of the patriarchs, he brought forth a nation of bold men, holy people, the race of Israel, rightly God's. So the old in their wisdom explain it, those who have most heard tell of the genealogy, the origin and ancestry of each of men. Noah travelled over the new flood, the glorious leader with his three sons, the deepest deluge of those that have occurred in the world. He had the holy covenant in his heart, therefore he led the greatest of treasure hoards over the seas, as I have heard tell. To save the life of the earth he had the everlasting survivors, each first generation, father and mother, of all the races of the earth producing descendants, counted by numbers, more diverse then men knew, wise sailor. In addition, in the bosom of the ship they carried each seed that men under the heavens enjoy the use of. As wise men tell with words, Abraham's father was ninth from Noah in the genealogy. That is the Abraham for whom the God of the angels created a new name; and in addition gave the holy troops into his protection, the control of nations. He lived in exile.' *Ex.* 353–83.

The lines not only serve to establish the Israelites' heritage and birthright, but also to parallel their passage through the sea to that of Noah and his ark – both passages being types of baptism.[13] The poet then repeats the story of the sacrifice of Isaac, ending with a repetition of the innumerability topos:

he að swereð. engla þeoden.
wyrda waldend. and wereda god.
soðfæst sigora. þurh his sylfes lif.
þæt þines cynnes. and cneowmaga.
randwiggendra. rim ne cunnon.
yldo ofer eorðan. ealle cræfte.
to gesecgenne. soðum wordum.
nymðe hwylc þæs snottor. in sefan weorðe.
þæt he ana mæge. ealle geriman.
stanas on eorðan. steorran on heofonum.
sæbeorga sand. sealt yða.
ac hie gesittað. be sæm tweonum.
oð egipte. ingeðeode.[14]
land cananea. leode þine.
freobearn fæder. folca selost.[15]

[13] Both passages appear in the lections for the Easter Vigil in Anglo-Saxon England. See B. Raw, *The Art and Background of Old English Poetry* (New York, 1978), pp. 1 and 84. See also J. W. Bright, 'The Relation of the Cædmonian *Exodus* to the Liturgy', *MLN* 27 (1912), 97–103; P. Salmon, *The Breviary through the Centuries*, trans. D. Mary (Collegeville, MN, 1962), p. 65; J. E. Cross, 'The Old English Period', in *The Middle Ages*, ed. W. F. Bolton, The New Hist. of Lit. 1 (London, 1987), pp. 168–73; S. Foot, '"By Water in the Spirit": the Administration of Baptism in Early Anglo-Saxon England', in *Pastoral Care before the Parish*, ed. J. Blair and R. Sharpe (Leicester, 1992), pp. 171–92; Remley, *Biblical Verse*, pp. 168–73.

[14] The manuscript reads *incaðeode*.

[15] 'He swears an oath, the Lord of angels, Controller of fate, God of hosts, trustworthy of victories, through his own life that the number of your kin and kinsmen, warriors, cannot be known to men over the earth by any skill of telling with true words, unless anyone becomes so wise in mind that he alone can count all the stones on the earth, the stars in the heavens, the sand in the cliffs, the salt in the sea; but they will occupy the land of Canaan between the two seas as far as Egypt, your people, noble sons of the father, the best of peoples.' *Ex.* 432–46. Lucas, ed., *Exodus*, p. 131, notes that the final reference to 'father' here is ambiguous, and could be understood as referring to either God or Abraham.

A lacuna comprising an entire section of the poem follows,[16] but the last line of the passage brings us back to the present time of the poem. Although the section of the poem dealing with the completion of the Israelites' crossing of the Red Sea and the pursuit of the Egyptians is missing, it is clear that the genealogical 'digression' represents a turning point. Like Noah and Abraham the Israelites at this moment are marked as triumphant. The crossing is a type of baptism, and here, at the point of total immersion, their progress towards salvation begins.

The same formula that was used to make the transition from *Genesis* to *Exodus* is used to make the transition from *Exodus* to *Daniel*. *Exodus* ends with Moses and the Israelites rejoicing in their triumph and their treasure, and *Daniel* opens with a reference back to Moses, Exodus, and God's covenant with Abraham and his descendants, followed by a renewal of tribulation. In this instance, the drawings might well have helped to establish the contrast between the fortunes of the Israelites, probably depicting their gathering of treasure at the end of *Exodus*, and their loss of the same in the illustrations intended for pages 174 and 175 in *Daniel*. The intervention of a possible picture of Daniel writing on page 172 might have served as a sign of scribal or authorial continuity and a guarantee of the seamless narrative of recorded history. But this last image is the most hypothetical,[17] and is by no means necessary to a reading of the two poems as a coherent narrative.

Again, the protagonists of one part of the poem, the three Hebrew boys, are explicitly identified as *Abrahames bearn* ('the children of Abraham', *Dan*. 193b). The line occurs just prior to Nabuchodonossor's sentencing of the boys to the fire, and is a mark of their true faith. Again, the turning point in their fortunes is signalled by the invocation of Abraham and Isaac and another repetition of the innumerability topos:

Ne forlet þu usic ana. ece drihten.
for ðam miltsum. ðe ðec men hligað.
and for ðam treowum. þe þu tirum fæst.
niða nergend. genumen hæfdest.
to abrahame. and to isaace.
and to iacobe. gasta scyppend.
þu him þæt gehete. þurh hleoðorcwyde.

16 Lucas, ed., *Exodus*, 14.

17 Lucas's suggestion (in 'On the Blank *Daniel* Cycle') is based on the evidence of Spanish manuscripts.

þæt þu hyra frumcyn. in fyrndagum.
ican wolde. þætte æfter him.
on cneorissum. cenned wurde.
and seo mænigeo mære wære.
hat to hebbanne. swa heofonsteorran.
bebugað bradne hwyrft. oðþe brimfaroþes.[18]
sæfaroða sand. geond sealtne wæg.
in eare gryndeð.[19] þæt his unrima.
in wintra worn. wurðan sceolde.[20]

Azarias's call to the Lord is immediately answered by the appearance of the shining angel sent by God. And here too there is a typological relationship established in addition to the genealogical one. The three boys, like Isaac, are not only *Abrahames bearn*, but also innocent victims offered to the flames, and saved through faith and the intervention of the angel of God.

The appearance of Abraham at the moments in which salvation is in sight in *Exodus* and *Daniel* prepares us for the final triumph, the journey of *Abrahames cynn* ('Abraham's race', *Christ and Satan* 459) to heaven in *Christ and Satan*.[21] In the Harrowing of Hell it is Christ, rather than a heavenly angel or a pillar of fire, who descends to rescue the children of Abraham from their suffering, but both the structural and typological relationship between this and the references to Abraham and his children in the Old Testament poems are clear. The possible depiction of the Harrowing between pages 222 and 223 would have helped to extend this message of hope to the Anglo-Saxon readers who counted themselves amongst the children of Abraham awaiting salvation, and for whom the Harrowing provided a model of struggle and redemption in the liturgy as well as in daily life.[22] Even if a drawing of the Harrowing was not

[18] The manuscript reads *oðþ brimfaro þæs*. Farrell emends to present reading.

[19] The manuscript reads *me are gryndeð*. Farrell emends to present reading.

[20] 'Do not forsake us, eternal Lord, for that kindness that men attribute to you, and for that covenant that you, firm in glories, Saviour of men, have given to Abraham and to Isaac and to Jacob, Creator of spirits. You promised them with prophetic words in days of old that their lineage would be increased, that from them a mighty nation would be born, and that host would be famous, a nation to be exalted as the stars in heaven that turn in a broad circuit, or the sand of the seashore that lies beneath the sea; they should become a multitude, numberless in years.' *Dan*. 309–24.

[21] They are also identified as *Adames cyn* (*Christ and Satan* 406a).

[22] Gatch, *Preaching and Theology*, p. 57; Openshaw, 'Weapons in the Daily Battle'.

planned, the repetition of the blessing 'increase and multiply' at key points in the manuscript would have been enough to make this point. Remley notes that the blessing was 'exceedingly popular' in Anglo-Saxon England, appearing in everything from liturgical texts to popular charms, and that its presence in Junius 11 'may be viewed as an extrabiblical augmentation of the narrative'.[23] On another level, the appearance of Abraham and the return to the theme of genealogy at key moments in each of the four poems may well have helped to remind a learned Anglo-Saxon audience of the omnipresence of Christ, who states in John VIII.58: 'I say to you, before Abraham was, I am', and to the eternal present of the manuscript in which history and lineage are united.[24]

Interestingly, while the Old Testament patriarchs are identified as the children of Adam and Abraham, Christ and Mary are identified as the children of Eve. Eve makes her maternal body the argument for her salvation,[25] articulating her biological and genealogical relationship to Mary and Christ: 'þu fram minre dohtor, drihten, onwoce' ('you from my daughter, Lord, awoke', *Christ and Satan* 437), and subtly subverting the patrilinear descent from Christ to Adam, replacing it with the cognatic lineage. Her words also move us back through the manuscript's narrative to her own appearance as first mother at the head of the generations of *Genesis* (pl. XXI).

If the genealogical narratives of Junius 11 focus our attention on men as leaders of their people, they also focus our attention on women as fertile bodies, the bearers of sons. The illustrations do serve to keep women tied to biological function and domestic space, but their iconography, like Eve's words, links them to Mary, ideal mother and queen of heaven, and beyond that to images of contemporary Anglo-Saxon queens for whom Mary served as a model (pls. XXI, XXIVa, XXVI, XXXI, XXXII).[26]

23 Remley, *Biblical Verse*, p. 133.

24 For an interesting interpretation of these lines see J. Kristeva, 'From Signs to Subject', in *New Maladies of the Soul*, trans. R. Guberman (New York, 1995), pp. 129–30. Kristeva notes the way in which language works in the incorporation of a community of bodies into one in this and similar passages, as well as the mulitfaceted movement of time and body reflected in the final words 'I am'.

25 See above, p. 59.

26 Eve also appears enthroned after the Fall in the Genesis mosaics in the church of S. Marco, Venice, but there Eve is shown with uncovered head, and a distaff held idly in one hand. See P. H. Jolly, *Made in God's Image? Eve and Adam in the Genesis Mosaics of S. Marco, Venice* (Berkeley, CA, 1997), pp. 59–60 and pl. 2.

This is a problematic subject in that it clearly places our attention on women as sexualized bodies, a category that men, for the most part, manage to avoid. Clare Lees notes a similar binary division in homiletic accounts of men and women, concluding that what we are being presented with is a cultural construction of female and male in which 'Anglo-Saxon women have sex and rank; men have rank and weapons'.[27] Yet it is also a construction which Anglo-Saxon women did at times turn to their own advantage. The iconography associating the Anglo-Saxon queen with Mary was first developed at Æthelwold's Winchester, and stuck.[28] The coronation of Mary in Æthelwold's Benedictional (fol. 102v) is the first depiction of this subject in a western manuscript, and it is surely not coincidental that the first of the West Saxon queens to be titled *regina* and anointed and crowned with her husband was Æthelwold's ally, Ælfthryth, in 973.[29] While there are no surviving images of Ælfthryth, there are two of her daughter-in-law, Emma/Ælfgyfu. The first is in the New Minster *Liber Vitae* (fol. 6r), and positions Emma to Christ's right, in the place of honour and beneath the figure of Mary. The second, in the *Encomium Emmae* of 1041–2, shows her crowned and enthroned like a king, receiving the manuscript from the scribe, probably a monk of the monastery of Saint-Bertin (pl. XLVIIIa).[30] But unlike surviving images of kings, Emma is accompanied by her sons; they receive the book with her much as Mary and Christ receive the homage of the magi (pl. XLVIIb), or the women of *Genesis* receive the attention of the reader.[31] In the tenth and eleventh centuries Anglo-Saxon queens could and did manipulate sons as a way of expressing and maintaining personal power, and both the portrait of Emma in the *Encomium* and the image of the largely nameless

27 Lees, *Tradition and Belief*, p. 138.

28 Deshman, *Benedictional*, pp. 204–7 and 213–14.

29 J. Nelson, 'The Second English *Ordo*', in her *Politics, Law and Ritual in Early Medieval Europe* (London, 1986), pp. 361–74, at 372. The text is from the Sherborne Pontifical (Paris, Bibliothèque Nationale, lat 943, fol. 74).

30 A. Campbell and S. Keynes, *Encomium Emmae Reginae* (Cambridge, 1998), p. xxxix.

31 Mary Clayton has recently suggested that Ælfric's *Esther* may have been written as a 'mirror for queens' text for Emma in response to the St Brice's day massacre. If true, this provides a telling example of the use of Old Testament models for contemporary royal women. Esther as a model for queens was to become a commonplace in the later Middle Ages. See M. Clayton, 'Ælfric's Esther: a Speculum Reginae?' in *Text and Gloss. Studies in Insular Learning and Literature Presented to Joseph Donovan Pheifer*, ed. H. C. O'Briain, A. M. D'Arcy and J. Scattergood (Dublin, 1999), pp. 89–101.

matriarchs of *Genesis* displaying their sons like badges of office must be viewed within this context. The word for pregnant used in the poem, *eacne*, can also mean 'increased' or 'made powerful',[32] and it seems likely on the evidence of royal marriage practices alone that Anglo-Saxon women were fully aware of the power that went along with the bearing of sons.

As already noted, the date of Junius 11 remains uncertain, and the manuscript cannot be safely dated more precisely than to the late tenth or early eleventh century. It is a highly literate and lavishly illustrated manuscript, quite possibly intended for a court audience. In her work on female book ownership and production, Michelle Brown has commented on the fact that vernacular poetry, in both written and oral form, seems to have been popular amongst aristocratic women in the mid-ninth century.[33] There is no reason to assume that it did not remain popular into the tenth and eleventh centuries, particularly as evidence for the cultural patronage of women increases greatly during this time; nor is there reason to assume that Junius 11 could not have been produced for a woman, or at least for an audience that included aristocratic women. We should therefore bear in mind that it was at precisely the time of the manuscript's production that our evidence for powerful and manipulative queens and queen-mothers is strongest. Eadgifu, third wife of Edward the Elder, was a minor figure during the reign of her husband and his son, Athelstan, but played a prominent role during the reign of her two sons Edmund and Eadred. She continued to take an interest in the struggle for the throne that broke out between her grandsons in 955–6, and was handsomely rewarded when Edgar, her favourite, eventually came to power. Ælfthryth, Edgar's third wife, promoted the cause of her son Æthelred II over that of her stepson, Edward, after Edgar's death in 975, eventually having Edward put to death. It was partially in support of Ælfthryth and Æthelred that Æthelwold is thought to have developed the strong iconographic association between the English queen and the Virgin. Emma/Ælfgyfu, second wife of both Æthelred II and Cnut, is said to have made the succession of a son by her body a condition of her second

32 *Gen.* 2238, 2607 and 2767. This is not to say that the word always carried connotations of power. Cf. The reference to Beadohilde's pregnancy in the Exeter Book poem *Deor*, line 11 (ASPR III, p. 179).

33 M. P. Brown, 'Female Book-ownership and Production in England during the Ninth Century: the Evidence of the Prayerbooks', in *Lexis and Texts in Early English*, ed. C. Kay and L. Sylvester (Amsterdam and Atlanta, forthcoming).

marriage, and possibly her first.[34] Politically she supported Harthacnut, her son by Cnut, over her stepson Harold Harefoot and her own sons by her first marriage. Illegitimacy was the primary charge Emma and Harthacnut levelled against their rivals, Ælfgifu of Northampton and Harold. The Chronicle entry for 1035 simply questions Harold's legitimacy,[35] which was dependent upon his paternity. The *Encomium* goes further, implying not only that Cnut was not Harold's father, but that Ælfgifu of Northampton was not his mother, denying her all claim to the position of queen-mother, a position that Emma cultivated:

Unde factum est, ut quidam Anglorum pietatem regis sui iam defuncti obliti mallent regnum suum dedecorare quam ornare, relinquentes nobiles filios insignis reginae Emmae et eligentes sibi in regem quendam Haroldum, quem esse filium falsa aestimatione asseritur cuiusdam eiusdem regis Cnutonis concubinae; plurimorum uero assertio eundem Haroldum perhibet furtim fuisse subreptum parturienti ancillae, inpositum autem camerae languentis co(n)-cubinae, quod ueratius credi potest.[36]

This, then, was a battle fought through and with the maternal body, and one which would have given the images of aristocratic mothers and sons in Junius 11 special potency.

The need to establish legitimacy and the succession of the rightful son and heir brings us back to the issue of genealogy. In Junius 11, genealogy was a means of uniting the body of the reader with the bodies described and depicted in the book. For the Anglo-Saxons, these were their ancestors

34 P. Stafford, 'The Portrayal of Royal Women in England, Mid-Tenth to Mid-Twelfth Centuries', *Medieval Queenship*, ed. J. C. Parsons (New York, 1993), pp. 143–62.

35 MSS CD and EF. 'And Harold sæde þæt he Cnutes sunu wære and Ælfgyfe þære Hantumisca, þeh hit soð nære.' ('Harold and Ælfgifu of Northampton said that he was Cnut's son, but it was not the truth.') G. P. Cubbin, *MS D*, vol. VI of *The Anglo-Saxon Chronicle: A Collaborative Edition*, ed. D. Dumville and S. Keynes (Cambridge, 1996), 65.

36 'And so it came to pass that certain Englishmen, forgetting the piety of their lately deceased king, preferred to dishonour their country than to ornament it, and deserted the noble sons of the excellent Queen Emma, choosing as their king one Haraldr, who is declared owing to a false estimation of the matter, to be a son of a certain concubine of the above-mentioned King Knútr; as a matter of fact, the assertion of very many people has it that the same Haraldr was secretly taken from a servant who was in childbed, and put in the chamber of the concubine, who was indisposed; and this can be believed as the more truthful account'. Campbell and Keynes, *Encomium*, pp. 38–41.

clearly united to them by a carefully recorded line of descent. The genealogy of King Alfred in Asser's *Life of Alfred* extends back through the historical royal line to include Alfred's legendary Germanic ancestors and his biblical ancestors,[37] the very men, though not the women, that we see in Junius 11. The genealogy of Alfred's father Æthelwulf, recorded in the Chronicle under the year 855 (in manuscripts A, D, E; 856 in C, F) does the same but goes one step further, tracing his lineage not just back to Adam but beyond him to Christ:

855–58 On se Ęþelwulf wæs Ecgbrehtin `g´, Ecgbryht Ealhmunding, Ealhmund Eafing, Eafa Eopping, Eoppa Ingilding; Ingild wæs Ines broþur Westseaxna cyninges, þæs þe eft ferde to Sancte Petre and þær eft his feorh gesealde; and hie wæron Cenredes suna, Cenred wæs Ceolwalding, Ceolwald Cuþaing, Cuþa Cuþwining, Cuþ `wine´ Ceaulining, Ceawlin Cynricing, Cynric Cerdicing, Cerdic Elesing, Elesa Esling, Esla Giwising, Giwis Wiging, Wig Freawining, Freawine Friþogaring, Friþogar Bronding, Brond Bęldæging, Bęldæg Wodening, Woden Friþowalding, Friþuwald Freawining, Frealaf Friþuwulfing, Friþuwulf Finning, Fin Godwulfing, Godwulf Geating, Geat Tętwaing, Tętwa Beawing, Beaw Sceldwaing, Sceldwea Heremoding, Heremod Itermoning, Itermon Hraþraing, se wæs geboren in þære earce, Noe, Lamach, Matusalem, Enoh, Iaered, Maleel, Camon, Enos, Sed, Adam primus homo; et pater noster est Christus, amen.[38]

Like *Genesis*, Æthelwulf's genealogy declares the existence of Christ beyond time and before Creation. Like the Junius 11, manuscript, it

[37] S. Keynes and M. Lapidge, *Alfred the Great* (Harmondsworth, 1983), p. 67.

[38] 'Æþelwulf was the son of Egbert, Egbert the son of Ealhmund, Ealhmund the son of Eafa, Eafa the son of Eoppa, Eoppa the son of Ingild. Ingild was the brother of Ine, king of the West Saxons, who afterwards went to St Peter's and ended his life there. And they were sons of Cenred. Cenred was the son of Ceolwald, Ceolwald the son of Cuþa, Cuþa the son of Cuþwine, Cuþwine the son of Ceawlin, Ceawlin the son of Cynric, Cynric the son of Cerdic, Cerdic the son of Elesa, Elesa the son of Esla, Esla the son of Gewis, Gewis the son of Wig, Wig the son of Freawine, Freawine the son of Friþogar, Friþogar the son of Brond, Brond the son of Bældæg, Bældæg the son of Woden, Woden the son of Friþowald, Friþowald the son of Frealaf, Frealaf the son Friþuwulf, Friþuwulf the son of Fin, Fin the son of Godwulf, Godwulf the son of Geat, Geat the son of Tætwa, Tætwa the son of Beaw, Beaw the son of Sceldwea, Sceldwea the son of Heremod, Heremod the son of Itermon, Itermon the son of Hraþra. He was born in the ark. Noe, Lamech, Matusalem, Enoh, Iaered, Maleel, Camon, Enos, Sed, Adam the first man, and our father is Christ. Amen.' J. M. Bately, *MS A*, vol. III of *The Anglo-Saxon Chronicle: A Collaborative Edition*, ed. D. Dumville and S. Keynes (Cambridge, 1986).

creates a temporal continuum in which present and past become one, and the end is implied in the beginning. All three are examples of the belief that earthly power and wise rule, like life itself, come from God.[39]

The narrative structure of the genealogy, read within the context of the Chronicle or the pictorial genealogy of Junius 11, is particularly interesting. The Chronicle is a record of human events the grammar of which is juxtaposition[40] and the framework of which is the eternal progression of time; the images of the patriarchs and their families in Junius 11 are an illustration of succession, the progression from father to son. But genealogies move backwards, from son to father. They introduce a temporary rupture in the textual fabric of history, reversing the flow of the narrative, chronological and biological time, yet simultaneously furthering the bond between present and past, the living and the dead. They provide a map by means of which the here and now of lived experience is united with a point of origin beyond memory. No matter how fictional the content, the appearance of a carefully kept record that the genealogy presents gives it an aura of factual accuracy akin to that of a scientific observation.[41] The very ability of the genealogical material to project a sense of documented continuity between present and past may have served in turn to bolster the claims of the Chronicle, or the poem, to historical validity.[42] The mapping of events from present to past and from

[39] In her analysis of time and history in the homilies of Ælfric, Clare Lees demonstrates the ways in which belief becomes part and parcel of Anglo-Saxon historiography: 'Creation, rule, and power all derive from God and from a body of knowledge . . . that is the basis for wisdom. The wisdom that comes from knowledge, which is the wisdom of salvation history, governs the recording of history . . . History reveals the presence of divine governance – a perspective that informs Bede's account of the saints in the *Historia ecclesiastica* as well as Ælfric's understanding of the politics of the world' (*Tradition and Belief*, p. 94). But as Spiegel has shown (see above, p. 143), salvation history also becomes modelled on the narrative structures of human history.

[40] J. Thormann, 'The Anglo-Saxon Chronicle Poems and the Making of the English Nation', in *Anglo-Saxonism and the Construction of Social Identity*, ed. A. J. Frantzen and J. D. Niles (Gainesville, FL, 1997), pp. 60–85, at p. 60. See also P. Clemoes, 'Language in Context: *Her* in the 890 *Anglo-Saxon Chronicle*', *Leeds Studies in English* 16 (1985), 27–36, at p. 31.

[41] LaCocque and Ricoeur, *Thinking Biblically*, pp. 50–1.

[42] On the significance of poetry to manuscripts of the Anglo-Saxon Chronicle see P. W. Conner, *The Abingdon Chronicle, A.D. 956–1066*, vol. 10 of *The Anglo-Saxon Chronicle: A Collaborative Edition*, ed. D. Dumville and S, Keynes (Cambridge, 1996), lxxxi–lxxxiii; O'Keeffe, *Visible Song*, ch. 5.

past to present (usually with an implication of projection into the future) reinforce each other, providing a mutually supportive sense of order that doubles the claim to truth and historicity, while perhaps also reaffirming the reader's belief in a divinely ordered plan. Indeed, it is both a metaphor for and copy of it. Spiegel, amongst others, has noted that 'The procreative process by which human beings engender successive generations is the human shape of history generating events over time, events which stand in a filiative relation to one another that mirrors the reproductive course of human life.'[43] The reproduction of bodies thus parallels the production of books, or at least the recording of history. For an Anglo-Saxon audience familiar with the structure and content of the royal genealogies, the physical bond between lived and depicted bodies and times would have been strong, and made stronger still by the depiction of their biblical ancestors in contemporary aristocratic dress and settings.

While everyone may not have read with the same dynastic and genealogical interests, the case of ealdorman Æthelweard demonstrates just how clearly Genesis and genealogy could be united in the aristocratic mind. Ælfric translated and wrote on the meaning of Genesis for Æthelweard and his son Æthelmær. In the late tenth century this same Æthelweard sent his cousin Matilda, Abbess of Essen, a copy of his own translation of the Anglo-Saxon Chronicle, prefaced by a mutual and somewhat informal genealogy:

Scilicet Ælfred rex Athulfi regis filius, ex quo nos originem trahimus; cui filii quinque subiiciuntur, ex quibus ego de Etheredo rege, et tu de Ælfredo rege progeniti uidemur filiis supradicti regis Athulfi. Misit Ælfthrythe filiam suam ad partes Germaniæ Baldwino in matrimonium, et genuit ab ea filios duos Athulfum uiz. et Earnulfum, duas filias quoque Ealhswid et Earmentruth; quippe ex Ælfdryde seriem ducit Earnulfus comes, qui et uicinus uester.

Siquidem Eadgyfu nominata est Eadwerdi regis filia, filii Ælfredi supra scripti regis quæ et abmatertera tua ipsa in matrimonium Galliarum ad partes minori Karulo mittitur regi. Eadhild etiam in coniugium mittitur Hugoni filio Hrodbyrhti. Alias vero duas Ædestanus rex tali ratione misit ad Oddonem, ut quæ ab eis placuisset sibi in matrimonium elegisset; cui uisa melior Eadgyde, ex qua tu principium tenes natiuitatis. Alteram etiam subiunxit cuipiam regi iuxta Iupitereos montes.[44]

[43] 'Geneaology: Form and Function', p. 51.

[44] 'Alfred was the son of Æthelwulf, from whom we are descended. Five sons followed him. Of these, I am descended from King Æthelred, and you from King Alfred, both

While Æthelweard's genealogy does not go all the way back to Genesis, it does indicate that both he and his cousin belonged to branches of the West Saxon royal family whose genealogy purported to do so. It also has an interesting structure, beginning in the past (with Alfred), moving to the present (with the reference to Æthelweard and Matilda), moving back to the past (with the sons of Alfred) and then forward from Alfred to Matilda. In fact a projection into an unwritten future is implied by Æthelweard's request a few lines later that Matilda send him news of the descendants of Eadgyth's sister.

Æthelweard's request to his cousin also indicates that women can be assumed to have had both a knowledge of and interest in family history, even though they rarely appeared in official genealogies.[45] The *Encomium Emmae*, and the *Vita Ædwardi* commissioned by Edward the Confessor's widow Edith do the same.[46] Anglo-Saxon women thus became the invisible means by which the genealogies were maintained, both biologically and, more rarely, textually. The Junius 11 illustrations place them visibly at the heart of the progression from father to son. Moreover, the iconography of birth and childbed highlights the pivotal role of the maternal body in the process of succession and the resulting creation of both history and its record.

sons of King Æthelwulf . . . Alfred sent his daughter Ælfthryth to the land of Germany to marry Baldwin, who had by her two sons, Æthelwulf and Earnwulf, and also two daughters, Ealhswith and Eormenthryth. From Ælfthryth, as a matter of fact, Count Earnwulf, who is your neighbour, is descended.

'Eadgyfu was the name of the daughter of King Eadweard, the son of Alfred . . . and she was your great-aunt and was sent into the country of Gaul to marry the younger Charles. Eadhild, furthermore, was sent to be the wife of Hugo, son of Robert. King Æthelstan sent another two [of his sisters] to Otho, the plan being that he should choose as his wife the one who pleased him. He chose Eadgyth, from whom you spring in the first place. The other sister he married to a certain king near the Alps.' A. Campbell, *The Chronicle of Æthelweard* (London, 1962), pp. 1–2.

45 The significant exceptions are Osburh, mother of Alfred the Great, whose genealogy is included in informal form in Asser's life of Alfred (*Alfred the Great*, ed. Keynes and Lapidge, p. 68), and Emma/Ælfgyfu. While the latter is not included in the offical recorded genealogies, the fact that her name was changed from Emma to Ælfgyfu (the name of Æthelred II's grandmother and of his first wife) on her arrival in England seems, at the very least, an attempt to proclaim her a part of the West Saxon dynasty.

46 Campbell and Keynes, eds., *Encomium*; F. Barlow, ed., *Life of King Edward who Rests at Westminster, Attributed to a Monk of Saint-Bertin*, 2nd edn (Oxford, 1992).

For both men and women, the genealogical material and the images of creation and procreation in Junius 11 provided lessons in proper conduct. Leaders who were faithful to the Lord prospered in lineage, wealth and kingdom. Women had the added responsibility of being loyal to their lords, and their prosperity was guaranteed through their obedient bodies, as the examples of Eve, Sarah and Mary make clear. If a king's role was to lead his people through adversity into plenty, a queen's role was to bear sons and ensure the continuation of both people and dynasty. The reward for the proper conduct of both groups was not just earthly prosperity but inclusion amongst the chosen, the family of Christ in heaven. In the Junius 11 manuscript Christ is God's 'noble child',[47] and is surrounded in heaven by his 'blessed children'.[48] *Genesis* describes and depicts God as the Creator of the earth and its family of inhabitants; *Christ and Satan* ends with a statement to the same effect, and a summary of both the primary message of the manuscript and the hope of the reader:

þu eart hæleða helm. and heofendema.
engla ordfruma. and eorðan tudor.
up gelæddest[49] to þissum eadigum ham.[50]

This is very much a synopsis of the manuscript. The Creation and Fall of the angels was followed by the Creation and Fall of Adam and Eve and the continuing cycle of Creation and Fall of their descendants. From the institution of God's covenant with Abraham on through *Exodus* and *Daniel*, God has quite literally led the family of the saved towards heaven. The deliverance of Adam, Eve and the patriarchs at the Harrowing indicates that they have finally reached their long-awaited goal. The reader too is positioned amongst those being led towards salvation by both the first-person voice of the lines quoted above and the suggestion in the remaining lines of the poem that the cycle will continue, before ending ultimately in salvation. The lines are followed by a description of the heavenly family gathered around the Lord singing words of praise, a reflection of the opening of *Genesis* and its accompanying frontispiece. The

47 *Freobearn godes* (*Christ and Satan* 288b).

48 'þær sunu meotodes. / habbað eadige bearn. ealle ymbfangen. / seolfa mid sange.' *Christ and Satan*, 142b–144.

49 This half-line is not in the manuscript, but is inserted by modern editors.

50 'You are the leader of men and heavenly Judge, Creator of angels and earth's family, [you] lead us up to this blessed home.' *Christ and Satan* 656–8.

song merges imperceptibly into a brief account of the Temptation of Christ, paralleling the Temptation of Adam and Eve in *Genesis*.[51] In the first Temptation Satan brings Christ *brade stanas* ('broad stones', *Christ and Satan* 670b). Both Clubb and Finnegan have commented on the theological significance of the line and the scene as a whole,[52] the final reminder of Christ's human nature in the manuscript. If an illustration of the Temptation of Christ was originally located after page 228, it may well have echoed visually the earlier Temptation of man. The 'broad stones' are sometimes represented as small and round, and very like the apple with which Adam and Eve are tempted. In the Odbert Psalter of *c.* 990–1012 (Boulogne-sur-Mer, Bibliothèque Municipale, 20) the historiated initial of Psalm XCI includes the detail of the tree and combines the Temptation with Christ's trampling on the beasts (pl. XLVb).[53] Christ's victory over the demon here again provides a contrast to Satan's victory over Adam and Eve. Similarly, Satan's offering of the earthly kingdom to Christ is reminiscent of his offering Eve the heavenly kingdom. Both Christ and Eve are instructed to look and to see, but Christ, of course, sees rightly and with his own eyes. The poem ends with the final condemnation of Satan to hell and a warning to those who 'would not do rightly'.

THE OUTCAST BODY

But there were also those who were not amongst the chosen. As the creative power of God and the richness of the heavenly kingdom is contrasted with Satan's inability to create coupled with the barrenness of hell, so the men and women of *Abrahames cynn* are consistently contrasted with the outcasts of Junius 11, namely Cain, Hagar and Ismael, Lot and his daughters, and the people of Sodom. The generations of these people do not extend beyond the *Genesis* poem. Cain's male lineage ends with the

[51] It is also typologically related to Exodus and the trials of the Israelites after the crossing of the Red Sea. Danielou, *From Shadows to Reality*, pp. 158–9. As the poem *Exodus* ends with the crossing of the Red Sea it is doubtful that the parallels would have been picked up in the illustrations.

[52] Clubb, *Christ and Satan*, p. 131; Finnegan, *Christ and Satan*, p. 119.

[53] The psalter was produced at Saint-Bertin for Abbot Odbert (990–1007) and is thought to contain contributions by an Anglo-Saxon artist (Temple, *Anglo-Saxon Manuscripts*, 23 and 100).

sons of his slayer Lamech: Iared, Iabal and Tubal-Cain. The Egyptian Hagar and Ismael disappear into the wilderness,[54] while the death of the Egyptian first-born is the only one of the ten plagues to be documented by the *Exodus* poet. As Peter Lucas notes, within this manuscript and its conception of power, the *frumbearn* ('first-born') is the most important link in the establishment and maintenance of genealogy.[55] The landscape inhabited by these people is also decidedly different from the *ælgrene* land of the patriarchs. The Egyptians are clearly labelled as *burhweardas* ('city-dwellers', *Ex.* 39), inhabiting a *ðrysmyde* ('thirsty', *Ex.* 40b) land. Cain is doomed to inhabit a land that is entirely without green[56] and that will be developed by his son Enoch into the city of blood.[57] The Sodomites too inhabit a city that is not only deprived of greenness but transformed into a truly apocalyptic wasteland:

lig eall fornam.
þæt he grenes fond.   goldburgum in.
swylce þær ymbutan.   unlytel dæl.
sidre foldan.   geondsended wæs.
bryne and brogan.   bearwes wurdon.
to axan and to yslan.   eorðan wæstma.
efne swa wide.   swa ða witelac.
reðe geræhton.   rum land wera.[58]

As the fertility of the earth and human race are joined in Abraham, sterility and barrenness are joined in the Sodomites. The Sodomites, as Allen Frantzen documents, are contrasted with Abraham at every level. Their sterility and non-procreative sex is opposed to his fertility and 'proper' heterosexual conduct, and they are city-dwellers living in a

54 According to the Canterbury biblical commentaries Ismael's race was that of the Saracens, 'a race which is never at peace with anyone': 'sic fuit genus eius Saracenis, numquam cum omnibus pacem habentes se semper contra aliquos certantes'. Bischoff and Lapidge, *Biblical Commentaries*, pp. 324–5.

55 *Ex.* 52 and 65.

56 *forþon heo þe hroðra oftihð, glæmes grene folde* ('therefore the earth withdraws the brightness of the green land', *Gen.* 1017b–18).

57 *Gen.* 1056b–7; Doane, ed., *Genesis A*, 249.

58 'Fire destroyed all that it found of green in the rich cities, and also an un-little portion of that wide earth around was covered with fire and terror. The forests were ashes, and ashes the fruits of the earth. Just as wide as the severe punishment reached the spacious land of men.' *Gen.* 2550–7.

disordered world, while Abraham and his true line inhabit an orderly rural landscape.[59]

Lot and his two daughters have been spared the fate of Sodom, yet dwell in isolation, like animals, in their mountain cave. Their incestuous relationship produces the founders of the Moabites and Ammonites, both traditional enemies of the Israelites.[60] Again, a contrast with Abraham is established. The poet does not dwell on the sin of incest, but indicates the disorderly nature of the act by emphasizing Lot's passive role in it:

ne wiste blondenfeax.
hwonne him fæmnan to. bryde him bu wæron.
on ferhðcofan. fæste genearwot.
mode and gemynde. þæt he mægðe sið.
wine druncen. gewitan ne meahte.[61]

In his passivity he is like the Sodomites, whom the poet associates with women, passivity and defeat,[62] markedly different from the virile and active Abraham, who 'makes Hagar with child' and gives life to Isaac.[63] Lot's daughters too are associated with the Sodomites, as well as with Cain, by the poet's description of them as '*willgesweostor*' ('dear sisters', *Gen.* 2608), recalling his description of the Sodomites as '*willgesteallum*' ('dear companions', *Gen.* 2147) and '*willgesiððas*' ('dear comrades', *Gen.* 2003), and of Cain and Abel as '*willgebroðor*' ('dear brothers', *Gen.* 971).[64] The outcasts of Junius 11 have no genealogy, at least not in this version of biblical history, and certainly they have no place in the royal genealogies. We may meet their descendants from time to time in such isolated characters as the fatherless Grendel, but their histories go largely

59 Frantzen, *Before the Closet: Same-Sex Love from 'Beowulf' to 'Angels in America'* (Chicago, 1998), pp. 187–200.

60 On the construction of the origin narratives of these peoples see J. M. Miller, 'Moab and the Moabites', *Studies in the Mesha Inscription and Moab*, ed. J. A. Dearman (Atlanta, GA, 1989), pp. 18–19.

61 'The gray-haired man did not know when both the women were brides to him, firmly constrained in mind, heart and thought, so that the wine-drunk man was not able to know the maidens' actions.' *Gen.* 2602b–2606.

62 Frantzen, *Before the Closet*, p. 217; and see *Gen.* 2123–35 and 2139–61.

63 *Gen.* 2237–8; *Gen.* 2764b–2765: 'Abrahame woc bearn of bryde.'

64 Frantzen, *Before the Closet*, 223; Doane, ed., *Genesis A*, 246, 301, 314. We should note, however, that *willgeðoftan* ('dear comrades') is also used to describe Abraham's companions in *Genesis* 2026. Of Lot's daughters Doane comments 'the first element seems to be used ironically where the family relationship is somewhat amiss' (246).

unrecorded. However, it is not just the absence of genealogy that unites these figures, they are also united through the emphasis on their bodies: the naked body of Satan, the marked body of Cain, and the sexualized bodies of Hagar, the Sodomites and Lot's daughters.

BODILINESS

Within the cycle of creation and procreation that leads from Genesis to the Last Judgement, the body is a central image and issue. In general, genealogy is anchored in biology and the physical body. It is through the succession of bodies from generation to generation that the link between past and present is made real. In illustrated manuscripts such as Junius 11 or Claudius B. iv this becomes all the more evident as the illustrations literally embody the events about which we read. But events also leave their mark on the body. Obedience and disobedience, for example, are as irrevocably marked on the body in the bible and in Junius 11 as they were in Anglo-Saxon England. Disobedience leads to disfigurement, usually a bodily loss that at the same time emphasizes human bodiliness, and exile. In her study of the body and the law in Anglo-Saxon England, Katherine O'Brien O'Keeffe points out that 'whatever its function as deterrence, juridical mutilation produces a body about which things may be known. The spectacle of such a body continually announces both crime and punishment.'[65] Depictions and descriptions of the body in Junius 11 function in much the same way. Satan and the rebel angels receive naked bodies as signs of their disobedience and lower nature, their movement into bodiliness led by Satan contrasting with the journey of the Israelites towards salvation, and Christ leading the patriarchs from hell to heaven. The bodies of Satan and his contemporaries are sexed as male (pls. VIII, IX), perhaps as a means of connecting yet contrasting their bodies with those of Adam, Noah, Abraham and Christ, and they are made to suffer bodily. They are tormented by heat and icy cold, surrounded by writhing serpents and wailing clamour, and Satan is forced to labour vainly attempting to measure hell with his hands. The description of hell and its inhabitants in *Christ and Satan* picks up where Satan's speeches and the illustrations of hell in *Genesis* left off (pls. VIII, Xa, XV). Satan laments:

[65] See K. O'Brien O'Keeffe, 'Body and Law in Late Anglo-Saxon England', *ASE* 27 (1998), 209–32, at p. 230.

ic eom limwæstmum. þæt ic gelutian ne mæg.
on þyssum sidan sele. synnum forwundod.
hwat her hat and ceald. hwilum mencgað.
hwilum ic gehere. hellescealcas.
gnornende cynn. grundes mænan.
niðer under næssum. hwilum nacode men.
winnað ymb wyrmas.[66]

The isolation of Satan within a crowded hell, and his bodily torments, are suggested by the image of Satan chained and immovable within the mouth of hell on pages 3 and 16 (pls. IIb, VIII). The direct appeal of the passage to the body of the reader/viewer, however, has a much earlier parallel in the hell scene on the ninth-century Rothbury cross, in which a tiny naked and screaming figure, isolated against the darkness of the deeply cut stone, grasps the legs of two of a series of intertwined beasts and serpents while looking directly into the eyes of the viewer.[67] Satan's appeal to our ears is like the Rothbury figure's appeal to our eyes. It makes real the abstract torments about which we read.

Like the Fall of the angels, the Fall of Adam and Eve brings about a new bodiliness, demonstrated this time in a new awareness of and shame in their bodies (pls. XIV, XVI). Desiring eternal bodilessness in the kingdom of heaven, they sin through the body and receive labour, bodily pain and death as a result. Moreover, their bodies now carry clear marks of sexed and gendered difference (Adam's beard, their different hairstyles, clothing and occupations) that were not present before the Fall. The disobedience of their son, Cain, also results in a marked body, the *tacen* the Lord sets upon him in *Genesis* 1044b echoing the *tacen* that Adam claims marks his body after the Fall in *Genesis* 885b. Cain's mark is said to be visible for all to see, with the exception of his blind kinsman, Lamech. Cain slew Abel in spiritual blindness, while Lamech's blindness is physical. The two cannot, however, be separated as Cain's crime has left

[66] 'I am in limbsize such that I may not hide in this broad dwelling, wounded with sins. Lo, here hot and cold at times mingle, at times I hear hell retainers, a lamenting race, lament the abyss down under the earth; at times naked men struggle around worms.' *Christ and Satan* 129–35.

[67] Cramp, *County Durham and Northumberland*, Rothbury 1cD, part 1, pp. 217–21 and part 2, pl. 215, no. 1224; J. Hawkes, 'The Rothbury Cross: an Iconographic Bricolage', *Gesta* 35 (1996), 77–94.

its mark on the bodies of his descendants as well as his own.[68] Lamech himself makes this clear in his speech to his two wives, Ada and Sella, in which he identifies himself as the slayer of Abel's murderer, and one who shall suffer mortal pain, death and sevenfold vengeance for it.

> ic on morðor ofsloh.   minra sumne.[69]
> hyldemaga.   honda gewemde.
> on caines   cwealme mine.
> fylde mid folmum.   fæder enoses.
> ordbanan abeles.   eorðan sealde.
> wældreor weres.   wat gearwe.
> þæt þam lichryre.   on last cymeð.
> soðcyninges   seofonfeald wracu.
> micel æfter mane.   min sceal swiðor.
> mid grimme gryre.   golden wurðan.
> fyll and feorhcwealm.   þonne ic forð scio.[70]

Curiously, the Junius 11 *Genesis* does not mention Lamech's blindness, making his crime all the more akin to Cain's original crime.

The poet and the artist both depict Cain as an exile but, as noted above, he is an exile within a city rather than an animal-like wanderer in the wastelands. Nevertheless, the animal masks in the border of the illustration on page 51 (pl. XXIII), and the possible paralleling of God's eternal curse on Cain with his curse on the serpent hint at his animal nature.[71] A similar combination of the urban and the animal occurs in *Daniel*, where Nabuchodonosor is portrayed as both city-dweller and exile, in his case a city-king suffering seven years of torture in the wasteland of wild animals:

> seofon winter samod.[72]   susl þrowade.
> wildeora westen.   winburge cyning.[73]

68 Just as the mark of the Fall given first to Adam and Eve leaves its trace on their descendants.

69 The manuscript reads *sune*.

70 'In murder I slew one of my near relations, defiled my hands in the destruction of Cain, killed with hands the father of Enos, the original murderer of Abel, gave the earth the blood of a murdered man. I know certainly that sevenfold vengeance, great evil will result from that true-king's death. My [act] of death and mortal pain will be requited with grim terror when I die.' *Gen*. 1093–1103.

71 Doane, ed., *Genesis A*, p. 248, commenting on line 1015a.

72 The manuscript reads *winter*.

73 'Seven winters together he suffered torture in the wasteland of wild animals, the king of the capital city.' *Dan*. 620–1.

Obedience, like disobedience, can be marked on the body. Circumcision, the sign of God's covenant with Abraham, is also a sign placed on the body, though the *Genesis* poet focuses more on the spiritual nature of the mark than on its physical nature,[74] and thus on its fulfilment in the sacrament of baptism and spiritual circumcision. Ælfric writes:

God bebead abrahame þæt he sceolde and his ofspring his wed healdan þæt sum tacen wære on heora lichaman to geswutelunge þæt hi on god belyfdon. and het ðæt he name scearpecgedne flint. and forcurfe sumne dæl þæs felles ætforeweardan his gesceape. and þæt tacen wæs ða swa micel on geleaffullum mannum. swa micel swa nu is þæt halige fulluht buton þam anum þæt nan man ne mihte godes rice gefaran ær þan ðe se come þe þa ealdan æ. sette and eft on his andwerdnysse hi to gastlicum þingum awende . . .

Se ylca hælend þe nu egefullice. and halwendlice clypað on his godspelle. buton gehwa beo geedcenned of wætere. and of þam halgan gaste. ne mæg he faran into heofenan rice. se ylca clypode gefyrn þurh ða ealdan æ. swa hwilc hysecild swa ne bið ymbsniden on þam fylmene his flæsces. his sawul losað. for þan ðe he aydlode min wed.[75]

The mark of circumcision is yet another sign of the special status granted to men in Genesis, their ability to create dynasty, genealogy and history by seminally imparting it from one generation to the next.[76] The generations between Seth and Abraham are the 'seedbearers' (*sædberende*, *Gen.* 1145), and the verbs used for their begetting of children, *strynan* and *astrienan*, reflect their special status.[77] Unlike the mark of Cain, the mark of circumcision is not immediately visible to all, it is a mark of faith that

74 In contrast to the tenth-century Joshua Roll (Vatican, Biblioteca Apostolica, gr. 431), in which blood drips from the wounds of the agonized Israelites.

75 'God commanded Abraham that he and his offspring should hold his covenant and that a certain sign that they believed in God should be made manifest on their bodies; and commanded him to take a sharp-edged flint and cut off a portion of the foreskin. And that sign was then as great amongst believing men as holy baptism is now, except only that no man could travel to the kingdom of God before the One came who would set the old law, and thereafter in his presence turn it to a spiritual act . . . The same Saviour who now awfully and salutarily cries in his gospel, "Unless each one be born again from the water and from the Holy Ghost, he may not travel to the heavenly kingdom". The same cried formerly through the old law, "Whichever male-child shall not be circumsised on the foreskin of his flesh, will lose his soul, because he profaned my covenant".' 'Kalendas Ianvarii Octabas et Circumcisio Domini', lines 49–57 and 61–5, in *Ælfric's Catholic Homilies. The First Series* (ed. Clemoes), pp. 225–6.

76 Speigel, 'Genealogy: Form and Function', p. 50.

77 Butcher, 'Formulaic Invention'.

holds dynasties and peoples together. Like Ælfric's sign of the cross, it must be marked on the body and carried in the heart.[78] It is also remarkably potent. The birth of Isaac is the direct result of Abraham's faithful marking of the male body with the sign of the covenant (*Gen.* 2326–7). Isaac is born out of faith, the product of God and Abraham, with Sarah as the sceptical vessel. The Claudius B. iv artist illustrates this point by depicting Abraham blessed by the hand of God alongside the birth of Isaac on folio 35r.

The body made visible also becomes a sign and is used to distinguish the chosen from the outcasts. While we do not see the mark of the chosen cut on the bodies of the men of *Abrahames cynn*, we have seen the bodies of the women who brought forth the outcast generations, Hagar and Lot's daughters. Their bodies are disruptive bodies, so it is not surprising that in each of these episodes it is the woman who takes the initiative in the begetting of sons, the disorderliness of their behaviour indicated by the lesser status of their children. Certainly it is Sarah rather than Hagar who convinces Abraham that Hagar should bear his child, but it is Hagar who grows proud, exulting in her pregnancy and, like Cain, becoming jealous and hateful, as well as attempting to usurp the position of the rightful wife and mother.[79] Both Hagar and Ismael's inferior status may have been picked up in the illustrations intended for page 102 and the bottom of page 105, which are likely to have depicted the conception and birth of Ismael.[80] Conception, with its reference to the sexual body, is not usually depicted in Anglo-Saxon art. In Claudius B. iv, and most probably in Junius 11, such illustrations served (or would have served) to indicate the problematic nature of the relationship between the men and women involved, and the resulting otherness of their offspring. Several of the birth scenes in Claudius B. iv, like those in Junius 11, are modelled on images of the Nativity, and it is only the depiction of the moment of

78 'And we sceolan mearcian ure forewearde heafod. and urne lichaman mid cristes rodetacne. þæt we beon ahredde fram forwyrde. þonne we beoð gemearcode ægðer ge on foranheafode. ge on heortan mid blode þære drihtenlican ðrowunge.' ('And we shall mark our forehead and our body with the sign of Christ's cross so that we may be saved from destruction. Therefore let us be marked either on the forehead or in the heart with the blood of the Lord's suffering'.) 'Sermo de sacrificio in die Pascae', *CH*, ed. Godden, p. 151.

79 *Gen.* 2234–43. See above, p. 160.

80 See appendix, p. 204.

conception that sets certain episodes apart. The birth of Isaac is illustrated, but his conception is not, nor is there any evidence to suggest that it would have been depicted in Junius 11. The drawing of the conception of Ismael on folio 27v of Claudius B. iv, on the other hand, positions us as voyeurs looking into the private space of the bedroom and witnessing what is ultimately a private act (though genealogy is not of course a private matter), and the artist draws our attention to this by covering Sarah's body with a curtain while exposing the bodies of Abraham and Hagar. The impropriety of our looking parallels and makes clear the impropriety of the act, and marks Ismael as the product of the body and sex outside of marriage, and hence outside of the true lineage. Ismael's future as an exiled hunter and fighter is a reflection of his beginnings. Similarly, the illustrations intended for pages 122 and 123 of Junius 11 are likely to have shown the conception and birth of Moab and Ammon. In Claudius B. iv the cave in which Lot and his daughter have taken refuge is sliced open like a doll's house, again allowing us a forbidden look at a forbidden moment (pl. XLVIb). As with the birth of Ismael, the births of Moab and Ammon are not treated differently from the other birth scenes in the manuscript; it is the moment of conception that makes the difference. With respect to the improper look we should also note that the distribution of spaces for drawings suggests that we too would have witnessed the destruction of Sodom, our look paralleling the ultimate forbidden look, the look back of Lot's wife.

The outcast nature of Lot's daughters and their sons is doubled by their improper knowledge of their father's body, although this is not necessarily a specifically female sin. Noah's son, Cham, is also guilty of wrongful knowledge of the father's body, this time through the impropriety of his gaze. Here, as with the daughters of Lot, the result is disorder and rupture within the family. In both cases also the exposed body of the father is rendered senseless through drink, ensuring its passivity and inability to maintain order and control. Once more, the depiction of this episode in Junius 11 aligns us with the misguided look by representing Noah with his genitals exposed (pl. XL) so that we gaze on the body along with Cham. This is highly unusual if not unprecedented in early medieval art, and the reasons for it are not revealed by reference to the text of the poem. Certainly we can equate the body of Noah with birth, rebirth and fertility, as the story of the ark and the lush vegetation of the vineyard make clear. The only other figures drawn with exposed genitals in this manuscript are the fallen angels (pls. VIII, IX), so a reference to the fallen nature of man is doubtless intended. As we have seen, the poets and artists of the Junius 11 manuscript consistently present the reader/viewer with a choice, so that, like the protagonists of the poems, we are asked to read and interpret properly. In this larger context Noah's exposed genitals may be nothing more than a sign of the danger of the misguided look. Eve, after all, is guilty of just this act of disobedience with her eyes. Her gazing at the apple and the messenger is not presented as in any way sexual or related to bodily desire; rather, she is tempted through her eyes. She looks at and believes in the false angel and the vision placed before her eyes, and desires a knowledge of the Father which has been forbidden.

THE BODY OF CHRIST

The offering of bodies to the eyes of both the characters within the poems and the reader contrasts with the offering of bodies to God. Isaac, the three Hebrew boys and Christ are all offered, are tested and triumph through the spirit, which in this manuscript leaves the body intact.[81] Of this group, the body of Christ is the most complex, an omnipresent yet elusive subject. Unlike the bodies of mortal men and women, or even the body of Satan, Christ's body escapes definition, containment and history.[82] In Junius 11 it is at once present and absent, human and eternal, Word and body, divine light, and indivisible Father and Son – its nature capturing something of the mystery of the body itself. It descends from heaven to destroy the false idols of the Egyptians and free the Israelites in *Exodus*,[83] is referred to ahistorically in the invocation of the Trinity in *Daniel*,[84] and is present throughout *Genesis*. The cruciferous nimbus of the Creator in the majority of *Genesis* illustrations indicates that he is meant to be understood as incorporating the figure of Christ *logos*.[85] He appears most prominently in the illustrations preceding the Creation of

[81] As opposed to saints' lives in which the body is repeatedly opened up and dismembered.

[82] Although she deals with a later period, on Christ's body see M. Rubin, *Corpus Christi: The Eucharist in Late Medieval Culture* (Cambridge, 1991).

[83] Lucas, ed., *Exodus*, pp. 58–9, line 466.

[84] See above, p. 138.

[85] The artists are not consistent. The cruciferous nimbus is present in eighteen out of twenty-five images. In six there is no nimbus, and in one (page 23), a nimbus but no cross.

man (pls. I, IIa, IIIa, IIIb), embodying the eternal existence of the Son, his indivisibility from the Father, and the act of Creation in and through the Word.[86] The frontispiece (fol. 2) to Claudius B. iv has no such complexity, nor is the Creator depicted with a nimbus, though he is shown with a cruciferous nimbus elsewhere in the manuscript. While not generally the subject of visual narrative, this making visible of the Word was very much a feature of Anglo-Saxon culture. Both Bede and Ælfric taught that one of the purposes of Christ's incarnation was to make God visible.[87] Following Bede, Ælfric wrote:

> On frymðe wæs word. and þæt word wæs mid gode. and þæt word wæs god. word bið wisdomes geswutelung. and þæt word, þæt is se wisdom, is acenned of ðam ælmihtigum fæder butan anginne. For ðan ðe he wæs æfre god of gode. wisdom of ðam wisan fæder. nis he na geworht. for þan þe he is god and na gesceaft: Ac se ælmihtiga fæder gesceop þurh ðone wisdom ealle gesceafta. and hi ealle þurh ðone halgan gast geliffæste; Ne mihte ure mennisce gecynd crist on ðære godcundlican acennydnesse geseon: ac þæt ilce word wæs geworden flæsc and wunode on us. þæt we hine geseon mihton.[88]

While Ælfric and Bede both claimed that we could not see Christ before his incarnation, the Junius 11 artists keep the body of Christ *logos* present before our eyes by giving God the Father the cruciferous nimbus that is a sign of the Son. In doing so they emphasize the divine, spiritual nature of

86 Although he appears with greatest frequency in the illustrations of Creation and paradise, the Creator-Logos retains his cruciforous nimbus after the Fall of man. Here the Junius 11 illustrations differ markedly from those of the Cotton Genesis and related manuscripts in which the Creator-logos disappears after the expulsion. See Weitzmann and Kessler, *Cotton Genesis*, p. 37.

87 Raw, *Trinity and Incarnation*, pp. 66–7, and texts cited therein. See also Bede, *Homilae* (CCSL 122) I.7, pp. 47–8. See also Hannover, Kestner Museum WM XXIa 36, 147v, discussed above, p. 48, n.10, and in J. O'Reilly, 'St John as a Figure of the Contemplative Life: Text and Image in the Art of the Anglo-Saxon Benedictine Reform', in *St Dunstan: His Life, Times and Cult*, ed. N. Ramsay, M. Sparks and T. Tatton-Brown (Woodbridge, 1992), pp. 165–85, at p. 178–9.

88 'In the beginning was the word, and the word was with God, and the word was God. The word is the manifestation of wisdom, and that word that is wisdom is born from the almighty Father, without beginning, because he was always God from God, wisdom from the wise Father. He was not created because he is God and not a creature; but the almighty Father created all Creation through that wisdom, and he gave life to all through the Holy Spirit. Our human nature could not see Christ in that divine birth, but that same word became flesh and dwelt among us so that we might see him.' *CH*, ed. Clemoes, p. 195.

Christ rather than his earthly, human nature. With the exception of the Crucifixion which might have been planned for *Christ and Satan*, the drawings become signs of the coming incarnation, while showing us the intact and eternal body rather than the broken and mortal one. On the other hand, the text, particularly the text of *Christ and Satan*, allows us glimpses of the latter. Together, the two work to make the human body more mystical and the mystical body more human, possibly reflecting the notion expressed by John of Damascus that the divine is knowable only through images, visual or verbal. (John also makes it clear that perception is itself a bodily, not just a mental process.)[89] In effect, the unknowable God reveals himself in the knowable form of his Son. The dual nature of Christ and his twofold birth was the focus of Ælfric's *Sermo de sacrificio in die pascae*. Ælfric wrote of Christ's body in the following terms:

Se lichama soðlice ðe crist on ðrowade wæs geboren of Marian flæsce. mid blode. and mid banum. mid felle. and mid sinum. on menniscum limum. mid gesceadwisre sawle geliffæst. and his gastlica lichama ðe we husel hatað is of manegum cornum gegaderod buton blode. and bane. limleas. and sawulleas. and nis for ði nan ðing þæron to understandenne lichamlice. ac is eall gastlice to understandenne.[90]

89 'Anyone would say that our inability immediately to direct our thoughts to contemplation of higher things makes it necessary that familiar everyday media be utilized to give suitable form to what is formless, and make visible what cannot be depicted, so that we are able to construct understandable analogies. If, therefore, the world of God, in providing for our every need, always presents to us what is intangible by clothing it with form, does it not accomplish this by making an image using what is common to nature and so brings within our reach that for which we long but are unable to see? A certain perception takes place in the brain, prompted by the bodily senses, which is then transmitted to the faculties of discernment, and adds to the treasury of knowledge something that was not there before. The eloquent Gregory says that the mind which is determined to ignore corporeal things will find itself weakened and frustrated. Since the creation of the world the invisible things of God are clearly seen by means of images.' John of Damascus, *De imaginibus* I.11 (PG 94, 1241); St John of Damascus, *On the Divine Images: Three Apologies Against Those who Attack the Divine Images*, trans. D. Anderson (Crestwood, NY, 1980), p. 20.

90 'Truly the body in which Christ suffered was born of Mary's flesh, with blood and with bones, with skin and with sinews, and with human limbs, brought to life with a wise soul. And his spiritual body which we call the Eucharist is gathered from many corns without blood or bone, limbless and soulless. And there is not therefore anything of the body to understand; but it is all to be understood as spirit.' *CH*, ed. Godden, p. 154.

Like the Junius 11 poems, Ælfric's words focus us simultaneously on Christ as body and bodiless, his limbed yet limbless body providing a telling contrast to the body of Satan for whom 'limbsize' remains a problem.[91] The twofold nature of Christ's birth encapsulated in Ælfric's homily is used by the compiler of Junius 11 to frame the poetic narrative. At the opening of *Genesis* the artist's depiction of the cross-nimbed God and the poet's stress on Creation as Word reflect the divine Christ born without body from the Father, while the iconography of the birth scenes in *Genesis* and Eve's words at the Harrowing of Hell in *Christ and Satan* are reminders of the human Christ born bodily from the mother, Mary, and of the Trinity. According to Ælfric we can identify the site of our likeness to God, and it is a spiritual rather than a bodily likeness:

On hwilcum dæle hæfð se man godes anlicnysse. on him? on þære sawle na on þam lichaman; þæs mannes sawul hæfð on hire gecynde þære halgan þrynnysse anlicnysse. for þan ðe heo hæfð on hire ðreo ðing. þæt is gemynd. and andgit. and willa . . . ðeahhwæðere nis nan þæra þreora seo sawul ac seo sawul þurh ðæt gemynd gemanð. þurh þæt andgit heo understent. þurh ðone willan heo wile swa hwæt swa hire licað and heo is hwæþere an sawul and an lif. Nu hæfð heo for ði godes anlicnysse on hire. for þan ðe heo hæfð þreo þing an hire untodæledlice wyrcende.[92]

The ultimate symbol of Christ's humanity was, however, not his birth but his suffering and broken adult body. We do not see this body in the manuscript as it survives, and in general the suffering body was not a popular subject in Anglo-Saxon art. Christ's wounds, on the other hand – especially the wound in his side – were sites of particular interest, as much for their sacramental symbolism as for their evidence of his humanity. On the early free-standing stone crosses, five bosses representing the five wounds frequently stood for the Crucifixion,[93] while Christ displaying his wounds became a popular subject in late Anglo-

[91] See above, p. 162.

[92] 'In which part does man have God's likeness in him? In the soul, not in the body. Man's soul has in its nature the likeness of the Holy Trinity, because it has within it three things, that is memory, and understanding and will . . . However the soul is none of these three things, but the soul remembers through memory, it understands through understanding, through the will it wills whatever pleases it, and yet it is one soul and one life. Now it has, therefore, God's likeness within it, because it has three things working undividedly within it.' 'De fide catholica', *CH*, ed. Clemoes, p. 342.

[93] R. Bailey, *Viking Age Sculpture* (London, 1980), pp. 148–50.

Saxon manuscript illumination, most memorably in the image of Christ enthroned in the Galba Psalter,[94] and the images of doubting Thomas in the Benedictional of St Æthelwold and the Tiberius Psalter.[95] In *Christ and Satan* the doubting rather than the Nativity or Crucifixion provides the focus for Christ's human body and nature, though it is textually and symbolically linked to both earlier events. Indeed, in the poem the doubting is framed by two references to the Crucifixion, helping to establish the episode as a revelation of Christ's humanity and bodily presence, over and above its more usual role as theophany; this interweaving of the human and divine is typical of *Christ and Satan*. The divine, resurrected Christ recounts in summary fashion the events of his incarnation, including his virgin birth and culminating in his account of the Crucifixion:

> þa me on beame.   beornas sticedon.
> garum on galgam.[96]

The line even manages to capture the dual nature of the cross as living tree and gallows of death.[97] The poet then writes:

> sume hie ne mihton   mode oncnawan.
> þæt wæs se deora.   didimus wæs haten.
> ær he mid hondum.   hæland genom.
> sylfne be sidan.   þær he his swat forlet.
> feollan to foldan.   fulwihtes bæðe.
> fæger wæs þæt ongin.   þæt freodrihten.
> geþrowode.   þeoden ure.
> he on beame astah.   and his blod ageat.
> god on galgan.   þurh his gastes mægen.[98]

94 London, British Library, Cotton Galba xviii, 2v.

95 BL, Add. 49598, 56v; BL, Cotton Tiberius C. vi, 14v. See Deshman, *Benedictional*, pp. 69–77, for a discussion of these images and some of their continental parallels.

96 The manuscript reads *galgum*, Finnegan emends to *galgan*. *Christ and Satan* 508–9. 'When on the tree soldiers pierced me with spears on the cross [gallows].'

97 The dual nature of the cross is also taken up in *The Dream of the Rood* and the runic poem on the Ruthwell monument.

98 'Some could not understand with their minds. That was the dear one. [He] was called Didmus, before he with his hands took hold of the Lord himself by the side where he sent forth his blood; the bath of baptism fell to earth. Fair was that undertaking, the suffering of the Lord, our Lord. He ascended onto the cross and shed his blood, God on the cross, through the strength of his spirit'. *Christ and Satan* 540–8.

The syntax of the passage is difficult, with the sudden change from plural to singular subject in the first two lines,[99] but rather than a poetic flaw this may be the poet's way of indicating that the individual (Thomas) here stands for the many (the weak of faith). In terms of its intertextuality the scene is one of the most powerful in the manuscript. It is also the culmination of the theme of the desire to know God that has run throughout the poems. The Old English version of the gospels describes the episode as a *tacen* worked by Christ,[100] allowing us to connect the real body of Christ revealed here to the false vision of God enthroned offered to Eve in *Genesis*. Thomas's true belief and physical blindness replace Eve's false belief and spiritual blindness. John records that Christ makes just this point when he says: 'You believe because you can see me. Happy are those who have not seen and yet believe.'[101] The wound as a site of entrance into or exit from Christ's body is also stressed. Thomas reaching for the wound in Christ's side reminds us of Eve born of Adam's side. We have already read of Eve at the Harrowing reaching for Christ with her hands and pleading for her release from hell on the grounds that she is mother of both Mary and Christ, and we have seen her in a similar pose reaching out to God at the moment of her Creation (pl. IV). Moreover, Eve born from Adam's side is a prefiguration of Ecclesia, born from the side of Christ at the Crucifixion, and by this time associated with Mary.[102] Mary reaching up towards her son's wounded body or Ecclesia catching the blood from the wound in her chalice were standard figures in early medieval Crucifixion scenes. In the drawings of the Crucifixion from the tenth-century Arenberg Gospels, the mid-eleventh-century Winchcombe Psalter, the *c.* 1060 Red Book of Darley and the mid-eleventh-century Weingarten (or Judith of Flanders) Gospels, Mary is shown gazing up at or reaching for the wound.[103] The way in which the description of

99 See Finnegan, *Christ and Satan*, pp. 115–16; C. R. Sleeth, *Studies in Christ and Satan* (Toronto, 1982), p. 128.

100 John XX.30; R. Liuzza, *The Old English Gospels*, EETS 304 (Oxford, 1994), p. 201.

101 John XX.29; Liuzza, *Gospels*, p. 201.

102 Ecclesia with her chalice does not appear in Anglo-Saxon art but is a popular subject in contemporary Ottonian art. See the Fulda Sacramentary: Bamberg, Staatsbibliothek, cod. lat. 1, 165v; H. Mayr-Harting, *Ottonian Illumination: An Historical Survey*, 2 vols. (London and New York, 1991), pl. XIV.

103 New York, Pierpont Morgan Library, 869, 9v; Cambridge, University Library, Ff. 1. 23, 88r; Cambridge, Corpus Christi College 422, pp. 27–586, at p. 53; New York, Pierpont Morgan Library, 709, 1v. See B. C. Raw, *Anglo-Saxon Crucifixion Iconography*

Thomas standing beside the body of Christ is linked literally and symbolically with the second reference to the Crucifixion and the shedding of Christ's blood helps to affirm his connection with the figure of Mary (though admittedly Mary is not mentioned in this section of the poem). Barbara Raw notes that similar connections are established in the Tiberius Psalter, where the Crucifixion, three Maries at the tomb and doubting Thomas work together to make the point that 'Christ was truly God and truly man . . . The presence of his human mother, her faith in his divinity, the testimony of John, the experience of Thomas all witness to the truth of the Christian message and to the link between Christ's incarnation and his redemption of men on the cross.'[104]

If the story of Thomas was intended to give strength to those who were weak of faith,[105] it was also intended to provide a point of contact with Christ's body for all humanity. In *Christ and Satan* the reader, like Thomas, Mary or Ecclesia, is offered Christ's body and blood via the story's reference to the sacraments, the water of baptism and the bread and wine of the eucharist.[106] Christ's blood is a 'bath of baptism' (*fulwihtes bæðe*, *Christ and Satan* 544) that 'fell to earth' (*feollan to foldon*, *Christ and Satan*, 544) not just to Thomas or Mary.[107] Christ's Resurrection, of which the doubting provides tangible bodily proof, thus offers the hope of final resurrection for all humanity. We may all handle and enter into Christ's body and consume it in the form of the eucharist. As Ælfric tells us: 'we ðicgað nu gastlice cristes lichaman . and his blod drincað . þonne we mid soðum geleafan þæt halige husel ðicgað'.[108] Julia Kristeva has pointed out that the 'signs-miracles' of the body of Christ, the 'son of man', also evoke a generational link between Son and Father and between Christ and congregation that is manifested physically, bodily, in the mass.[109] It is also mirrored in the words of *Christ and Satan*. On a spiritual

and the Art of the Monastic Revival, CSASE 1 (Cambridge, 1990), pls. II, X, XIIb and XVI.

104 Raw, *Crucifixion Iconography*, p. 109.

105 *Ibid.*, p. 60; Ælfric, *Homilies*, ed. Thorpe, I, 234.

106 See Bede, *In Lucam* VI (CCSL 120), 418–20.

107 Cf. B. Raw, 'Why does the River Jordan Stand Still? (the Descent into Hell, 103–6)', *Leeds Studies in English* NS 23 (1992), 29–47; P. W. Conner, 'The Liturgy and the Old English "Descent into Hell"', *JEGP* 79 (1980), 179–91.

108 'We consume now the holy body and drink his blood when we with true belief receive the holy eucharist'. 'In die pascae', *CH*, ed. Godden, pp. 151–2.

109 Kristeva, *New Maladies of the Soul*, p. 129.

level, the handling of the body of Christ is a sign that, like Thomas or the Israelites before him, those who believe in both the body and its resurrection will be led to glory. The *Christ and Satan* poet addresses his readers on this subject directly after his account of Thomas and the Crucifixion:

> forþon men sceolon. mæla gehwylce.
> secgan drihtne þanc. dædum and weorcum.
> þæs ðe he us of hæftum ham gelædde.
> up to eðle. þær we agan sceolon[110]
> drihtnes domas.
> and we in wynnum. wunian moton.
> us is wuldres leoht.
> torht ontyned. þam þe teala þenceð.'[111]

The words of thanks in this passage recall the opening lines of the manuscript, themselves an echo of the canon of the mass, which instruct us to offer words of praise to God and to love him in our hearts. The reference to the mass helps to bring the bodies of Christ, Thomas and the reader together in contemplation of the Crucifixion and its meaning. The poet then turns to a description of God enthroned in heaven and surrounded by music (*wolcna sweg*, *Christ and Satan* 563b)[112] and hosts of angels (*engla þreatas*, *Christ and Satan* 567b), recalling the false vision granted to Eve by Satan and the genuine vision of God/Christ in majesty given to us in the frontispiece. But it is not just specific lines that recall the mass, the very structure of the poem echoes the liturgy. The alternation of voice from third person narrative to direct invocation of the audience by which the poem progresses mirrors the liturgical structure of statement (or lection) and multiple-voice response, and draws the reader into active participation in the songs of praise that recur throughout the poem. This is a pattern that began in *Daniel* with the song of the three Hebrew boys, but is expanded into a primary narrative technique in *Christ and Satan*.[113]

[110] *sceolon* is not in the manuscript.

[111] 'Therefore each of times men shall say thanks to the Lord with deeds and with works, because he led us out of bondage home up to the homeland where we shall possess the glory of the Lord, and we may dwell in joys. The bright glory of light is revealed to us, to those who think rightly.' *Christ and Satan* 549–56.

[112] Literally 'the sound of clouds'.

[113] See below, p. 178.

It is important to remember, however, that the doubting did not provide a guarantee of salvation. The display of Christ's wounds in this episode is also associated with the display of Christ's wounds at the Last Judgement, the moment at which humanity will either be united with or separated from the body of Christ for all eternity.[114] Christ the Judge displaying his wounds at the second coming is a feature of a number of late Anglo-Saxon representations of the Last Judgement,[115] and the Last Judgement is the penultimate episode in *Christ and Satan*. Those who have not maintained their faith, who have neither seen nor believed in Christ's suffering body and its resurrection, are doomed themselves to suffer bodily. Those who refused to know Christ are no longer known to him (*nu ic eow ne con*, *Christ and Satan* 627), and are doomed to remain in the darkness beneath the ground from which Christ and the family of believers ascend.

The poem closes with the Temptation of Christ and a return to the theme of the knowing and recognition of Christ's two natures. Like Thomas or the good Christian receiving the eucharist, Satan here takes Christ's body in his hands, though with evil and mockery (*atol þurh edwit*, *Christ and Satan* 680), rather than with reverence and belief. The episode also provides a stark contrast to the Harrowing of Hell in which Christ's body is lifted up by *Abrahmes cynn*, amongst whom the Anglo-Saxons of course counted themselves. Satan refuses to see past the human body to the divine and is doomed to the measureless darkness and torments of hell, with the bodies of the devils rising up before him like the bodies of the resurrected before Christ. The poem and the manuscript end with a warning rather than an unequivocal message of salvation, and a warning that might have been picked up in the drawing of the Last Judgement,

114 See Bede, *In Lucam* VI.419–20; Bede, *Homilies on the Gospels*, trans. L. T. Martin and D. Hurst (Kalamazoo, MI, 1991), 2 vols., II, 82 (Homily II.9 on the Gospels). 'Although he could have shown his body to his disciples with all indications of his passion abolished, he certainly preferred to keep the indications of his passion on it, by the grace of the divinely arranged plan. First of all [this was] so that the disciples who saw these things could clearly discern that what they saw was not a spirit without a body, but a spiritual body, and that they might preach to the world certain faith in his complete resurrection, and certain hope in the future resurrection of all human beings.'

115 See Deshman, *Benedictional*, p. 72. Deshman cites both the page from the Galba Psalter and an early-eleventh-century ivory in the Cambridge University Museum of Archaeology and Ethnicity (fig. 68).

the hypothetical final image in the manuscript.[116] The final words are spoken not by Christ, nor by the reader, nor even by the poem's narrator, but by the hoard of wretched spirits who say in torment 'noldæs ær teala' ('You would not ever before do rightly', *Christ and Satan* 729). This is a grim message, but one that again situates the reader in the balance. There is a hint here that while we might not have done rightly in the past, the opportunity to do so is still before us, but only if we have seen and read correctly and grasped the message of the book.

BOOK AND BODY

In the Junius 11 poems the reader does not handle Christ's body directly, but via the intercessory body of the book, itself the product of poets, scribes, artists and compilers. They are all creative bodies, and the traces of their bodies within the manuscript have also become a crucial part of its meaning and its voice. The poets repeatedly call our attention to the fact that they have a presence in the text by interrupting the flow of the biblical narrative to remind us of past events, highlighting the didactic nature of an event with a gnomic statement, or by shifting to a first-person voice. For example, *Daniel* begins:

> GEfrægn ic hebreos. eadge lifgean.
> in hierusalem.[117]

And in lines 223–5 of *Christ and Satan* the poet writes:

> Đa get ic furðor gefregen. feonda ondetan.[118]
> wæs him eall ful strang. wom and witu.[119]

Such statements obviously serve to help link originally separate poems together in a continuous narrative, but they also place the body of the poet before the mind's eye of the reader. The poets become active scholarly figures, reliable narrators, gathering information from books,[120] from the witnessing of events, and from information gleaned from third parties.[121]

[116] See appendix page 206.

[117] 'I learned that the Hebrews lived happily in Jerusalem.'

[118] The manuscript reads *feonda*.

[119] 'Then I further heard tell that the enemy confessed that to him all was full of wailing and torment.'

[120] E.g. *Gen.* 939, 2565, 2612, or *Ex.* 531.

[121] E.g. *Ex.* 1.

The process echoes that by which history is written, underscoring the connection between biblical and Anglo-Saxon history. Bede, for example, relies on exactly this narrative technique.[122] His presence in the *Historia ecclesiastica*, while much more prominent than that of any of the four Junius 11 poets in their poems, is established in basically the same way, and he explains this to us in great detail in his preface and his final chapter:[123]

Haec de historia ecclesiastica Brittaniarum, et maxime gentis Anglorum, prout uel ex litteris antiquorum uel ex traditione maiorum uel ex mea ipse cognitione scire potui, Domino adiuuante digessi Baeda famulus Christi et presbyter monasterii beatorum apostolorum Petri et Pauli, quod est ad Uiuraemuda et Ingyruum.[124]

Furthermore, if the text of Junius 11 was meant to be read aloud the voice and body of the reader would have seemed to become those of the poets, adding a flesh-and-blood presence to the anonymous 'I' of the text. This union of poet and reader is made particularly evident in lines 939–40 of *Genesis*:

> Hwæt we nu gehyrað. hwær us hearmstafas.
> wraðe onwocan. and woruldyrmðo.[125]

It is picked up again in the opening verse of *Exodus*, with its sombre challenge to the listener:

> HWÆT, WE FEOR AND NEAH. gefrigen habbað.
> ofer middangeard. moyses domas.
> wræclico wordriht. wera cneorissum.
> in uprodor. eadigra gehwam.
> æfter bealusiðe. bote lifes.

122 D. K. Fry, 'The Art of Bede II: the Reliable Narrator Persona', *Acta* 6 (1982 for 1979), 63–82.

123 See also *HE* IV.32, p. 447.

124 *HE*, V.24, p. 566. 'This history of the church in Britan and of the English people in particular, according to either ancient documents or from the tradition of predecessors, or from my own knowledge, with the help of God and to the best of my abilities, I, Bede, servant of Christ and priest of the monastery of the blessed apostles Peter and Paul which is at Wearmouth Jarrow, put together.' As Fry notes ('Art of Bede II', p. 76), Bede's words foreground the text and its sources and downplay the presence of the author (something lost in the Colgrave translation); nevertheless, Bede is insistently present in his text.

125 'Lo, now we shall hear where troubles arose for us, evil and world miseries awoke.'

lifgendra gehwam. langsumne ræd.
hæleðum secgan. gehyre se ðe wille.[126]

All four poets also use the first person plural to unite themselves with the book and the bodies displayed in it, as well as with their audience. This is perhaps made clearest at the very beginning when the *Genesis* poet states:

US IS RIHT MICEL ÐÆT we rodera weard.
wereda wuldorcining. wordum herigen.
modum lufien.[127]

The *us* and *we* unite the voices of poet and audience, while the frontispiece of God enthroned (pl. I) provides the focus for their prayers. The poet's injunction that we love God in our hearts brings audience and image together physically; what we see is within us and our Creator. The use of the personal pronoun *ure* ('our') eight times in variations of the phrase 'our Lord' in the *Genesis* poem does the same.[128] In fact, the use of first-person-plural pronouns to involve the reader in the action of the poems, or drive home their meaning, is significant. In *Genesis*, *we* or *us* is used at least eleven times to unite narrator and reader before the lesson offered by the text.[129] In *Exodus* and *Daniel* they are used in similar constructions four times and twice, respectively,[130] while in *Christ and Satan* there are seventeen such constructions,[131] many part of the lection and multiple-voice response that characterize this particular poem.[132] The small number of instances of the first person plural applied to the reader and/or reader and poet in *Exodus* and *Daniel* may correspond to the relative absence of the body of Christ from these two poems.[133] In *Exodus* God/

[126] 'Lo. We have heard far and near over earth men tell of the judgements of Moses, wonderful laws, for generations of men – for each of the blessed in heaven, after a terrible journey, life's reward, long-enduring counsel. Hear he who will' *Ex.* 1–7.

[127] 'It is our great duty that we praise with words and love in our hearts the Guardian of heaven, the Lord of glory.'

[128] *Gen.* 40, 65, 92, 137, 140, 147, 206 and 2827.

[129] *Gen.* 1, 227, 939 (× 2), 964, 995, 997, 1121, 1630, 1723 and 2013.

[130] *Ex.* 1, 529, 530 and 531; *Dan.* 394 and 404.

[131] *Christ and Satan* 201, 203, 207, 286, 288, 289, 290, 291, 293, 298, 300, 382, 551, 552, 554, 588, 589.

[132] See also Stévanovitch, 'Envelope Patterns and the Unity of the Old English *Christ and Satan*'.

[133] See below, pp. 204–6.

Christ is present only in symbolic forms which demand both our recognition and that of the Israelites, while in *Daniel* he is present only in the two anachronistic references to the Trinity in lines 394 and 404, part of the canticle in which our voices are joined with those of the three children and of all Creation. *Genesis* and *Christ and Satan*, however, involve the body of the reader more directly, dealing as they do with the creation of the body and its final judgement, rather than with relatively straightforward narratives of Old Testament events, albeit ones designed to provide parallels to, and antecedents for, contemporary life. *Christ and Satan* in particular, with its presentation of the body of Christ in its two natures, evokes the body of Christ as present in the mass. It is in the mass, as Ælfric emphasizes, that our bodies are united both physically and spiritually with that of Christ:

Æne þrowade christ ðurh hine sylfne. ac swa ðeah dæghwomlice bið his ðrowung geedniwod þurh gerynu þæs halgan husles, at ðære halgan mæssan; For ði fremað seo halige mæsse micclum. ge þam lybbendum. ge ðam forðfarenum. swa swa hift foroft geswutelod is.

Us is eac to smeagenne þæt þæt halige husel is ægðer ge cristes lichama ge ealles geleaffules folces æfter gastlicere gerynu.[134]

While the Junius 11 poems may not unite us physically with the body of Christ, the book does reveal mysteries; we see the representations of heaven and hell, and the acts of Creation and Fall, Temptation and Judgement, places and events about which we can normally just read. Though likely to be a later addition to the manuscript,[135] the little figure sketched in the margins of page 7 provides the ultimate metaphor for the position of artists, poets, scribes and readers in relation to the manuscript and its narratives. We stand outside of the biblical acts described and depicted, yet within Creation; we observe and are observed, judge and are judged at the same time. The addition of the figure also highlights the process of the creation of the manuscript itself, a process which took place over time rather than as a single stroke. A reader brought together a

[134] 'Christ suffered once through his self, but still his suffering is renewed daily through the mystery of the holy eucharist at the holy mass; therefore, the holy mass benefits greatly both the living and the dead, as is very often made manifest.

'We should consider that the holy eucharist is both Christ's body and the body of all believers, according to a spiritual mystery.' 'In die Pascae', *CH*, ed. Godden, pp. 156–7.

[135] How much later remains an open question.

selection of preexisting poems to form a new narrative, illustrations were added, and then in turn added to, and new histories and interpretations were provided for both the book and its poems from the moment of its creation down to the present day. The interactions of these bodies with the body of the book have left their traces on it, and have helped to keep it very much alive. The physical interaction of the body of the reader and the book was allegorized in the monastic practice of *ruminatio*, and made visible in the image of St John eating the Book of Revelation. Indeed, in his study of texts and feasting in the Renaissance, Michael Jeanneret describes the act of reading as one in which 'The reader-eater takes possession of the object being read, assimilates this foreign body and makes it part of his own being.'[136] Somewhere within our bodies we carry the memory of the images and events we have seen and read of in books, just as somewhere within our souls we carry the likeness of God, a memory of divine authorship.

[136] M. Jeanneret, *A Feast of Words: Banquets and Table Talk in the Renaissance* (Chicago, IL, 1991), p. 129.

6

The historical narrative

> Sicut enim librorum corpora, ex contrariorum commixtione compacta, suae compositionis continuum sentiunt detrimentu, sic per prudentiam clericorum reperiri debet remedium, per quod liber sacer solvens naturae debitum, haereditarium obtineat substitutum et simile semen fratri mortuo suscitetur verificeturque statim illud Ecclesiastici 30: Mortuus est pater illius et quasi non est mortuus, similem enim sibi reliquit post se.
>
> Sunt igitur transcriptiones veterum quasi quaedam propagationes recentium filiorum, ad quos paternum devolvatur officium, ne librorum municipium minuatur. Richard de Bury, *Philobiblon*.[1]

This book has been concerned primarily with the narratives of the Junius manuscript and the importance of reading the book as a book and not as a series of isolated and unillustrated poems, or poetic fragments. Useful as the editions of the four poems may be, they can provide us only with fragments, and cannot reveal the full intertextuality or intervisuality of the culture in which Junius 11 was produced. But there is still much more to know, and what is needed above all is an edition of the *manuscript* complete with illustrations, translation and commentary. The Bodleian

[1] 'For as the bodies of books seeing that they are formed of a combination of contrary elements, undergo a continual dissolution of their structure, so by the forethought of the clergy a remedy should be found, by means of which the sacred book paying the debt of nature may obtain a natural heir and may raise up like seed to its dead brother and thus may be verified by that saying of Ecclesiasticus 30: "His father is dead, and he is as if he were not dead; for he hath left one behind him that is like himself." Thus the transcription of ancient books is as it were the begetting of fresh sons, on whom the office of the father may devolve, lest the commonwealth of books suffer detriment.' Ed. and trans. E. C. Thomas (Oxford and New York, 1970), pp. 146–7.

webpages have certainly provided a step in the right direction, though they are not without their own practical and theoretical problems.[2] The consideration of existing problems and possible solutions brings us finally to the issue of the editorial history of the manuscript, and the narratives that have been created around it.

Unlike Richard de Bury's fictional book, Junius 11 has not one, but many sons and each son has a prominent editorial 'father'. The book has thus produced its own patriarchal lineage and family, much like the one it records and the Anglo-Saxon ones with which it resonated at the time of its production. The history of the Junius 11 manuscript has been well rehearsed by the editors of its individual poems, but as it is important to its editorial genealogy, it will be summarized briefly here. The arguments for or against a Canterbury provenance have already been discussed. Both the style of the drawings and the palaeography have proved difficult to localize to any one centre, but the entry in the early-fourteenth-century catalogue of Christ Church, Canterbury recording a '*Genesis anglice depicta*' amongst the monastery's holdings continues to have its appeal despite all the obvious problems of identity.[3] The entry could as easily refer to Claudius B. iv or to a now lost manuscript as it could to Junius 11, and even if it could be shown to refer to Junius 11, it still does not prove that the manuscript was written and illustrated in Canterbury.[4] Be that as it may, the continuing weight given to the possibility of the connection is a typical manifestation of the scholarly desire not only to pin down the source of a manuscript – which is reasonable enough – but also to secure its origins to a documentary record with which it often has the most tenuous of relationships. We desire, in other words, a birth certificate.

Nothing certain is known about the location of Junius 11 until the early 1640s when Johannes De Laet (1581–1649) is recorded as having the manuscript with him in Leiden. De Laet used the manuscript in the completion of his unpublished dictionary of Old English (destroyed in the English siege of Copenhagen in 1728), and was the first scholar known to have recognized it as a poetic manuscript.[5] De Laet had apparently

[2] See images available at www.bodley.ox.ac.uk.

[3] The connection was first made by M. R. James, *Ancient Libraries of Canterbury and Dover*, pp. xxv–xxvi, 51 and 509.

[4] All points raised by Lucas (*Exodus*, p. 2).

[5] R. H. Bremmer, Jr., 'The Correspondence of Johannes De Laet (1581–1649) as a Mirror of his Life', *Lias* 25 (1998), 139–64, at p. 160 n. 104; B. J. Timmer, 'De Laet's Anglo-

borrowed the manuscript from its first known owner, John Ussher, Archbishop of Armagh (1581–1656), and Ussher is thought likely to have acquired it *c.* 1650 from fellow antiquary Sir Simonds d'Ewes (1602–50).[6] D'Ewes, like De Laet, was working on the publication of an Anglo-Saxon dictionary, and it is possible that the manuscript was originally acquired and lent as part of this project. Ussher gave the manuscript to Francis Junius (1591–1677), the Dutch scholar and librarian to Thomas Howard, Earl of Arundel,[7] most probably at the time of Junius' return to the Netherlands from England in 1651, and certainly before 1652 when it is mentioned in a letter to Junius from the Nuremburg scholar Christopher Arnold.[8] Both D'Ewes and Ussher were particularly interested in Anglo-Saxon texts and studies, but Junius, who is regarded as 'the father of Anglo-Saxon philology', may have been judged the most appropriate scholar for this volume of poetry. Junius published the first 'facsimile' of the manuscript in 1655.[9] It was the first edition of any Anglo-Saxon poetic manuscript, and thus of seminal importance to the history of Anglo-Saxon literature on many levels. Junius returned to England in 1674 and bequeathed the book to Oxford University at his death in 1677. It was acquired by the Bodleian Library in 1678 along with the rest of his collection of books and manuscripts.

Junius' 1655 edition of the manuscript was its first comprehensive, serious and scholarly treatment. However, it included neither translation

Saxon Dictionary', *Neophilologus* 41 (1957), 199–202. See also O. Worm, *Olai Wormii et ad eum Doctorum virorum Epistolae, medici, anatomici, botanici, physici & historici argumentii Rem vero Linguasque & Antiquitates Boreales potissimim illustrantes*, 2 vols. (Copenhagen, 1751), II, no. 786 (4 March 1643).

6 On De Laet see Bremmer, 'Correspondence', p. 160. On Ussher and D'Ewes see Gollancz, *Cædmon Manuscript*, p. xiv; on the ambiguity of ownership and the exchange of the manuscript between Ussher and D'Ewes see A. G. Watson, *The Library of Sir Simonds D'Ewes* (London, 1966), pp. 9–10.

7 P. Lucas, *Franciscus Junius: Cædmonis Monachi Paraphrasis Poetica Genesios ac praecipuarum Sacrae paginae Historiarum* (Leiden and Atlanta, GA, 2000), pp. xiv and xix. Junius served as Arundel's librarian from 1621 to 1651. I would like to thank Peter Lucas and Rolf Bremmer for allowing me to consult the introduction to this facsimile prior to its publication.

8 R. Bremmer, 'Retrieving Junius' Correspondence', in *Franciscus Junius F. F. and His Circle*, ed. R. Bremmer (Leiden and Atlanta, GA, 1998), pp. 199–235, at p. 208.

9 *Cædmonis Monachi Paraphrasis Poetica Genesios ad præcipuarum Sacræ paginæ Historium abhinc annos M.LXX Anglo-Saxonice conscripta & nunc primum edita à Francisco Junio F. F.*, printed in Amsterdam by C. Cunrad.

nor notes, and printed *Genesis*, *Exodus* and *Daniel* as one uninterrupted text. It was criticized for its many errors of transcription, particularly in the metrical points.[10] Equally importantly, the Junius 'facsimile' did not include the illustrations, thereby beginning the practice of studying the two as separate, sometimes seemingly unrelated 'programmes', and the privileging of text over illustration. It also omitted the decorated capitals and sectional divisions, creating a false sense of uninterrupted continuity between the poems and between their constituent parts.[11] As a philologist, Junius' interests were no doubt predominantly, if not exclusively, in the text. His art historical tastes were strictly for the classical, which was hardly surprising in his day, and the Junius 11 drawings may well have struck him as crude and artistically unimportant when compared to some of the 'masterpieces' of the Arundel collection.[12] Nevertheless, his arguments for the importance of the visual arts as a means of personal and social inspiration in *De Pictura Veterum* strike an ironic chord in light of his indifference to Anglo-Saxon art. It is one of the quirks of history that Junius was apparently allowed only limited access to the late-fifth-century Cotton Genesis, one of the great treasures of Sir Robert Cotton's collection and a manuscript which would eventually come to be seen as the ultimate source for the Junius 11 drawings.[13] In 1630, the Cotton Genesis (BL, Cotton Otho B. VI) was lent, together with the Utrecht Psalter, by Cotton to the Earl of Arundel, and was not returned before Cotton's death in 1631.[14] It went with the Arundel family to the Continent in 1642 and had to be bought back from them by Sir John Cotton, Robert's grandson,

[10] Thorpe, *Cædmon's Metrical Paraphrase*, p. xiii.

[11] P. Lucas, *Franciscus Junius*, pp. xix and xx.

[12] Junius published his *De Pictura Veterum* in Amsterdam in 1637. An English translation, *The Painting of the Ancients*, was published in London in 1638. His *Catalogus Architectorum, Mechanicorum, se praecipe Pictorum Statuariorum, Caelatorum, aliorumque Artificium, et Operum quae fecerunt, secundum serien litterarum digestus* was published posthumously in Rotterdam in 1694 by Johannes Georgius Graevius. See Keith Aldrich, Philipp Fehl and Raina Fehl, *Franciscus Junius: The Literature of Classical Art*, 2 vols. (Berkeley, 1991). As the Earl of Arundel's librarian Junius took a great interest in the Arundel Marbles, complaining to Sir William Dugdale in a letter of 21 April 1656 that many of the pieces had been stolen or cut up since their publication in John Selden's *Marmora Arundelliana* in 1628. See G. Parry, *Trophies of Time: English Antiquarians of the Seventeenth Century* (Oxford and New York, 1995), p. 128 n. 49.

[13] See above, p. 5.

[14] Weitzmann and Kessler speculate that it may have been sent to Arundel as a way of

at the end of the seventeenth century.[15] Two letters from Junius to Sir William Dugdale, who repeatedly tried to retrieve the manuscript after Cotton's death, reveal that Junius had seen the Cotton Genesis, but that 'Since the late Countess Arundel carried over a vast treasure of rarities, I heard the mentioned Old Genesis to have beene also convaighed away out of England; but seemeth to have beene hid somewhere without coming in her librarie; even as at London itselfe it was kept close, and came not in her librarie whilest I kept it.'[16] He continues that he was unable to find it amongst her books when he catalogued them in Antwerp in 1644, nor could he find it when she left Antwerp for Alkmaer, nor at Amersford shortly before her death.[17] The countess's illicit desire for her borrowed manuscript is in marked contrast to the scholarly sharing of Junius 11, but, given her taste for collecting art, perfectly in keeping with the enormous art historical importance – and lineage – that would later come to be attributed to it. An account of the manuscript by Junius before its near destruction in the Cotton Library fire would have been illuminating indeed, and it is particularly ironic that he was searching for the manuscript at the same time that he was preparing his facsimile for publication.[18]

The Junius 11 illustrations do not appear to have generated much interest until the second quarter of the eighteenth century. In 1732 an edition of the drawings by the Society of Antiquaries was proposed, but it was not until 1794 that engravings of fifteen of the drawings were made,

freeing it from the Cotton library after it was closed by King Charles in 1629 (*Cotton Genesis*, p. 3).

15 The Utrecht Psalter and several other manuscripts were never returned. See C. G. C. Tite, 'Lost, Stolen or Strayed: a Survey of Manuscripts Formerly in the Cotton Library', *British Library Jnl* 18.2 (1992), 107–47, at pp. 116–18. Junius' employment with the Howards of Arundel itself ended badly and he was eventually forced to take legal proceedings against William Howard, Viscount Stafford. See R. H. Bremmer and R. Rácz, 'Junius's Case against William Howard, Viscount Stafford', in *Franciscus Junius and His Circle*, pp. 121–7.

16 W. Dugdale, *The Life, Diary and Correspondence of Sir William Dugdale*, ed. W. Hamper (London, 1827), pp. 299 and 300; Weitzmann and Kessler, *Cotton Genesis*, pp. 3 and 6. Surviving accounts of the manuscript while it was in the possession of the Arundel family indicate that it was rarely, if ever, shown to anyone (Weitzmann and Kessler, *Cotton Genesis*, p. 6).

17 Dugdale, *Life, Diary and Correspondence*, p. 300.

18 *Ibid.*, pp. 301–2.

preparatory to a new fully illustrated edition by Edward Rowe Morris and a group of his fellow antiquaries. The edition was never completed, but the engravings were issued with a brief preface referring the purchaser to the copies of Junius' facsimile which included his notes, published by James Fletcher's Oxford bookshop (and printed by Mores).[19] The drawings themselves were accompanied by short descriptions in Latin that often failed to identify the scenes correctly, or to relate them to the poems. The plates were reproduced by Sir Henry Ellis, secretary of the Society of Antiquaries, in his *Account of Cædmon's Metrical Paraphrase of Scripture History* presented to the Society and published in 1832 as a separate volume, and as volume 24 of *Archaeologia*. Ellis's plates were intended to accompany the new edition of the poems edited by Benjamin Thorpe which also appeared in 1832 under the title *Cædmon's Metrical Paraphrase of Parts of the Holy Scriptures*. This arrangement, at least partially dictated by financial considerations,[20] naturally meant that the illustrations and text continued to be read as separate narrative programmes. While Thorpe did include Ellis's descriptive catalogue of the plates as part of his introductory material, he did not include the pictures themselves and he made no further mention of their location within the poem or of their content.[21] The purpose of the new edition was to provide a text 'freed from the inaccuracies, both editorial and typographical' of the Junius facsimile.[22] In order to place the manuscript in its 'historical' context Thorpe included the preface to the Junius facsimile, as well as the text and translation of Bede's account of Cædmon and its Old English translation. Yet despite its stated purpose and attempts at inclusiveness, Thorpe had problems when it came to *Christ and Satan*. He saw the poem as little more than a 'series of unconnected fragments', and expressed his surprise that 'both in the manuscript and in Junius' edition, these

[19] Junius' notes on his facsimile edition are now contained in Oxford, Bodleian Library, Junius 73.

[20] Ellis, *Account of Cædmon's Metrical Paraphrase*, p. 3.

[21] Ellis's descriptive catalogue does include the number of the page on which an illustration is located in the original manuscript, and references to the page and line to which that illustration might relate, but does not include any discussion of the style or content of the drawings. The ornamented initials are reproduced separated from the text and in alphabetical order on the last two plates.

[22] Thorpe, *Cædmon's Metrical Paraphrase*, p. vii.

fragments appear on the page as entire parts of the poem, unnoticed as fragments either by the Saxon scribe or the modern editor'.[23]

Thorpe's edition was quickly followed by those of Bouterwek and Grien, as well as a host of editions and translations of the separate poems.[24] Gollancz's 1927 edition of Junius 11 for the Early English Text Society was the first true facsimile of the manuscript,[25] providing both a photographic reproduction of each page and discussion of the style and iconography of the illustrations and the way in which they might relate to the poetic narrative. It remains an invaluable resource for anyone interested in the manuscript. Equally invaluable are the images now available through the Bodleian Library website. Digitalized from the original manuscript, these images allow study of both the overall programme of illustration and details of each page in new ways. An introductory page of thumbnail images (an electronic form of photographic proof sheet) provides an overview of the programme of illustration at a glance, while the excellent resolution of the individual pages permits unprecedented study of the manuscript's punctuation, palaeography, and the drawing style of the artists. Unfortunately, in its present state the digital facsimile lacks a transcription and translation of the text, as well as any form of commentary.

EDITORS AND ORIGINS

One of the most controversial aspects of Junius' work was his identification of the author of all four of the poems as the seventh-century cowherd (and later monk) of Whitby, Cædmon, whose story is told by Bede in Book IV.24 of the *Historia ecclesiastica*. Junius was not the first to identify the poems as the work of Cædmon, and he may simply have been following the list of works attributed to the poet by John Bale in his *Illustrium Maioris Brittaniae scriptorum* of 1548. The attribution is not discussed in the preface to his facsimile but is made explicit in its title. The reader is also referred to Junius' *Observationes in Willerami Abbatis Francicam paraphrasin cantici canticorum*, printed in Amsterdam shortly

23 *Ibid.*

24 K. Bouterwek, *Cædmon's des Angelsachsen biblische Dichtungen*, vol. I (Elberfeld, 1849–51), vol. II (Gütersloh, 1854); C. W. M. Grien, *Bibliothek der angelsächsischen Poesie*, vol. I (Göttingen, 1857).

25 Gollancz, *Cædmon Manuscript*.

before the appearance of the Junius 11 facsimile, in which he wrote that throughout the Junius 11 poems there were numerous passages that had the flavour of antiquity and which were certainly in the spirit of the verses of sacred poetry attributed to Cædmon in Book IV, cap. 24 of Bede's *Historia ecclesiastica*, and equally in accord with the verses contained in 'King Alfred's paraphrase' of Bede's text.[26] According to Bede, Cædmon composed poems on:

De creatione mundi et origine humani generis et tota Genesis historia, de egressu Israel ex Aegypto et ingressu in terram repromissionis, de aliis plurimis sacrae scripturae historiis, de incarnatione dominica, passione, resurrectione et ascensione in caelum, de Spiritus Sancti aduentu et apostolorum doctrina; item de terrore futuri iudicii et horrore poenae gehennalis ac dulcedine regni caelestis multa carmina faciebat.[27]

For the most part these were subjects and themes covered by the Junius 11 poems. Moreover, according to Bede, Cædmon's first song began with an Old English version of the words 'Nunc laudare/debemus auctorem regni caelestis', ('Now we must praise the maker of the heavenly kingdom'), words close to those of the opening of the *Genesis* poem.[28] Without citing specific examples, Junius identified numerous echoes of Cædmon's words in his manuscript's texts, no small feat as the 'Hymn' consists of only nine lines of verse.[29] He met with immediate opposition,

[26] 'innumera in ea passim occurrere, quæ penitiorem sapiunt antiquitatem, et quoniam ipse stilus ac totius operis cum argumentum tum genius ex amussim respondent isti veteris poësios specimini quod adduxit ven. Beda lib. iv. hist. gentis Anglorum, cap. 24. ipse quoque posthac aliquid ex nobilissimo reconditæ antiquitatis thesauro citaturus, utar nomine istius Cædmon (in Anglo-Saxonica Regis Alvredi paraphrasi est Cedmon vel Ceadman) quem sacrae illius poësios authorem facit Beda ibidem.' Wülker, *Grundriss*, p. 120.

[27] 'The creation of the world, the origin of the human race, the whole history of Genesis, on the departure of Israel from Egypt and the entry into the promised land, on many other of the stories taken from the sacred Scriptures: on the incarnation, passion, and resurrection and ascension into heaven of the Lord, on the coming of the Holy Spirit and the teaching of the apostles. He also made many songs about the terrors of future judgement, the horrors of the pains of hell, and the joys of the heavenly kingdom'. *HE*, IV.24, pp. 418–19.

[28] (*HE* IV.24, p. 416). Bede's version of the OE original reads: 'Nu sculon herigean heofonrices ward' (*The Old English Version of Bede's Ecclesiastical History*, ed. T. Miller, EETS 96 (Oxford, 1891), part I, vol. II, 344); 'Us is riht micel ðæt we rodera weard. / wereda wuldorcyning. wordum herigen.' (*Gen.* 1–2).

[29] See above, n. 27.

most notably from George Hickes. Hickes believed that the style and dialect of the poems differed significantly from those of the song of Creation quoted in Bede.[30] In a letter of 25 April 1699 to Bishop Nicolson, Hickes stated his opinion that the words of Cædmon's 'Hymn' were sufficiently different from those of *Genesis* as to cast serious doubt on their joint authorship, and that the Junius poems showed the influence of the Danish language on Old English, and hence had to be of much later date.[31] Hickes was supported by Humfrey Wanley;[32] Junius was supported by such scholars as Conybeare,[33] Thorpe,[34] Jakob Grimm,[35] Wright,[36] and Bouterwek.[37] Ellis believed that while 'it cannot be a matter of great difficulty to determine whether the substance of the Hymn translated by Alfred may not yet be found in the Metrical Paraphrase', the fragment of Cædmon's poetry quoted in Bede was too short to allow any decision on the matter.[38] Both Thorpe and Wright, while agreeing with the attribution to Cædmon, noted that the Junius manuscript was not written by or contemporary with Cædmon, and that in reading the poems due allowance had to be made for 'such interpolation, omissions, and corruptions of the original text, as Cædmon . . . may be supposed to have suffered at the hands of ignorant transcribers'.[39]

From its first appearance in the modern historical record, the Junius manuscript has been caught up in the contemporary concerns of the scholars who have studied it. In many ways this is simply a continuation of the validation of a contemporary order by reference to the past that also seems to have concerned the manuscript's creators or compilers. While we cannot be certain of Ussher's motives in acquiring this particular manu-

30 G. Hickes, *Linguarum Vett. Septentrionalium Thesaurus Grammatico-Criticus & Archaeologicus* (Oxford, 1703), p. 133.

31 Quoted in R. Wülker, *Grundriss zur Geschichte der angelsächsischen Litteratur* (Leipzig, 1885), p. 121; Thorpe, *Cædmon's Metrical Paraphrase*, p. ix.

32 H. Wanley, *Librorum Vett. Septentrionalum, qui in Angliæ Biblioth. Extant, Catalogus Historio-Criticus* (Oxford, 1705), p. 77.

33 W. D. Conybeare, *Illustrations of Anglo-Saxon Poetry* (London, 1826), p. 183.

34 *Cædmon's Metrical Paraphrase*, pp. viii–xii.

35 *Andreas & Elene* (Cassel, 1840), p. xlvii.

36 T. Wright, *Biographia Britannica Literaria* (London, 1842), I, 23, 197.

37 K. Bouterwek, *Cædmon's des angelsächsischen biblische Dichtungen*, I, 6; II, 10.

38 *Account of Cædmon's Metrical Paraphrase*, p. 5.

39 Thorpe, *Cædmon's Metrical Paraphrase*, p. viii. Wright described the manuscript as 'much corrupted in passing through three centuries' (*Biographia*, I, 197).

script – issues of bibliomania aside – it seems reasonable to assume that it appealed in general to his interest in matters Anglo-Saxon, and in particular to his interest in universal chronology, particularly Old Testament chronology, and the progress of the church in the world. Ussher had calculated that Creation had begun on the night preceding Sunday, 23 October 4004 BC, that the binding of Satan was contemporary with either the birth or the death of Christ, or with the destruction of the temple in Jerusalem, that the coming of the Antichrist could be dated to the sixth century; and that the loosing of Satan took place under one of the eleventh-century popes.[40] This last date brought the 500-year reign of Satan to an end at the time of the Reformation, and the contemporary church now stood cleansed and powerful, and ready for the second coming of Christ. Seventeenth-century Britain was thus located in much the same position of reformed anticipation as was Anglo-Saxon England in the years following the late-tenth-century Benedictine reform; and Ussher's calculations were very much in the tradition of those of Byrhtferth of Ramsey or Hrabanus Maurus. Ussher's work on church history and biblical chronology was brought together in his two most important publications: his *Britannicarum ecclesiarum antiquitates*, a study of the early church in Britain and Ireland published in 1639, and his *Annales veteris et novi testamenti* published in 1650 (part 1) and 1654 (part 2). An English translation of the latter, *The Annals of the Old and New Testament or the Annals of the World deduced from the Origin of Time*, appeared in 1858. Clearly the poems of the Junius manuscript could have had a role in the creation of Ussher's chronology, though there is no concrete evidence that he ever consulted them for this purpose.

Junius was of course primarily a philologist and a lexicographer, and seems to have inherited an interest in the Old Testament from his father,[41] but his comments in his *Observationes in Willerami Abbatis*

[40] See Parry, *Trophies of Time*, pp. 141–50. Parry speculates that Ussher's locating the appearance of the Antichrist in the sixth century might have been intended to relate it to the birth of Muhammad or to the arrival of St Augustine's mission in England (*ibid.*, p. 141 n. 12). Certainly Ussher's work as a scholar and collector must be understood within the context of his Protestant Elizabethan upbringing and his concern with the theological and political issues of the Reformation. On Ussher's collection in general see W. O'Sullivan, 'Ussher as a Collector of Manuscripts', *Hermathena* 88 (1956), 34–58.

[41] Aldrich, Fehl and Fehl, *Franciscus Junius*, I, xxviii.

Francicam paraphrasin cantici canticorum make it clear that it was the identification of the 'long-lost poetry of Cædmon' that appealed to him above all else. Moreover, his words connect the poems in his manuscript not only to the verses of Cædmon recorded by Bede, but also to the Anglo-Saxon paraphrase of Bede (and hence Cædmon) traditionally thought to have been written by Alfred (*in Anglo-saxonica regis Alvredi paraphrasi*). As many scholars have noted, the bulk of Junius' transcripts are of Alfredian material,[42] and he may have had a particular interest in works associated with this first king of all England famous for his wisdom, his love of books, and his abilities as a translator. But whatever his interests in Alfredian texts may have been, his words establish a scribal and intellectual genealogy that links Junius to Cædmon via Alfred and Bede. The manner in which Bede creates, or 'fathers', Cædmon in his text of the *Historia ecclesiastica* has received quite a bit of attention,[43] but the process extends far beyond Bede. Moreover, it is certainly possible to question exactly how much of Bede's account of Cædmon is history, and how much is fiction. Analogues for Bede's story of Cædmon and Cædmon's 'Hymn' are numerous.[44] Similar myths of divine poetic origins occur in classical writings,[45] as well as in medieval Ireland and Scandinavia. One legend attributes the origins of Irish literature to the mid-seventh-century Cennfaeled mac Ailella, an aristocratic cleric with considerable knowledge of ecclesiastical learning, literature and law. Cennfaeled, like Cædmon, became a teacher, but unlike Cædmon he was also a gifted writer.[46] In Scandinavia the originary poem is the *Vǫluspá* ('Prophecy of the Sibyl') in which the seeress remembers the past and

42 E. G. Stanley, 'The Sources of Junius's Learning as Revealed in the Junius Manuscripts in the Bodleian Library', in *Franciscus Junius F. F. and His Circle*, ed. R. Bremmer (Amsterdam and Atlanta, GA, 1998), pp. 159–76; S. D. Keynes, 'The Cult of King Alfred the Great' *ASE* 28 (1999), 225–356, at pp. 266–7.

43 See Lees and Overing, 'Birthing Bishops and Fathering Poets: Bede, Hild and the Relations of Cultural Production', *Exemplaria* 6 (1994), 35–65.

44 See especially G. A. Lester, 'The Cædmon Story and its Analogues', *Neophilologus* 58 (1974), 225–37; A. Orchard, 'Poetic Inspiration and Prosaic Translation: the Making of *Cædmon's Hymn*', in *Studies in English Language and Literature*, ed. M. J. Toswell and E. M. Tyler (London and New York, 1996), pp. 402–22.

45 Orchard, 'Poetic Inspiration'.

46 D. Dumville, '*Beowulf* and the Celtic World: The Uses of the Evidence', *Traditio* 37 (1981), 109–60.

prophecies the future from the creation of the world to the destruction of the gods.

More problematically, as Lees and Overing have stressed,[47] Bede is our only source for Cædmon and this is unusual. Why is such an important figure and such an originary moment mentioned in no other source? Above all, why is there no mention of Cædmon in the *Life of Gregory* composed at Whitby a generation after Bede places Cædmon there, and a text very much concerned with origins, language and translation, teaching, and the prominent place of Whitby within the Anglo-Saxon church?[48] Chapter 13 of the *Life* considers the linguistic relationship between *Angulorum* (Angli) and *angelorum* (angels), one of the latter of whose properties it is to praise God (*pro certo celis laudere*). The angels sing 'alleluia', which means 'God's praise', and which, when divided into syllables, contains a reference to the Trinity in *alle* (*Patrum*), *lu* (*Filium*) and *ia* (*Spiritum sanctum*). The word also resonates of course with the name of the Northumbrian king, Ælli.[49] According to the anonymous author, who could as easily have been a nun as a monk of Whitby, words of praise directed to God are very much a part of Whitby's own legend of origin, quite apart from the Cædmon story. Moreover, Edwin, father of Abbess Ælfflæd under whom the *Life* was written, is associated with a miracle of song and conversion located between hall and church.[50] Edwin was on his way to church to receive instruction along with a crowd of heathen courtiers, when the party was halted by the song of a bird, as if mistaking it for the 'new song' of praise within the church ('quasi illud canticum novum carmen Deo nostro non esset vero futurum in eclesia, sed falso ad nihile utile'). Edwin's people are naturally converted and Edwin, like Cædmon, becomes a teacher of the faith ('quod ille docebat qui mones ad se invitat batizatos in nomine Patris et Filli et Spriitus sancti').[51]

Both Bede and the author of *The Life of Gregory* associate Whitby with learning, teaching and songs of praise, but while the author of the *Life* sets these activities within a royal context, Bede describes them as exclusively monastic. The difference between the two texts may be, at least in part, the result of the differing agendas of their respective authors.

47 'Birthing Bishops'.

48 B. Colgrave, ed., *The Earliest Life of Gregory the Great by an Anonymous Monk of Whitby* (Lawrence, KA, 1968).

49 *Ibid.*, pp. 90, 94 and 97.

50 *Ibid.*, p. 102.

51 *Ibid*, p. 96.

The *Life* was written under Abbess Ælfflæd who, as the text tells us, was actively building Whitby into a royal cult centre, the focus of which were the royal graves surrounding the high altar within the church.[52] Bede does not seem to have entirely approved of Ælfflæd and her interest in court and dynasty, as a comparison of the portraits of her drawn by Bede in his prose *Life of Cuthbert* with that of the author of the anonymous *Life of Cuthbert* reveals.[53] Given this background, Bede may well have been anxious to downplay the monastery's contemporary royal focus by shifting the reader's attention to a lost past of spiritual and educational glory, and how better to do it than with a miracle (for which Bede provides no source). The *Historia ecclesiastica* was dedicated to the devout Northumbrian king, Ceolwulf, for whom Bede seems to have had a genuine admiration.[54] It may be that Bede, while not daring overtly to criticize an abbess who was also a princess royal in this text, chose to emphasize, and perhaps embellish, the piety and importance of the Whitby community under Ælfflæd's predecessor. It is also possible that Ælfflæd in turn suppressed the earlier history of the monastery – there is after all no mention of Hild in the *Life of Gregory* – in order to foreground her own role in the shaping of its history. However, this still does not explain why there is no mention of Cædmon outside of Bede.

Whether Cædmon was a genuine historical figure or simply a combination of traditional history and a literary trope, the words Bede attributes to him are not his but Bede's paraphrase and translation, as Bede himself makes clear.[55] David Dumville was one of the first to address the problems in the relationship between Bede and Cædmon, and Bede and Cædmon's 'Hymn'.[56] The earliest version of Cædmon's 'Hymn' in Old English

[52] *Ibid.*, pp. 100–4.

[53] See C. E. Karkov, 'Whitby, Jarrow and the Commemoration of Death in Northumbria', in *Northumbria's Golden Age*, ed. J. Hawkes and S. Mills (Stroud, 1999), pp. 126–35.

[54] Fry, 'Art of Bede II', p. 79; C. W. Jones, *Saints' Lives and Chronicles in Early England* (Ithaca, 1947), p. 80.

[55] 'Hic est sensus, non autem ordo ipse uerborum, quae dormiens ille canebat; necque enim possunt carmina, quamuis optime conposita, ex alia in aliam linguam ad uerbum sine detrimento sui decoris ac dignitatis transferri.' ('This is the sense but not the order of the words which he sang as he slept. For it is not possible to translate verse, however well composed, literally from one language to another without some loss of beauty and dignity.') *HE* IV.24, pp. 416–17.

[56] Dumville, '*Beowulf* and the Celtic World', pp. 147–8. (Though seminal, the article does contain a number of errors and should be used with caution.)

survives only as a marginal gloss or addition to Bede's Latin paraphrase,[57] and is as likely to be a retranslation of Bede's Latin back into Old English as it is Cædmon's original verse.[58] In either case it is in the Old English Bede that the 'Hymn' first becomes part of the main text,[59] and thus it must be seen as a reworking of the 'original' to some degree. Biblical origins, the origins of England and English poetry, and the origins of Anglo-Saxon scholarship are thus united in the production of the Junius facsimile. Junius may, in fact, have seen himself as taking on something of the role of Cædmon in his editorial practices, modelling his marking of the versification in his transcript of *Judith* not on what was actually in the manuscript but, apparently, on the metrical pointing of the 'Cædmonian' poems – which may have represented for him the 'authentic Anglo-Saxon manner'.[60] A potent merging of bodies and books indeed!

The authorial/editorial genealogy constructed by Junius is in keeping with the scholarly interests of the mid-seventeenth century. This was an era very much concerned with English origins: Ussher was busily exploring the origins of the English church; D'Ewes, Somner and Junius, amongst others, were investigating the origins of the English language; Sir John Spelman was at work on his life of King Alfred, published in Latin in 1678 and in English in 1709;[61] and Abraham Whelock furthered study of the origins of the English nation with the publication of his edition of Bede's *Historia ecclesiastica*, accompanied by its 'Alfredian' translation into Old English and a text and translation of

57 St Petersburg, Public Library, lat. Q. v. i. 18 (marginal gloss); Cambridge, University Library, Kk. 5. 16 (addition to originally blank last page); Ker, *Catalogue*, pp. 158 and 38. On the manuscript record of Cædmon's 'Hymn' see O'Keeffe, *Visible Song*, ch. 2; and K. Kiernan, 'Reading Cædmon's "Hymn" with Someone Else's Glosses', *Representations* 32 (1990), 157–74.

58 A suggestion first made by John Lingard in *The Antiquities of the Anglo-Saxon Church*, 2 vols. (Newcastle, 1806), II, 521–2.

59 O'Keeffe, *Visible Song*, p. 25.

60 Lucas, 'Franciscus Junius and the Versification of *Judith: Francisci Junii in memorium*: 1591–1991', in *The Preservation and Transmission of Anglo-Saxon Culture*, ed. P. E. Szarmach and J. T. Rosenthal (Kalamazoo, MI, 1997), pp. 369–404, at pp. 371–2. Lucas notes that while the pointing of the *Judith* transcript does not follow that of the original text, Junius' sense of versification was good and his marking of the verse is 90 percent accurate (*ibid.*, pp. 385–7).

61 Keynes, 'Cult', p. 254.

the Anglo-Saxon Chronicle in 1643.[62] It was in and through these works that King Alfred the Great 'became a creature of national mythology . . . in all his essentials a product of the first half of the seventeenth century'.[63] While Junius might be seen as building on the combination of Bedan and 'Alfredian' texts begun by Whelock, the first to identify Alfred as the author of the Old English translation of Bede, he can perhaps take credit for being the first to explicitly link Alfred and Cædmon as authors. Alfred, father of the English nation, thus becomes author of the first translation of the works of the first English poet in the writings of his intellectual son and heir, Junius, father of Anglo-Saxon philology.

So strong was Cædmon's spell that even those who did not agree with Junius' attribution of the biblical poems to him could not resist it. George Hickes, the earliest and most influential of the critics, labelled the author of the Junius 11 poems 'pseudo-Cædmon', a term which suggests derivation from if not dependence on the work of the master. Indeed, in his letter to Bishop Nicolson, Hickes states his belief that the author of the Junius poems wrote 'in imitation of the true Cædmon'.[64] The letter also displays an interesting confusion of authors and texts. While Hickes clearly believed that there was an historical Cædmon, this figure gradually disappears in the letter, becoming 'the fragment in Bede, which was the beginning of the true Cædmon', an interesting turn of phrase that hints at the possibility of Cædmon's being nothing more than a product of Bede's literary imagination. In a similar vein the author of the Junius 11 poems becomes 'Junius' Cædmon'.[65] Conybeare took something of a middle ground when it came to Cædmon's authorship of the Junius 11 poems, but in the process made Cædmon the head of a whole 'Cædmonian School'. He suggested that if the poems were not the work of Cædmon himself, they must surely be the work of the 'extensive school of imitators' that Bede tells us adopted the poet as

[62] On Whelock see A. J. Frantzen, *Desire for Origins: New Language, Old English and Teaching the Tradition* (New Brunswick, NJ, and London, 1990), pp. 151–63. Frantzen states that the Chronicle text was not included until the second edition of 1644, but this is incorrect. I would like to thank Simon Keynes for verifying the contents of the two editions for me.

[63] Keynes, 'Cult', p. 246.

[64] Quoted in Thorpe, *Cædmon's Metrical Paraphrase*, pp. viii–ix; Wülker, *Grundriss*, p. 121.

[65] Thorpe, *Cædmon's Metrical Paraphrase*, p. ix.

their 'great model'.[66] Of course, Bede says nothing about a Cædmonian school, stating merely that while later Englishmen attempted to compose religious poetry, none could compare with Cædmon.[67]

While Junius made the biblical poems available to the scholarly community for the first time, Thorpe was the first to provide a fully translated and glossed edition with the text of the poems printed in half-lines, and in it he continued the association between Anglo-Saxon author and modern editor. As noted above, he identified himself as the first to recognize the fragmented nature of Liber II, and expressed surprise at the failure of both the Anglo-Saxon scribe and Junius to do so.[68] (Gollancz points out that there are indications that Junius too had his doubts about the authenticity of Liber II.[69]) The implication is that Thorpe is the more sensitive editor, and hence closer to the spirit and sense of the lost original text. In places he resorts to 'conjectural interpretation',[70] actively taking on the role of author as part of the editorial process, but for the most part he felt the poems were written in 'Saxon as pure as the works of Alfred himself'.[71] Once again, Alfred intervenes in the transmission of the original 'Cædmonian' text, perhaps in this instance spurred on by the rampant 'Alfredophilia' of the early nineteenth century.[72] Indeed, Alfred has a far more prominent place in Thorpe's edition than he had in Junius', and plays a more prominent role in the processes of translation and textual production. Thorpe recognized the likely difference between the song composed by Cædmon and the words of the 'Hymn' as it has come down to us. He points out that Bede's Latin is only a translation, and echoes Lingard's suggestion that the Old English version of the 'Hymn' is an Alfredian retranslation,[73] but for Thorpe the differences between each translation and the opening of *Genesis* merely provided additional proof of

66 Quoted in Wülker, *Grundriss*, p. 122.

67 'Et quidem et alii post illum in gente Anglorum religiosa poemata facere temtabant, sed nullus eum aequiperare potuit' (*HE* IV.24, p. 414); 'Ond eac swelce monige oðre æfter him in Ongelþeode ongunnon æfeste leoð wyrcan: ac nænig hwæðre him þæt gelice don meahte' (*Old English Version of Bede's Ecclesiastical History*, p. 342).

68 Thorpe, *Cædmon's Metrical Paraphrase*, p. vii. He conjectured that *Christ and Satan* was the product of an 'illiterate man writing from recitation' (*ibid.*).

69 Gollancz, *Cædmon Manuscript*, p. xlix.

70 Thorpe, *Cædmon's Metrical Paraphrase*, p. vii.

71 *Ibid.*, p. x.

72 Keynes, 'Cult', p. 332.

73 Lingard, *History and Antiquities of the Anglo-Saxon Church*, II, 521–2.

the genuineness of the latter. The differences are 'such as might naturally be expected to exist between an original composition and a retranslation from a translation of it'.[74] It was perhaps to help make this point, as much as to provide some historical background on Cædmon the poet, that he included the story of Cædmon from both Bede's *Historia ecclesiastica* and 'King Alfred's Anglo-Saxon Translation' amongst his prefatory material.

Nationalism was a continuing problem in Thorpe's scholarship and may also have played a role in the increased presence of Alfred within his book. In 1830 Thorpe published *A Grammar of the Anglo-Saxon Tongue, with a Praxis*, a translation of the Dane Rasmus Rask's *Angelsaksisk Sproglære tilligemed enkort Læsebog*, leaving out Rask's own highly nationalistic dedicatory epistle with its references to a glorious pagan Scandinavian past. The third edition of the same translation, published in 1879, went further, eliminating Rask's introduction along with the epistle because 'The Grammar as originally published was obnoxious to at least one objection, which, in the present edition, will not be found, it was, perhaps, too Scandinavian, owing, no doubt, to the very natural bias of its author.'[75] Thorpe has also been accused of stealing N. F. S. Grundtvig's 1830 prospectus for the publication of key Anglo-Saxon texts, a move which 'eradicated Grundtvig's name from the project and rendered Anglo-Saxonism distinctly, stubbornly British'.[76] Robert Bjork notes that Grundtvig, like Rask, was as caught up in Scandinavian nationalism as Thorpe was in its English counterpart.[77] There is no evidence that Junius could be accused of the same sort of nationalistic fervour; nevertheless, in his 1832 edition of Junius 11, Thorpe cast aspersions on the work of Junius, labelling him a 'learned foreigner', and, while acknowledging Junius' contribution to scholarship, he 'cannot avoid noticing' the numerous errors of his facsimile.[78] As has recently been pointed out,

[74] Thorpe, *Cædmon's Metrical Paraphrase*, p. ix.

[75] R. E. Bjork, 'Nineteenth-Century Scandinavia and the Birth of Anglo-Saxon Studies', in *Anglo-Saxonism and the Construction of Social Identity*, ed. A. J. Frantzen and J. D. Niles (Gainseville, FL, 1997), pp. 111–32, at pp. 121–2.

[76] Bjork, 'Nineteenth-Century Scandinavia', p. 112 and n. 6. See also P. Pulsiano, 'Benjamin Thorpe', in *Medieval Scholarship: Biographical Studies in the Formation of a Discipline*, vol. II of *Literature and Philology*, ed. H. Damico (New York and London, 1998), pp. 75–92.

[77] Bjork, 'Nineteenth-Century Scandinavia', p. 116.

[78] Thorpe, *Cædmon's Metrical Paraphrase*, p. xiii.

several of the emendations credited to Thorpe and other scholars were actually proposed by Junius in the notes to his facsimile.[79] Thorpe's criticisms of Junius resulted in his own immediate but ineffective censure by other scholars.[80] Thorpe, an Englishman, thus presents himself to us as heir to Alfred, Bede and Cædmon himself. The Cædmon manuscript was 'the first native volume on Old English verse', and Thorpe became the first to provide us with a 'faithful text' of the work of the first English poet. He ends his prefatory remarks with an address to the reader that drives home this very point: 'Cædmon's Paraphrase, with all its beauties and all its faults, is thus, for the first time, before the public in an English garb. Those readers who may rise disappointed from the perusal should reflect, that he is our earliest poet; that he lived (himself a herdsman) when all around him was barbarism; and that these mangled remains are all that time has spared us.'[81]

The first full facsimile of the manuscript was edited by Israel Gollancz for the British Academy in 1927. The introduction opens with an account of the great names associated with the preservation of Anglo-Saxon poetic manuscripts including, of course, James Ussher and Francis Junius. In contrast to Thorpe, Gollancz believed the flaws of Junius' original facsimile to be negligible when compared to his signal achievement in editing. (He also acknowledged the advances in editing made by Thorpe.[82]) When it came to the ascription of the poems to Cædmon, Gollancz was more circumspect. Following Ettmüller,[83] the first scholar to consider seriously the idea that the poems might be the work of different authors, Gollancz considered the separate themes, styles, and evidence for sources and date for each of the four poems. He concluded that he could find 'nothing against the authenticity of *Genesis A*, including even the paraphrase of the genealogies, as the work of Cædmon'.[84] *Exodus*, however, seemed to him to be the work of a different and more learned poet. Still, the spectre of Cædmon could not be entirely dispelled: 'No one would now identify the *Exodus* with Bede's reference to Cædmon's poem "De egressu Israel ex Ægypto", but it should be borne in

79 Lucas, *Franciscus Junius*, p. xxiv.

80 Pulsiano, 'Thorpe', p. 77.

81 Thorpe, *Cædmon's Metrical Paraphrase*, p. xvi.

82 Gollancz, *Cædmon Manuscript*, p. xvi.

83 L. Ettmüller, *Engla and Seaxna Scôpas and Bôceras* (Quedlinburg and Leipzig, 1850).

84 Gollancz, *Cædmon Manuscript*, pp. lxii and lix.

mind that the historian adds that others after Cædmon, in the English nation sought to make pious songs ("religiosa poemata"). The present poem may have been known to Bede and included in the latter category.'[85] Once again, the school of Cædmon is invoked by Gollancz's conclusion that the poem may have been the work of 'Cædmon's followers'.[86] *Christ and Satan*, though not written by Cædmon, may have been a later addition to the manuscript prompted by Bede's reference to Cædmon's composing poetry on New Testament subjects, while *Daniel* is simply the work of a poet 'in every respect differentiated from the poet of *Exodus*'.[87] Despite his separate analyses of the individual poems, Gollancz retains the title *The Cædmon Manuscript* for his facsimile, and opens the volume with the Old English version of Cædmon's 'Hymn', thereby perpetuating the very associations he claims he wishes us to examine more critically.

Perhaps it was the spectre of Cædmon that led to the selection of the Junius 11 manuscript as the first volume of the Anglo-Saxon Poetic Records to be published. While seriously questioning Cædmon's actual authorship of the poems, the editor, George Krapp, never denies it completely, and opens his introduction with a sentence that perpetuates the bond between first poet and first editor: 'Two names must always be associated with the venerable manuscript . . . the name of Cædmon as possible author and the name of Franciscus Junius, the earliest of the modern scholars to enter on the task of restoring to the world the knowledge of the poetry of the Anglo-Saxons.'[88] Krapp goes on to state that even though few today would regard Cædmon as author, 'the content of the manuscript accords so closely with the description of Cædmon as poet given by Bede, especially the first poem in the manuscript, that it requires no stretching of probability to assume that the example and incentive of Cædmon's own verse accounts in large measure for the existence of these poems, and, in consequence, of this manuscript'.[89] Alfred does not make an appearance until the discussion of *Genesis* on page xxvi of the edition. Krapp sees *Genesis* as the work of at least two poets, and divides the poem into the traditional '*Genesis A*' and '*Genesis B*'. '*Genesis B*', he believes, was translated from its Old Saxon exemplar in the

85 *Ibid.*, p. lxviii. 86 *Ibid.*, p. lxxxiv.

87 *Ibid.*, pp. cvi, xcviii and lxxxviii.

88 Krapp, *Junius Manuscript*, p. ix.

89 *Ibid.*, p. xi.

ninth century and may have been the result of the 'cosmopolitan activity of Alfred's court'.[90] Alfred, or at the very least someone connected with his court, again appears as translator, this time not just of Cædmon's 'Hymn' but of a major portion of *Genesis*. Cædmon the poet remains hovering ambiguously in the background when it comes to the origins of '*Genesis A*'. 'If the poem was written in the north of England, about the year 700', Krapp writes, 'time and theme fit so exactly the description of Cædmon as poet given by Bede that the ascription of the poem to Cædmon might seem to be beyond cavil'.[91] His conclusion is inconclusive at best, suggesting that while most scholars would assign '*Genesis A*' to the school of Cædmon, or an author working in a deliberately Cædmonian style, the question of authorship must ultimately remain open.

What Krapp and the Anglo-Saxon Poetic Records claimed with some reservation in 1931 is probably true today: no scholar would now consider any of the four poems to be the work of Cædmon. But we are still, as Allen Frantzen has shown, fascinated by desire for and stories of origins.[92] With the Junius 11 manuscript this may be in part due to the fact that the stories of Cædmon and Bede are all about reading, writing and scholarship, the very acts in which we are engaged when reading and studying the manuscript. The originary significance of Bede and Cædmon are entirely the creation of scholars[93] anxious to pin down the origins of Anglo-Saxon poetry, history and historiography. One could also add Alfred to the mix; our relationship to the 'Alfredian' text is a trope for its author's relationship to Bede,[94] just as our relationship to Bede is a trope for Bede's relationship to Cædmon, itself a trope for divine Creation through the Word, one of the primary subjects of the Junius 11 poems. Clare Lees and Gillian Overing view the situation slightly differently, pointing out that for all its power and importance as an originary moment, the story of Bede and Cædmon is also one of loss. In their view, 'The paraphrase in Latin – the prestige language of Christian culture – only makes the reader more aware of the vernacular poem that it supplants and that the Old English version seeks to redeem. Bede identifies ancient traditions with emerging institutions and his text produces a reordering

90 *Ibid.*, p. xxvi. 91 *Ibid.*, p. xxvii.

92 Frantzen, *Desire for Origins*.

93 *Ibid.*, p. 144; Dumville, '*Beowulf* and the Celtic World', pp. 147–8; Lees and Overing, 'Birthing Bishops'.

94 Frantzen, *Desire for Origins*, p. 138.

in terms of his priorities and desires, which inevitably involves a forgetting.'[95] Yet Cædmon and his originary 'Hymn' are not just forgotten, they are lost – to us if not to Bede. In Freudian terms the desire to identify Cædmon and his 'Hymn' in the words and texts of later authors is an acknowledgement of the very loss we seek to deny.[96] Similarly, translation, transcription, and the production of facsimiles are forms of repetition; they represent a desire for identity between two objects or events, for the interpenetration of the bodies of books and authors, for the 'begetting of fresh sons'. At the same time they also demonstrate the impossibility of literal identity. This process is of course a central concern of postmodern literary theory, and one perhaps most effectively demonstrated in Borges's story, 'Pierre Menard, Author of Don Quixote'.[97]

With each repetition of 'Cædmon's Hymn' we are reminded both of the search for the real Cædmon and of his loss. For Junius, whose poetic sensibilities seem to have been based on what he thought were those of Cædmon, the difference between model and copy, father and son, begins to blur. The process has been completed by modern scholarship which now refers to Junius 11 as both the 'Cædmon manuscript' and the 'Junius manuscript' of biblical poetry.[98] But the point of this story, like that of Richard de Bury's account of textual production, is not just the impossibility of literal identity, but the fact that we copy in order to update; rather than repeating the historical text we reenact it in the present. Junius altered the punctuation and metre of the manuscripts he transcribed to accord with those of the Junius 11 poems – an updating which was clearly based on a desire for the lost original.[99] Thorpe

95 'Birthing Bishops', p. 41.

96 On repetition and identity see S. Freud, 'Three Essays on the Theory of Sexuality', in *The Standard Edition of the Complete Psychological Works*, 24 vols., ed. and trans. J. Strachey, vol. VII (1905), 123–245; E. Bronfen, 'Risky Resemblances: on Repetition, Mourning and Representation', in *Death and Representation*, ed. S. W. Goodwin and E. Bronfen (Baltimore, MD and London, 1993), pp. 103–29, esp. pp. 103–6. On the application of Freud's theories to books and book collecting see J. Derrida, *Archive Fever: A Freudian Impression* (Chicago, 1996).

97 J. L. Borges, 'Pierre Menard, Author of Don Quixote', *Ficciones* (New York, 1962), pp. 45–55.

98 A point noted by Frantzen, *Desire for Origins*, p. 138. See also the Bodleian webpage cited in n. 2.

99 Lucas, 'Versification of *Judith*', pp. 371–2.

presented himself as heir to Alfred, Bede and Cædmon, his objective juxtaposition of texts belying the nineteenth-century nationalism that was so much a part of his editorial process. But we too are a part of this process. Writing is an act of reading, and reading an act of rewriting; neither occurs in a vacuum, but in a space filled with the present. The authors and artists of the Junius 11 manuscript both recognized this fact and made it a part of their narrative. Biblical history was updated, rewritten (and drawn) into Anglo-Saxon history. Their interest was in biblical origins and the connection of the present order to those origins in a universal framework in which individuals like Cædmon, Bede or Alfred are ultimately unimportant. Their narrative strategies locate modern readers right alongside their Anglo-Saxon counterparts, still standing in expectation of the Last Judgement, and still engaged in the process of reading, writing and rewriting the book of poems. But is this a process that is likely to survive in our present era of the 'post-human'? As Michael Camille notes: 'the whole history, development, and to some extent the institutional aims of the modern library have been to exclude the body from the site of reading, to make a silent and desomatized optics of the *biblioteca* the simulacrum of purely mental experience, a process that will only accelerate in the future with the increasing incorporeality of the electronic word'.[100] Digital facsimiles allow us to scroll through manuscripts in ways that we never could before, to see previously unnoticed details, and to compare and reconstruct images and texts in new ways, but their incorporeality may also provide us with the ultimate example of transcription and translation as simultaneous acts of reproduction and of loss. These are not the ways in which 'books' as objects were intended to be read. At the same time that such facsimiles make image and text more accessible, they make the body of the book less accessible. In separating the body of the book from that of its reader we may lose nothing in terms of our understanding of textual production and analysis, but we do lose all sense of the physical act of reading, the act for which the narrative techniques of the authors and artists of Junius 11 (and, one might add, the narrative strategies of its editors) were designed.

[100] M. Camille, 'The Book as Flesh and Fetish in Richard de Bury's *Philobiblon*', in *The Book and the Body*, ed. D. W. Frese and K. O'Brien O'Keeffe (Notre Dame, IN, 1997), pp. 34–77, at p. 40. See also Derrida, *Archive Fever*; and N. Basbanes, *A Gentle Madness: Bibliophiles, Bibliomanes, and the Eternal Passion for Books* (New York, 1995).

Appendix: suggested subjects of blank picture spaces

GENESIS[1]

page	
99	Abraham before God
101	Sarah troubled, or Sarah offering Hagar to Abraham (Henderson)
102	Hagar in Abraham's bed (Henderson)
103	Sarah's persecution of Hagar, or Hagar's flight (Henderson)
104	Hagar's flight, or Hagar with the angel (Henderson)
105	Top: Return of Hagar (Henderson)
	Bottom: Birth of Ismael (Henderson)
108	God's covenant with Abraham
110	God and his two companions walk with Abraham to Sodom (Henderson)
111	Lot greeting angels (Henderson)
112	Attack on the house of Lot (Henderson)
113	Lot speaking to Sodomites (Henderson)
114	Rescue of Lot and blinding of Sodomites (Henderson)
115	Angels speaking to Lot inside his house (Henderson)
116	Lot warning his sons-in-law (Henderson)
117	Lot's request to go to Zoar (Henderson)
118	Lot's safe arrival at Zoar (Henderson)
120	Destruction of Sodom (Henderson)
121	Lot's wife
122	Lot in cave with daughters (Henderson)

[1] Where indicated, these suggestions are based on G. Henderson, 'The Programme of Illustrations in Bodleian MS XI', in G. Henderson, *Studies in English Bible Illustration* (London, 1985), I, 138–83; otherwise they derive from my own comparisons with Claudius B. iv.

The following page is missing. Henderson (p. 158) believes that it 'must have contained two large picture spaces destined for two more scenes of Lot with his daughters in the cave'.

123 Lot's daughters give birth
124 Abimelech's reception of Sarah (Henderson)
125 God appears at the bed of Abimelech (Henderson)
126 God haranguing Abimelech (Henderson)
127 Abimelech consults his counsellors (Henderson)
128 Abraham addresses Abimelech (Henderson)
129 Abimelech's restitution of Sarah and gifts to Abraham (Henderson)
130 Abimelech speaking with Abraham and Sarah (Henderson)
131 The childlessness of Abimelech's people (Henderson)
132 Lifting of blight against Abimelech (Henderson)
133 Isaac playing with Ismael
134 Abraham sends Sarah and Ismael away
135 Abraham and Abimelech
136 Abraham's pledge to Abimelech
137 Abraham makes offering to God
138 God tells Abraham to sacrifice Isaac
139 Abraham leads Isaac to sacrifice
140 Isaac carrying wood
141 Sacrifice of Isaac
142 Abraham makes offering to God.

EXODUS[2]

144 Slaying of the first-born
145 Israelites depart from Egypt
147 God leads Israelites in a pillar of cloud by day
150 Israelites fearful at the advance of the Egyptians
151 Egyptians pursue Israelites
152 Pillar of cloud divides Israelites and Egyptians
155 Israelites ready to cross the Red Sea
157 Moses divides the Red Sea
159 Israelites cross the Red Sea
164 Abraham is restrained from killing Isaac
165 Drowning of the Egyptians in the Red Sea

[2] All suggestions for the subjects of the illustrations intended for *Exodus* are from P. J. Lucas, ed., *Exodus* (London, 1977).

168 Moses and Israelites rejoice
171 Israelites collect booty on further shore.

DANIEL[3]

172 Daniel writing
174 (Two pages missing after 174. Lucas suggests two full-page pictures of Nabuchodonosor's troops attacking Jerusalem, and the capture of Jerusalem.)
175 Israelites led to Babylon
176 Three children learning Chaldean language and literature
177 Top: Nabuchodonosor receives three children into his service
Bottom: Nabuchodonosor asleep, dreaming
178 The helpless wise men before Nabuchodonosor
179 Nabuchodonoser commands wise men to be executed
180 Daniel before Nabuchodonosor.
(Pages missing after 180. Lucas suggests they included pictures of Nabuchodonosor receiving Daniel and the worship of the statue.)
181 Accusation of the three children
182 Three children brought before Nabuchodonosor
183 Nabuchodonosor condemns the three children to the fire
184 The three children bound in the fire
185 The three in the open furnace with the angel of protection
186 The Babylonian officers burnt by the flames
187 The three children worship God in the closed furnace
189 Azarias
193 Nabuchodonosor conferring with his courtiers
194 The three children released from the furnace
195 Nabuchodonosor with the three children
196 Nabuchodonosor honours the three children
197 Nabuchodonosor confers with his council
198 Nabuchodonosor ignores God and continues his evil ways
199 Nabuchodonosor's dream of the tree
200 An angel orders the tree to be cut down
201 Daniel speaking with Nabuchodonosor
203 Nabuchodonosor deprived of his throne
204 Nabuchodonosor among the beasts
206 Nabuchodonosor acknowledges God

[3] All suggestions for the subjects of the illustrations intended for *Daniel* are from P. J. Lucas, 'On the Blank *Daniel* Cycle in MS Junius 11', *JWCI* 42 (1979), 207–13.

207 Nabuchodonosor restored to his throne
210 Darius' troops march on Babylon
211 Baltasar's feast with the writing on the wall
212 (Lucas suggests a page missing after 212 with a scene of Daniel interpreting the writing.)

CHRIST AND SATAN

Gollancz suggested that missing leaves between pages 212 and 213, 216 and 217, 222 and 223, 224 and 225, and 228 and 229 might have contained illustrations of Satan in hell, the Harrowing of Hell, the Crucifixion and the Temptation of Christ.[4] James Hall thought it most likely that the illustrations consisted of a depiction of God creating the universe or the Fall of Lucifer (after 212); Satan in hell (after 216); the Harrowing of Hell (after 222); and the Temptation of Christ and the Last Judgement (after 228).[5]

4 I. Gollancz, ed., *The Cædmon Manuscript of Anglo-Saxon Biblical Poetry: Junius XI in the Bodleian Library* (London, 1927), p. cv.

5 J. R. Hall, 'The Old English Book of Salvation History: Three Studies on the Unity of MS. Junius 11' (unpubl. PhD dissertation, University of Notre Dame, 1974), pp. 25–43.

Bibliography

Ælfric, *Ælfric's Catholic Homilies, the First Series*, ed. P. Clemoes, EETS SS 17 (London, 1997)

Ælfric's Catholic Homilies, the Second Series, ed. M. Godden, EETS SS 5 (London, 1979)

Ælfric's Lives of the Saints, ed. W. W. Skeat, EETS OS 76, 82, 94 and 114 (London, 1966)

Exameron Anglice or The Old English Hexameron, ed. S. J. Crawford (Darmstadt, 1968)

Homilies of Ælfric: a Supplementary Collection, ed. J. C. Pope, 2 vols., EETS OS 259–60 (London, 1967–8)

The Homilies of the Anglo-Saxon Church, ed. B. Thorpe, 2 vols. (London 1844–6)

The Old English Version of the Heptateuch, Ælfric's Treatise on the Old and New Testament and his Preface to Genesis, ed. S. J. Crawford, EETS OS 160 (Oxford, 1922; repr. 1969 with additional texts transcribed by N. R. Ker)

Alcuin, *De fide sanctae et individuae Trinitatis*, PL 101, 11–58

Aldrich, K., Philipp Fehl and Raina Fehl, *Franciscus Junius: The Literature of Classical Art*, 2 vols. (Berkeley, 1991)

Alexander, J. J. G. 'Dancing in the Streets', *Jnl of the Walters Art Gallery* 54 (1996), 147–62

Ambrose, *De Abraham*, ed. K. Schenkl, CSEL 32.1 (Vienna, 1897), 501–638

De Noe et arca, ed. K. Schenkl, CSEL 32.1 (Vienna, 1897), 413–97

De sacramentis, ed. O. Faller, CSEL 73 (Vienna, 1962)

Astell, A. W., 'Holoferne's Head: *Tacen* and Teaching in the Old English *Judith*', *ASE* 18 (1989), 117–33

Augustine of Hippo, *Confessiones*, ed. P. Knöll, CSEL 33.1 (Vienna, 1846)

De civitate dei, ed. B. Dombart and A. Kolb, CCSL 47–8 (Turnhout, 1955)

De doctrina christiana, PL 34, 15

De Genesi ad litteram, ed. J. Zycha, CSEL 28 (Vienna, 1894), 1–435
De utilitate credendi, ed. J. Zycha, CSEL 25 (Vienna, 1891), 1–48
Enchiridion, ed. M. P. J. van den Hout, CCSL 46 (Turnhout, 1969), 49–114
Ennarrationes in Psalmos, PL 36, 67
Anderson, E. R., 'Style and Theme in the Old English *Daniel*', *English Studies* 68 (1987), 1–23
Bailey, R. N., *Viking Age Sculpture* (London, 1980)
England's Earliest Sculptors (Toronto, 1996)
Bailey, R. N. and R. Cramp, eds., *Cumberland, Westmorland and Lancashire North-of-the-Sands*, vol. II: *Corpus of Anglo-Saxon Stone Sculpture* (Oxford, 1988)
Bal, M., *Reading 'Rembrandt': Beyond the Word–Image Opposition* (Cambridge, 1991)
Bal, M. and N. Bryson, 'Semiotics and Art History', *Art Bull.* 73.2 (1991), 174–208
Barker, N., ed., *The York Gospels* (London, 1986)
Barlow, F., ed., *Life of King Edward who Rests at Westminster, Attributed to a Monk of Saint-Bertin*, 2nd edn (Oxford, 1992)
Barthes, R., 'Rhetoric of the Image', in his *The Responsibility of Forms* (New York, 1985), pp. 21–40
Bately, J. M., *MS A*, vol. 3 *The Anglo-Saxon Chronicle: A Collaborative Edition*, ed. D. Dumville and S. Keynes (Cambridge, 1986)
Bäuml, F. 'Medieval Texts and the Two Theories of Oral-Formulaic Composition: A Proposal for a Third Theory', *New Literary History* 16 (1984), 31–49
Bede, *Bede's Ecclesiastical History of the English People*, ed. B. Colgrave and R. A. B. Mynors (Oxford, 1969)
De schematibus et tropis, ed. C. Kendall, CCSL 123A (Turnhout, 1975)
Homilae, ed. D. Hurst, CCSL 122 (Turnhout, 1955)
Homilies on the Gospels, trans. L. T. Martin and D. Hurst, 2 vols. (Kalamazoo, MI, 1991)
In Genesim, ed. C. W. Jones, CCSL 118A (Turnhout, 1967)
In Lucam, ed. D. Hurst, CCSL (Turnhout, 1960)
The Old English Version of Bede's Ecclesiastical History, ed. T. Miller, 4 vols. EETS 96 (Oxford, 1891)
Belanoff, P., 'The Fall (?) of the Old English Female Poetic Image', *PMLA* 104 (1989), 822–31
Bethurum, D., ed., *The Homilies of Wulfstan* (Oxford, 1952)
Biggs, F., '"*Englum gelice*": *Elene* line 1320 and *Genesis A* line 185', *NM* 86 (1985), 447–52
Bischoff, B. and M. Lapidge, *Biblical Commentaries from the Canterbury School of Theodore and Hadrian*, CSASE 10 (Cambridge, 1994)
Bjork, R. E., 'Nineteenth-Century Scandinavia and the Birth of Anglo-Saxon

Studies', in *Anglo-Saxonism and the Construction of Social Identity*, ed. A. J. Frantzen and J. D. Niles (Gainseville, FL, 1997), pp. 111–32

Bloch, R. H., *Etymologies and Genealogies: A Literary Anthropology of the French Middle Ages* (Chicago, 1986)

Blum, P. 'The Cryptic Creation Cycle in MS Junius xi', *Gesta* 15 (1976), 211–26

Bouterwek, K., *Cædmon's des Angelsachsen biblische Dichtungen*, vol. I (Elberfeld, 1849–51), vol. II (Gütersloh, 1854)

Bremmer, R. H. Jr., 'Retrieving Junius' Correspondence', in *Franciscus Junius F. F. and His Circle*, ed. R. Bremmer (Leiden and Atlanta, GA, 1998), pp. 199–235

'The Correspondence of Johannes De Laet (1581–1649) as a Mirror of his Life', *Lias* 25 (1998), 139–64

Bremmer, R. H. and R. Rácz, 'Junius's Case against William Howard, Viscount Stafford', in *Franciscus Junius F. F. and His Circle*, ed. R. Bremmer (Leiden and Atlanta, GA, 1998), pp. 121–7.

Bright, 'The Relation of the Cædmonian *Exodus* to the Liturgy', *MLN* 27 (1912), 97–103

Broderick, H. R., 'The Iconographic and Compositional Sources of the Drawings in Oxford Bodleian Library, MS Junius 11' (unpubl. PhD dissertation, Columbia University, 1978)

'Observations on the Method of Illustration in MS Junius 11 and the Relationship of the Drawings to the Text', *Scriptorium* 37 (1983), 161–77

'The Influence of Anglo-Saxon Genesis Iconography on Later English Medieval Manuscript Art', in *The Preservation and Transmission of Anglo-Saxon Culture*, ed. P. E. Szarmach and J. T. Rosenthal (Kalamazoo, MI, 1997), pp. 211–39

Bronfen, E., 'Risky Resemblances: on Repetition, Mourning and Representation', in *Death and Representation*, ed. S. W. Goodwin and E. Bronfen (Baltimore, MD and London, 1993), pp. 103–29

Brown, M. P., *The Book of Cerne: Prayer, Patronage and Power in Ninth-Century England* (London and Toronto, 1996)

'Female Book-Ownership and Production in England during the Ninth Century: The Evidence of the Prayerbooks' in *Lexis and Texts in Early English*, ed. C. Kay and L. Sylvester (Amsterdam and Atlanta, forthcoming)

Bruce-Mitford, R. L. S., *The Art of the Codex Amiatinus*, Jarrow Lecture, Jarrow, 1967

Budny, M., *Insular, Anglo-Saxon and Early Anglo-Norman Manuscript Art at Corpus Christi College, Cambridge* (Kalamazoo, MI, 1998)

Butcher, J. W., 'Formulaic Invention in the Genealogies of the Old English *Genesis A*', in *Comparative Research on Oral Traditions: A Memorial for Milman Perry*, ed. J. M. Foley (Columbus, OH, 1985), pp. 73–92

Byrhtferth, *Byrhtferth's Enchiridion*, ed. P. Baker and M. Lapidge, EETS SS 15 (Oxford, 1995)

Camille, M., 'Seeing and Reading: Some Visual Implications of Medieval Literacy and Illiteracy', *Art History* 8 (1985), 26–49

'Gothic Signs and the Surplus: The Kiss on the Cathedral', *Yale French Studies*, special issue: *Contexts: Style and Values in Medieval Art and Literature* (1991), 151–70

'Mouths and Meanings: Towards an Anti-Iconography of Medieval Art', in *Iconography at the Crossroads*, ed. B. Cassidy (Princeton, NJ, 1993), 43–57

'The Book as Flesh and Fetish in Richard de Bury's *Philobiblon*', in *The Book and the Body*, ed. D. W. Frese and K. O'Brien O'Keeffe (Notre Dame, IN, 1997), pp. 34–77

Campbell, A., ed., *The Chronicle of Æthelweard* (London, 1962)

Campbell, A. and S. Keynes, eds., *Encomium Emmae Reginae* (Cambridge, 1998)

Campbell, J. J., 'To Hell and Back: Latin Tradition and Literary use of the "Descensus ad Inferno" in Old English', *Viator* 13 (1982), 107–58

Chance, J., *Woman as Hero in Old English Literature* (Syracuse, NY, 1986)

Clayton, M., *The Cult of the Virgin Mary in Anglo-Saxon England*, CSASE 2 (Cambridge, 1990)

'Ælfric's Esther: a Speculum Reginae?' in *Text and Gloss. Studies in Insular Learning and Literature Presented to Joseph Donovan Pheifer*, ed. H. C. O'Briain, A. M. D'Arcy and J. Scattergood (Dublin, 1999), 89–101

Clemoes, P., 'Cynewulf's Image of the Ascension', in *England Before the Conquest: Studies in Primary Sources Presented to Dorothy Whitelock*, ed. P. Clemoes and K. Hughes (Cambridge, 1971), pp. 293–304 (repr. in *Cynewulf: Basic Readings*, ed. R. E. Bjork (New York, 1996), pp. 109–32)

'Language in Context: *Her* in the 890 *Anglo-Saxon Chronicle*', *Leeds Studies in English* 16 (1985), 27–36

Clubb, M. D., ed., *Christ and Satan: An Old English Poem* (New Haven, CT, 1925)

Colgrave, B., ed., *Felix's Life of Saint Guthlac* (Cambridge, 1956)

The Earliest Life of Gregory the Great by an Anonymous Monk of Whitby (Lawrence, KA, 1968)

Conner, P. W., 'The Liturgy and the Old English "Descent into Hell"', *JEGP* 79 (1980), 179–91

Anglo-Saxon Exeter: A Tenth-Century Cultural History (Woodbridge and Rochester, NY, 1993)

The Abingdon Chronicle, A.D. 956–1066, vol. X of *The Anglo-Saxon Chronicle: A Collaborative Edition*, ed. D. Dumville and S. Keynes (Cambridge, 1996)

Conybeare, W. D., *Illustrations of Anglo-Saxon Poetry* (London, 1826)

Copeland, R., *Rhetoric, Hermeneutics, and Translation in the Middle Ages: Academic Traditions and Vernacular Texts* (Cambridge, 1991)
Cramp, R., ed., *County Durham and Northumberland*, vol. I of *Corpus of Anglo-Saxon Stone Sculpture* (Oxford, 1984)
Cross, J. E., 'The Old English Period', in *The Middle Ages*, ed. W. F. Bolton, The New Hist. of Lit. 1 (London, 1987), pp. 168–73
Cubbin, G. P., *MS D*, vol. VI *The Anglo-Saxon Chronicle: A Collaborative Edition*, ed. D. Dumville and S. Keynes (Cambridge, 1996)
Danielou, J., *From Shadows to Reality: Studies in the Biblical Typology of the Fathers* (Westminster, MD, 1960)
de Bury, R., *Philobiblon*, trans. E. C. Thomas (Oxford and New York, 1970)
Deshman, R., 'The Leofric Missal and Tenth-Century English Art', *ASE* 6 (1977), 145–73
The Benedictional of Æthelwold (Princeton, NJ, 1995)
'The Galba Psalter: Pictures, Text and Context in an Early Medieval Prayer-book', *ASE* 26 (1997), 109–38
Dleéani-Nigoul, S., 'L'utilization des modèles bibliques du martyre par les écrivains du IIIe siècle', in *Le monde latin antique*, ed. J. Fontaine and C. Pietri (Paris, 1985), II, 334–8
Doane, A. N., ed., *Genesis A: A New Edition* (Madison, WI, 1978)
The Saxon Genesis: An Edition of the West Saxon Genesis B and the Old Saxon 'Vatican Genesis' (Madison, WI, 1991)
Dockray-Miller, M., 'Mixed Pairs: Gender Construction in Anglo-Saxon Art and Poetry' (unpubl. PhD dissertation, Loyola University, 1996)
Dodwell, C. R., *Anglo-Saxon Gestures and the Roman Stage*, CSASE 28 (Cambridge, 2000)
Dombart, B. and A. Kalb, eds., *Sancti Aurelii Augustini De civitate Dei*, CCSL 47and 48 (Turnhout, 1955)
Dubs, K., '*Genesis B*: A Study in Grace', *American Benedictine Review* 33 (1982), 47–64
Dugdale, W., *The Life, Diary and Correspondence of Sir William Dugdale*, ed. W. Hamper (London, 1827)
Dulaey, M., *La rêve dans la vie et la pensée de saint Augustin* (Paris, 1973)
Dumville, D. '*Beowulf* and the Celtic World: The Uses of the Evidence', *Traditio* 37 (1981), 109–60
Dutton, P. E., *The Politics of Dreaming in the Carolingian Empire* (Lincoln, NB and London, 1994)
Earl, J. W., 'Christian Traditions and the Old English *Exodus*', *NM* 71 (1970), 541–70
Eco, U., *A Theory of Semiotics* (Bloomington, IN and London, 1976)

Ellis, H., *Account of Caedmon's Metrical Paraphrase of Scripture History, Archaeologia* 24 (1832)

Ettmüller, L., *Engla and Seaxna Scôpas and Bôceras* (Quedlinburg and Leipzig, 1850)

Fadda, A. M. L., '"De descensu Christi ad inferos": una inedita omelia anglo-sassone', *Studi medievale* 13 (1972), 989–1011

Farr, C., *The Book of Kells: Its Function and Audience* (London, 1997)

Farrell, R. T., ed., *Daniel and Azarius* (London, 1974)

Finnegan, R. E., 'Christ as Narrator in the Old English *Christ and Satan*', *English Studies* 75.1 (1994)

'The Man in "Nowhere": A Previously Undiscovered Drawing in Bodleian MS Junius11', *English Studies* 79.1 (1998), 23–32

Finnegan, R. E., ed., *Christ and Satan: A Critical Edition* (Waterloo, 1977)

Foot, S., '"By Water in the Spirit": the Administration of Baptism in Early Anglo-Saxon England', in *Pastoral Care before the Parish*, ed. J. Blair and R. Sharpe (Leicester, 1992), pp. 171–92

Frank, R. 'Some Uses of Paronomasia in Old English Scriptural Verse', *Speculum* 47.2 (1972), 207–26

Frantzen, A. J., *The Literature of Penance in Anglo-Saxon England* (New Brunswick, NJ, 1983)

Desire for Origins: New Language, Old English and Teaching the Tradition (New Brunswick, NJ and London, 1990)

Before the Closet: Same-Sex Love from 'Beowulf' to 'Angels in America' (Chicago, IL, 1998)

Freud, 'Three Essays on the Theory of Sexuality', in *The Standard Edition of the Complete Psychological Works*, 24 vols., ed. and trans. J. Strachey, vol. VII (1905), 123–245

Fry, D. K., 'The Art of Bede II: the Reliable Narrator Persona', *Acta* 6 (1982 for 1979), 63–82

Gameson, R., 'English Manuscript Art in the Mid-Eleventh Century: The Decorative Tradition', *Antiquaries Jnl* 71 (1991), 64–122

The Role of Art in the Late Anglo-Saxon Church (Oxford, 1995)

Gameson, R., and F. Gameson, 'The Anglo-Saxon Inscription at St Mary's Church, Breamore, Hampshire', *ASSAH* 6 (1993), 1–10

Gatch, M. McC., 'Noah's Raven in *Genesis A* and the Illustrated Old English Hexateuch', *Gesta* 14.2 (1975), 3–15

Preaching and Theology in Anglo-Saxon England: Ælfric and Wulfstan (Toronto, 1977)

Godden, M., 'Money, Power and Morality in late Anglo-Saxon England', *ASE* 19 (1990), 41–65

Gollancz, I., ed., *The Cædmon Manuscript of Anglo-Saxon Biblical Poetry: Junius XI in the Bodleian Library* (London, 1927)

Gregory the Great, *Homilies .xl. in evangelia* 9 PL 76, 1075–1312

Grien, C. W. M., *Bibliothek der angelsächsischen Poesie*, vol. I (Göttingen, 1857)

Hall, J. R., 'The Old English Book of Salvation History: Three Studies on the Unity of MS. Junius 11' (unpub. PhD dissertation, University of Notre Dame, 1974)

'Niwe Flodes: Old English "*Exodus*" 362', *N&Q* NS 22 (1975), 1243–4

'The Old English Epic of Redemption: The Theological Unity of MS. Junius 11', *Traditio* 32 (1976), 185–208

Hall, T. N., 'The Cross as Green Tree in the *Vindicta Salvatoris* and the Green Rod of Moses in *Exodus*', *English Studies* 72.4 (1971), 297–307

Harbus, A., 'Old English *Swefn* and *Genesis B* line 720', in *Studies in English Language and Literature*, ed. M. J. Toswell and E. M. Tyler (London and New York, 1996), pp. 157–74

Hardison, O. B., *Christian Rite and Christian Drama in the Middle Ages* (Baltimore, MD, 1965)

Hawkes, J., 'Mary and the Cycle of Resurrection: the Iconography of the Hovingham Panel', in *The Age of Migrating Ideas*, ed. R. M. Spearman and J. Higgitt (Edinburgh and Stroud, 1993), pp. 254–60

'The Rothbury Cross: An Iconographic Bricolage', *Gesta* 35 (1996), 77–94

Head, P., *Representation and Design: Tracing a Hermeneutics of Old English Poetry* (Albany, NY, 1997)

Heimann, A., 'Three Illustrations from the Bury St Edmunds Psalter and their Prototypes', *JWCI* 29 (1966), 39–59

Henderson, G., 'The Programme of Illustrations in Bodleian MS Junius XI', in *Studies in Memory of David Talbot Rice*, ed. G. Robertson and G. Henderson (Edinburgh, 1975), pp. 113–45. Reprinted in G. Henderson, *Studies in English Bible Illustration*, 2 vols., vol. I (London, 1985), pp. 138–83

'Cassiodorus and Eadfrith Once Again', in *The Age of Migrating Ideas: Early Medieval Art in Northern Britain and Ireland*, ed. R. M. Spearman and J. Higgitt (Edinburgh and Stroud, 1993), pp. 82–91

Vision and Image in Early Christian England (Cambridge, 1999)

Hermann, J. P., *Allegories of War: Language and Violence in Old English Poetry* (Ann Arbor, MI, 1989)

Hesbert, R.-J., ed., *Corpus antiphonalium officii*, vol. III: *Invitatoria et Antiphonae* (Herder, 1968)

Hickes, G., *Linguarum vett. septentrionalium thesaurus grammatico-criticus & archaeologicus* (Oxford, 1703)

Higgitt, J., 'Glastonbury, Dunstan, Monasticism and Manuscripts', *Art History* 2 (1979), 275–90

Hill, T. D., '"Byrhtword" and "Hælendes Heafod": Christological Allusion in the Old English *Christ and Satan*', *ELN* 8 (1970), 6–9

Howe, N., *Migration and Mythmaking in Anglo-Saxon England* (New Haven, CT and London, 1989)

Hughes, A., ed., *The Portiforium of Saint Wulstan* (London, 1960)

Innis, R., ed., *Semiotics: An Introductory Anthology* (Bloomington, IN, 1985)

Irvine, M., *The Making of a Textual Culture: 'Grammatica' and Literary Theory, 350–1100* (Cambridge, 1994)

Irving, E. B. Jr., ed., *The Old English Exodus* (New Haven, CT, 1953; reprinted and revised New York, 1970)

Isaacs, N. D., *Structural Principles in Old English Poetry* (Knoxville, TN, 1968)

Jager, E., 'Invoking/Revoking God's Word: The *Vox Dei* in *Genesis B*', *English Studies* 71.4 (1990), 307–21

James, M. R., *The Ancient Libraries of Canterbury and Dover. The Catalogues of the Libraries of Christ Church Priory and St Augustine's Abbey at Canterbury and of St Martin's Priory at Dover* (Cambridge, 1903)

Jeanneret, M., *A Feast of Words: Banquets and Table Talk in the Renaissance* (Chicago, IL, 1991)

Jerome, *Commentarii in Danielem*, ed. F. Glorie, CCSL 75A (Turnhout, 1969)

In Esaiam, ed. M. Adriaen, CCSL 73–73A (Turnhout, 1963)

John of Damascus, *De imaginibus* I. 11 (PG 94, 1241); translated by D. Anderson in St John of Damascus, *On the Divine Images: Three Apologies Against Those who Attack the Divine Images* (Crestwood, NY, 1980)

Johnson, R., 'Archangel in the Margins: St Michael in the Homilies of Cambridge, Corpus Christi College 41', *Traditio* 53 (1998), 63–91

Jolly, K. L., *Popular Religion in Late Saxon England: Elf Charms in Context* (Chapel Hill, NC, 1996)

Jolly, P. H., *Made in God's Image? Eve and Adam in the Genesis Mosaics of S. Marco, Venice* (Berkeley, CA, 1997)

Jones, C. W., *Saints' Lives and Chronicles in Early England* (Ithaca, 1947)

Jones, L. W., ed., *Cassiodorus. An Introduction to Divine and Human Readings* (New York, 1946)

Junius, F., ed., *Cædmonis monachi paraphrasis poetica Genesios ac præcipuarum sacrae paginae historiarum, abhinc annos M.LXX. Anglo-Saxonice conscripta & nunc primum edita . . .* (Amsterdam, 1655)

Karkov, C. E., 'Whitby, Jarrow and the Commemoration of Death in Northumbria', in *Northumbria's Golden Age*, ed. J. Hawkes and S. Mills (Stroud, 1999), pp. 126–35

'The Anglo-Saxon Genesis: Text, Illustration and Audience', in *The Old English*

Hexateuch: Aspects and Approaches, ed. B. Withers and R. Barnhouse (Kalamazoo, MI, 2000), pp. 187–223

'Margins and Marginalization: Representations of Eve in Oxford, Bodl. Lib. MS Junius 11', in *Texts in Margins*, ed. S. L. Keefer and W. Schipper (forthcoming)

'Naming and Renaming: The Inscription of Gender in Anglo-Saxon England', in *Theorizing Anglo-Saxon Stone Sculpture*, ed. C. E. Karkov and F. Orton (Morgantown, WV, forthcoming)

Keefer, S. L., 'Respect for the Book: A Reconsideration of "Form", "Content" and "Context" in Two Vernacular Poems', in *New Approaches to Editing Old English Verse*, ed. S. L. Keefer and K. O'Brien O'Keeffe (Cambridge, 1998), pp. 21–44

Kemble, J. M., ed., *The Dialogues of Solomon and Saturn* (London, 1848)

Kennedy, C. W., *The Cædmon Poems Translated into English Prose* (Gloucester, MA, 1965)

Ker, N. R., *Catalogue of Manuscripts Containing Anglo-Saxon* (Oxford, 1957)

Kermode, F., *The Sense of an Ending: Studies in the Theory of Fiction* (New York, 1966)

Kessels, M., 'Ancient Systems of Dream Classification', *Mnemosyne* 4th ser. 22 (1969), 389–424

Kessler, H. L., *The Illustrated Bibles from Tours* (Princeton, NJ, 1977)

Keynes, S. D., 'The Cult of King Alfred the Great', *ASE* 28 (1999), 225–356

Keynes S. and M. Lapidge, *Alfred the Great* (Harmondsworth, 1983)

Kiernan, K., 'Reading Cædmon's "Hymn" with Someone Else's Glosses', *Representations* 32 (1990), 157–74

Kirkland, J. W. and C. E. Modlin, 'The Art of *Azarias*', *MÆ* 41 (1972), 9–15

Krapp, G. P. and E. V. K. Dobbie, eds., *The Anglo-Saxon Poetic Records*, 6 vols. (New York, 1931–42)

Kristeva, J., 'From Signs to Subject', in *New Maladies of the Soul*, trans. R. Guberman (New York, 1995), pp. 127–34

Kruger, S., *Dreaming in the Middle Ages* (Cambridge, 1992)

Kuypers, B., ed., *The Prayer Book of Aedelvald the Bishop, Commonly Called the Book of Cerne* (Cambridge, 1902)

LaCocque A., and P. Ricoeur, *Thinking Biblically*, trans. D. Pellauer (Chicago, IL, 1998)

Lang, J., *York and Eastern Yorkshire*, vol. III of *Corpus of Anglo-Saxon Stone Sculpture* (Oxford, 1991)

Lees, C., 'Engendering Religious Desire: Sex, Knowledge and Christian Identity in Anglo-Saxon England', *Jnl of Medieval and Early Modern Studies* 27.1 (1997), 17–45

Tradition and Belief: Religious Writing in Anglo-Saxon England (Minneapolis, MN, 1999)

Lees, C. and G. Overing, 'Birthing Bishops and Fathering Poets: Bede, Hild and the Relations of Cultural Production', *Exemplaria* 6 (1994), 35–65

Lerer, S., *Literacy and Power in Anglo-Saxon Literature* (Lincoln, NB and London, 1991)

Lester, G. A., 'The Cædmon Story and its Analogues', *Neophilologus* 58 (1974), 225–37

Lingard, J., *The Antiquities of the Anglo-Saxon Church*, 2 vols. (Newcastle, 1806)

Liuzza, R., *The Old English Gospels*, EETS 304 (Oxford, 1994)

Lucas, P. J., 'Old English Christian Poetry: the Cross in *Exodus*', in *Famulus Christi: Essays in Commemoration of the Thirteenth Centenary of the Birth of the Venerable Bede*, ed. G. Bonner (London, 1976), pp. 193–209

'On the Blank *Daniel* Cycle in MS Junius 11', *JWCI* 42 (1979), 207–13

'On the Incomplete Ending of *Daniel* and the Addition of *Christ and Satan* to MS Junius 11', *Anglia* 97 (1979), 46–59

'MS Junius 11 and Malmesbury', *Scriptorium* 34 (1980), 197–220; and 35 (1981), 3–22

'Franciscus Junius and the Versification of *Judith: Francisci Junii in memorium*: 1591–1991', in *The Preservation and Transmission of Anglo-Saxon Culture*, ed. P. E. Szarmach and J. T. Rosenthal (Kalamazoo, MI, 1997), pp. 369–404

Lucas, P. J., ed., *Exodus* (London, 1977)

Franciscus Junius: Cædmonis monachi paraphrasis poetica Genesios ac praecipuarum sacrae paginae historiarum (Leiden and Atlanta, GA, 2000)

Luria, M., 'Why Moses' Rod is Green', *ELN* 17 (1980), 161–3

Marmo, C., ed., *Vestiga, Imagines, Verba: Semiotics and Logic in Medieval Theological Texts (XIIth–XIVth century)* (Turnhout, 1997)

Marsden, Richard, *The Text of the Old Testament in Anglo-Saxon England*, CSASE 15 (Cambridge, 1995)

Martin, E. E., 'Allegory and the African Woman in the Old English *Exodus*', *JEGP* 81 (1982), 1–15

Mayr-Harting, H., *Ottonian Illumination: An Historical Survey*, 2 vols. (London and New York, 1991)

McGurk, P., 'An Edition of the Abbreviated and Selective Set of Hebrew Names found in the Book of Kells', in *The Book of Kells: Proceedings of a Conference at Trinity College, Dublin 6–9 September 1992* (Aldershot, 1999), 102–32

Michel, L., '*Genesis A* and the *praefatio*', *MLN* 62 (1947), 545–50

Miller, J. M., 'Moab and the Moabites', in *Studies in the Mesha Inscription and Moab*, ed. J. A. Dearman (Atlanta, GA, 1989), 18–19

Morris, R., ed., *The Blickling Homilies of the Tenth Century*, EETS 58, 63, 73 (London, 1874–80; reprinted in one vol., 1967)

Muir, B. J., *The Exeter Anthology of Old English Poetry* (Exeter, 1994)

Nelson, J., 'The Second English *Ordo*', in J. Nelson, *Politics, Law and Ritual in Early Medieval Europe* (London, 1986), pp. 361–74

Neuman de Vegvar, C., 'The Origin of the Genoels-Elderen Ivories', *Gesta* 29.1 (1990), 8–24

Nichols, S., *Romanesque Signs: Early Medieval Narrative and Iconography* (New Haven, CT, 1996)

Noel, W., *The Harley Psalter* (Cambridge, 1995)

Ó Carragáin, É.,'Crucifixion as Annunciation: The Relation of the *Dream of the Rood* to the Liturgy Reconsidered', *English Studies* 63 (1982), 487–505

'The Ruthwell Crucifixion Poem in its Iconographic and Liturgical Contexts', *Peritia* 6–7 (1987–8), 1–71

'Seeing, Reading, Singing the Ruthwell Cross: Vernacular Poem, Old English Liturgy and Implied Audience', *Art and Symbolism*, pre-printed papers 7, Medieval Europe: Conference on Medieval Archaeology (York, 1992), pp. 91–6

'Rome, Ruthwell, Vercelli: "The Dream of the Rood" and the Italian Connection', in *Vercelli tra Oriente ed Occidente tra Tarda Antichità e Medioevo: atti delle Giornate di studio: Vercelli 10–11 aprile 1997, 24 novembre 1997*, ed. V. D. Corazza (Alessandria, 1999), pp. 59–99

Liturgical Thought and the Dream of the Rood (London, forthcoming)

Ohlgren, T. H., 'The Illustrations of the Cædmonian Genesis as a Guide to the Interpretation of the Text' (unpubl. PhD dissertation, University of Michigan, 1969)

'The Illustrations of the Cædmonian Genesis: Literary Criticism through Art', *Medievalia et Huministica* 3 (1972), 199–212

'Some New Light on the Old English *Caedmonian Genesis*', *Studies in Iconography* 1 (1975), 38–73

Anglo-Saxon Textual Illustration: Photographs of Sixteen Manuscripts with Descriptions and Index (Kalamazoo, MI, 1992)

Okasha, E., '"Beacen" in Old English Poetry', *N&Q* 23 (1976), 200–7

'The Inscriptions', in *The Anglian Helmet from Coppergate*, ed. D. Tweddle, The Archaeology of York, The Small Finds 17/8 (London, 1992), 1012–16

O'Keeffe, K. O'Brien, *Visible Song: Transitional Literacy in Old English Verse*, CSASE 14 (Cambridge, 1990)

'Body and Law in Late Anglo-Saxon England' *ASE* 27 (1998), 209–32

Ong, W. J., *Orality and Literacy: The Technologizing of the Word* (London, 1982)

Openshaw, K. M., 'The Battle between Christ and Satan in the Tiberius Psalter', *JWCI* 52 (1989), 14–33

'The Symbolic Illustration of the Psalter: An Insular Tradition', *Arte medievale* 2nd ser. 6 (1992), 41–60

'Weapons in the Daily Battle: Images of the Conquest of Evil in the Early Medieval Psalter', *Art Bull.* 75 (1993), 17–38

Orchard, A., 'Poetic Inspiration and Prosaic Translation: The Making of *Cædmon's Hymn*', in *Studies in English Language and Literature*, ed. M. J. Toswell and E. M. Tyler (London and New York, 1996), pp. 402–22

O'Reilly, J., 'Early Medieval Text and Image: the Wounded and Exalted Christ', *Peritia* 6–7 (1987–88), 72–118

'St John as a Figure of the Contemplative Life: Text and Image in the Art of the Anglo-Saxon Benedictine Reform', in *St Dunstan: His Life, Times and Cult*, ed. N. Ramsay, M. Sparks and T. Tatton-Brown (Woodbridge, 1992), pp. 165–85

Ó Riain-Raedel, D., 'Edith, Judith, Matilda: the Role of Royal Ladies in the Propagation of the Continental Cult', in *Oswald: Northumbrian King to European Saint*, ed. C. Stancliffe and E. Cambridge (Stamford, 1995), pp. 210–29

Orton, F., 'Rethinking the Ruthwell Monument: Fragments and Critique; Tradition and History; Tongues and Sockets', *Art History* 21 (1998), 65–106

'Northumbrian Sculpture (the Ruthwell and Bewcastle Monuments): Questions of Difference', in *Northumbria's Golden Age*, ed. J. Hawkes and S. Mills (Stroud, 1999), pp. 216–26

O'Sullivan, W., 'Ussher as a Collector of Manuscripts', *Hermathena* 88 (1956), 34–58

Overing, G., 'Nebuchadnezzar's Conversion in the Old English *Daniel*: A Psychological Portrait', *Papers on Language & Literature* 20.1 (1984), 1–14

Language, Sign and Gender in Beowulf (Carbondale, IL and Edwardsville, 1990)

'On Reading Eve: *Genesis B* and the Reader's Desire', in *Speaking Two Languages: Traditional Disciplines and Contemporary Theory in Medieval Studies*, ed. A. J. Frantzen (Albany, NY, 1991), pp. 35–63

Owen-Crocker, G. R., *Dress in Anglo-Saxon England* (Manchester, 1986)

Parkes, M. B., *Pause and Effect: Punctuation in the West* (Aldershot, 1982)

Parry, G., *Trophies of Time: English Antiquarians of the Seventeenth Century* (Oxford and New York), 1995

Pasternack, C. B., 'Stylistic Disjunctions in *The Dream of the Rood*', *ASE* 13 (1985), 167–86

The Textuality of Old English Poetry, CSASE 13 (Cambridge, 1995)

Portnoy, P., '"Remnant" and "Ritual": the Place of Daniel and *Christ and Satan* in the Junius Epic', *English Studies* 75.5 (1994), 408–21

Prudentius, *Aurelii Prudentii Clementis Carmina*, ed. M. P. Cunningham, CCSL 126 (Turnhout, 1966)

Pulsiano, P., 'Psalters', in *The Liturgical Books of Anglo-Saxon England*, ed. R. W. Pfaff, *OEN* Subsidia 23 (Kalamazoo, MI, 1995), pp. 61–85

'Benjamin Thorpe', in *Medieval Scholarship: Biographical Studies in the Formation of a Discipline*, vol. II: *Literature and Philology*, ed. H. Damico (New York and London, 1998), pp. 75–92

Raw, B. C., 'The Probable Derivation of Most of the Illustrations in Junius 11 from an Illustrated Old Saxon *Genesis*', *ASE* 5 (1976), 133–48

The Art and Background of Old English Poetry (New York, 1978)

'The Construction of Oxford, Bodleian Library, Junius 11', *ASE* 13 (1984), 187–207; reprinted in *Anglo-Saxon Manuscripts Basic Readings*, ed. M. Richards (New York and London, 1994), pp. 251–75

Anglo-Saxon Crucifixion Iconography and the Art of the Monastic Revival, CSASE 1 (Cambridge, 1990)

'Why does the River Jordan Stand Still? (the Descent into Hell, 103–6)', *Leeds Studies in English* NS 23 (1992), 29–47

Trinity and Incarnation in Anglo-Saxon Art and Thought, CSASE 21 (Cambridge, 1997)

Remley, P. G., *Old English Biblical Verse*, CSASE 16 (Cambridge, 1996)

Renoir, A., 'Eve's I.Q. Rating: Two Sexist Views of Genesis B', in *New Readings on Women in Old English Literature*, ed. H. Damico and A. H. Olsen (Bloomington, IN, 1990), pp. 262–72

Ricoeur, P., *Time and Narrative*, trans. K. McLaughlin and D. Pellauer, 3 vols. (Chicago, IL, 1984–8)

'Fides quaerens intellectum: Antécédents bibliques?' *Archivo di Filosofia* 68 (1990), 19–42

Rosenthal, J. E., 'Three Drawings in an Anglo-Saxon Pontifical: Anthropomorphic Trinity or Threefold Christ?' *Art Bull.* 43.4 (1981), 547–62

'The Pontifical of St Dunstan', in *St Dunstan: His Life, Times and Cult*, ed. N. Ramsay, M. Sparks and T. Tatton-Brown (Woodbridge, 1992), pp. 143–63

Rubin, M., *Corpus Christi: The Eucharist in Late Medieval Culture* (Cambridge, 1991)

Salmon, J. W. P., *The Breviary Through the Centuries*, trans. D. Mary (Collegeville, MN, 1962)

Salmon, P., 'The Site of Lucifer's Throne', *Anglia* 81 (1963), 118–23

Schabram, H., *Superbia: Studien zum altenglischen Wortschatz. Teil I: Die dialektale und zeitliche Verbreitung des Wortguts* (Munich, 1965)

'Das altenglische *superbia* – Wortgut. Eine Nachlese', in *Festschrift Prof. Dr. Herbert Koziol zum siebzigsten Geburtstag*, ed. G. Bauer *et al.* (Vienna, 1973), pp. 272–9

Schapiro, M., 'The Image of the Disappearing Christ: the Ascension in English Art around the Year 1000', *Gazette des Beaux-Arts* 6th ser. (March 1943), 135–52; reprinted in M. Schapiro, *Late Antique, Early Christian and Medieval Art: Selected Papers* (New York, 1979), pp. 267–87

'Frontal and Profile as Symbolic Forms', in M. Schapiro, *Words, Scripts, and Pictures: Semiotics of Visual Language* (New York, 1996), pp. 69–114

Shepherd, G., 'Scriptural Poetry', in *Continuations and Beginnings*, ed. E. G. Stanley (London, 1966), pp. 1–36

Sleeth, C. R., *Studies in Christ and Satan* (Toronto, 1982)

Spiegel, G., 'Genealogy: Form and Function in Medieval Historical Narrative', *History and Theory* 22.1 (1983), 43–53

'History, Historicism, and the Social Logic of the Text in the Middle Ages', *Speculum* 65.1 (1990), 59–86

The Past as Text (Baltimore, MD, 1997)

Stafford, P., 'The Portrayal of Royal Women in England, Mid-Tenth to Mid-Twelfth Centuries', in *Medieval Queenship*, ed. J. C. Parsons (New York, 1993), pp. 143–62

Stancliffe C. and E. Cambridge, eds., *Oswald: Northumbrian King to European Saint* (Stamford, 1995)

Stanley, E. G., 'The Sources of Junius's Learning as Revealed in the Junius Manuscripts in the Bodleian Library', in *Franciscus Junius F. F. and His Circle*, ed. R. Bremmer (Amsterdam and Atlanta, GA, 1998), 159–76

Stévanovitch, C., 'Envelope Patterns and the Unity of *Christ and Satan*', *ASNSL* 233 (1996), 260–7

'Envelope Patterns in *Genesis A* and *B*', *Neophilologus* 80.3 (1996), 465–78

'The Translator and the Text of the Old English *Genesis B*', *The Medieval Translato*r 5 (1996), 130–45

Tannenhaus, G. H., 'Concerning Figures and Tropes', in *Readings in Medieval Rhetoric*, ed. J. M. Miller, M. H. Prosser and T. W. Benson (Bloomington, IN and London, 1973), pp. 96–122

Temple, E., *Anglo-Saxon Manuscripts 900–1066*, Survey of Manuscripts Illuminated in the British Isles 2 (London, 1976)

Tertullian, *De baptismo*, ed. J. Borleffs, CCSL 1 (Turnhout), 277–95

Thacker, 'Membra Disjecta: the Diffusion of the Body and the Diffusion of the Cult', in *Oswald: Northumbrian King to European Saint*, ed. C. Stancliffe and E. Cambridge (Stamford, 1995), pp. 97–127

Thormann, J., 'The Anglo-Saxon Chronicle Poems and the Making of the English Nation', in *Anglo-Saxonism and the Construction of Social Identity*, ed. A. J. Frantzen and J. D. Niles (Gainesville, FL, 1997), pp. 60–85

Thornley, G. C., 'The Accents and Points of MS. Junius 11', *Trans. of the Philological Soc.* (1954), 178–205

Thorpe, B., ed., *Cædmon's Metrical Paraphrase of Parts of the Holy Scriptures in Anglo-Saxon* (London, 1832)
Timmer, B. J., ed., *The Later 'Saxon Genesis' Edited from Manuscript Junius 11*, 2nd edn (Oxford, 1954)
'De Laet's Anglo-Saxon Dictionary', *Neophilologus* 41 (1957), 199–202
Tite, C. G. C., 'Lost, Stolen or Strayed: A Survey of Manuscripts Formerly in the Cotton Library', *British Library Jnl* 18/2 (1992), 107–47
Toswell, M. J. and E. M. Tyler, eds., *Studies in English Language and Literature* (London and New York, 1996)
Trask, R. M., 'Doomsday Imagery in the Old English *Exodus*', *Neophilologus* 57 (1973), 295–7
Vickrey, J. F., '*Exodus* and the Battle in the Sea', *Traditio* 28 (1972), 119–40
Walsh, M. and D. Ó Cróinín, eds., *Cummian's Letter 'De Controversia Paschali' and the 'De Ratione Conputendi'* (Toronto, 1988)
Wanley, H., *Librorum vett. septentrionalum, qui in Angliæ biblioth. extant, catalogus historio-criticus* (Oxford, 1705)
Watson, A. G., *The Library of Sir Simonds D'Ewes* (London, 1966)
Weitzmann, K., *Illustrations in Roll and Codex: A Study of the Origins and Method of Text Illustration*, 2nd edn (Princeton, NJ, 1970)
Weitzmann, K. and H. L. Kessler, *The Cotton Genesis: British Library Cotton Otho B.VI* (Princeton, NJ, 1986)
Woolf, R., 'The Fall of Man in *Genesis B* and the *Mystère d'Adam*', in *Studies in Old English in Honor of Arthur G. Brodeur*, ed. S. B. Greenfield (Eugene, OR, 1963), pp. 187–99
Worm, Ole, *Olai Wormii et ad eum Doctorum virorum Epistolae, medici, anatomici, botanici, physici & historici argumentii Rem vero Linguasque & Antiquitates Boreales potissimim illustrantes*, 2 vols. (Copenhagen, 1751)
Wormald, F., 'Decorated Initials in English MSS, from A.D. 900 to 1100', *Archaeologia* 91 (1945), 107–35
Wright, C., 'The Blood of Abel and the Branches of Sin: *Genesis A*, *Maxims I* and Aldhelm's *Carmen de uirginitate*', *ASE* 25 (1996), 7–19
Wright, T., *Biographia Britannica Literaria* (London, 1842)
Wülker, R., *Grundriss zur Geschichte der angelsächsischen Litteratur* (Leipzig, 1885)
Zarnecki, G., J. Holt and T. Holland, eds., *English Romanesque Art 1066–1200*, (London, 1984)

Index